Wassily Leontief and Input-Output Economics

Wassily Leontief (1905–1999) was the founding father of input-output economics, for which he received the Nobel Prize in 1973. This book offers a collection of papers in memory of Leontief by his students and close colleagues. The first part, "Reflections on input-output economics," focuses upon Leontief as a person and scholar as well as on his personal contributions to economics. It includes contributions by Nobel laureate Paul A. Samuelson, who shares his memories of a young Professor Leontief at Harvard, and ends with the last joint interview with Wassily and his wife, to date previously unpublished. The second part, "Perspectives of input-output economics," includes new theoretical and empirical research inspired by Leontief's work and offers a wide-ranging sample of the current state of interindustry economics, a field Leontief founded. This is a strong collection likely to appeal to a wide range of professionals in universities, government, industry and international organizations.

ERIK DIETZENBACHER is Associate Professor of International Economics and Business at the University of Groningen, the Netherlands. He is co-editor of *Input-Output Analysis: Frontiers and Extensions* (with Michael L. Lahr, 2001) and *Input-Output Analysis* (three volumes, with Heinz D. Kurz and Christian Lager, 1998), and is currently editor of *Economic Systems Research*, the official journal of the International Input-Output Association.

MICHAEL L. LAHR is Associate Research Professor at the Center for Urban Policy Research, Rutgers University, New Jersey. He is co-editor of *Input-Output Analysis: Frontiers and Extensions* (with Erik Dietzenbacher, 2001) and *Regional Science Perspectives in Economics: A Festschrift in Memory of Benjamin H. Stevens* (with Ronald E. Miller, 2001).

Wassily Leontief and Input-Output Economics

Erik Dietzenbacher

University of Groningen, the Netherlands

Michael L. Lahr

Rutgers University, New Jersey

CAMBRIDGE
UNIVERSITY PRESS

CAMBRIDGE UNIVERSITY PRESS
Cambridge, New York, Melbourne, Madrid, Cape Town, Singapore, São Paulo

Cambridge University Press
The Edinburgh Building, Cambridge CB2 8RU, UK

Published in the United States of America by Cambridge University Press, New York

www.cambridge.org
Information on this title: www.cambridge.org/9780521832380

First published 2004
This digitally printed version 2008

A catalogue record for this publication is available from the British Library

ISBN 978-0-521-83238-0 hardback
ISBN 978-0-521-04943-6 paperback

Contents

Part I   Reflections on input-output economics

Contributors

CLOPPER ALMON is Professor of Economics at the Department of Economics, University of Maryland, College Park.

HENRI AUJAC was formerly head of the Bureau d'Informations et de Prévisions Economiques (BIPE) and formerly Professor of Economics at the Ecole des Hautes Etudes en Sciences Sociales, Paris.

ANDREW BRODY is Professor at the Institute of Economics, Hungarian Academy of Sciences, Budapest.

ANNE P. CARTER is the Fred C. Hecht Professor of Economics at the Department of Economics, Brandeis University, Waltham, Massachusetts.

CHRISTIAN DEBRESSON is Professor at the Département de Management et Technologie, Ecole des Sciences de la Gestion, Université du Québec à Montréal, and (since 1997/98) Visiting Professor at the School of Economics and Management of Tsinghua University, Beijing.

ERIK DIETZENBACHER is Associate Professor of International Economics and Business at the University of Groningen, the Netherlands.

FAYE DUCHIN is Professor of Economics at the Department of Economics, Rensselaer Polytechnic Institute, Troy, New York.

VIJAYA G. DUGGAL is Professor of Economics at the MIS and Decision Sciences Department, School of Business Administration, Widener University, Chester, Pennsylvania.

EMILIO FONTELA is Professor at the Universidad Autónoma de Madrid.

MAURIZIO GRASSINI is Professor at the Dipartimento di Studi sullo Stato, Università degli Studi di Firenze, Italy.

LAWRENCE R. KLEIN is Benjamin Franklin Professor Emeritus of Economics at the University of Pennsylvania, Philadelphia, and the 1980 winner of the Nobel Memorial Prize in Economic Sciences.

ROBERT E. KUENNE is Emeritus Professor of Economics at Princeton University and Director, General Economics Systems Project.

MASAHIRO KURODA is a professor and former director at the Faculty of Business and Commerce, Keio University, Tokyo.

MICHAEL L. LAHR is Associate Research Professor at the Center for Urban Policy Research, Rutgers University, New Brunswick, New Jersey.

BART LOS is Assistant Professor at the Department of International Economics and Business, University of Groningen, the Netherlands.

WILLIAM H. MIERNYK is Benedum Emeritus Professor of Economics and Director Emeritus at the Regional Research Institute, West Virginia University, Morgantown.

KOJI NOMURA is Associate Professor at the Institute for Economic and Industry Studies, Keio University, Tokyo.

IWAO OZAKI is Professor at the Keio Economic Observatory (Sangyo Kenkyujo), Keio University, Tokyo.

JEAN H. P. PAELINCK is Emeritus Professor at Erasmus University, Rotterdam.

KAREN R. POLENSKE is Professor of Regional Political Economy and Planning in the Department of Urban Studies and Planning at the Massachusetts Institute of Technology, Cambridge, Massachusetts.

THIJS TEN RAA is Senior Lecturer in Econometrics at the Centre for Economic Research, Faculty of Economics and Business Administration, Tilburg University, the Netherlands.

CYNTHIA SALTZMAN is Associate Professor and head of the Department of Economics, Business School, Widener University, Chester, Pennsylvania.

PAUL A. SAMUELSON is Professor Emeritus at the Department of Economics, Massachusetts Institute of Technology, Cambridge, Massachusetts, and the 1970 winner of the Nobel Memorial Prize in Economic Sciences.

SHUNTARO SHISHIDO is Professor Emeritus, International University of Japan and University of Tsukuba.

ALBERT E. STEENGE is Professor at the Department of Economics in the Faculty of Public Administration and Public Policy, University of Twente, Enschede, the Netherlands.

EDWARD N. WOLFF is Professor in the Department of Economics, New York University.

Figures

Tables

Preface

Wassily Leontief (1905–1999) was the founding father of input-output economics, for which he received the Alfred Nobel Memorial Prize in 1973. Comparisons have been made between Leontief's framework and those developed by other great economists who came before him (e.g. François Quesnay, Karl Marx, Léon Walras and Ladislaus von Bortkiewicz). By making input-output an inherently large-scale empirical work, however, Leontief clearly distinguished his contribution from those of his "predecessors." While most economists of the time respected the mathematical rigor of his new system, Leontief took greatest pride in input-output's empirical grounding. Indeed, throughout his career Professor Leontief periodically admonished his colleagues (including John Maynard Keynes) for overemphasizing mathematical and theoretical elegance at the expense of empirical verification.

Since his path-breaking contribution in 1936, input-output analysis has become a major tool in quantitative economics. In addition to creating its own set of followers, input-output analysis helped to revive classical Ricardian and Marxian theories and inspired the analysis of the linear production systems used in neo-Walrasian theory. Input-output tables and techniques continue to be used widely to analyze all sorts of economic and policy issues. They are important in many subdisciplines of economics, such as economics of growth, economics of trade, development economics, energy and environmental economics, labor economics, regional science, structural economics, and national accounting. Input-output studies are important not just for academic economists but also for business analysts, policy-makers and consultants. Over sixty nations have current input-output accounts of their economies.

Today, the field of input-output analysis embraces any study that uses data in the format of (or somehow related to) input-output tables, employs an input-output technique as an analytical tool, or develops techniques for producing input-output accounts. The input-output literature covers material across a wide range of: theoretical backgrounds (e.g. classical, neoclassical, Walrasian, Keynesian, Ricardian, Marxian, and Sraffian economics); topics (e.g. growth, welfare, interdependence, (dis)equilibrium, and prices); policy issues (e.g. income distribution, employment, investments, migration, energy consumption, and environment); analytical frameworks (e.g. static, comparative static, dynamic, structural, spatial, and open versus closed); units and levels of analysis (e.g. enterprises, industries, metropolitan areas, regions, multiple regions, single nations, groups of countries, and the world); objects of analysis (e.g. goods and services, materials in physical quantities, prices, innovations, patented inventions, citations, information, and people); and technical focuses (e.g. data collection and compilation of input-output tables, economic theory, and applied mathematics).

Needless to say, developments in input-output analysis have been crucial for the evolution of economics as a science. As a simple example, the construction of large-scale computable general equilibrium (CGE) models, which are often used today in policy analysis, would not have been possible without Leontief's seminal contributions. Leontief also championed the evolving connections between economics and the world of physical relations, including science and technology. His last work, for example, focused on the interdependence of scientific disciplines, as measured by citations. Three of his students – Paul Samuelson, Robert Solow and James Tobin – have themselves received Nobel Prizes. Thus, it is clear that Wassily Leontief's impact on economics runs both broad and deep.

When questioned about his approach to economics, Wassily Leontief chaffed that he was simply a collector of facts. Further, the balletomane and connoisseur of fine wines confessed that another true passion was landing a nice Vermont brook trout. It was such charm and love of life that attracted people to him.

Not long after Leontief's death on February 5, 1999, we organized – with the help of Anne P. Carter – a set of plenary sessions in his memory at the Thirteenth International Conference on Input-Output Techniques (Macerata, Italy, August 2000). Such conferences are held every two to three years – a tradition that harkens to 1950, when the founder of our science organized the first one. For the memorial sessions we invited a group of renowned scholars in the field; all have made major contributions themselves and many were Leontief's students. Few declined the invitation to present a paper at the conference simply because they were detained elsewhere. The papers in this book were selected from the memorial sessions and the submissions of invitees who could not attend.

The contributions in this volume fall roughly into two categories. The papers in the first part, "Reflections on input-output economics," focus upon Leontief as a person and scholar or on Leontief's contributions to economics. The pieces that develop a personal view offer the reader a deeper understanding of the composition of Wassily Leontief. In this part, each paper reviews certain aspects of input-output economics as developed by the 1973 Nobel laureate. It starts with a contribution by Paul A. Samuelson, who shares with us his memories of a young Professor Leontief at Harvard, and it ends with the last joint interview of Wassily Leontief and his wife Estelle. The second part, "Perspectives of input-output economics," includes new scientific research following the lines of Leontief's own work. This latter set of papers is a sample of the state of the art of the field, covering a wide range of topics.

We heartily thank Anne P. Carter for her dedication and input in organizing the memorial sessions and in making the early preparations for this volume. She truly owns part of the credit, and we regret that we were not able to persuade her to sign on as a co-editor.

Erik Dietzenbacher, Groningen
Michael L. Lahr, New Brunswick, NJ

Part I

Reflections on input-output economics

1   A portrait of the master as a young man

Paul A. Samuelson

1.   The Harvard background

Leontief had a long and picturesque life in three countries, on two con-
tinents. Over sixty years his was a first-rate lectureship at Harvard University and New York University (NYU).[1] At the editors' invitation, I
speak here for an early generation of Leontief's boys: those in his special
workshop within a golden pre-war Cambridge age. Listed in approximate
chronological order, I bear witness for Abram Bergson, Sidney Alexander, Shigeto Tsuru, Lloyd Metzler, Dick Goodwin, Jim Duesenberry,
Hollis Chenery, Bob Solow and myself. A baker's half dozen that, owing
only to age-related inadvertence, omits to mention a few other celebrated
names.[2]

For a long time I was as much younger than Leontief as Solow is
younger than I am. However, late in the era of the Soviet Union, revisionist
research into Czarist vital statistics pushed back from 1906 to 1905 the
birth year of my beloved master. But what signifies age? When I first
glimpsed Wassily, brown-suited, dark, scarred and handsome, at the 1934
Palmer House Chicago meeting of the American Economic Association
(AEA), he looked much the same as when at 69 he left Harvard in a huff
for NYU. Even in the months before he died, in 1999, his appearance
had not changed much. I may also add that his foreign accent softened
little over the years; but, after my first hour of hearing him lecture, his
soft-spoken words came through loud and clear.

We graduate students spun legends in the junior common room about
our mentor. At the age of puberty, as a Menshevik, his life was spared by
the Bolsheviks in the hope that he would grow up to know better. The
scar on his neck was not the wound from a student's duel; actually the

---

[1] It was a nineteenth-century Harvard graduate who said: "Good Americans, when they
die, go to Paris." It is I who says: "Good economists, before they die, go to NYU." Fritz
Machlup, Oskar Morgenstern, Will Baumol and Wassily Wassilyovitch Leontief will know
I state the truth.

[2] Marion Crawford (Samuelson) was at least one gender exception; her 1937 summa senior
honors thesis was written as Leontief's Radcliffe tutee.

German operation that produced it did provide him the exit visa to leave the Soviet Union.[3] Like an earlier immigrant, Simon Kuznets, the young Leontief at first seemed quite apolitical in America. Later he reversed the usual life cycle: with age, conservative cynicism peeled off – particularly after the Republicans cut back on input-output development.

In 1935 Harvard was just moving from torpor into an Elizabethan renaissance. Frank Taussig had aged. Allyn Young had died prior to returning from the London School of Economics to Harvard. Failing to achieve tenure, Laughlin Currie had recently been banished to Washington. Charles Jesse Bullock and Thomas Nixon Carver had at long last retired. Economic historian Edwin Gay, although he may not have known it, was in his last year at Harvard (thereby liberating Abbott Payson Usher to teach graduate students). John Williams led dynamic seminars that were respectable and, after Alvin Hansen arrived (in 1937, by a Harvard miscalculation!), the two made a great macroeconomic duo. Edward Chamberlin at 35 was, judged retrospectively, at the zenith of his scholarly career; Edward Mason was not yet the important elder statesman he was to become. Other local worthies can mostly be overlooked.

Thanks only in part to Adolf Hitler, the foreign rescuers were on their way: Schumpeter from Austria and Weimar Germany; Haberler from Vienna and the League of Nations. It must have been the newly-arrived-in-Cambridge Schumpeter who plucked Leontief from a brief National Bureau stint to Harvard. I suspect Schumpeter fastened on Leontief as a genius on the basis of the 24-year-old's German article (Leontief, 1929) on how to identify demand and supply elasticities from a time-series sample – a brilliant investment decision even if not 100 percent cogent.

2.   Early teaching

It was only in the calendar year 1935 that Schumpeter and Leontief were permitted to lecture on their specialties. That was luck for me since it provided both a telescopic and a microscopic add-on to my training. It rescued me from my miscalculation, which had diverted me from Morningside Heights to the Harvard Yard.[4]

---

[3] Unlike Prokofiev he never went back, except to preach to his fatherland the virtues of input-output analysis.

[4] When the Social Science Research Council (SSRC), my Medicis, dictated that I leave Chicago, midway locals without exception advised choosing the Columbia of Wesley Mitchell, Harold Hotelling and J. M. Clark. Joseph Schumpeter, I was told, was the eccentric who believed in a zero interest rate for the stationary state. Leontief neither I nor they knew anything about. Before Seymour Harris was an "inflationist," Lloyd Mints warned me against him as one. Independently of any Chicago reading list, I had

That first registration day I gladly burned my bridges. Defying inde-scribable high authority, William Tell refused to take economic history from Gay. (I already knew it from John U. Nef.) That made room to take two advanced courses – one of which was from Chamberlin. Twenty-one years later, when I substituted for him to teach the basic elementary Harvard graduate course in theory, I encountered precisely the same unchanged reading list: J. S. Mill, A. Marshall, E. H. Chamberlin and J. V. Robinson! Eschewing Gay in the spring semester, I was able to learn genuine modern statistics from E. B. Wilson, bypassing Edwin Frickey (who, with Leonard Crum, taught at Harvard courses *against* modern statistics!). But all was not lost.

For the first time Wassily gave a one-semester mathematical economics seminar; it was camouflaged as "Price Analysis" but that didn't fool me. We were a small class. Abe Bergson, then a third-year graduate student, was one attendee. Another was Harvard honors senior Sidney Alexander. Maybe Shigeto Tsuru and Philip Bradley were auditors, as was Schum-peter occasionally.

Here is what we learned from late September to almost November Thanksgiving. (a) Specified two-good indifference contours, non-intersecting and "convex to the origin." (b) A negatively sloped bud-get line. (c) No indicator of *cardinal* utility at all. The commodity (numbered 2) on the vertical axis was specified to be numeraire good, so that P_1/P_2 determined the absolute slope of the budget line. (d) As this price ratio changed, the budget line pivoted around the intercept where it hit the vertical axis. (e) What could we *prove* about the signs of $\partial q_1/\partial(P_1/P_2)$ and $\partial q_2/\partial(P_1/P_2)$? But first, (f), what might be true of the signs of income elasticities or of $\partial q_i/\partial(I/P_1)$ when I/P_1 is defined as $(P_2/P_1)q_1 + q_2 = I/P_1$, the budget constraint?

We learned that, in so-called "normal" case(s), *both income* elasticities would be positive. But also there could be cases where one, but *not both*, of the income elasticities could be negative. Finally, somewhere between Columbus Day and Thanksgiving, we found the Holy Grail at the North Pole.

Theorem. In all "normal" cases, own-price elasticities were indeed negative. However, in a case where a good's income elasticity was neg-ative and much was spent on it, Giffenosity could obtain to make $\partial q_i/\partial(P_i/P_j) > 0$!

discovered on my own the *Theory of Monopolistic Competition* (Chamberlin, 1933) on the SSRC reserve room shelf. That predisposed me toward Harvard. But, truth to tell, it was because I expected Harvard to be like Dartmouth – located around a New England green common, with a white chapel tower and much ivy on the walls – that I arrived by tram, unannounced, at the Harvard Yard.

We didn't learn this by writing down in our notebooks the professor's dictated statements of the theorem. We *proved* it by 2 × 2 determinants! Ah, bliss.

No other course I ever took so profoundly set me on the way of my life career. It was, so to speak, slow motion, and all the better for that. It prepared me to master Edwin Bidwell Wilson's exposition of Willard Gibbs' thermodynamic analysis. Leontief assigned no readings in Pareto or Allen-Hicks; or, for that matter, W. E. Johnson (1913) or Eugen Slutsky (1915) – only our own laboratory work. Then, after Thanksgiving, we replaced the linear budget equation by Haberler's (1933) concave "opportunity-cost" curve – thereby mastering Leontief's (1933) own vindication of Marshallian (1879) offer curves in international trade. Obviously we were prepared for James Meade's (1952) later graphics of international trade.

I have told more than once how Haberler's resistance to indifference curves provoked from one brash Leontief student the rebuke: "Well, without indifference curves, your 1925 Vienna Ph.D. thesis on index numbers evaporates into thin air" (see Haberler, 1927). The theory of revealed preference (see Samuelson, 1938a, and 1938b) was born one second later as I listened to what *I* was saying.

Although Wassily rarely lectured on *his* current researches, this was a golden decade in his own life. (Also, it was that for Abba Lerner far away in London. And for the Oskar Lange whose muse left him after his patriotic return to post-war Soviet-satellite Poland.) Notable and already mentioned was Leontief's (1933) paper on indifference curves in international trade. Less noticed was his (1934) paper – in German, but translated in Leontief (1966) – on cobweb dynamics of non-linear supply and demand curves. Here his topological explorations into multiple periodic motions came close to chancing on modern *chaos* theory. Already his Harvard lectures introduced testable partial differential equations for disaggregation separability. In my 1941 thesis (see Samuelson, 1947, p. 178), I referred to the *Leontief* condition for additive-utility independence of goods x and y, namely the vanishing of $\partial^2 \log M(x, y)/\partial x \partial y$, where M denotes the observable marginal rate of substitution between x and y.

3.   Afterthoughts on input-output

Leontief's middle and final decades were increasingly preoccupied by input-output researches (see Leontief et al., 1953; Leontief, 1966). These were of tremendous value to society and to him. His Nobel Prize properly cited them. Well and good; a scholar should follow his own instincts and volitions. Still, I have to confess to a certain regret. Max

Born (the physics Nobel laureate who helped to found the better post-Planck and post-Bohr quantum mechanics theory) expressed my sentiments when he wrote to the Albert Einstein who, from the age of 45 on, concentrated all his energies on creating a new unified field theory combining gravity, relativity, quantum theory and cosmology. To do this, Einstein chose to cut himself off from most of the frontier developments in 1925–1955 physics. Born wrote to his admired master: "We are left to struggle on without our leader." I am much like Oliver Twist, who always asks for "More!" So original and lively an economist as Leontief, in my contra-factual history, could well have given us another volume of diverse and sparkling collected papers like those in his classic 1966 book. The whole world appreciated the genius of Wassily W. Leontief. But we his disciples knew the full measure of his inspiration and potential.

At Berlin Leontief was lucky in his teacher Ladislaus von Bortkiewicz, a keen contributor to statistics and to mathematical economics. Matching this depth came the width from Werner Sombat, the grandiose creator of theories for economic history. From von Bortkiewicz's improvements on Marx must have come an early interest in the Quesnay-like circular interdependence of input-output. But, from my later explicit quizzing of him, I can rebut the innuendo that he ever did know the work of Vladimir Dmitriev (1898). Just as Sraffa's (1960) book on input-output never cited Leontief, Leontief's 1925–1999 writings seem never to have cited the work of Sraffa.

I try not to make those venial mistakes. I am conscious of how much I have benefited from teachers like Leontief: at Chicago Jacob Viner, Henry Simons, Frank Knight and Paul Douglas; at Harvard Edwin Bidwell Wilson, Joseph Schumpeter, Leontief, Gottfried Haberler and Alvin Hansen. It is humbling when one weighs accomplishments against advantages. Old school ties are dummy variables that unfairly boost one's R^2. And, when your teachers pass off the stage, your students step in to add on their push. All the while the wind is broken for us by contemporaries such as Abram Bergson, Robert Solow, Kenneth Arrow, Gerard Debreu, Abraham Wald, Lionel McKenzie and the rest of the Invisible College.

Sixty-five years have not dimmed memories of that golden age in the Harvard Yard: so to speak, Wassily Leontief on one end of the log and I on the other.

REFERENCES

Chamberlin, E. H. (1933) *The Theory of Monopolistic Competition* (Cambridge, MA, Harvard University Press, 6th edn., 1948).

Dmitriev, V. K. (1898) The theory of value of David Ricardo: an attempt at a rigorous analysis, in *Economic Essays on Value, Competition and Utility* (London, Cambridge University Press, 1974), 37–95. [Translated by D. Fry from a 1904 Moscow Russian-language publication, and published with an introduction by D. M. Nuti.]

Haberler, G. (1927) *Der Sinn der Indexzahlen* (Tübingen, J. C. B. Mohr).

  (1933) *Der internationale Handel. Theorie der weltwirtschaftlichen Zusammenhange sowie Darstellung und Analyse der Aussenhandelspolitik* (Berlin, Julius Springer). [Translated as: *The Theory of International Trade with its Applications to Commercial Policy* (London, William Hodge & Co., 1936).]

Johnson, W. E. (1913) The pure theory of utility curves, *Economic Journal*, 23, 483–515.

Leontief, W. W. (1929) Ein Versuch zur statistischen Analyse von Angebot und Nachfrage, *Weltwirtschaftlichs Archiv*, 30, 1–53.

  (1933) The use of indifference curves in the analysis of foreign trade, *Quarterly Journal of Economics*, 47, 493–503.

  (1966) *Essays in Economics: Theories and Theorizing* (New York, Oxford University Press).

Leontief, W. W., et al. (1953) *Studies in the Structure of the American Economy* (New York, Oxford University Press).

Marshall, A. (1879) *The Pure Theory of International Trade. The Pure Theory of Domestic Values.* [Privately printed 1879. First published (London, London School of Economics, 1930), reprinted (Clifton, New Jersey, Augustus M. Kelley, 1974).]

Meade, J. (1952) *A Geometry of International Trade* (London, Allen & Unwin).

Samuelson, P. A. (1938a) A note on the pure theory of consumer's behavior, *Economica*, 5, 61–71.

  (1938b) An addendum, *Economica*, 5, 353–354.

  (1947) *Foundations of Economic Analysis* (Cambridge, MA, Harvard University Press).

Slutsky, E. (1915) Sulla teoria del bilancio del consumatore, *Giornale degli Economisti e Rivista di Statistica*, 51, 1–26. [Translated as: On the theory of the budget of the consumer, in K. E. Boulding and G. Stigler (eds.) *Readings in Price Theory* (London, Allen & Unwin, 1953).]

Sraffa, P. (1960) *Production of Commodities by Means of Commodities. Prelude to a Critique of Economic Theory* (Cambridge, Cambridge University Press).

2 Leontief's "magnificent machine" and other contributions to applied economics

Karen R. Polenske

1. Introduction

Wassily W. Leontief was an excellent theorist. As I note below, others have reviewed his extensive contributions to economic theory. In this paper, I focus instead on the many major contributions to applied economics he made by conducting detailed empirical analyses. He was often ahead of his time, especially by sensing that computers would soon be able to handle the difficult and complex empirical studies he kept saying needed to be done. I begin with a brief review of his most important empirical contribution, namely the development and extensions of the input-output model. Then I discuss five areas of applied economics in which he made an innovative set of insights: (1) automation; (2) disarmament; (3) the environment; (4) foreign and interregional trade; and (5) spatial and world analyses. In each area of study, he usually constructed a novel framework in which to conduct a unique analysis.

2. Linking theory and applications

One of Leontief's major contributions to economics, of course, was to economic theory. Others (e.g. Dorfman, 1973; Carter and Petri, 1989) have discussed most aspects of his theoretical work, so I will not focus on them here. In order to understand his contribution to applied economics, I do review his important thinking on linking theory and applications. He mentioned this link in many of his articles, feeling it was critical for superb economic analyses. As recently as 1998, Leontief stated: "My tendency was to combine empirical and theoretical. In economics that combination requires mathematical concepts, such as systems analysis" (Foley, 1998, p. 126).

Leontief was extremely critical of most economic theorists, especially of those who failed to understand economics as an empirical and applied science. As an example, he sharply criticized the neo-Cambridge group of economists who supported Keynes (Leontief, 1937), arguing that analysts needed to beware of defining theoretical arguments in such a way as to ensure that given conclusions would be reached. This is most likely to occur when theory is not tested by empirical observations. In an early article on the interrelationship of subsets of variables (Leontief, 1947), as well as in his 1970 presidential address to the American Economic Association (AEA) (Leontief, 1971), he wrote about the need to confirm theory with the use of detailed data. In a 1958 article, he went even further in arguing that supporting theory with data should be done by the same person. He sharply criticized Koopmans, who wanted to help correct problems with econometric work by separating the pure theorists from the empirical investigators, with the first building internally consistent models, and the second testing them with observed facts. Leontief (1958, p. 104) said that such a separation, "instead of alleviating the trouble, is bound to make it very much worse." He referred to a quote from Quesnay, who said that "theory and observation, which are reconciled perfectly, if combined in a single person, whenever they are separated wage against each other an incessant, but futile, war" (p. 106, fn. 1). Leontief was as ruthless in his criticism of most empirical economic analysts as he was of the economic theorists, saying that an empirical analysis should be a "descriptive complement of its theoretical analysis" (Leontief, 1954, p. 229). He expressed dismay that some economic theorists believe they are doing empirical studies, but try to "depict the operation of the entire economic system in terms of five, four, or even only three aggregative variables" (p. 229).

During the late 1930s and throughout the 1940s and early 1950s, when others at Harvard University and elsewhere were not using mathematics, Leontief encouraged his students to learn it (see Solow, 1998). By the late 1960s, however, Leontief felt that most economists were spending far too much time in developing more sophisticated mathematical models, rather than in working on data issues that would help them assess the way the real world worked. He stated his concern in the following blunt words (Leontief, 1967a, p. 2): "I submit that already the greatly perfected engine of economic theory is using up the available factual information much faster than the limited resources devoted to collection and organization of such basic data can now supply." Leontief also said, "I am essentially a theorist. But I felt very strongly that theory is just a construction of frameworks to understand how real systems work. It is an organizing principle, while, for many economists, theory is a separate object" (Foley, 1998, p. 123). He was also adamant that techniques of statistical inference "yield only marginal improvements in terms of solid, factual results" (Leontief, 1967a, p. 5). As an alternative, he claimed that data had to be collected first-hand, tedious though it may be to do so, and organized into appropriate frameworks. The input-output accounts and the models developed from those accounts are part of his solution to this perception of what was missing in economics.

3.   The input-output model – the "magnificent machine"

What is the magnificent input-output machine that Leontief designed? How did he come to develop it? Leontief indicated that his development of the input-output model of an economy was influenced by Quesnay and Walras, not by Marx, and that he conceived of the input-output structure in 1927 at the Institute for World Economics in Kiel, Germany, after leaving Russia in 1925 (Foley, 1998, p. 118).[1] He had studied mathematics and was well aware of Frobenius matrices, which economic analysts today know of as Leontief matrices. Underlying his interest in the mathematical/theoretical construct of the model was an even deeper desire to see how an economy actually operated.[2] This desire seems to have been the prime motivation for his theoretical and empirical input-output work (Foley, 1998). He wanted to open the "black boxes of economic theory"; or, to use one of Leontief's many analogies, he wanted to look under the hood of the machine (the economy), in fact, to take the motor apart and "subject each of its components to many desired tests and measurements," whereas most theorists were interested only in building the machine (Leontief, 1954, p. 228).

His first paper on input-output analysis appeared in 1936, entitled "Quantitative input and output relations in the economic system of the United States." Although this was a "novel and important contribution to economic theory," Leontief laid stress in the paper on "the numerical description of the American economic structure" (Dorfman, 1973, p. 434). Based upon that work, the US government asked him to come to Washington, DC, to construct a 1939 input-output table. He refused

---

[1] It was in Kiel that he met a group of Chinese, who had the Chinese ambassador in Berlin ask him to go to Nanking, China, as an economic adviser to the Ministry of Railroads. In his usual innovative manner, while in Nanking, he had photographs taken from an aircraft in order "to make estimates of farm production by region as a basis for planning rail lines" (Silk, 1976, p. 157).

[2] There is some dispute as to whether or not Leontief developed several of his input-output theory and accounting ideas while still in the Soviet Union (Kurz and Salvadori, 2000). He claims he did not (Foley, 1998), but he did publish a critique of the work of Popov, a Soviet statistician, on the balance of the economy of the USSR. Popov developed detailed accounting systems somewhat like the input-output tables (Leontief, 1964). Leontief learned later that Remak "proposed a theoretical input-output formulation of an economy seven years before Leontief's earliest paper on the subject, [and] a mathematician, H. E. Bray, had written in a similar vein seven years before that" (Dorfman, 1973, p. 431). Regardless, none of his predecessors structured the accounts in as explicit and comprehensive a way as Leontief, and none tried to collect such detailed data as he did for the US economy.

to go, saying Washington did not have the data, but he did accept having a sub-office of the Bureau of Labor Statistics (BLS) of the US Department of Labor set up at Harvard, so that he could construct the table there with a team of BLS workers. Kohli (2001, p. 29) maintains that the "Department of Labor's interest stimulated the development of an analytical model and tables that were more useful for policy-makers than Leontief's first formulation."

To develop the input-output model, Leontief reformulated the Walrasian fully determinate general equilibrium system, in which intermediate goods were expressed as a set of equations with the sales and purchases of the intermediate industries forming the core of the system (Leontief, 1941). At this point he was retaining Walras's concept of an entirely self-contained, self-determining system of economic interrelationships, and the model was what we now refer to as a "closed model." In fact, it was completely closed, with all final demand and value added components taken as endogenous. Ten years later, Leontief (1951a) reformulated the system to what we know today as an "open model," with the final demand and value added components treated exogenously.

Leontief's first input-output tables were for ten sectors and were constructed for the 1919 and 1929 US economy. Although these tables seem to be very small by today's standards, and because the automatic computing machine was not yet developed, he calculated the first Leontief inverses using punchcard machines. Leontief eventually used the Harvard Mark II computer to invert a 42-sector table for 1939, a calculation that required fifty-six hours (Leontief, 1951a, p. 20).[3]

The rest is history in terms of the US input-output research. The US government continued to construct input-output tables for 1947, 1958 and 1963, and – starting in 1967 – for every year ending in a "2" or a "7." The gap between 1947 and 1958 was caused by the closing down of input-output work under the Eisenhower administration, because it was considered to be too closely related to planning in the Communist countries (Polenske, 1999). Equally important, input-output research soon spread to Europe and Asia, partially through the start of the international input-output conferences in 1950, which were held approximately every five years until recently. Now, they are scheduled for once every two years. As a result of the adoption of the input-output accounting

---

[3] As far as I know, we have no estimate of the number of labor months required to assemble the 1919, 1929 and 1939 tables. The task was awesome, to say the least, even for skilled data handlers. All data were in printed form, some handwritten on unpublished worksheets. For the 1919 and 1929 tables, Leontief inverted them on punchcard machines, because there were – of course – no computers, computer tapes, computer disks, or CD-ROMs.

framework into the 1968 United Nations System of National Accounts (United Nations, 1968), analysts throughout the world began to use this manual (called "the Blue Book" because of its blue cover) to construct not only the national income and product accounts, but also the more comprehensive set of input-output accounts. No doubt another important source of information about input-output analysis, especially among scientists, was the appearance over the years in *Scientific American* of many input-output articles by Leontief (1951b, 1952, 1963, and 1985), Leontief and Hoffenberg (1961), Carter (1966) and others, and the distribution by *Scientific American* of input-output wall charts whenever a new national input-output table was released by the US government, with the strong encouragement of the editor, Gerard Piel (Piel, 1999).

4.   Automation

Leontief's fascination with automation and its effect on workers was an obvious outgrowth of his desire to understand how the economy worked and the effects of technological change. Here is a case where he guessed wrong, but he also later admitted his mistake (Duchin, 1995). Leontief should actually be attributed with the development of two paradoxes. The Leontief trade paradox is well known (see below). His other paradox about "horse productivity" is not well known (Leontief, 1979). Economists conventionally measure the productivity of labor (capital) by dividing total output (value of shipments) by the number of laborers (amount of capital). Leontief was fascinated with the idea that, as the economy developed, tractors replaced horses in agriculture. As this happened, he speculated that perhaps economists should divide the annual agriculture output by the number of tractors (horses). Because the number of tractors was rising, the tractor productivity should be falling, and because the number of horses was decreasing, the horse productivity should be rising. He was wiser than to be tricked by such a reasoning, noting that "in fact, the cost-effectiveness of horses, of course, diminished steadily as compared to that of the more and more efficient tractors" (Leontief, 1979, p. 48). Until 1986, Leontief did believe that, with the continuation of the computer revolution, the use of automation (robots and other machinery) in the economy would quickly lead to the replacement of people by machines.

In 1952 he published an article, "Machines and man," in *Scientific American* to explain the effect that the instrumentation of the US economy was having on employment. His question was: will automatic control systems lead to technological unemployment? He reasoned that the use of automatic equipment could be introduced at a much more rapid rate than the introduction of mechanical equipment to industries in the nineteenth century, because capital requirements are much lower (Leontief, 1952, p. 154). The result of automation on workers, he said, was not to reduce the number of workers, but to decrease the working week from 67.2 hours in 1870 to 42.5 in 1950. Whether or not workers can adapt to automation or become unemployed, he said, will depend upon whether or not the workforce can train and retrain itself (p. 156).

This type of reasoning unsupported by quantitative measures was not very satisfactory to Leontief. Thus, he and Duchin embarked on an important, detailed quantitative study of automation (Leontief and Duchin, 1986). They used a dynamic input-output model, adapted from Duchin and Szyld (1985), to project sectoral outputs and investment and labor requirements year by year for 1963 through 2000, and tested four alternative paths for changes in technology between 1980 and 2000. They concluded that workers would not become obsolete; rather, workers would adjust from the old technologies to the new ones with less disruption than originally thought.[4] This conclusion countered Leontief's earlier conviction that people would become obsolete as workers, but he accepted the results "with characteristic pragmatism, integrity, and grace" (Duchin, 1995, p. 269).

5.   Defense conversion

Leontief was not directly involved in politics, but he kept abreast of many political events, especially those concerning defense conversion and the welfare of workers. During World War II he was head of the Russian Economic Subdivision of the Office of Strategic Services. As the war was coming to a close, the BLS staff used the 42-sector 1939 input-output table to determine how much steel capacity would be required in the post-war US economy. They discovered that, instead of having to close steel plants, which would no longer have to supply the armament industry, US steel plants would have to expand production to accommodate the huge pent-up demand by civilians for appliances and cars, most of which were made of steel (Duncan and Shelton, 1978, p. 110). After World War II (in 1948) the US Air Force included funding for what was eventually a 450-sector 1947 input-output table (published in 192- and 50-sector format) in a project called SCOOP (Scientific Computation Of Optimum Programs), which was for defense planning purposes. Leontief's

---

[4] Typical of most publications by Leontief, he and Duchin pay special attention not only to a description of the theoretical model, but also to the type of data collected and the way they are adjusted (Leontief and Duchin, 1986, appendices A and B).

first published work on defense conversion (Leontief, 1944) concerned the conversion of the US economy after World War II and the effect this would have on workers and output in different economic sectors. Military spending has been and still is a major way in which the US output and employment levels are maintained at such a high level.

Leontief was concerned about having so much money spent (wasted) on military expenditures. He was therefore pleased when, in the early 1960s, Senator Proxmire, who was then head of the US Joint Economic Committee, asked him to assess the effect on the US economy of a hypothetical 20 percent reduction in US military spending in Vietnam and a compensating increase in US civilian final expenditures so as to keep total US employment the same. Rather than look at the economy as one region, as he had done for a disarmament study four years previously (Leontief and Hoffenberg, 1961), Leontief and his colleagues decided to use some of his new thinking on regional input-output analyses to study the effect on nineteen US regions (which were aggregates of the fifty states and Washington, DC) and fifty-eight industries (forty-one national industries and seventeen local industries). This seemingly simple exercise required use not only of the relatively new theoretical intraregional construct for the input-output model (Leontief, 1953a), but the estimation of both regional data, where available, and proxies for unavailable regional data. In the intranational input-output table he and his colleagues used, all industries were divided into either national or local industries (Leontief et al., 1965). They assumed that the demand for the output of the national industries, such as aircraft, came from throughout the United States, while the demand for the output of local industries came from a particular region. For the technologies, they assumed that they were the same throughout all the regions. They therefore used the 1958 national table of direct input coefficients for all sectors. To estimate the outputs for the national industries, they multiplied the inverse of the matrix $(I-A)$ by the national final demands. Thus, it was only regional data that they needed to estimate for the final demands of the local industries – certainly a less arduous task than doing it for both local and national industries.

This was the era of President Johnson's "Great Society" programs. In keeping with the Great Society concept, Proxmire asked Leontief to conduct the analysis assuming that the total employment in the nation would remain the same; only the regional and sectoral allocations would change. To make this happen, Leontief and his associates increased the amount of spending on the Great Society by 2 percent (by augmenting each non-military final demand component by that percentage), which was sufficient to offset the 20 percent decline in military spending. Thus, they were able to show the Joint Economic Committee and Congress the effects of the reduction on a region-by-region and industry-by-industry basis; details that were previously unavailable. One of the important findings was that such a military spending reduction with the compensating increase to maintain full employment would drastically alter the regional and industrial distribution of employment. It would increase, rather than reduce, employment and output in the Midwest (the heartland of the United States), where the iron and steel and agricultural sectors were concentrated, but it would have large negative effects on industries and regions located along the periphery (coastal areas) of the country, where the aircraft, space, and other military industries were located. In the early 1960s analysts could see the initial effects of industrial and regional restructuring as major defense industries relocated away from the iron and steel belt in the Midwest, but this movement was not yet fully occurring.

How true were the findings from the computations to what actually happened? During the mid-1960s, Vietnam expenditures increased by 20 percent, rather than declining by 20 percent. Leontief just sadly shook his head to those of us who had worked on the study and said, "Well, all we have to do is change all our minuses to pluses and vice versa."[5] Later, Leontief (1967b) testified before Congress concerning the computations he had made. For reasons that are not entirely clear to this author, it was about this time that he became fascinated with environmental issues.

6.   Environment

By the late 1960s – long before it became fashionable to conduct research on the environment – Leontief decided to examine environmental pollution on a sector-by-sector basis. He was dissatisfied with the types of environmental analyses his colleagues were conducting. Once again, he made an innovation to the structure of the input-output equations, so that he could conduct another unique type of analysis. In early environmental modeling, some of his colleagues, such as Isard and others (1968), had used the input-output framework for their models, but they simulated the interaction between the economy and the environment in a totally closed relationship. In these systems, the analyst monitors the interactions between the two sectors and uses policy alternatives as modifying agents. Leontief wanted a model that was more relevant for policy

[5] He was not as happy with the war itself and worked hard as a member of the American Academy of Arts and Sciences (AAAS) to get as many AAAS members as possible to sign a petition to stop the war in Vietnam.

analysis than those of his colleagues in order to focus directly on the implications of different policy interventions, especially pollution abatement policies.

During the late 1960s, Cumberland (1966), Daly (1968), Isard et al. (1968) and Ayres and Kneese (1969) had used four distinct types of frameworks. Cumberland's was a standard input-output model to which he added three rows to designate the environmental benefits, the environmental costs, and the net balance between the two, and a single environmental column. This column contained information on the costs of restoring the environment to its pre-project condition. It may be a precursor, but for a very different use, to Leontief's abatement-cost column. An analyst using Cumberland's model would have difficulties in estimating the data, and there is a lack of consistency in its accounting units. This internal accounting problem arises again in different ways both in Daly's (1968) input-output environmental model and in the model by Isard et al. (1968). To implement Daly's model, an analyst would need to calculate market prices for ecological goods. Isard and his colleagues overcame part of Daly's problem by using commodity-by-industry accounts rather than industry-by-industry accounts, so that each industry can produce more than one product. As with Daly's model, however, data for the ecological sector are not available. Finally, Ayres and Kneese (1969) framed a Walras-Cassel general equilibrium model, in which all materials pass through the economy and environmental sectors. Their formulation required that an analyst know all the preference and production functions, all factor and process substitutions, and the relationship between residuals discharged and external costs. The difficulty, obviously, was the impossibility of implementing the model, because, in their own words, the model "implies a central planning problem of impossible difficulty" (Ayres and Kneese, 1969, p. 295).

Leontief's (1970) formulation of a model to examine environmental pollution issues was an important and ingenious one. His resourceful solution to the dilemma faced by the other analysts was to reverse the positions of two of the quadrants: the quadrant representing the amount of pollution produced by each industry as a function of its total output; and the quadrant representing the industrial inputs required to produce pollution control equipment. Thus, Leontief treats pollution emissions as outputs of an industrial process. He assumed that each air, water, or land pollutant was generated as a fixed function of output; therefore, if output doubled, so would the emissions of – say – a given gas, particulate, or other pollutant. With this information, an analyst can relatively easily assess the economic and emission impacts of given pollution control policies, including the effects of changes in pollution control technologies.

Leontief does eliminate the environmental sector; however, this loss is not as serious as it may seem, because the other environmental analysts were not able to specify data for that sector in any case. Leontief and Ford (1972) implemented the environmental model, using pollution emission coefficients from the Resources for the Future (a major environmental organization in the Washington, DC, area).

7.   Foreign and interregional trade

Most international trade economists, even if they do not know about input-output analysis per se, are well aware of the "Leontief Paradox" and Ohlin's work on international trade (Ohlin, 1933). Ohlin, in fact, attributes his important factor-price equalization work to Heckscher (1919), thus giving rise to what analysts began to call the "Heckscher-Ohlin (HO) theorem." The HO theorem states that countries, such as the United States, with an abundance of capital and a shortage of labor should export capital-intensive goods and import labor-intensive goods.

This seemed almost intuitive, until, in the early 1950s, Leontief used the 1947 input-output table to test whether or not the HO theorem was true for the United States. He concluded that "an average million dollars' worth of our exports embodies considerably less capital and somewhat more labor than would be required to replace from domestic production an equivalent amount of our competitive imports" (Leontief, 1953b, p. 343). Leontief's finding was the reverse of that predicted by the HO theorem, and it soon came to be known as the "Leontief Paradox." Vanek (1968) contributed to the theoretical argument by specifying clearly the factor content of international trade; consequently, the HO is sometimes referred to as the Heckscher-Ohlin-Vanek (HOV) theorem. Williams (1978) was the first to use Vanek's version of the model of the factor content of international trade data to criticize Leontief's argument. Two years later, Leamer (1980) examined the HOV model using both theoretical arguments and Leontief's own data (pp. 502–503) to challenge the Leontief Paradox, basically saying that Leontief overlooked the exports/imports of capital and labor services.

Two main sets of analysts have tried to prove or disprove the HO (or HOV) theorem or the Leontief Paradox. The first are the analysts, some of whom we have discussed above, who have tried to explain theoretically the factor content and commodity content of international trade. The second are analysts who have used national or regional data to test the accuracy of the Leontief Paradox. The regional analysts actually have developed some new tests and have used regional, rather than national, data.

Many of the theoretical analysts start from the Samuelson (1948) article on the equalization of factor prices. He examines the theoretical possibilities of free factor movements and free commodity movements to show impediments to complete factor price equalization. Deardorff (1982) provides a more general proof of the HO theorem than previous analysts, examining theoretically both the factor content and commodity content of international trade.

Although Leontief's own explanation is sometimes overlooked by analysts (Leontief, 1953b, p. 345), he explained the paradox by observing that the productivity of US workers was three times as great as that of their foreign counterparts; therefore, the export of labor-intensive goods was essentially the export of goods in which a high level of labor productivity was present. One group of economists (e.g. Kreinin, 1965; Chacholiades, 1978; Duchin, 1989, 1990) supported Leontief's explanation with specific information on the increases in US labor productivity. Especially during the years immediately following the publication of Leontief's article, economists offered numerous alternative explanations as to why the paradox exists, as summarized by Caves (1960, pp. 268–282). Many of these alternative explanations centered around the issue of comparative advantage, namely (1) the abundance of research and development; (2) skill differentials; (3) high education levels and other human capital factors; (4) the failure to account for the role of natural resources, including land; and (5) the possibility of a factor intensity reversal. Others (e.g. Becker, 1952; Ellsworth, 1954; Kenen, 1959) countered Leontief by saying that the factor contents of US exports were consistent with the HO theorem, because US exports were material-capital- plus human-capital-intensive, rather than labor-intensive. Some of the most relevant literature is contained in the "Foreign trade and international models" section of the three-volume collection of input-output papers by Kurz et al. (1998, pp. 131–208). Few of the national analysts have taken actual trade data from countries to do tests.

In contrast to the relatively wide attention given to tests of the Leontief Paradox using international trade data, very few analysts seem aware of the tests made using interregional trade data within a single country. The main finding from regional tests, with one or two exceptions, is that they do not support the Leontief Paradox. Yet few economists note this finding, perhaps because economists generally have not followed the regional literature.

Regional analysts have not made major theoretical contributions to the trade theory upon which the HO theorem is based, but they have done extensive empirical testing of the theorem both for regions in the United States (e.g. Moroney and Walker, 1966; Horiba and Kirkpatrick, 1981;

Madresehee, 1993) and in Japan (e.g. Horiba, 1973; He, 1996; He and Polenske, 2001). Only Davis et al. (1996, and 1997) have tested the HO theory both internationally and interregionally. Most of these analysts assume that the HO theorem would be supported at the regional level, because, for regions within a country, distortions from tariffs, import quotas, government subsidies, depletion allowances, institutions, and other extraneous factors should be minimal. At the same time, they were confident that the HO assumption of identical production technologies and demand conditions would be met.

Findings from these tests also help to explain some of the limitations of the data that both national and regional analysts use for the tests. First, Heckscher's definition of factors of production includes not only the quantities, but also the qualities of land, labor and capital, whereas analysts testing the HO theory have no information on qualities. Second, Ohlin's definition of factor endowments includes mineral deposits, special-use land, and climate. Third, certain products, such as chemicals, paper products, petroleum and tobacco, can be produced only in areas where the natural resources (including good climate) are present; consequently, an analyst needs to expand the definition of factor endowments to say that comparative advantage is determined by natural resources as well as by capital and labor endowments (Madresehee, 1993). In fact, "the initial endowment of natural resources may be more important than [the] relative abundance of material capital or labor in determining the *initial structure* [their emphasis] of comparative advantage . . . [After this is established, however,] relative endowments of material capital and labor are important in influencing the pattern of industrial growth" (Moroney and Walker, 1966, p. 584).

Horiba and Kirkpatrick (1981) have tested whether the changes in endowment ratios across regions were systematically related to changes in factor proportions. The latest testing of the Leontief Paradox by other economists, of which I am aware, is reported in two relatively recent articles by Davis et al. (1996, and 1997) and one article by He and Polenske (2001). He and Polenske take pairs of regions, rather than assuming a region exports to (and imports from) a single homogenous aggregate region. For some of these pairs the HO theorem holds, while for other pairs the Leontief Paradox holds. The next step is to obtain data to conduct more extensive tests of labor migration than any analysts were able to conduct so far and to perform additional tests of capital flows as well.

Instead of testing the old comparative advantage trade theory, some analysts advocate the use of New Trade Theory. Helpman and Krugman (1986) build upon the earlier work of Dixit and Norman (1980),

Vanek (1968) and others, as well as their own separate research (e.g. Krugman, 1979, 1980, 1981, 1987, and 1996; Helpman, 1983, 1984a, and 1984b), to show theoretically how international trade operates in an imperfectly competitive world market that is characterized by increasing returns. They make an important theoretical contribution to trade theory not only by building an alternative (to the comparative cost) theoretical framework, but also by starting the bridge to theories of industrial organization. Their purpose is to build a framework for an integrated economy with differentiated products that analysts can use to determine the pattern of international trade and whether or not it is useful. Not only do they start from the premise that the factors of production are perfectly mobile, but they also either sidestep, or deal only implicitly with, the issue of the factor content or commodity content of international trade.

One major problem with the New Trade Theory is that, as far as this author knows, no analysts have conducted extensive empirical tests of it. Testing the New Trade Theory is difficult because considerable data are required to account for the economic, environmental, geographical, cultural and social factors that probably help determine particular trade patterns. The regional analysts mentioned above have noted many of these factors in their studies, but neither they nor the national trade analysts have been able to collect appropriate data. Leontief believed that a theory to be useful must be tested empirically with real data.

In summary, the HO theorem assumes historically static regional conditions and costless movements of labor and capital between regions. As shown in testing the HO theorem to date, these two conditions are not usually met; in addition, analysts have not yet located sufficient data to show how regional variations in different resource endowments might affect trade. It is surprising that so few economic analysts have tested the Leontief Paradox at the regional level. As Leontief would stress, additional national and regional data are needed for analysts to conduct more robust empirical tests than have been possible to date.

8.   Spatial and world models

Leontief conducted a limited number of spatial analyses, including intranational and multiregional analyses. The theoretical structures of both models are unique compared with other work ongoing in the field at the time he developed them. In both cases, Leontief took into consideration the need to work with very limited quantities of regional data.

For the intranational accounts and model, Leontief designed them so that analysts had to obtain only these items: (1) a national input-output table, including final demands; (2) allocation factors to distribute the so-called national outputs (see above) to the regions; and (3) final demands for the regional (local) industries, specified for each region. Very few data are needed in comparison to almost any other multiregional system proposed. Although Leontief developed the theoretical intranational model, which was his first spatial input-output model, in 1953 (Leontief, 1953a), he did not implement it fully until the arms reduction analysis noted above (Leontief et al., 1965).

Thus, in terms of amount of data required to implement the model, Leontief's intranational accounts and model stood in sharp contrast to the interregional input-output (IRIO) accounts and model that Isard (1960) proposed. On the one hand, Isard's IRIO model requires separate input-output matrices for each region. If there are n regions in the study, this alone requires $(n - 1) \times n$ more matrices than Leontief's intranational model. On the other hand, Leontief did not propose to use the intranational model for transportation analyses, but an analyst can use the IRIO model for such studies. To implement Isard's model, an analyst not only needs an input-output table for each region, but he/she must specify all inputs (and outputs) by industry and region of origin, and industry and region of destination.[6]

For the multiregional accounts and model, Leontief and Strout (1963) designed a theoretical regional structure that was unique in two ways. First, Leontief believed in working with conceptual frameworks, such as the multiregional input-output (MRIO) model, that would be easy to explain to engineers and others. The IRIO model is not designed in a way that engineers can readily follow. What is the difference? To make one widget, an engineer needs to know how many pounds of steel, kilowatts of electricity, etc. are needed, which is the information present in the MRIO technical coefficient matrices. The region of origin (information present in the IRIO technical coefficient matrices) of each of the inputs is not of direct interest to the engineer (although it may be to the purchasing agent). As just mentioned, for the IRIO model the analyst needs to obtain a complete set of input data, by region and industry, of origin and destination. In the Leontief multiregional model, the analyst needs only to know, for a given industry in a given region, how much of each input is used (the region of origin of the input is not required for implementing

---

[6] Staff at the Ministry of International Trade and Industry (MITI) in Japan followed Isard's suggestions and constructed an IRIO table for Japan for nine regions and ten industries. The Japanese IRIO tables are available on a five-year basis since 1960 (MITI, 1970); in 2003, the most recent one was for 1995.

the model). Hartwick (1971) and Polenske (1995) provide additional details about the theoretical structure of these two models. The data for the multiregional model are easily obtainable from census data in the United States. That is where Polenske (1970) and her research team at the Harvard Economic Research Project (HERP) obtained much of the data for the US MRIO model, the first full implementation of the Leontief-Strout multiregional input-output framework.

The second unique characteristic of the Leontief-Strout model is the use of gravity coefficients instead of column coefficients to designate flows between regions. Leontief and Strout maintained that the flow of a good between region g and region h is equal to the amount of production in region g and amount of consumption in region h, divided by the overall production/consumption in the country. That fraction is then multiplied by the gravity coefficient, which can be represented as the inverse of the distance between regions g and h. Here, as in the case of automation, Leontief did not completely work through the empirical models. If he had done so, he would have found that the Leontief-Strout gravity model cannot be implemented with actual large-scale data. Rather than invert a large matrix (more than 4,000 rows and columns), the HERP researchers decided to use the iterative procedure for calculating the inverse of the I-A matrix. The iterations never converged. After consulting with many mathematicians and others, Bon (1975) determined that the Leontief-Strout gravity coefficients, which are demand- and supply-driven, are not mathematically consistent with the input-output coefficients, which are demand-driven.

People throughout government agencies heard about Leontief's Vietnam War arms reduction study. That knowledge probably is part of the reason that Benjamin Chinitz and other staff in the Economic Development Administration (EDA), US Department of Commerce, approached Leontief in 1965 to construct a set of multiregional input-output accounts for the United States. Leontief and his researchers at the HERP decided to undertake the project, and EDA gave them a three-year grant for the work. The HERP staff decided to construct the accounts for fifty-one regions (the fifty states plus Washington, DC) and for seventy-nine industries (the size of the 1958 published national input-output table, which was the latest one available when work was begun). EDA officials tried to get Leontief to undertake the project for all counties (about 3,076). He rejected their suggestion for two reasons. First, actual data for the accounts were not readily available at the county level from the census, because of non-disclosure rules. Second, computers in the late 1960s were limited in capacity, and the calculations for the approximately 3,076 counties would have been too time-consuming and costly compared with those for the fifty-one regions. In any case, he was deeply immersed in working on the theory of the dynamic model and did not want to oversee the work on the accounts.

Polenske became the person whom he asked to be in charge of the multiregional accounts and modeling activity. In 1966 Polenske was just completing her Ph.D., and, as today, few young scholars in the Harvard Economics Department were interested in regional issues. No one else was willing to undertake such an heroic endeavor. After all, the IBM 7094 was still the main computer being used, so that the calculation of such huge sets of data (4,029 × 4,029 matrices) was an awesome, time-consuming and expensive operation, even with all the free computer time frequently available at Harvard. Polenske and her team of three full-time staff and seven students worked on the first detailed set of MRIO accounts and models until 1970, having started work in the summer of 1966. They implemented the model using 1963 input-output tables constructed from actual census and other data for each of the fifty-one regions, and 1947, 1958 and 1963 actual final demand data and 1970 and 1980 projected final demands (Polenske, 1980). Because the gravity version of the MRIO model would not converge, the team reverted to using the so-called Chenery-Moses (Chenery, 1953; Moses, 1955) column coefficient model.

Work on the dynamic model distracted Leontief from the multiregional model until the early 1970s (Leontief, 1975). At that point, the Dutch government offered a grant to the United Nations to sponsor a comprehensive study of the sustainability of the world economy. Leontief was asked by the United Nations to develop the world model (Leontief et al., 1977). Leontief sketched the basic model in a simple and elegant two-sector form, classifying the world into the "developed countries" and the "less developed countries." This sketch was published as his Nobel Prize address (Leontief, 1975). Carter and Petri helped design and then elaborated the basic model to fifteen regions, each with roughly two hundred activities, including sectoral outputs, minerals, specific pollutants and a set of macroeconomic current and capital account variables. They organized the data collection and the processing and modeling of alternatives (on a PDP-10!) at Brandeis University. As with earlier versions of Leontief's multiregional model, one of the unique characteristics of the world model was the use of supply and demand pools. Rather than deal with the individual origins and destinations of each input and output, Leontief, Carter and Petri assumed that a good went into a supply pool from which an industry or final user within or outside the region could demand it. Thus, once again in this field, Leontief and his colleagues designed several unique ways of working with the limited data available.

9.   Conclusion

In this paper, I have shown how Leontief systematically made advances in theory at the same time that he was contributing to the knowledge of the working of the US and world economies. For him, economic theory and empirical research had to be closely linked, and he illustrated, time after time, why this link was so important. His first major work, the development of the input-output theory and his application of the model to the US economy in 1919 and 1929 (Leontief, 1936, and 1941) is the best-known achievement. It is a major one, especially considering the lack of computers and data at the time he was doing the research. Amazingly, he was not deterred from thinking of working with the massive amounts of data that exist in the real world. I can only wonder why other great theorists shy away from such work.

ACKNOWLEDGEMENTS

The author deeply appreciates comments by Professor Anne P. Carter, Martin C. Kohli, Ali Shirvani-Mahdavi and two anonymous referees. The author, however, takes full responsibility for the views presented. Earlier versions of this paper were presented at the Allied Social Science Association meetings, Union of Radical Political Economists, in Boston, MA, January 8, 2000, and at the Thirteenth International Conference on Input-Output Techniques, Macerata, Italy, August 21–25, 2000. Both were special sessions in memory of Wassily W. Leontief.

REFERENCES

Ayres, R. A., and A. V. Kneese (1969) Production, consumption, and externalities, *American Economic Review*, 59, 282–297.

Becker, G. S. (1952) A note on multi-country trade, *American Economic Review*, 42, 558–568.

Bon, R. (1975) *Some Conditions of Macroeconomic Stability in Multiregional Models*, Ph.D. dissertation (Cambridge, MA, Massachusetts Institute of Technology, Department of Urban Studies and Planning).

Carter, A. P. (1966) The economics of technological change, *Scientific American*, 214, 25–31.

Carter, A. P., and P. Petri (1989) Leontief's contributions to economics, *Journal of Policy Modeling*, 11, 7–30.

Caves, R. E. (1960) *Trade and Economic Structure: Models and Methods* (Cambridge, MA, Harvard University Press).

Chacholiades, M. (1978) *International Trade Theory and Policy* (New York, McGraw-Hill).

Chenery, H. (1953) Regional analysis, in H. Chenery and P. Clark (eds.) *The Structure and Growth of the Italian Economy* (Rome, United States Mutual Security Agency), 96–115.

Cumberland, J. H. (1966) A regional interindustry model for the analysis of development objectives, *Papers of the Regional Science Association*, 16, 69–94.

Daly, H. E. (1968) On economics of a life science, *Journal of Political Economy*, 76, 392–407.

Davis, D. R., D. E. Weinstein, S. C. Bradford and K. Shimpo (1996) *The Heckscher-Ohlin-Vanek Model of Trade: Why Does It Fail? When Does It Work?*, NBER Working Paper W5625 (Cambridge, MA, National Bureau of Economic Research).

(1997) Using international and Japanese regional data to determine when factor abundance theory of trade works, *American Economic Review*, 87, 421–446.

Deardorff, A. V. (1982) The general validity of the Heckscher-Ohlin theorem, *American Economic Review*, 72, 683–694.

Dixit, A., and V. Norman (1980) *Theory of International Trade* (Cambridge, Cambridge University Press).

Dorfman, R. (1973) Wassily Leontief's contribution to economics, *Swedish Journal of Economics*, 75, 430–449.

Duchin, F. (1989) International trade and the use of capital and labor in the US economy, *Economic Systems Research*, 1, 345–350.

(1990) Technological change and international trade, *Economic Systems Research*, 2, 47–52.

(1995) In honor of Wassily Leontief's 90th birthday, *Structural Change and Economic Dynamics*, 6, 267–269.

Duchin, F., and D. B. Szyld (1985) A dynamic input-output model with assured positive output, *Metroeconomica*, 37, 269–282.

Duncan, J. W., and W. C. Shelton (1978) *Revolution in United States Government Statistics, 1926–1976* (Washington, DC, US Department of Commerce).

Ellsworth, P. T. (1954) The structure of American foreign trade: a new view examined, *Review of Economics and Statistics*, 36, 279–285.

Foley, D. K. (1998) MD interview: an interview with Wassily Leontief, *Macroeconomic Dynamics*, 2, 116–140.

Hartwick, J. M. (1971) Notes on the Isard and Chenery-Moses interregional input-output models, *Journal of Regional Science*, 11, 73–86.

He, S. (1996) *An Interregional Test of the Heckscher-Ohlin Theory: The Case of Japan*, Master in City Planning thesis (Cambridge, MA, Massachusetts Institute of Technology, Department of Urban Studies and Planning).

He, S., and K. R. Polenske (2001) Interregional trade, the Heckscher-Ohlin-Vanek theorem, and the Leontief Paradox, in M. L. Lahr and E. Dietzenbacher (eds.) *Input-Output Analysis: Frontiers and Extensions* (Basingstoke, Palgrave), 161–186.

Heckscher, E. (1919) The effect of foreign trade on the distribution of income, *Ekonomisk Tidskrift*, 21, 497–512. [Reprinted in abridged form in H. S. Ellis and L. A. Metzler (eds.) *Readings in the Theory of International Trade* (Homewood, IL, Irwin, 1949), 272–300.]

Helpman, E. (1983) Variable returns to scale and international trade: two generalizations, *Economics Letters*, 11, 167–174.

(1984a) Increasing returns, imperfect markets, and trade theory, in R. W. Jones and P. B. Kenen (eds.) *Handbook of International Economics* (Amsterdam, North Holland), 325–365.

(1984b) The factor content of foreign trade, *Economic Journal*, 94, 84–94.

Helpman, E., and P. R. Krugman (1986) *Market Structure and Foreign Trade: Increasing Returns, Imperfect Competition, and the International Economy* (Cambridge, MA, MIT Press).

Horiba, Y. (1973) Factor proportions and the structure of interregional trade: the case of Japan, *Southern Economic Journal*, 34, 381–388.

Horiba, Y., and R. C. Kirkpatrick (1981) Factor endowments, factor proportions, and the allocative efficiency of US interregional trade, *Review of Economics and Statistics*, 63, 178–187.

Isard, W. E. (1960) *Methods of Regional Analysis: An Introduction to Regional Science* (Cambridge, MA, MIT Press).

Isard, W. E., et al. (1968) On the linkage of the socioeconomic and ecological systems, *Papers of the Regional Science Association*, 21, 79–99.

Kenen, P. B. (1959) Distribution, demand, and equilibrium in international trade: a diagrammatic analysis, *Kyklos*, 12, 629–638.

Kohli, M. C. (2001) The Leontief-BLS partnership: framework for measurement, *Monthly Labor Review*, 124 (6), 29–37.

Kreinin, M. E. (1965) Comparative labor effectiveness and the Leontief scarce factor paradox, *American Economic Review*, 64, 143–155.

Krugman, P. R. (1979) Increasing returns, monopolistic competition, and international trade, *Journal of International Economics*, 9, 469–479.

(1980) Scale economies, product differentiation, and the pattern of trade, *American Economic Review*, 70, 950–959.

(1981) Intraindustry specialization and the gains from trade, *Journal of Political Economy*, 89, 959–974.

(1987) Increasing returns and the theory of international trade, in T. F. Bewley (ed.) *Advances in Economic Theory* (New York, Cambridge University Press), 301–328.

(1996) *Rethinking International Trade* (Cambridge, MA, MIT Press).

Kurz, H. D., E. Dietzenbacher and C. Lager (eds.) (1998) *Input-Output Analysis*, 3 vols. (Cheltenham, Edward Elgar Publishing).

Kurz, H. D., and N. Salvadori (2000) 'Classical' roots of input-output analysis: a short account of its long prehistory, *Economic Systems Research*, 12, 153–179.

Leamer, E. E. (1980) The Leontief Paradox, reconsidered, *Journal of Political Economy*, 88, 495–503.

Leontief, W. W. (1936) Quantitative input and output relations in the economic system of the United States, *Review of Economics and Statistics*, 18, 105–125.

(1937) Implicit theorizing: a methodological criticism of the neo-Cambridge school, *Quarterly Journal of Economics*, 51, 337–351.

(1941) *The Structure of American Economy, 1919–1929* (Cambridge, MA, Harvard University Press).

(1944) Output, employment, consumption, and investment, *Quarterly Journal of Economics*, 58, 290–313.

(1947) Introduction to the internal structure of functional relationships, *Econometrica*, 15, 361–373.

(1951a) *The Structure of American Economy, 1919–1939: An Empirical Application of Equilibrium Analysis* (New York, Oxford University Press).

(1951b) Input-output economics, *Scientific American*, 185, 15–21.

(1952) Machines and man, *Scientific American*, 187, 150–160.

(1953a) Interregional theory, in W. W. Leontief et al. *Studies in the Structure of the American Economy* (New York, Oxford University Press), 93–115.

(1953b) Domestic production and foreign trade: the American capital position re-examined, *Proceedings of the American Philosophical Society*, 97, 332–349.

(1954) Mathematics in economics, *Bulletin of the American Mathematical Society*, 60, 215–233.

(1958) The state of economic science, *Review of Economics and Statistics*, 40, 103–106.

(1963) The structure of development, *Scientific American*, 209, 148–166.

(1964) The balance of the economy of the USSR, in N. Spulber (ed.) *Foundations of Soviet Strategy for Economic Growth: Selected Soviet Essays, 1924–1930* (Bloomington, IN, Indiana University Press), 88–94.

(1967a) *The New Outlook in Economics* (Sir Ellis Hunter Memorial Lecture No. 3, July 6, University of York).

(1967b) Economic effect of Vietnam spending, in *Hearings before the Joint Economic Committee, Congress of the United States*, Vol. I: *Statements of Witnesses and Supporting Materials* (Washington, DC, US Government Printing Office), 242–263.

(1970) Environmental repercussions and the economic structure: an input-output approach, *Review of Economics and Statistics*, 52, 262–271.

(1971) Theoretical assumptions and nonobserved facts, *American Economic Review*, 61, 1–7.

(1975) Structure of the world economy – outline of a simple input-output formulation, *Proceedings of the Institute of Electrical and Electronics Engineers*, 63, 345–350.

(1979) Is technological unemployment inevitable?, *Challenge*, 22, 48–50.

(1985) The choice of technology, *Scientific American*, 252, 36–45.

Leontief, W. W., A. P. Carter and P. Petri (1977) *The Future of the World Economy* (New York, Oxford University Press).

Leontief, W. W., and F. Duchin (1986) *The Future Impact of Automation on Workers* (New York, Oxford University Press).

Leontief, W. W., and D. Ford (1972) Air pollution and the economic structure: empirical results of input-output computations, in A. Brody and A. P. Carter (eds.) *Input-Output Techniques* (Amsterdam, North Holland), 9–30.

Leontief, W. W., and M. Hoffenberg (1961) The economic effects of disarmament, *Scientific American*, 204, 47–55.

Leontief, W. W., A. Morgan, K. R. Polenske, D. Simpson and E. Tower (1965) The economic impact – industrial and regional – of an arms cut, *Review of Economics and Statistics*, 47, 217–241.

Leontief, W. W., and A. Strout (1963) Multiregional input-output analysis, in T. Barna (ed.) *Structural Interdependence and Economic Development* (New York, St Martin's Press), 119–150.

Madresehee, M. (1993) Factor prices, factor proportions, and factor endowments in the Pacific Northwest: a regional test of the Heckscher-Ohlin theorem for the N-factor case, *Annals of Regional Science*, 27, 143–152.

Ministry of International Trade and Industry (1970) *Interregional Input-Output Table for Japan* (Tokyo, Ministry of International Trade and Industry).

Moroney, J. R., and J. M. Walker (1966) A regional test of the Heckscher-Ohlin hypothesis, *Journal of Political Economy*, 74, 573–586.

Moses, L. N. (1955) The stability of interregional trading patterns and input-output analysis, *American Economic Review*, 45, 803–832.

Ohlin, B. (1933) *Interregional and International Trade* (Cambridge, MA, Harvard University Press).

Piel, G. (1999) *Wassily W. Leontief*, memorial service for Wassily Leontief, April 8, New York University.

Polenske, K. R. (1970) An empirical test of interregional input-output models: estimate of 1963 Japanese production, *American Economic Review*, 60, 76–82.

(1980) *The U.S. Multiregional Input-Output Accounts and Model* (Lexington, MA, Lexington Books).

(1995) Leontief's spatial economic analyses, *Structural Change and Economic Dynamics*, 6, 309–318.

(1999) Wassily W. Leontief, 1905–1999, *Economic Systems Research*, 11, 341–348.

Samuelson, P. A. (1948) International trade and the equalization of factor prices, *Economic Journal*, 58, 163–184.

Silk, L. (1976) *The Economists* (New York, Basic Books).

Solow, R. M. (1998) On rereading "The Structure of the American Economy," *Economic Systems Research*, 10, 299–306.

United Nations (1968) *A System of National Accounts*, Studies in Methods, Series F, No. 2, Rev. 3 (New York, United Nations, Department of Economic and Social Affairs, Statistical Office of the United Nations).

Vanek, J. (1968) The factor proportions theory: the N-factor case, *Kyklos*, 21, 749–756.

Williams, J. R. (1978) *The Canadian-United States Tariff and Canadian Industry: A Multisectoral Analysis* (Toronto, University of Toronto Press).

3 Leontief and the future of the world economy

Emilio Fontela

1. Historical background

In the 1950s and 1960s the world economy recorded extremely high growth, reaching, on average, an annual gross domestic product (GDP) growth rate of 4.5 percent. This high economic growth raised problems of sustainability, taking into account the increase in pollution and the significant consumption of finite resources such as minerals and hydrocarbons. At the end of the 1960s a thorough analysis of these problems was greatly stimulated by the Club of Rome's active promotion of a world model using systems dynamics methodologies. The model was first developed by Forrester (1971) and expanded by Meadows et al. (1972). The latter study, entitled "Limits to Growth," pointed quantitatively to the impending dangers of world shortages of energy and raw materials, and to vast environmental problems, should the world population, capital formation, and economic production continue to grow exponentially at rates such as those observed in the preceding decades.

Systems dynamics deals with "multi-loop non-linear feedback systems, a class to which all our social systems belong" (Forrester, 1971, p. 123). The design of the model was fairly simple, the world being treated as a single unit. The structural specification and calibration of the model, however, turned out to be extremely difficult due to a lack of relevant information. As a consequence, arbitrary levels and rates had to be used for most variables. Despite the efforts toward a better quantification by a larger research team, the resulting final world model raised considerable objections. Yet the debate in itself served the purpose of diffusing the Club of Rome's idea of the "World Problematique." Substantial improvements in the methodology and data were introduced in a second report to the Club of Rome by Mesarovic and Pestel (1974). Although they used a set of interacting regions of the world – this being the first time that such a model had been employed – the nature of the debate on world modeling was not substantially changed. The idea of "limits to growth" was also developed by Ward and Dubos (1972) and was presented to the United

Nations Conference on Human Environment held in Stockholm in 1972. However, in their study they used other means – such as the biospheric concept of "only one earth."

The United Nations had been pressing for an international development strategy for the 1970s (see UN, 1971). In particular, the organization wished this strategy to aim at reducing the disparities between rich and poor countries and to take account of the new consciousness of the limited capacity of the earth. The interesting progress of modeling these relevant topics moved the United Nations to launch a study dealing with environmental issues raised by world development and looking for "possible alternative policies to promote development while at the same time preserving and improving the environment" (UN, 1973, p. 2). To embark on such a study, the United Nations required a solid methodological basis. Wassily Leontief, who had already analyzed the relations between the economy and the environment (Leontief, 1970), had a long-standing relationship with the organization (having hosted the International Conferences on Input-Output Techniques in Geneva in the 1960s). Leontief was, therefore, the United Nations' first choice.

Leontief was enthusiastic about the UN project and, by 1973, he had already developed his first theoretical model. This model provided the content for the Stockholm lecture of December 1973, when he received the Nobel Memorial Prize in Economic Sciences (Leontief, 1974). The model was built around a hypothetical case of two regions (developed and less developed countries), three commodities (the product of the extraction industry, other production, and pollution abatement), two components of final demand (domestic and trade), and two components of value added (labor and capital returns). Its theoretical formulation included both a quantity model and a dual price model, relying on the basic input-output relations.

With seventeen equations and twenty-nine unknowns, this simple model required twelve exogenous values for actual computation. The choice of these values, as well as possible changes in technical coefficients, was made in the framework of scenarios. Peter Petri provided rough estimates of the necessary technical coefficients. "The numbers are, strictly speaking, fictions. But their general order of magnitude reflects crude, preliminary estimates . . ." (Leontief, 1974, p. 825). On this basis, three scenarios were computed for 2000.

In the base scenario (case 1), the productivity of labor was expected to be three times as high in 2000 as in 1970, and the developed region would strictly enforce the standards of the 1967 US Clean Air Act, whereas there was to be no abatement activity in the less developed region. In case 2, the less developed region would introduce an abatement policy to limit pollution to twice its initial level. In case 3, the productivity of labor in the extraction industry of the developed countries would grow at half the initial rate, and the technical coefficients for inputs in this extraction industry were to be doubled. This reflected a move toward the exhaustion of natural resources and to increasing extraction costs. As might be expected in a simple linear accounting system, without price-sensitive behavioral equations either for demand or for trade, the results of the three scenarios in real terms were not radically different. However, in cases 2 and 3 there was a substantial shift of the terms of trade – leading to a redistribution of income favoring the less developed countries.

Leontief ended his Nobel lecture by stating (1974, p. 833):

All theories tend to shape the facts they try to explain; any theory may thus turn into a Procustean bed. Our proposed theoretical formulation is designed to protect the investigator from this danger: it does not permit him to draw any special or general conclusions before he or someone else completes the always difficult and seldom glamorous task of ascertaining the necessary facts.

This less than glamorous task was expected of Anne Carter, Peter Petri and, of course, Wassily Leontief himself during the following two years. It led to the report to the United Nations on the future of the world economy (UN, 1976) – which was later to be published in book form in several languages (Leontief et al., 1977). It was widely discussed in both developed and developing countries, by all sorts of economic and environmental organizations.

Before its release, the report was discussed by an ad hoc group of experts (Chakravarty, Courcier, el Iman, Klein, Linneman, Mesarovic, Porwit, Ridker, Shishido and the present author) that proposed further extensions of the model and the consolidation of permanent UN activity around it, under the heading of "UN Project 2000." This was in line with Leontief's own wishes: "It is hoped that the model will have a continuing life in which fresh data are used as they become available and in which the model is eventually applied to other development questions" (UN, 1976, p. 7).

Earlier in that same year Richard Stone (1976) had confirmed that developing a world model based on national accounting data, including sectoral disaggregation, raised "serious but not in principle insoluble" problems. As Stone observed (1976, p. 32):

In so far as they are due to the uneven development of the relevant subject areas, all that is needed is for the interest and energies of social scientists and historians to be channelled towards a quantitative approach to their subject: once these scientists had set up the appropriate framework, the data will flow in like pins towards a magnet, as has happened with national accounts statistics in the last thirty years.

Some UN agencies, such as the United Nations Industrial Development Organization (UNIDO), made efforts to develop and quantify new generalized world models. The Seventh International Conference on Input-Output Techniques, held at Innsbruck in 1979, devoted an entire session to the discussion of several world models developed by international organizations (UNIDO, 1984).

As often happens in large organizations, the United Nations was not interested in funding the refinements, the UN agenda changed, and Project 2000 progressively lost momentum. Rather, the United Nations concentrated on shorter-term macroeconomic analyses implementing Project LINK under the methodological guidance of Lawrence Klein (see Klein and Peeterssen, 1973).[1] In 2003 LINK was still a UN project, coordinated by teams at the Universities of Toronto and Pennsylvania, including almost a hundred national macro-models interrelated by a trade matrix.

At a later stage, Leontief made further runs with the model (together with Faye Duchin at the NYU's Institute of Economic Analysis), dealing with alternative population forecasts and other issues (Leontief et al., 1978). Leontief had proven the point: given adequate resources, it is possible and useful to build regionalized long-term world models, with the usual restrictions of input-output analysis.

2.   The model and the data

The final version of Leontief's world model (UN, 1976) included fifteen regions. There were four regions covering the advanced industrial countries, four regions for the centrally planned economies, and two groups of developing countries – namely resource-rich (three regions) and resource-poor (four regions). Each region was described in terms of forty-eight sectors of economic activities, including eight exhaustible mineral resources and hydrocarbons. In addition, eight types of major pollutants and five types of abatement activities were identified. The base year was 1970 and projections were made to 1980, 1990 and 2000. In total, the fifteen interconnected (through trade) sets of regional equations developed into a linear system of 2,625 equations.

In some senses, the world model was a partitioned hybrid input-output system, with agricultural crops, energy and minerals treated in terms of physical units and nominal prices, and the rest of the sectors treated in value terms with initial unit prices. An original feature of the model

---

[1] Project LINK is an international research consortium of more than sixty countries in the industrial and developing worlds. Its focus has been to integrate independently developed national econometric models into a single world model ("LINK"). Initiated in 1968 by the US Social Science Research Council (SSRC), the project has expanded from a core of eleven researchers and seven country models to more than two hundred and fifty participants and almost a hundred models.

was the use of "world pools" to deal with trade relations. Regions addressed their import requirements (as a function of their own activity levels) to a pool, which distributed the totals to the different exporting countries. The world pool idea avoided the need for building an input-output international trade model, with country-to-country flows for each commodity, along the lines initially suggested by Isard (1951). While, for Isard (1951, p. 320), "any given good or service produced in any region must be taken as a unique commodity distinct from the same good and service produced in any other region," with Leontief's idea of world pools, goods and services are the same and nothing is required to be known about the bilateral relations between regions. The imports of the different commodities were endogenous – a function of regional outputs. For each commodity, a region could export a fixed proportion of the total world requirements (the sum of country imports). This proportion could be established from statistical observation of past and present situations, or from estimates provided by sectoral experts, as is usually done with columns of technical coefficients in an input-output table.

The resulting trade flows between the region and the pools were valued at uniform world prices (eventually obtained from the dual system of the US model) – a rather crude assumption justified by the lack of relevant international information and the belief that the US economy was the best available example of a free-market international economy.

The behavioral relations were kept very simple, and household consumption of specific goods was allocated with coefficients proportional to the aggregate consumption per capita. "Slacks" were introduced as extra additive variables in many equations, simplifying the use of the model in alternative situations (for example, changes of variables from endogenous to exogenous and vice versa, or even changes in the shape of an equation) – an essential requisite for scenario simulation. Despite its comprehensiveness, the model was very simple in its structure and easy to run. The main difficulty lay in establishing a database for 1970, and projecting structural changes into the future.

Because the core of the model consisted of the fifteen regional input-output tables, assembling these tables raised many problems. Although input-output tables were available for more than seventy countries, these featured different classifications and prices, and not all of them were for 1970. Therefore, the regional tables were estimated mainly on the basis of cross-national regressions of national income per capita. The regressions used input-output coefficients for the eight countries for which comparable prices were actually available (Kravis, 1975). Whenever possible, adjustments were made to introduce region-specific information.

Considerable attention was devoted to the input structures for mining activities. Starting from the 485-sector US input-output table, the relevant columns were modified to take into account the interregional differences on average costs of extracting each specific resource. US data also helped to establish regional resource consumption coefficients. The structures of the consumption of commodities for 1970 were based on cross-country regressions on income per capita for the countries of the Kravis study. International trade data were obtained from UN statistics, and time series helped to identify trends in the relevant trade import and export coefficients.

The coefficients of this complex system were projected for the years 1980, 1990 and 2000 – either as a function of income (per capita or total) or as a function of exogenous techno-economic information. For natural resources, the input coefficients also depended on the difference between production cumulated in the past and assumptions for the existing reserves. These coefficients were expected to increase with the depletion of reserves, thus reflecting the increasing difficulty of extractive activities. Production determined the employment levels as well as the needs for different types of capital stocks. The investment requirements were the sum of the depreciation of past capital stock (that is, replacement investments) and of additional requirements to expand the current capital stock.

Table 3.1, which is directly extracted from the report, portrays at a glance the variety of the methods that were used to estimate the initial 1970 base and to project the coefficients for the target years. In this table, the first four rows and columns describe the hybrid input–output matrix; the row on pollution records emissions, and the corresponding column records de-pollution activities; the rows "capital" and "labor" decompose value added; final demand includes investment and inventories (gross capital formation), consumption, urban (consumption), and government (private and public consumption); and a specific column treats fisheries exogenously from the production system. Exports and imports close the relations with the rest of the world.

To keep the accounting balances in the projections, scaling procedures were adopted to fit the specific items to the totals. This scaling was either vertical (normalizing the inputs to meet the projected total input) or horizontal (normalizing the outputs to meet the projected total output).

The task of building a regionalized model of the world economy was so large that, even with the enormous amount of work that had been done by the authors, it became a tremendous challenge. Thus, the ad hoc expert group suggested that other methods for the endogenous determination of price changes should be considered, that trade relations

Table 3.1 *Coefficient estimation and projection for a single region*

	Agriculture	Metals	Energy	Industry and services	Investment	Inventory	Pollution	Consumption	Urban	Government	Fish	Exports
Agriculture	2	0	0	4	0	4	0	1,2	0		0	4
Metals	0	0	0	2	0	4	0	0	0	0	0	2
Energy	1,2	3	3	2,4	0	4	4	1	2	1	1	2
Industry and services (fertilizers)	4	3	3	1,2	4	4	4	1	2	1	4	1
	2											
Capital	1,2	3	3	1	0	0	4	1	2	1	1	0
Pollution	2	0	0	2	0	0	4	0	1,2	0	0	0
Labour	1,2	3	3	1,2	0	0	4	1	2	1	1	0
Imports	2	2	2	1	0	0	0	0	0	0	1	0

Coefficient projection methodology

1. Income-dependent (cross-national regressions of income per capita; the coefficients change with income).
2. Specially projected (expert opinions).
3. Changing with resource depletion (reflecting increasing extraction costs).
4. Held constant.

region-specific   other

column scaled   0   no entry

benchmarked   row scaled

should be specified again with a view to incorporating bilateral flows and price elasticities, and that the dynamic properties of the model should be extended beyond the areas of population, trade and capital formation.

However, no one questioned whether a model with such crude assumptions was able to provide some rough quantitative insights into the nature of world economic interdependence. It was a courageous and ambitious endeavor, a pioneering effort in international modeling, and it was recognized as such by the United Nations and by the academic community. Because it was essentially an accounting machine with limited behavioral relations, the world model was more transparent than other attempts that used more endogenous "black box" methodologies, such as system dynamics. Of course, as is typically the case with an input-output type of model, it yields more conservative projections. Also, because a considerable number of exogenous variables and technical coefficients have to be fixed, it leaves most of the responsibilities for the final results of the simulations to the user. The Leontief world model was a stepping stone for explorers of the long-term future of the world economy. Although it had many limitations, it was nevertheless a source of significant encouragement.

3.   Scenarios and results

Because the world model was built at the request of the United Nations, the scenarios that it explored were essentially relevant to UN issues. For the definition of the basic scenarios, it was essential to cover the elements mentioned in the International Development Strategy (IDS) for the 1970s by exploring longer-term horizons (up to 2000). The scenarios were defined as combinations of exogenous sets of variables and coefficients – that is, exogenous both in terms of which variables and coefficients were chosen and in terms of the values used. In total, the report discussed the hypotheses and results of eight scenarios, and analyzed in greater depth the basic scenario, called scenario X.

First, consider the scenario in which the objectives of the IDS are extended up to 2000. Due to higher population growth in developing countries, the income gap is observed to remain stable (that is, the ratio of GDP per capita of developed regions to developing regions would remain 12.0), as shown in table 3.2.

Therefore, in establishing scenario X, changes were introduced both for developed countries (where the average annual GDP rate of growth for the period 1950 to 1970 of 4.5 percent slowed down to 4.0 percent for 1970 to 2000, and the population growth rate also slowed down from 1.0 percent to 0.7 percent) and in the developing countries (where the

Table 3.2 *Growth rates under assumptions of the IDS minimum targets for developing countries, and extrapolation of long-term growth rates in the developed countries (percentage rates per annum, 1970–2000)*

		Developed countries	Developing countries
GDP		4.5	6.0
Population		1.0	2.5
Gross product per capita		3.5	3.5
Ratio of average GDP per capita[a]	1970	12.0	1
	2000	12.0	1

[a] Developing countries =1.
Source: UN (1976, p. 122).

Table 3.3 *Growth rates and the income gap in scenario X (percentage rates per annum, 1970–2000)*

	Developed countries	Developing countries
GDP	4.0	7.2
Population	0.7	2.5
Gross product per capita	3.3	4.7
Ratio in 2000 of average GDP per capita[a]	7.7	

[a] Developing countries =1.
Source: UN (1976, p. 124).

GDP growth rate increased to 7.2 percent per year). As a result of these changes, the ratio of average GDP per capita of developed countries to developing countries (reflecting the income gap) could be brought down to 7.7 in the pivotal scenario X. This outcome could be considered a reasonable UN policy target. In an alternative scenario (scenario C) this ratio could even go down to 7.0 – should the GDP growth rate in the developed countries be brought down to 3.6 percent. Table 3.3 summarizes the key components of scenario X – the basic scenario for the UN policies.

Needless to say, in scenario X the regional growth rates were exogenous. The model was used essentially to compute some consequences of this growth on employment, investment, food production, trade, the balances of payments, pollution, abatement activities, and extraction of minerals and energy. This was the usual way of running the model, and was

Table 3.4 *Growth rates and the income gap in scenario A (percentage rates per annum, 1970–2000)*

	Developed countries	Developing countries
GDP	3.9	5.4
Population	0.7	2.3
Gross product per capita	3.2	3.1
Ratio in 2000 of average GDP per capita[a]	11.2	1.0

[a] Developing countries = 1.
Source: UN (1976, p. 125).

also the case for scenarios C, D, E, H, R and M – which incorporated various alternative hypotheses, mainly related to the size of resource endowments and to changes in trade, aid and capital flow coefficients. In short: scenarios C and D considered alternative population projections (lower in C and higher in D in relation to those in scenario X), and lower economic growth in the advanced countries; scenarios E, H, R and M envisaged a situation with food self-sufficiency in Asia, with H and R incorporating a more optimistic resource endowment, R greater aid and reduced debt services, and M a reduction of import requirements and an increase of export shares of developing countries. All these alternative scenarios used scenario X as a reference point.

However, scenario A was run in an entirely different manner. In this case, the GDP growth rates were endogenously computed, and the exogenous constraints related to the need for (i) full employment in the developed countries and (ii) the balance of payments to be in equilibrium in the less developed countries. In this respect, the authors stated that (UN, 1976, p. 115)

the future growth of GDP would tend to be determined either by the projected rates of domestic savings supplemented by funds coming from abroad, or by foreign exchange constraints (operating through the balance of payments), which would limit the imports of raw materials and capital goods that these countries cannot yet produce themselves.

The main results for scenario A are portrayed in table 3.4.

Scenarios X and A provided the main arguments for discussing the future of the world economy. The essential point made by the authors of the report was that an attempt to reduce the income gap between developed and developing countries would necessarily lead to a substantial increase in the foreign debt of these countries (scenario X), and that constraining this level of indebtedness would automatically bring down economic growth in developing countries and postpone hopes for reducing the income gap (scenario A).

As could have been expected from a very large disaggregated model, the actual run of the scenarios provided an extremely large amount of information in relevant areas of interest. Thus, the report (UN, 1976) discussed in detail scenario X projections for issues such as the changing structure of world manufacturing by regions and sectors, the prospects for food supply and demand, the outlook for grain and animal products, the future for irrigation investments, and the need for fertilizers. The market equilibria for minerals (such as copper, bauxite and nickel) and hydrocarbons (such as petroleum, natural gas and coal) were related to costs and levels of resource endowment, and the capital stocks required for resource extraction were computed. Solid wastes, suspended solids in water, particulates in air pollution, and several other pollutants were analyzed by considering their long-term developments in terms of emissions and abatements.

All of these issues were matters of great concern for the United Nations, for many governments and, of course, for those who were devoting their efforts to the World Problematique. That is, it was apparent that there was a complex system of problems to be confronted by humanity in coming decades. But perhaps the most original feature of the Leontief world model was to be found in the area of future trade and capital movements, in which serious – and essentially economic – problems could reasonably be expected to arise in the not too distant future.

In scenario X, world trade (led by trade in manufacturing) was computed to grow at an annual rate of 5.9 percent, which is well above the GDP world average rate of 4.8 percent. At constant prices, the share of manufacturing in world trade was expected to jump from 65.4 percent in 1970 to 86.4 percent in 2000.

The detailed results showed that two important regions – (i) Latin America medium income (LAM), including Argentina, Brazil and Mexico; and (ii) Asia low income (ASL), including India, Pakistan and South-East Asia – could be expected to develop large trade deficits and to face a substantial indebtedness problem under the conditions of scenario X. Table 3.5 summarizes the findings for these two regions, which were close to equilibrium in 1970.

It was, therefore, rather clear from the exploration made with the world model that these two key regions of the developing world would be able to grow only with an insufficient level of local savings, and at the expense of a growing level of foreign indebtedness. As already pointed out, scenario A enforced a balance of payments equilibrium with normal levels of capital flows. It was designed specifically to explore this initial conclusion in

Table 3.5 *International financial flows in scenario X (billions of dollars, at current prices)*

	LAM		ASL	
	1970	2000	1970	2000
Balance of trade	−0.4	−84.7	−4.2	−81.7
Net capital inflows[a]	0.8	13.6	9.3	4.9
Net aid flows	0.9	0.8	−3.8	18.2
Foreign income or interest[b]	−1.3	−172.7	−0.8	−128.8
Balance of payments[c]	0.0	−243.0	0.5	−187.0

[a] Net capital inflows in these computations include additional capital movements that are necessary to balance the payments deficits.
[b] Foreign income or interest payments are calculated on total foreign capital and debt accumulated as a result of such net capital inflows.
[c] Balances of payments totals are calculated on the same basis.
Source: UN (1976, p. 265).

greater detail. In this case, the model computed endogenously the growth rate of GDP for all regions, the aggregated results of which were shown in table 3.4.

Direct comparison of tables 3.3 and 3.4 shows, as might have been expected, that the growth of developed countries was only slightly affected (from 4.0 percent to 3.9 percent) by the changing set of hypotheses. The developing countries, however, saw their GDP growth rates reduced from 7.2 percent in scenario X to 5.4 percent in scenario A. As a consequence, the income gap remained practically constant, as reflected in the GDP per capita ratio of developed countries to developing countries – which was computed as 11.2 in 2000 and 12.0 in 1970. Bringing per capita income in developing countries closer to the world average would not come by itself. Rather, massive capital transfers would be required. A UN report could not openly spell out such a conclusion – but the model was there, showing the evidence.

4. Looking backwards from 2000

Since the early 1970s the world economy has slowed down, and population growth has been lower than expected. Table 3.6 summarizes the most recent estimates for the period, in a form directly comparable to tables 3.3 (scenario X) and 3.4 (scenario A).

Inspection of table 3.6 shows that the growth rates of the IDS were quite different from the actual future course of events, for both developed and

Table 3.6 *Observed growth rates and income gaps, 1970–2000*

	Developed countries	Developing countries
Growth rates:		
GDP	2.5	4.1
Population	0.5	2.2
Gross product per capita (1987 prices)	2.0	1.9
Ratio of average GDP per capita:[a]		
In dollars at 1987 constant exchange rates	12.3	1.0
In dollars at current exchange rates	14.7	1.0
At PPP rates	5.4	1.0

[a] Developing countries =1.
Source: Own estimates, using data from UNDP (1999).

developing countries, for reasons that are tentatively explained below. But probably the most interesting observation lies in the fact that the main objective of reducing the income gap – that is, lowering the ratio of GDP per capita between developed and developing countries – has not been met, and the ratio remains very close to the initial level of 12.0. This result points to the fact that the world has been moving more in a scenario A configuration than in a scenario X pattern of fast development of international cooperation.

Scenario X was normative: it corresponded to the objectives put forward by the United Nations, which were never met. Scenario A simulated a situation in which constraints would set limits to the deficits in current account balances of developing countries, much in line with what the International Monetary Fund has recently termed "structural adjustment policies."

It should be noted that the gap can also be measured at current exchange rates, in which case the ratio for 2000 would be higher than the initial 1970 ratio. Obviously, it can also be measured at purchasing power parity (PPP) rates, in which case the welfare value of developing countries' income is considerably increased. However, the PPP measure is not relevant for a comparison with the initial current US dollar exchange rate measures used in the report, neither for 1970 nor for the target years.

It was impossible for the scenario writers in the mid-1970s, coming as they did from an historically unique period of continuous strong growth, to imagine such a sizeable slowdown. Even allowing for the "oil shock" and the dismantling of the Bretton Woods financial stability system signaling some dangers ahead, it was difficult for scenario writers in the 1970s to extract credible indications of long-term structural changes from such short-term events.

It was only later that Freeman (1984) was in a position to provide a convincing explanation of what had happened at the time that the Leontief world model had been built. In commenting on the Massachusetts Institute of Technology (MIT) models (Forrester, 1971; Meadows et al., 1972), Freeman stated (1984, p. 499):

The characteristics of the MIT models are those of the *fourth Kondratiev* upswing – a techno-economic paradigm based on cheap oil universally available as the foundation for energy-intensive, mass and flow production of standardized homogeneous commodities such as consumer durables, and the associated capital goods, components and services.

This techno-economic paradigm permitted the massive expansion of the world economy during and after World War II, following its successful development in the US automobile industry in the previous three decades and during the war itself. Although it enabled very big productivity increases in many branches of manufacturing and in agriculture, and an enormous associated proliferation of public and private service employment, it ultimately began to encounter *limits* to further growth in the late 1960s and 1970s. This was not *just*, or even *mainly*, a question of the oil price increases, but of a combination of factors including the exhaustion of economies of scale, diminishing returns to further technical advance along existing trajectories (Wolf's Law), market saturation factors, pressures on input prices, declining capital productivity and the erosion of profit margins arising from all these factors, as well as the culmination of the competitive pressures from the Schumpeterian *swarming* process.

These comments on the MIT models also apply to the model of Mesarovic and Pestel (1974), as well as to the Leontief world model.

At the end of the 1980s there was a general move towards free trade and market economies, and towards greater regional integration. No past trends were able to explain this radical transformation, although an analysis of such types of events had been carried out on the basis of subjective a priori probabilities (Fontela and Gabus, 1974).

The present is not what the future used to be, and it is useful to build long-term models – even if only to help us understand, a posteriori, the reasons for change. As T. S. Eliot noted – in *Four Quartets* – with such great eloquence: "We shall not cease from exploration, And the end of all our exploring, Will be to arrive where we started, And know the place for the first time."

From a strictly technical point of view, all of the world models built in the early 1970s probably shared the same difficulty in exploring the future: a failure to depict the processes of change brought about by introducing prices and technologies into the picture. Prices reflect scarcities, and their evolution induces technological change. In turn, technology changes costs and prices. Such are the Schumpeterian dynamics that determine the problem of "limits."

Of all the models built at the time, the Leontief model was the only one that, in principle, allowed for the introduction of this price-technology dynamic – using price-sensitive equations for demand and for technical coefficients. That said, in the version of the model that was left to us by Carter, Leontief and Petri, these elasticities were not even specified. They relied on an exogenous treatment with very simple and conventional assumptions. But the accounting system was open to these developments of the model. Unfortunately, circumstances never allowed for these developments to take place at later stages of the modeling exercise.

5.   A tentative research agenda

Exploring the future should never be identified with forecasting. Whereas forecasting is founded on determinism, futures research encompasses a view of the world based on freedom of choice. Leontief's world model has been one of the most ambitious methodologies ever attempted to explore the long-term future of an infinitely complex system subject to continuous deep structural changes.

The exercise was successful, among other things, in pinpointing the balance-of-payments constraints in developing countries, and in identifying signals of what was later to become the debt crisis. It helped to coordinate the policies of the many agencies of the United Nations, and most probably played an educational role for those involved in decision-making affecting the future of the world, both inside and outside the United Nations. Needless to say, Leontief was courageous enough to extend the "cooking recipe" beyond its traditional boundaries. As a consequence, he met enormous methodological and data problems, and risked severe criticism from the conventional academic community. But the final output was outstanding – thanks to Peter Petri and Anne Carter, who, with rudimentary data and little computer capacity, devoted extraordinary effort to an extraordinary endeavor, and to Faye Duchin, who has extended work with the model in more recent times.

Should research along these lines be continued? Of course, the answer should be "yes". The data have continuously improved, and a single statistical observation system for all countries of the world – the 1993 UN System of National Accounts and the System of Environmental Accounts – provides promise that some of the severe hypotheses used for data preparation in the world model can soon be withdrawn. The number of countries officially publishing input-output tables, or make and use matrices linking commodities and industries, has increased. The crude income regressions for technical or consumption coefficients could now be replaced by appropriate time-series models in many regions. Furthermore, the development of social accounting matrices offers a possibility for more complete descriptions of the regional subsystems.

Modeling has also developed new tools that could be incorporated in a world model. The private consumption coefficients might be derived from behavioral equations (allowing for price and income elasticities and utility maximization), and the determination of the future technical coefficients of the input-output tables might also incorporate more explicit technology and price-sensitive models. Experiments performed with general equilibrium models, under neoclassical assumptions, already point to the fact that a new world model could be considerably more closed, with more endogenous determination of variables.

Moreover, the concept of "scenario" has also evolved towards a more comprehensive understanding of overall economic, social and political variables, and new forms of linkages between broadly defined scenarios and world models can now be envisaged. Methodologies of futures research, such as cross-impact analysis (Helmer, 1972) or interpretive structural modeling (Warfield, 1976), could considerably improve the simulation aspects of world modeling (Fontela, 2000).

In a world in which the market economy extends to cover the entire globe, in which the new technologies of the "information society" induce a new long-term upswing for the world economy, and in which new, unexpected events challenge these expectations, it is apparent that futures research in the area of world modeling, with quantitative interdependent models, is again urgent and necessary. This is a key challenge for the input-output research community, and provides a full research agenda for the years to come. This imperative is, in part, a legacy of the work of Wassily Leontief.

ACKNOWLEDGEMENTS

The author thanks Anne Carter and Faye Duchin for their comments on the historical course of events.

REFERENCES

Fontela, E. (2000) Bridging the gap between scenarios and models, *Foresight*, 2, 10–14.
Fontela, E., and A. Gabus (1974) Events and economic forecasting models, *Futures*, 6, 329–333.
Forrester, J. W. (1971) *World Dynamics* (Cambridge, MA, Wright-Allen Press).
Freeman, C. (1984) Prometheus unbound, *Futures*, 16, 494–507.

Helmer, O. (1972) Cross-impact gaming, *Futures*, 4, 149–167.

Isard, W. E. (1951) Interregional and regional input-output analysis: a model of a space-economy, *Review of Economics and Statistics*, 33, 319–328.

Klein, L. R., and L. Peeterssen (1973) Forecasting world trade within project LINK, in R. J. Ball (ed.) *The International Linkage of National Economic Models* (Amsterdam, North-Holland), 429–460.

Kravis, I. B. (1975) *A System of International Comparisons of Gross Product and Purchasing Power* (Baltimore, Johns Hopkins University Press).

Leontief, W. W. (1970) Environmental repercussions and the economic structure: an input-output approach, *Review of Economics and Statistics*, 52, 262–271.

(1974) Structure of the world economy: outline of a simple input-output formulation, *American Economic Review*, 64, 823–834.

Leontief, W. W., A. P. Carter and P. Petri (1977) *The Future of the World Economy* (New York, Oxford University Press).

Leontief, W. W., F. Duchin and I. Sohn (1978) *Population Growth and Economic Development: Illustrative Projections*, paper presented at the International Union for the Scientific Study of Population, Helsinki, Finland.

Meadows, D., J. Randers and W. W. Behren III (1972) *The Limits to Growth: First Report to the Club of Rome* (New York, Universe Books).

Mesarovic, M., and E. Pestel (1974) *Mankind at the Turning Point: Second Report to the Club of Rome* (New York, Dutton).

Stone, R. (1976) *Major Accounting Problems for a World Model*, paper presented at the Working Seminar on Global Opportunities and Constraints for Regional Development, Harvard University, Cambridge, MA.

United Nations (1971) *International Development Strategy: Action Programme of the General Assembly for the Second United Nations Development Decade* (New York, United Nations, Department of Economic and Social Affairs).

(1973) *Brief Outline of the United Nations Study on the Impact of Prospective Environmental Issues and Policies on the International Development Strategy* (New York, United Nations, Department of Economic and Social Affairs).

(1976) *The Future of the World Economy: a Study on the Impact of Prospective Economic Issues and Policies on the International Development Strategy* (New York, United Nations, Department of Economic and Social Affairs).

United Nations Development Programme (1999) *Human Development Report 1999* (New York, United Nations Development Programme).

United Nations Industrial Development Organization (1984) *Proceedings of the Seventh International Conference on Input-Output Techniques* (New York, United Nations).

Ward, B., and R. Dubos (1972) *Only One Earth* (London, André Deutsch).

Warfield, J. (1976) *Societal Systems, Planning, Policy and Complexity* (New York, John Wiley).

4 International trade: evolution in the thought and analysis of Wassily Leontief

Faye Duchin

1. Introduction

Most contemporary research about international trade assumes that a nation's comparative advantage is a major determinant of the amount and mix of its imports and exports. Comparative advantage may reflect a country's fortune regarding natural endowments or, more generally, a variety of considerations that affect its cost structures relative to those of potential trade partners. Over the course of the twentieth century, the Heckscher-Ohlin theory of international trade was expanded in various directions and formulated in ways that lent themselves to analytic representation and quantification through systems of equations expressed in terms of variables and parameters. Theorems were stated and proved, and data were collected to test hypotheses and the basic theory itself. The work of Wassily Leontief contributed significantly at every stage of this progress.

Despite all this work, the empirical results of investigations of comparative advantage have been at odds with expectations from theory so frequently that some contemporary researchers have turned to explaining trade by other mechanisms. I believe, however, that the extent of the explanatory power of comparative advantage remains to be demonstrated and that, while Leontief left an unfinished research agenda, his later work indicates research directions that others will pursue in deepening our understanding of comparative advantage in the world economy.

Between 1933 and 1977 Wassily Leontief published four articles, two reviews of the work of other economists, his Nobel Memorial Lecture, and one book on international trade. These works were produced in three distinct chronological periods; he first made a major contribution to existing theory, and then tested the dominant theory and opened it to severe questioning before offering a new conceptual framework of his own. Despite the small number of publications on trade, the subject was central to his concern with economic interdependence. By 1973, in the third period, Leontief was speaking no longer about "international trade" but about the "structure of the world economy" – a focus that situated all countries' resource endowments, production and choice of technology, consumption patterns, and trade flows within a unified framework. For him international trade was the activity that ensured the *closure of the input-output model for all geographic regions.* Leontief's treatment of trade in the 1970s departed from standard treatments – and his own earlier work – in dramatic ways, including his pioneering formulations of scenarios about the future. For these reasons, the centrality of trade in Leontief's contribution to economics has not been fully recognized. In this paper I will review the three periods of his work on trade and comment on the evolution of this body of work, its significance at the present time, and its potential significance for the future. The story is a homage to Wassily Leontief, whose originality and independence have left us a legacy the intellectual influence of which is poised to grow.

2.   The early work: Leontief as neoclassical theorist

In the 1930s Leontief (1933) developed a geometric representation of the production and consumption of two goods in two countries and the trade that would take place between them. This widely cited piece of work, which the author explicitly situated in the tradition of Marshall, Edgeworth and Pareto, extended the notion of economic equilibrium by revealing the relations between national and international phenomena. It earned him a reputation along with these predecessors, as well as Haberler, Lerner and Meade, as a major contributor, while still in his twenties, to neoclassical theory. All assumptions and conventions are those that were current at the time; he graphed production possibility frontiers and social indifference curves. The innovation was to do this for two countries simultaneously in a single graph. In the article he claimed as the significance of this achievement the ability to assess the implications for trade of changes in one or more variables in either country – an advantage over the standard demonstration by numerical example because of the greater ease in handling all cases of theoretical interest. In the later work of Leontief (and, indeed, in the profession more generally) the geometry will be supplemented by algebra and then give way to systems of equations that would be difficult to graph. The geometry facilitated the analysis of the sensitivity of the entire two-country system to a change in a variable or parameter and anticipated the even more flexible algebraic representation that would later make scenario analysis possible.

This contribution of Leontief's has been fully absorbed by the profession and is today mainly of historical interest. The main hint of things to come is his closing observation (Leontief, 1933, pp. 499 and 501):

Without trying to make a point against the spirit of the theory of comparative costs, it may be interesting to observe that two countries with costs of production which are equal not only comparatively, but even absolutely, will start an exchange of their products if their systems of indifference lines, i.e. their relative demands are different . . . The case is not as artificial as it may appear at first sight. It may partly explain the highly developed interchange of commodities between countries with similar industrial structure.

While respectful of the Heckscher-Ohlin theory, the statement prefigures his later readiness not simply to "relax" but to abandon what he considered to be the unrealistic assumptions that lay behind it. This early work is not otherwise relevant to Leontief's mature contributions.

3.   The middle period: testing the dominant theory

There are two main reasons for disillusionment among contemporary economists with the Heckscher-Ohlin theory of international trade. First, the factor-price equalization theorem, which follows logically from the theory, is clearly violated by even the most casual empirical observation. The second reason is that the doubts instigated by Leontief's empirical analysis of half a century ago have never been dispelled. This outcome was achieved in the second period of Leontief's work on trade, when in the 1950s he utilized the input-output concepts he had recently invented to test the dominant theory of trade.

3.1   Establishing the Leontief Paradox

To explain actual patterns of trade in terms of cost comparisons and factor availability required two things that were not at hand in the first half of the twentieth century: a conceptual framework and computational methods for making the necessary comparisons; and data describing the empirical situation. By the early 1950s Leontief had created a general framework for studying economic interdependence: input-output economics provided a mathematical model relating factor use, production and consumption, on the one hand, and the dual model, relating factor prices and goods prices, on the other. He and his colleagues also built a database describing the US economy at an unprecedented level of detail that would be used with the model in a wide range of inquiries. Using the full power of the model and database, he performed a conceptually simple computation to quantify the labor and the capital embodied in the country's exports and in its imports (if they had been produced domestically, or at least using the same techniques) in 1947. There is no other way besides an input-output computation to calculate the factors required directly plus indirectly to produce a given bill of goods. The method has the added advantage, which has not lost its appeal to this day, of making it possible to infer conclusions regarding a country's comparative advantage based on data for that country alone. In a framework of general interdependency (or general equilibrium), a comparison of factor contents among all potential trade partners would be required.

Twenty years after his first paper on trade, Leontief (1953) published the numerical results that established what became known as the Leontief Paradox, notably that the United States in 1947 is revealed by the factor contents of its trade to have abundant supplies of labor but scarce capital. The article was followed a few years later (Leontief, 1956) by a second one, in which he reported that the initial results still held after substantial refinement of data and method. The work was presented as an empirical test of the Heckscher-Ohlin theory of comparative advantage according to which a country would specialize in the export of goods intensive in its abundant factor. This test was made possible by an unprecedented program of data collection on Leontief's part and a clever construction of variables – the "factor content" of an export or import bill of goods – that made it possible to derive conclusive results from these data on the basis of a simple matrix multiplication using data for the United States only. In these articles Leontief stressed that these simple computations are as far as one can go in an operational understanding of the structure of international trade, so long as comparable data have not been collected for at least one other major trading country. These influential articles were successful in demonstrating the power of input-output economics. Later Leontief would oversee a massive data collection effort to assemble input-output tables for all parts of the world economy.

Over the last half-century an enormous volume of research has attempted to explain, or confirm or refute, the Leontief Paradox.[1] The first reaction among economists was to stand by the theory and question the contention that the United States was a net exporter of labor. The argument was that, in so strikingly simplifying the problem to one that could be quantified, Leontief had naturally left out other variables (such as other factors of production or non-competitive imports) and that with their inclusion the apparent paradox could be explained. Leontief's explanation was that the United States was indeed richly endowed with labor relative to capital: the qualitative superiority of American labor was the equivalent of a larger labor force of standard quality.

---

[1] There are many reviews of this extensive literature; for a recent survey article that puts the Leontief Paradox in historical perspective, see Helpman (1999).

While the theoretical implications of the Leontief Paradox remain un-settled (see below), Leontief's example stimulated many empirical arti-cles that examined the factor contents of imports and exports for different countries and time periods. Stern and Maskus (1981) confirmed the para-dox for the United States in 1958 but found that it had been eliminated by 1972. Duchin (1990) found that the paradoxical results were strong in 1963 but substantially reduced by 1977, with the reduction attributable both to the adoption of new technologies and, especially, to the changing bills of imports and exports.

3.2   Leamer's challenge

A formal representation of any economy requires dramatic simplification that necessarily leaves out what may be relevant variables, and Leontief's framework was no exception. But Leamer (1980) offered a different cri-tique: he claimed that Leontief had made the wrong comparisons. He also claimed that, once the error was corrected, the paradox disappeared and the Heckscher-Ohlin theory held for the United States in 1947.

Leamer pointed out that the Heckscher-Ohlin theory had to be tested in terms of its assumptions: all countries have the same technologies and the same pattern of consumption and each country's factor endowments are fully utilized. Based on these assumptions, Vanek (1968) had shown that factor proportions in domestic consumption (for any country) are the same as the proportions in factor endowments for the world as a whole. Using Vanek's results, Leamer argued that Leontief's comparisons of the factor contents of an equal dollar value of imports and exports were con-ceptually inconclusive. Leamer used Leontief's data to compare instead the factor contents of net exports to that of domestic consumption – a comparison that revealed the United States to be capital-rich in 1947.

Leamer's article was extremely influential, but, while subsequent au-thors have agreed to his formal argument, the story did not end there. It has been argued that Leamer, in turn, also made the wrong comparisons and, since he acknowledged that the paradox *did* hold for years other than 1947 even using his comparisons, the theory he is defending is still very much in question.

3.3   Recent analyses of factor contents

Over the past twenty years, the still substantial literature stemming from the Leontief Paradox has taken several paths. One path follows Leamer in questioning whether or not there really is a paradox if the right comparisons are made. Along these lines, Brecher and Choudhri (1982) accepted Leamer's conclusion that Leontief's data reveal the United States to be capital-rich in 1947. However, assuming yet another standard result – factor-price equalization – they found that Leontief's data still exhibited paradoxical results: consumption per worker is too high relative to the world average for a country that is a net exporter of labor (regardless of whether it is also a net exporter of capital).

A lot of the ambiguity regarding Leontief's original computation arises from the fact that the United States was a net exporter of both labor and capital in 1947, since it had a substantial trade surplus that year (especially in Leontief's database, which excluded non-competitive imports). Casas and Choi (1985) showed that Leamer's arguments were inconclusive in the case of unbalanced trade (a frequent reality, of course, but one that is inconsistent with equilibrium assumptions). They modified Leontief's data to reflect an assumption of balanced trade and found that in this case the United States is revealed to be rich in capital and scarce in labor in terms of both Leontief's comparisons and Leamer's – removing the paradox. Nonetheless, they concurred with Brecher and Choudhri that Leontief's data are still not fully explained by Heckscher-Ohlin theories.

Within the community of input-output economists, there are lines of research that continue to test for the existence of a paradox in the data for different countries or regions at different time periods. Wolff (2004) has examined changes in the detailed qualities of labor embodied in US imports and exports as well as the associated labor productivity and labor costs. He and Polenske (2001) have examined the circumstances under which the theory may be more relevant at the regional than the national level and provide a review of the regional literature on comparative advantage.

Another line of inquiry was stimulated by Leamer's critique: whether actually observed patterns of trade can be better explained if selected assumptions associated with the Heckscher-Ohlin theories are dropped. Trefler (1993, and 1995) became interested by Leontief's explanation that in 1947 the United States was abundant in labor, measured in productivity-equivalent workers, independent of whether the statement is paradoxical. He relaxed the standard Heckscher-Ohlin-Vanek assumptions of identical technologies and identical factor prices and calculated the factor productivity differences that would need to be present among nations to explain the observed data on trade and endowments. He found these productivity differences to be consistent with observed factor prices, providing support for the argument, based on Leontief's original explanation of his 1953 findings, that has been called the "Leontief-Trefler

Hypothesis" by Repetto and Ventura (1998), who – like Trefler – found support for it in their own empirical investigations. More recently Hakura (2001), following a similar methodology, observed goods trade for four countries in the European Community in 1970 and 1980, computed net factor trade flows, and compared them to expectations based on theory, using input-output matrices to represent each country's technologies. Her important conclusion is that the results were substantially better when each economy was represented by its own input-output matrix than under the assumption of common technologies.

Thus the factor content variables created by Leontief continue to be used extensively to test aspects of the dominant theory of trade and to help modify the model to better fit actual data. The factor content variables are also used to evaluate empirical evidence supporting policy positions about the major questions of the day, such as the impact of technological change versus trade on changes in domestic wage rates. A recent special issue of the *Journal of International Economics* was devoted to exploring the usefulness of factor proportions in methods that serve as a short cut to a general equilibrium analysis. Two of the main commentators are Krugman (2000), who argues for the empirical significance of factor contents, and Leamer (2000), who believes that they are mostly misleading as a substitute for a general equilibrium analysis.

All the research cited in this section defines itself in relation to a general equilibrium conception of the world economy that is consistent with the assumptions behind Heckscher-Ohlin theories of trade. Some of the researchers cited, however, are prepared to modify the theory, assumption by assumption, so as to conform better to actually observed data. While the latter start from the HOV model and relax assumptions, Leontief chose instead in the work he began in the 1970s to rely on few of the familiar assumptions and to focus on building the database that would be needed for a new model of international trade.

In 1961 Linder had remarked: "Not even Leontief, who has made extensive empirical research and reached results conflicting with factor proportions hypotheses, dared to conclude that the factor proportions approach was unsatisfactory . . . There are, however, alternative ways of explaining differences in relative price structures" (Linder, 1961, p. 16). This may have been true in 1961, but not much beyond then.

4.   Later work: a new theoretical framework

By the time of his Nobel Memorial Lecture (Leontief, 1974), Leontief did dare to take an entirely new approach to trade (see below) that does not mention factor proportion hypotheses. Nor, however, was he mainly concerned with explaining differences in relative price structures. Instead his objective was to analyze the prospects for an improved quality of life in the developing world in view of the substantial interdependencies among nations. He constructed a dramatically simplified model that covered the main features of the entire world economy and supervised the assembly of a substantial database to go with it. The conceptual design of the model relied on a few fundamental propositions, and he used three short articles (two of them reviews of other economists' work) written between 1964 and 1973 to establish them. In this section I discuss the three articles and the input-output model of the world economy, ending with a discussion of the theoretical framework of the model.

4.1   Critiques of Minhas and Chipman

By 1974 Leontief had worked out the design of a model of the world economy that grew out of the framework he used in the computations that demonstrated the Leontief Paradox. In particular, the all-important production functions were described in terms of intermediate inputs and factor inputs required to produce a unit of output, just as they had been in the context of the Leontief Paradox. While the unique strengths of input-output models were quickly recognized, still Leontief's failure to employ price elasticities as production (or consumption) parameters placed him well outside standard practice in the profession. The credibility of input-output economics required that Leontief's unconventional representation of production be robust under a relevant range of circumstances.

In a monograph entitled *An International Comparison of Factor Costs and Factor Use*, Minhas (1963) posed the question: can a meaningful distinction be made between capital-intensive and labor-intensive sectors? He concluded that it cannot, because his analysis showed that "crossovers" in the capital versus labor intensity of different sectors are common in response to changes in factor prices. If these empirical results were valid, it would be hard to defend production functions where the quantities of inputs per unit of output were not intimately tied to marginal changes in input prices.

Leontief (1964) in his review of Minhas's book asserted that these results were implausible and traced the problem to a methodological error. Correcting the problem and then relying not only on Minhas's data but also on his basic methodology, Leontief found that relatively few industries experience crossovers even using Minhas's methods. Leontief subsequently also rejected the methodology, dismissing not only Cobb-Douglas but also the constant elasticity of substitution (CES) production functions featured in the monograph as not useful for empirical analysis from which detailed conclusions about factor use at the level of specific sectors could be drawn. He argued that a sector can legitimately be called capital-intensive, because any substitution among factors in a given country due to changes in factor prices occurs only within a narrow range. This being the case, "fixed" coefficients are a good approximation of factor requirements.

The model that Leontief would develop by the end of the 1970s had as its main purpose to explore the implications for the developing economies of their relationships with the rich economies. Chipman (1970), following his influential three-part survey of the theory of international trade that was published in the mid-1960s, reported the results of his investigation into the effects of technological change on imports of raw materials by the industrialized countries from the developing countries. In this paper he demonstrated that the deteriorating terms of trade of resource-rich poor countries cannot be due to technological change in the rich countries – a result reached on the basis of an aggregative growth model with endogenous technological change. Reviewing Chipman's paper, Leontief (1970) found this result implausible and attributed it to empirically unjustifiable assumptions about elasticities of substitution among inputs. In particular, technological change in Chipman's model could not eliminate any input that was formerly used, except in the limit case where the improvement in its efficiency of use was infinite. Dismissing these methods, Leontief showed that a declining share of expenditures in the rich countries on raw materials may well be due essentially to technological change brought on by investment in research and development. The plausibility of this conclusion calls attention to the importance of technology and technological change in determining comparative advantage, and serves as a concrete example of the advantage of representing different technologies in different countries and the potential superiority of technical input-output coefficients over elasticities of substitution.

4.2   Theoretical status of bilateral trade

Leontief's empirical investigations of the 1950s had made input-output theory well known among economists. There he had started from given data for the imports and exports of one country, calculated the factor contents, and then compared the calculated factor contents to what would be expected on the basis of existing theory. Much of the work following from the Leontief Paradox followed the same schema, and still does today. By the 1970s Leontief had a different strategy, however. He wanted to build a model based on a theory of international trade with input-output coefficients as parameters and use this model to calculate imports and exports – simultaneously with production levels. The model would have to accommodate many countries, many goods, and any number of factors. But what theory of international trade would he use? He was convinced that the prevailing theory was far too restrictive and that, despite some attempts in that direction, it had never been operationally generalized from the two-country, two-good, two-factor case.

In a short and little-known paper, Leontief (1973) worked out one necessary step toward formulating his model of the world economy: he examined the theoretical standing of bilateral trade flows and found it wanting. In the paper he pointed out that the literature explaining bilateral trade makes the implicit assumption that comparative cost theory can explain these flows. He observed that theorists know better but are silent about the limitations of that theory, much to the disadvantage of those engaging in empirical research or policy analysis. His claim about the non-uniqueness of bilateral trade patterns in a comparative advantage framework comes as a surprise, especially because one is accustomed to thinking about trade in terms of the textbook case of only two countries, where the distinction between total and bilateral flows has no significance.

In general, Leontief argued, bilateral flows are not uniquely determined by comparative cost comparisons; the most that can be deduced (and this only in principle, because an adequate database is not yet available) is each trade partner's total outflow and total inflow of individual goods and services. Only if the transfer costs are large and truly differential among trade partners can a determinate bilateral solution based on comparative costs be found. Leontief presented data for the United States in 1963 according to which the differential portion of the transfer costs amounted to only a small percentage of the value of the goods.

Toward the end of the article, Leontief made the following statement (1973, p. 157):

> In the discussion of the factor-price equalization theorem it is, however, not often enough emphasized that, under the (obviously quite unrealistic) set of conditions described above, not only one but many alternative distributions of industrial activities between different countries could yield the same combination of aggregate world outputs of all goods while satisfying at the same time the requirement of full utilization of all primary resources that happen to be available in each country. This means that under such conditions and in the absence of international costs not only the network of country-to-country commodity flow but even the level and the composition of each country's total exports and imports . . . could not be uniquely determined.

Leontief demonstrated the first claim (about non-unique bilateral flows) through a mind experiment; unfortunately, no proof was offered for the second, stronger claim (about the non-uniqueness of the level and composition of a country's total trade flows). While he still had not abandoned the assumption of the full utilization of factors, by this time he was clearly convinced of the inadequacy of the standard assumptions for an empirical understanding of the structure of international trade, including that of a single, optimal solution. His rethinking of workable assumptions led to the temporary solution of "trade pools" (in the place of a more complicated representation of bilateral flows, which he considered theoretically indeterminate), which would be used in his important model of the world economy.

4.3   The "World Model" as the framework for a theory of trade

Based on the design laid out in his Nobel Memorial Lecture (Leontief, 1974), Leontief went on to create a few blocks of linear equations that, for the first time, extended a static, one-country input-output model to many regions. The variables and parameters would be quantified using input-output matrices for all countries. Final deliveries would be exogenous, just like the trade bills in his earlier calculations. The challenge would lie in conceiving of the mechanism for determining trade among regions on the basis of information about technologies, consumption vectors and factor endowments. An equally formidable challenge was to construct the database.

The motivation for the model was to analyze scenarios – not to prove theorems or test theories or hypotheses. Leontief quoted from a UN document: "By thus indicating alternative future paths which the world economy might follow, the study would help the world community to make decisions regarding future development and environmental policies in as rational a manner as possible" (Leontief, 1974, p. 345).

No mention whatever is made of a theory of factor proportions. Instead, Leontief described the input-output formulation as a "framework for assembling and organizing the mass of factual data needed to describe and understand the world economy" in terms of twenty-eight groups of countries, about forty-five sectors producing goods and services, forty minerals and fuels, and thirty pollutants. Leontief took advantage of the incomparable prestige of the Nobel Prize to publish and then implement a very unconventional formulation of international trade. Funding to construct the model and database had already been obtained through the United Nations with the objective of exploring future prospects for the developing economies.

A slim volume with the fruits of this effort was published a few years later (Leontief et al., 1977). The model and database, which are used to explore the implications of several alternative scenarios about future developments, include fifteen regions, around fifty goods and three factors. The data describing production technologies and consumption preferences are specific to each region, and there is no restraint regarding common factor prices. Factor endowments need not be fully utilized, and the framework captures intermediate production and differences in scale between large and small countries. The resulting model is one of the general interdependency of production, consumption and trade, but it does not include all the feedback mechanisms (and elasticity parameters) required for a model of Walrasian competitive equilibrium.

Thus Leontief's framework is innovative in two ways: it does not provide a unique, optimal solution; and this must be so because not all phenomena of economic interest are endogenous. He was able to drop many of the clearly unrealistic assumptions characteristic of the familiar trade theory – common structures of production and consumption for all regions, full utilization of factors, balanced trade – not to mention the usual limitation to two countries, two goods and two factors of production. He achieved this increased realism by requiring a massive base of factual information and developing detailed scenarios that themselves required a major effort for the projection of parameter values. And his formulation lacked the convenience and conceptual power, which he found illusory, of treating many phenomena, such as technological change, as endogenous.

International trade is represented in Leontief's World Model through a "trade pool" for each traded item. For each good and each region there are two sets of parameters: import coefficients and export shares. Export shares specify the portion of the total amount of world exports of the item provided by each region to the pool; and import coefficients specify the volume of competitive imports as a fraction of domestic production of the same good. Thus the determination of import and export levels is not based on cost comparisons, so there is no claim that the model can determine a region's comparative advantage.

Leontief's model of the world economy is defined by his choice of the essential variables and parameters and the relationships among them. The model has to capture the most critical attributes of the real situation so as to perform well in hypothetical scenarios about the future or of what might have been in the past (counter-factuals, "but fors," or "what ifs"). However, its main theoretical contribution is to provide a framework for analyzing the data without constraining them. The reliance on what may appear as a massive quantity of data about the present and past permits an empirical content not otherwise available for economic analysis and not massive by contemporary standards in, say, the natural sciences. Leontief never made use of this remarkable database to make the cost comparisons needed for a general theory of comparative advantage. Nonetheless, he used the World Model in a number of empirical investigations.

Economists have for the most part ignored not only the World Model but also the one-country models that share its basic features. The departures from standard practice are too great to ignore, in particular the rejection of price elasticities and elasticities of substitution as the fundamental parameters and of competitive equilibrium as the solution concept. But within new fields, such as ecological economics and industrial ecology, input-output economics is a natural counterpart to such data-based models as those of physical stocks and flows of materials (used in material balances or material flow analysis and life cycle analysis). Researchers whose work involves phenomena in the natural world have become more wary of equilibrium concepts for representing the behavior of what are clearly *complex systems*. Data-rich models of interdependent systems have a very contemporary appeal.

Among economists, even those in the input-output community have paid relatively little attention to the World Model. It is a professionally risky direction because Leontief's model traded one set of simplifications that is accepted within the profession for another set that is not. There are practical considerations as well. Working within Leontief's framework is an ambitious undertaking that requires substantial collaboration to build and maintain the relevant database and to support the research model for analyzing it. In the current literature, several trade economists are relying on the kinds of simplifications Leontief favored, preferring structural analysis to statistical inference on the one hand, and input-output representations to CGE models on the other. However, the descendant of Leontief's World Model was last used for research completed in the early 1990s (Duchin and Lange, 1994), and the team that did the analysis has dispersed.

4.4   Models and theories

Within the economics profession, it was the profoundly unsettling effect of the Leontief Paradox and the evident absence, in the real world, of factor-price equalization that opened the way for the unprecedented questioning of received wisdom about international trade by the new trade theorists. There is a tension in their work between the embrace and the rejection of some of the most deeply ingrained economic concepts. In a recent article, Krugman (2000, pp. 63–70) provides a great deal of insight into what has gone wrong with trade theory, but I believe that he fails to articulate the logical conclusion of his analysis.

According to Krugman we need to think carefully about what questions we are trying to answer, and he makes the case for the formulation of relevant scenarios (although he does not use this word) and not just the testing of the mechanics of a theoretical model. He goes on to ask of economists making a claim about causal relationships, "can they produce a general equilibrium model . . . that is consistent both with their assertions and with the . . . actual volume of trade? If they cannot, they have not made their case" (pp. 65–66). Nonetheless, rather than using a general equilibrium model, he reports a "quick and dirty version of this exercise" (p. 65), pointing out that "many economists studying the impact of trade on wages have been reluctant to commit themselves to a specific CGE model" (p. 66). This is so because there are so many parameters that "it would be hard to do any systematic sensitivity analysis" (p. 68). But this is true of all such models, not just a "specific" one. Krugman provides a more persuasive explanation when he says: "In the end, of course, one must return to the data . . . The assessment of the causes of changes in factor prices is ultimately an empirical matter" (p. 69). He then proceeds to the following conclusion (p. 70, emphasis added):

Why then has the subject [the use of factor contents to explain the relation between trade and factor prices] become a matter of intense, sometimes bitter dispute? Not because of arguments about the appropriate model: *all players in the controversy agree that the relationships among trade, technology, and factor prices are indeed very well suited for analysis using the standard competitive trade model.* The dispute is, instead, philosophical: it hinges on the question of what thought experiments to perform.

This is a baffling statement to come from one of the main architects of the new trade theory, which is hardly built around the standard competitive trade model.

Economists agree that differences among countries drive trade, and that trade acts to diminish some of these differences. Abundant factors tend to be cheaper and thus are used more intensively, and trade tends to lower the price of scarce factors and raise that of abundant ones. Relative cost structures are of critical importance for understanding the structure of the world economy and anticipating changes in it. However, the conventional formalization of the standard assumptions in a mathematical model is arguably far too rigid to replicate the empirical reality at the level of detail of many sectors and many factors for the past, or to be useful for counter-factual scenarios or scenarios about the future. This is true of a model of even a single economy, let alone the world economy. Krugman is right to identify as a major challenge the formulation of scenarios that are sufficiently incisive to permit relatively definitive conclusions regarding complex interrelationships. But he stops short of acknowledging the failure of existing models to represent these relationships without being constrained by highly unrealistic assumptions. His solution is to legitimize the partial analysis based on inferences from factor contents – and even the "quick and dirty exercise." Leontief opted instead to build a less constrained model of the world economy. The major simplifications of Leontief's input-output models are that quantities do not automatically adjust to changes in prices, and that both final deliveries and factor prices are exogenous.

5.   Looking to the future: the analysis of scenarios

The analysis of alternative scenarios as a way of preparing for an uncertain future began in the corporate world and found fertile ground among military planners. In the 1970s economists began to develop scenarios for model-based analysis – an innovation relative to the standard methods of proving theorems and testing hypotheses. The early scenarios in particular were generally distinguished by assigning high, medium or low values to key variables, such as the growth of the labor force or of productivity. The implications of these assumptions for other variables – such as the growth of GDP or of investment – are then determined using the model.

The community of analysts engaged in futures research has developed techniques for elaborating much bolder and more imaginative visions about the future in terms of alternative scenarios. While they vary in scope, level of detail, and degree of documentation of assumptions, the scenarios involve constructing a story that cuts across disciplinary boundaries. According to Fontela (2000, p. 12), "The writing of the scenario is the activity that most stimulates futures researchers." This community tends to find economists' scenarios uninteresting, and their mathematical models and databases too narrow in scope and too short-term to accommodate an interesting story and too limited in structure to assess the relevant interactions. While it is hard to dispute these criticisms, there are also shortcomings in the futurists' approach; mainly that their scenarios are rarely subjected to quantification let alone analysis.

Both futurist and economist, Fontela (2004) has called for bridging the gap between the two communities through collaboration in developing scenarios and analyzing them using models of long-term structural change (see also Duchin and Hubacek, 2003). He describes Leontief's World Model as "one of the most ambitious methodologies ever attempted to explore the long-term future of an infinitely complex system subject to continuous, deep structural changes," and points out that Leontief faced "enormous methodological and data problems, and risked severe criticism from the conventional academic community" (2004, p. 44). Fontela notes the relatively complex scenarios that Leontief formulated and was able to analyze, and the empirical significance of the results regarding the economic prospects for the developing countries. While Fontela describes what in his opinion are shortcomings of the model and database, he notes that they can be corrected with relative ease. Building a new-generation World Model is, for him, "a key challenge for the input-output research community" (Fontela, 2004, p. 45).

Leontief's World Model was built to serve two distinct purposes. First, it is comprised of the database that bears on the comparative advantage of all geographic regions: it is the global equivalent of the database used by Leontief in his articles on trade in the 1950s. The data were crude and incomplete, but a much better job could be done today. While Leontief's World Model took only the first steps in analyzing the database, he and his collaborators succeeded in demonstrating the feasibility of such an ambitious undertaking.

Second, Leontief developed relatively complex scenarios about the world economy and devised a method for documenting the assumptions to enable an easy comparison of alternatives. Since the scenarios were formulated in terms of the detailed variables and parameters of the model, each scenario was clearly related to a distinct computation. The outcome was equally detailed, so it was described as a story – not in terms of a few growth rates only. What today would be considered a structured approach to developing scenarios (see, for example, Rotmans et al., 2000), Leontief had already anticipated in his Nobel lecture.

Leontief wanted to identify strategies that countries might adopt for economic development and to investigate how their implementation could be expected to affect production quantities, relative prices, standards of living, and the countries' entry into the world economy. He invented the simplifications that are characteristic of input-output economics in order to make it possible and practical to use a framework of general interdependence to explore responses to systemwide challenges. These are challenges that can yield to empirical analysis, but they will require concerted effort and an intellectual division of labor on the part of a new generation of scholars to make substantial headway. As long as I knew him, Wassily Leontief was convinced that it was only a matter of time until this was achieved.

REFERENCES

Brecher, R. A., and E. U. Choudhri (1982) The Leontief Paradox, continued, *Journal of Political Economy*, 90, 820–823.
Casas, F. R., and E. K. Choi (1985) The Leontief Paradox: continued or resolved?, *Journal of Political Economy*, 93, 610–615.

Chipman, J. (1970) Induced technical change and patterns of international trade, in R. Vernon (ed.) *The Technology Factor in International Trade* (New York, Columbia University Press, National Bureau of Economic Research Conference Series), 95–127.

Duchin, F. (1990) Technological change and international trade, *Economic Systems Research*, 2, 47–52.

Duchin, F., and K. Hubacek (2003) Linking social expenditures to household lifestyles, *Futures*, 35, 61–74.

Duchin, F., and G.-M. Lange (1994) *The Future of the Environment* (New York, Oxford University Press).

Fontela, E. (2000) Bridging the gap between scenarios and models, *Foresight*, 2, 10–14.

(2004) Leontief and the future of the world economy, chapter 3 in this volume.

Hakura, D. S. (2001) Why does HOV fail? The role of technological differences within the EC, *Journal of International Economics*, 54, 361–382.

He, S., and K. R. Polenske (2001) Interregional trade, the Heckscher-Ohlin-Vanek theorem and the Leontief Paradox, in M. L. Lahr and E. Dietzenbacher (eds.) *Input-Output Analysis: Frontiers and Extensions* (Basingstoke, Palgrave), 161–186.

Helpman, E. (1999) The structure of foreign trade, *Journal of Economic Perspectives*, 13 (2), 121–144.

Krugman, P. R. (2000) Technology, trade, and factor prices, *Journal of International Economics*, 50, 51–71.

Leamer, E. E. (1980) The Leontief Paradox, reconsidered, *Journal of Political Economy*, 88, 495–503.

(2000) What's the use of factor contents?, *Journal of International Economics*, 50, 17–49.

Leontief, W. W. (1933) The use of indifference curves in the analysis of foreign trade, *Quarterly Journal of Economics*, 47, 493–503.

(1953) Domestic production and foreign trade: the American capital position re-examined, *Proceedings of the American Philosophical Society*, 97, 332–349.

(1956) Factor proportions and the structure of American trade: further theoretical and empirical analysis, *Review of Economics and Statistics*, 38, 386–407.

(1964) Review of "An International Comparison of Factor Costs and Factor Use" by B. S. Minhas, *American Economic Review*, 54, 335–345.

(1970) Comments on John Chipman's "Induced technical change and patterns of international trade," in R. Vernon (ed.) *The Technology Factor in International Trade* (New York, Columbia University Press, National Bureau of Economic Research Conference Series), 132–142.

(1973) Explanatory power of the comparative cost theory of international trade and its limits, in H. C. Bos (ed.) *Economic Structure and Development: Essays in Honor of Jan Tinbergen* (Amsterdam, North Holland), 153–160.

(1974) Structure of the world economy: outline of a simple input-output formulation, *Swedish Journal of Economics*, 76, 387–401.

Leontief, W. W., A. P. Carter and P. Petri (1977) *The Future of the World Economy* (New York, Oxford University Press).

Linder, S. B. (1961) *An Essay on Trade and Transformation* (New York, John Wiley).

Minhas, B. S. (1963) *An International Comparison of Factor Costs and Factor Use* (Amsterdam, North-Holland).

Repetto, A., and J. Ventura (1998) *The Leontief-Trefler Hypothesis*, unpublished manuscript. [Available on-line at www.itam.mx/lames/papers/contrses/repetto.pdf.]

Rotmans, J., M. van Asselt, C. Anastasi, S. Greeuw, J. Mellors, S. Peters, D. Rothman and N. Rijkens (2000) Visions for a sustainable Europe, *Futures*, 32, 809–831.

Stern, R. M., and K. E. Maskus (1981) Determinants of the structure of U.S. foreign trade, 1958–76, *Journal of International Economics*, 11, 207–224.

Trefler, D. (1993) International factor price differences: Leontief was right!, *Journal of Political Economy*, 101, 961–987.

    (1995) The case of missing trade and other mysteries, *American Economic Review*, 85, 1,029–1,046.

Vanek, J. (1968) The factor proportions theory: the N-factor case, *Kyklos*, 21, 749–756.

Wolff, E. N. (2004) What has happened to the Leontief Paradox?, chapter 11 in this volume.

5 Leontief's input-output table and the French Development Plan

Henri Aujac

1. French problems at the end of World War II

In 1957 I was in charge of the application of Leontief's input-output table during the elaboration of France's third Development Plan. In retrospect, it appears this was the first time that his table had been used in the economic planning of an industrialized country. We analyzed the whole technological and economic situation in France with Leontief's table. We also used it to check if resource availability constrained the French economy's ability to meet its objectives. So, by experience, we learned input-output's advantages and drawbacks in this setting. In order to understand the reasons why Leontief's concept had been called into service, it is necessary to recall the French economic and political situation at the time.

Immediately after the end of World War II the French government faced an austere situation. First, it had an economy to restore – most factories not destroyed by the war were obsolete. This is because most of the then modern equipment in occupied France had been removed to Germany during the war. Moreover, the French population as a whole, including corporate managers, seems to have been generally satisfied with the nation's quasi-stagnant economy during the twenty-five years of the inter-war period and did not seek improvement. Perhaps worst of all, the nation had been dangerously divided, both socially and politically, since some citizens had collaborated with the occupying forces while others had actively resisted those forces. Upon their return home, thousands of Frenchmen – among them soldiers, prisoners and deportees – encountered an exhausted and dejected country.

To restore the national economy, the Communists, then a powerful party, sought to apply the Soviet model and advised launching an economic plan. They argued that the USSR owed its wartime success to formal plans. They claimed that, due to the existence of just such an economic plan, the Soviet army had been amply supplied as scheduled with strategic stores. The Communist concept was met with wide approval.

Many Frenchmen were concerned, however, that this brand of planning would in the long run lead to despotism on the part of the Communist Party.

So, at the end of the war, the French government had to meet three minimum requirements and do so as soon as possible. First, it needed to modernize the country's core industries. Nationalizing them helped it attain this requirement. By doing so, the government was quickly able to transform these industries from a large number of small, obsolete establishments into a single (few) big one(s) that could enjoy a public monopoly. This process essentially affected "strategic" industrial sectors – for instance, the gas and coal extraction and electric power industries. Second, the population had to be persuaded that economic growth, rather than stagnancy, should be the rule. Last, but not least, the social and political cohesion of the country's citizenry had to be promptly restored. Indeed, this – above all – was a vital necessity.

With such aims in view, the French government cautiously promoted a National Development and Equipment Plan. Its target was to achieve rapid growth in the national product. Keep in mind that the French Plan was distinct from its Soviet equivalents in place since World War I in that French firm-level production plans were compulsory only for those core sectors. For other activities the Plan was merely indicative: a set of demands that firms collectively should try to meet so that the nation could achieve its planned targets.

Therefore, public authorities wisely decided to meet with important public and private economic leaders, corporate managers and trade union members alike. In addition to being summits for filling in the details of the rough plan outlined by the government, these meetings served as forums for explaining the rationales for the specific aims and processes of the plan that eventually emerged. In this way, the whole population was able to feel intimately involved in the setting of goals and understand its role in making the Plan a success. Thus, the nationalization process and the creation of a National Plan were two different sides of the same policy coin. Ultimately, they both helped the government to ameliorate substantially the difficult problems that France faced in the immediate aftermath of World War II.

2.   Nationalizing meant modernizing

At the end of the war the necessary modernization of industrial infrastructure seemed rather unlikely. The near-total lack of competition and the deeply rooted torpor of management reinforced stagnation. Fortunately, nationalization was applied to sectors judged strategically important; they were precisely the sectors that needed modernization the most.

The electric power industry was the most significant sector to be nationalized. Formerly, in France, electricity was produced by a relatively large number of small firms scattered all over the country and by a few major ones providing electricity to several large cities. In general, the industry lacked vitality. The individual plants worked quite independently and were predominantly coal- or oil-fired, or used hydroelectric power. The firms produced electricity of various voltages, sold it at various prices, and made investments that were very different in nature and magnitude from one plant to the next. Obviously, something had to be done to bring better management to the industry's various modes of production and marketing. It was particularly important since the demand for electricity grew rapidly after the war, at a rate of 7 percent annually. In order to keep up with this demand increase, electricity production needed to double within ten years. Because the capacity to meet such a production level did not exist, this meant making huge investments. As none of the existing firms had the will or ability to organize such an uncontrollable, multifarious and quite anarchical combination of plants, the French government decided to nationalize the industry. It bought all the firms producing electricity and formed just one, which enjoyed a state monopoly.

Electricité de France, as it was called, became a powerful firm, benefiting from up-to-date management. Dynamic young men, most of them colleagues from the famous Ecole Polytechnique, were appointed as senior executives. They charged various teams of eminent economists to elaborate long-term forecasts, covering five years or more. Knowing the expected level of French electricity consumption was particularly useful to the managers, who used the information to build their economic development scenarios on a solid foundation.

The French government decided similarly to nationalize other industries with structures that were judged to be outmoded. In this way, collieries were gathered into a single firm called Les Charbonnages de France. Soon afterwards Gaz de France, i.e. France's nationalized natural gas production and distribution company, was created. The various air transport firms were merged into Air France. The various firms connected with the air industry were included in the Société Nationale d'Etude et de Construction de Moteurs d'Aviation (SNECMA). Banque de France and the other four largest banks were nationalized, as were the nation's insurance companies. The various rail companies had already been nationalized in 1936, when on the verge of bankruptcy. Renault's motor vehicle plants were also nationalized, but for political rather than technological reasons. The then extremely powerful French Communist trade union Confédération Générale du Travail (CGT) lobbied heavily for national ownership of Renault.

So, by nationalizing those firms with outdated management and techniques, the state would become the creator, owner and manager of a great number of powerful industries. Nationalization could enable the industries to modernize quickly and at the same time yield some significant social benefit through the fact that a public monopoly allowed a policy of low prices. The concept seemed to provide a clear advantage to almost everyone involved. Hence, it was almost certain the state would grant priority to the financial resources such nationalization would require.

A few large firms, and most small and medium-sized ones, escaped nationalization as they were efficiently managed already. Energetically pushed forward by the Chambre Syndicale (the industry associations), the steel industry, for one, had modernized its infrastructure and had become sufficiently powerful to avoid nationalization. This was also the case for aircraft producer Dassault, and several other firms.

So, now, the country had at its disposal several efficient monopolies. The situation obviously had many advantages for the government: by providing these firms with investment funds, it had a permanent right to interfere in their management. Thereby it found itself in a position of allocating and overseeing nearly two-thirds of all industrial investments in France. When it was identifying the nature and volume of this magnitude of investment, the French government was also deciding about the economic future of the country. Thus, it seemed as though the state had acquired extraordinary power in the management of the nation's economic matters. But had the state really gained that power, or had the managers of the nationalized firms? Subsequently the government has frequently been blamed for having unintentionally created a few "states within the state" through nationalization. As a matter of fact, experience proved in due course that this reproach was not completely unfounded, as some of these states within the state have on occasion seemed more powerful than the state itself. But, when the first plans were set up, the French government and the nationalized firms had quite similar interests, and it was easy for them to work together harmoniously.

Planners, working in efficient teams within the nationalized firms, were expected to anticipate future production levels (only a few years out) that had to be attained by the core industries, and the level and type of investment that would likely be required to achieve the anticipated production. So, when the National Development Plan was implemented, they greatly helped the promoters of the Plan, who needed such information to estimate the final demand required by France's new national input-output table. National planning thus led to a gradual improvement in the planning abilities of private firms and public administrations. Immediately after the end of the war only about a dozen private firms had professional economists on their staff. The Plan compelled these firms to forecast changes in their markets; as a result they had to engage more of these specialists.

3.   The spirit of the National Development and Equipment Plan

Besides modernization, the French government had to keep in mind its other major post-war objectives: economic growth and national unity. Both aims could be fulfilled, so it seemed, by establishing a National Development and Equipment Plan. The government took the risk and was rewarded with success.

In 1945 Jean Monnet, a man who a few years later became the main promoter of the European Economic Community, volunteered to establish a national planning system. General De Gaulle, who was then president of the provisional government, agreed to this proposal and supported it thoroughly. Two years later the first plan was established.

In order to restore national unity, Jean Monnet conceived a straightforward policy: to stimulate contact and cooperation among as many French citizens as possible. This was done by getting the population as a whole to become involved in the choice and definition of the targets and in the establishment of a National Development Plan. Clearly, the only chance of success for this Plan was to require everybody's contribution, or – better still – to gain everyone's approval. So, not only was the established plan clearly explained and announced to the public, but its various intermediate forms and evolutionary processes were as well. This is because civil servants in charge did their best to give accurate information about the contents of the plan, its scheme and its evolution. At appointed times they even presented brief synopses of the situation.

First of all, from an economist's perspective, it was necessary to determine the magnitude and composition of national final demand, which consists of household consumption, the demand of private and public firms for capital goods, the various demands of the state (e.g. armaments), and foreign demand (i.e. exports). It was also necessary to forecast future needs, especially the likely import levels from the United States, with an emphasis on equipment. Secondly, future production levels had to be set for the goods and services needed to meet the projected final demand while taking into account the forecasts for imports and exports.

Several Plan Committees were assigned to elaborate and execute the Plan. They first had to forecast the various constituents of future demand and to identify the means that would be necessary to meet them. Further, they had to suggest the best methods for enhancing productivity at existing plants and for inducing the formation of firms that would produce new products using new techniques. The United States helped French managers by organizing visits to its state-of-the-art plants.

Jean Monnet's organization of Plan Committees remains a model for any democratic society. A Committee initially was composed of about twenty members. Each was allowed to create as many subcommittees as deemed necessary. The Committees enjoyed complete autonomy and could consult with any willing public or private expert. They regularly tried to bring together the critical economic public or private actors – journalists who heavily influenced public opinion, the radio personalities (TV was not yet popular in homes), members of the universities, etc. It was thought to be "an undeniable duty" for every Frenchman – as General De Gaulle would say later on – to cooperate in defining and implementing the Plan's objectives concerning the desirable level of private consumption, the required magnitudes of various investments, and the production level of the different economic activities.

It was a considerable advantage to the Committees that they were fully independent of public agencies. Their membership was composed of social partners, experts and the administration. Each Committee elected its own president, who was seldom a civil servant and more often from some other walk of life (e.g. corporate manager, banker, trade union member, production worker, newsman, academic). Any decision of a Committee required a majority vote, but the final report of the Committees was to include the size of any opposition to the decision and the reasons for it. Trade unions took on an active role in the Committees, even the one closely connected with the Communist Party, the CGT.

The Plan was not compulsory for private firms but various types of assistance were granted to those that followed its recommendations. Tax incentives were available to induce them to make judicious investments. Only those that followed the recommendations could obtain licenses to import machines that could not be purchased from anywhere but the United States. In fact, most chairmen and managing directors of private and nationalized firms were eager to take part in the Committee meetings. It was of the utmost interest for any employer to be aware of the key elements of the Plan, especially since so many people – his colleagues, civil servants, trade unions, and all sorts of private and public experts – had been so deeply involved in their creation.

The Plan Committees had been set up as early as the start of the first Plan. They appeared to be very efficient and were credited with the success of the first two French plans. They played a similar part in the development and implementation of the third Plan. But their weight gradually diminished thereafter. By and by, the Plan lost most of its democratic organization as the private executives and trade unionists progressively shirked active participation in Committee activities. Hence, from a meaningful political beginning, the Plan Committees evolved into a technical function, essentially managed and manned by civil servants of France's planning services.

4.   The third Plan (1958–1961) and the use of the input-output table

The aims of the first two five-year Plans – modernization, economic growth, and national unity – were essentially met by the terminal year of the second Plan in 1957. There had been a large increase in the production of coal, electricity, steel, building materials, etc. Freight trains as well as passenger trains were running faster and more punctually than ever before. Roads, bridges, harbors, and other civil engineering works that had been destroyed during the war had been repaired. In part, the success of the first two Plans was thanks to substantial American financial support, which enabled France to import a variety of needed capital goods.

The third Plan, which was to start in 1958, was intended to be a triennial one. It was expected to initiate a strong rise in France's standard of living, to develop consumer industries, and to provide full employment. Stimulated by the Common Market, at the foundation of this Plan was the objective of enabling French industries to contend well against foreign competition. It was during the preparation of *this* Plan that Leontief's input-output table was first used in support of national planning.

4.1   The National Accounting System and national planning

Claude Gruson, an eminent civil servant in the Finance Ministry, created the Office of Economic and Financial Studies (Service des Etudes Economiques et Financières – SEEF) because he wanted France to have a modern National Accounting System (Comptabilité Nationale). This accounting system required three interrelated tables expressed in value terms: the economic table, the financial table and the Leontief table. This intricate set of tables was not easy to manage, since it was necessary to account for the interdependencies of data among the tables. That is, each time one datum was modified, one had to check up the consequences of this change in the whole set of tables.

The government tentatively entrusted the SEEF with the task of establishing a preliminary forecast for 1961; the Plan Committees would make their own as in the previous years. Thus it was that two forecasts of the desired economic future in 1961, the final year of the third Plan, would be available: one established by the Plan Committees, the other by the team at the SEEF. They would be worded differently: the first using a technical vocabulary, and the second the language of the Comptabilité Nationale. In addition, they would comply with different requirements: the first meeting requirements of pragmatism, the second – necessarily – requirements of economic coherence. It appeared that a good way to improve the aims and means of the French planning process would be to compare the two forecasts for 1961. It was thought that the Plan would only be strengthened by the exercise of comparing them and aligning them into something more like a single vision. It must be kept in mind that the use of the input-output table in the SEEF forecast had been prescribed only tentatively, to see whether it could be used for establishing long- and medium-term forecasts.

A detailed sketch of the economic future desired for 1961 had to be drawn up; this 1961 situation would be the result of the political program developed prior to 1958 by the French government to increase public welfare. The vocabulary available for the design of the survey was that used by the National Accounting System. The latest available economic survey, issued in 1955, had gathered statistical data that could be used to produce the National Accounting System. These data, valid for 1955, first had to be extrapolated to 1958, the starting year of the third Plan, then further to 1961, its final year. So, two sets of expectations were needed: one covering three years, from 1955 to 1958, in order to update the survey data; the other covering the three years of the Plan, from 1958 to 1961 – the desired forecast. For brevity's sake, I discuss only the 1961 forecast in the present paper.

4.2   *The growth rates of GNP and final demand*

The most important decision made during the preparation of this third Plan was to fix the growth rate of PIB ("produit interieur brut," or, in English, gross national product – GNP) at the highest possible level capable of achieving the main economic objectives of the Plan: a strong rise in the standard of living, the development of consumer industries, full employment, and successful entry into the European Common

Market. To fix the desired growth rate, my colleagues and I (all members of SEEF), had to use an iterative method. Starting from a hypothetical growth rate, we would discover its probable consequences and modify that initial hypothesis to ameliorate them. If inflation threatened, we reduced the prospective growth rate; if any risk of high unemployment loomed, we would raise the growth rate somewhat; if the financial means required for various investments looked as if they might be dampened, we would cut back anticipated increases in salaries and employment levels – and so on. Thanks to the tables provided by the Accounting System, and – of course – a lot of hard work, we more or less succeeded in analyzing and measuring the consequences of various possible growth rates on the myriad components of the general economic equilibrium.

Then we had to compute the corresponding value of the components of final demand. These components were:

1. Household demand. A semi-public office, the Centre de Recherche pour l'Etude et l'Observation des Conditions de vie (CREDOC), had already created a detailed analysis and forecast of household consumption and was quite willing to collaborate. Democratically programming the economic situation for 1961 required taking into account the wishes expressed by most Frenchmen in 1958 regarding their then current economic situation. Since each social group wished to attain the standard of living of the social group ranked immediately above, it was rather easy to forecast the future demand for consumer goods such as refrigerators, washing machines and automobiles.
2. National investment demand. This included demand from the state and demand from many firms. The state wanted weaponry, research (especially atomic research), hospitals, schools, bridges, roads, motorways, and other civil engineering works. Public authorities were asked to indicate the probable level of infrastructure and equipment they would require by 1961. The demands of nationalized firms were strictly dependent on the Plan objectives. The forecasts of private firms mostly relied on information gathered by the Plan Committees.
3. International exchanges. Civil servants dealing with international commerce attempted to anticipate the evolution of French imports and exports three years in advance. They also accounted for government regulations that limited current account deficits. Such forecasting was rather uneasy; so experts were trusted.

4.3   The French input-output table

Leontief's input-output table was meant to calculate the production of the various industrial commodities required to satisfy final demand. The

French input-output table had about one hundred such commodities, each concerned with an equal number of products and services. Many similar or related products were aggregated and called by a single name: that of the main product of the composite. This composite product was a single commodity in the input-output table. All plants producing a component of the commodity were aggregated together and termed a "sector." So, about one hundred commodities and one hundred sectors were supposed to stand for the thousands – or, rather, millions – of products circulating all over the country, and for the thousands of establishments producing them.

Leontief's table was composed of rows and columns. Each row indicated the two main destinations assigned to the goods produced by each sector: either the products were ascribed to final demand or to other sectors that needed them to insure their own production (intermediate demand). Each column displayed the accounts of a sector, including the value of its production, the value of the purchases from various other sectors (i.e. the value of the intermediate demand), total payroll, various tax payments, and – finally – the balance: positive or negative.

When the 1955 table was constructed, SEEF experts calculated the technology coefficients specific to each sector. The so-called "technology coefficient" of a sector was found by dividing the amount of each element of intermediate demand by the sector's production total. Thanks to these technology coefficients, it was possible to calculate the level of production that each sector had to attain in order to satisfy not only final demand, in so far as the expected final demand was known, but also intermediate demand – the purchases of a sector's products by other sectors to meet their production needs.

More than forty years ago, SEEF was a very small research office intended to create the National Accounting System. Because of its small contingent of staff, I was the one entrusted by Claude Gruson with using Leontief's table. I was expected to calculate the production levels of the various activities playing their part in the desired final demand. To fulfill this task, I was given a secretary; an "ordinary" adding machine that could multiply and divide (as well as add and subtract); and a great number of blank index cards, upon which I wrote down the numbers resulting from my calculations. These index cards displayed the framework of either the sales accounts of each sector or the resources-employment accounts for each commodity.

Since computers were not yet available at the French Finance Ministry in 1957 and the calculations had to be performed by hand, it was essential to avoid being caught in the webs of interdependence and the consequent countless reckonings by iteration (see, e.g., Aujac, 1960). My thought was that, if by any chance it could be performed on Leontief's table, matrix triangulation would save us lots of time and trouble. I figured that, if it were triangulable, the interdependence of values within the table would not cause near-unending iterations of recalculation; sequential reckonings could be used instead. But was the French table triangulable?

The triangulation process required classification of the sectors and of their products. For instance, we decided that sectors serving mainly and directly final demand, such as agriculture and agro-food industries, should occupy the first lines, while the sectors catering to a great number of other intermediate sectors, such as the energy industries, should be placed at the bottom of the list. Thus, in case of perfect triangulation, null or low numbers would be located above (i.e. "north-east" of) the main diagonal of the table and large ones would be concentrated below (i.e. "south-west" of) it.

It should be noted that the French table contained no auto-consumption (i.e. a sector's consumption of its own product). If triangulation was possible and correctly carried out, the first row should be filled solely with final demand, but no intermediate demand. Hence, production for the first sector in the list could be obtained directly from final demand. Consequently, it was possible to calculate the fixed amount of its intermediate consumption that results. To calculate the desirable production amount for the second sector on the list, we would have at our disposal the final demand for this product and, possibly, the intermediate consumption of the first sector, being the only sector using product no. 2. This value of intermediate consumption would be the sector's "true value," which no iteration would ever modify. Of course, this logic could follow for other sectors if triangulation was possible. That is why we sought triangulation: it was a kind of computational "necessity."

In the end, the French table was roughly triangulable. Of the largest intermediate demands, only three were located above the diagonal, and they required some lengthy iterative reckoning. Fortunately, thanks to provisional hypotheses about the likely production amount of each sector, by using these large demands (assumptions based on the analysis, for each sector involved, of the relative weight of final demand and other consumption), it was often possible to build on sufficiently solid grounds a reasonable provisional account of these intermediate demands. As a result the number of necessary iterations was considerably reduced, and sequential reckoning could be used for the remaining sectors.

Before anything else, we had to update the technology coefficients in the input-output table. It was a rather easy task for the sectors that consisted of nationalized firms, and for certain large private firms (the steel industry, for instance). This is because it was a critical part of the Plan for these industries to attain a well-defined production level and a corresponding amount of investment. So the engineers of these firms were able to provide us with nearly every piece of information we needed. It was much more difficult, if not impossible, to do the same with the other sectors. But we were able to estimate the likely trends for the evolution of the most important of these coefficients by poring over the reports drawn up by the Plan Committees. So, by relying on what seemed to be credible estimates, we assigned values to the 1961 technology coefficients.

With this concept in hand, we were theoretically able to calculate all sectoral base production levels required to meet the final demand anticipated in the Plan. With the help of my secretary, I started on it one Monday morning, not knowing how long it would take. Beginning that day, we sort of lived inside a tornado of multiplication, division, subtraction and addition, using lots of pencils and erasers. At noon the following Friday we were met with an incredible surprise: our results, i.e. production levels for each of the model's 100 sectors to be implemented within the context of the Plan.

With the advent of inexpensive computer power, such calculation "tricks" essentially have become useless. Nonetheless, it is still worthwhile to investigate the kind of economic structure revealed by input-output table triangulability. The degree to which an economy is triangulable may well be related to its stage of development. We had to inquire into French economic history in order to discover the economy's order of triangulation. Indeed, it depends largely on history. Based on our work, it would seem that a table of a less developed or industrializing economy would probably be easy to triangulate. The economic structure of industrialized countries would tend to be less easy to triangulate since the interdependence of the system would be notably enhanced by the entry of new products with wider usage across the spectrum of industries.

4.4   The two forecasts for 1961

While we were working on the input-output table, the Plan Committees had made their own forecasts. Since my SEEF colleagues had taken part in the work of several Plan Committees, we tried together to draw some lessons by comparing the forecasts from the use of Leontief's table to that from the work of the Plan Committees.

It appeared that the content of both forecasts was a mixture of real planning and mere forecasting. For clarity's sake, I thought it convenient to reshuffle the industries, and their Plan Committees, into two groups based upon the degree of their interest and participation in the elaboration and achievement of the Plan targets.

The first group included the Committees essentially formed with the employers' associations of the firms directly concerned with the Plan targets. This group consisted of the nationalized firms and a few large private firms, all of them belonging to areas deemed of "strategic interest" by public authorities. For this group, the so-called forecasts were strictly the Plan targets. The forecasts dealing with the "basic strategic" products were established, in fact, by the planning departments of the nationalized firms and the few private firms, working in cooperation with the related administrations. The National Planning Department had simply declared their results as official ones.

Let us consider, for instance, the work done by the Steel Industry Committee, one of the most efficient Committees within the Plan organization. This Committee brought together, besides a few managing directors, representatives of steel's industry association, of other industries that provided the steel industry with raw materials or machinery, of the major steel-consuming industries (motor vehicle industries or machine industries), as well as tradesmen in the metal products industry and the like. A few trade union workers, most of them belonging to the CGT, joined the Committee as well. When needed, the Committee invited consultants. Economic journalists were also invited to attend the meetings.

All these people, diverse in origin and training, worked together for many hours. In order to derive a near-term forecast of steel production and to define the appropriate qualities and prices to be secured by the steel industry at the end of the planning period, it was obviously extremely useful to maintain a permanent dialogue among the representatives of the many facets of the steel industry. Whenever steel firm representatives had to define the volume of production to be achieved at the end of the Plan, they would inquire from the delegates of the supplying industries whether enough coke could be produced in France to meet the demand of the steel industry or whether it would be necessary to import German coke; whether new techniques could reduce the input of coke; whether electrical foundries would eventually make the use of coke obsolete; etc. They would talk to their customers about the efficiency of the new steel, the quantities required, and prices. They would ask them for delivery schedules and their needs for specialty steel, glass, plastic and other substitute materials. They wanted to know their demand for workers by occupation and skill. Workmen, through their unions, played their part in the main discussions and very often gave sound advice on solid grounds.

Thanks to such work by the steel industry's Plan Committee, their forecasts of steel production became the Plan targets. Consequently, the forecasts concerning associated activities were also turned into Plan targets.

The second group of Plan Committees consisted of a few big private firms and a large family of small and medium-sized firms (petites et moyennes entreprises – PME). The larger firms generally had their own industry association, which was almost entirely supported by them. Since they each had their own planning offices, they did not feel the need to create such an office within the association. The small and medium-sized firms were generally too poor to set up forecasting offices, and their industry association could not afford to create one. Anyway, their own forecasts did not meet the requirements of being categorized as mandatory Plan targets.

So, whenever there was a need for a forecast, a member of the firm or association was entrusted with the research. This person, even when quite efficient, had to be supervised and helped by someone else. So he/she tried to relate the forecast of the production of his/her firm or the firms represented by his/her industry association to the provisional forecast determined by the technology coefficients of the input-output table. In fact, the small and medium-sized firms were, unexpectedly, the largest users of our draft report. The difficulty was that, as we knew, the lists of products by firm were much longer than that admitted by the system of national accounts, and even those listed were recorded in the system of national accounts in quite different terminology. So, the PME delegate would have to figure it out himself/herself and invent a way of translating from the language of the official accounts and into that he/she used back at his/her office. Hence the delegate often would have to meet a member of our office and thrash it out with him. Experience proved that, by working together, they would reach a sensible accord. Hence, more frequently than expected, the provisional draft based upon the input-output table proved useful. It enabled the firm-level planner to develop a forecast for his/her firm that was in accord with the Plan targets, but based in the language used by his/her firm. Above all, it supplied him/her with a solid, well-regarded method that lent confidence to his/her own forecast.

In short, the Committees had established the forecasts that became Plan targets. As for those obtained independently through the input-output table, we feared that they would be useless, since the definitions of the sectors and commodities in the input-output table were very different from the commodities and industries familiar to the industry layman. Nonetheless, with some surprise, the input-output forecasts were thoroughly appreciated by small and medium-sized firms, since it gave them the otherwise expensive opportunity to get a sense of their likely future.

So, the input-output table was a definite help in the preparation of the French Development Plan, even though this help had been less efficient than expected.

5.   A few lessons from this experiment

Our struggle to apply the input-output table to the French planning process led us to reflect on various problems.

5.1   *Triangulation and the democratization of planning*

The research on triangulation suggested that, whenever it was possible to triangulate the table for a given economy, there could be a complete change in the power relations between a state and its citizens. The French experience showed that centralized planning, often thought necessary to establish any national plan, could profitably be replaced by a more decentralized organization – indeed, a nearly democratic one.

Let us imagine, for instance, national planning in the Soviet mode (if the USSR had developed a true input-output table of its own). If the Soviets' input-output table could not be triangulated, their planning organization would have been forced to remain authoritarian since only the state's planning office would have been able to produce and make use of the input-output table. It alone could have scheduled the target production levels to be attained by each sector and consequently issued production orders to managers of the establishments of the sectors. While some undoubtedly would have been first-rate civil servants, the managers could only have complied.

If by any chance the table were triangulable, a different scenario could take place. The previous relations between the almighty state (the only one to have at its disposal the input-output table) and the economic managers (if not the ordinary citizens) could, basically, be transformed – to the benefit of the latter. They would no longer have to depend on the central planning office, except regarding the schedule of meetings of the various managers. (This order would be the same as that used in classifying sectors for the triangulation scheme.) They could perform simple provisional reckoning. So, surprisingly enough, if they needed to calculate the production level of their own sector, they could be provided with every useful piece of information regarding the final or intermediate demand of the sectors positioned ahead of them in the triangulation list.

Economists and politicians continue to this day to seek normative economic tools that thrive in a decentralized political economy. It has indeed been proven that centralized administrations – even if efficient and benevolent – are unable to assimilate the knowledge necessary to develop a viable forecast or a plan, or to mobilize the experience of the various divisions of labor and social strata, in particular of different links in the supply-demand chain. So it was worth showing that, at least in the field of technology relations, a strict hierarchy in an industrial society could permit a decentralized economic management of human society.

5.2   The appearance of new techniques

As is typical in most undertakings, a difficulty appeared very early on. In our case it was due to the need to forecast technological progress. Soon after the war I had met a Renault engineer who, as a war prisoner, had succeeded in working out the concept of numerically controlled machine tools. These are highly sophisticated machines, now often called "robots." In any case, this man was convinced (and convinced me) that this kind of machine would be a huge success. As we are all now well aware, he was right. So I suggested that one of the aims of the third Plan should be to develop this new kind of machine. But how could we work such a program into an accounting system that dealt at best only with a sector and product called "machine tools"? Boldly enough, we "created" a sector and product, labeled "robot," that we tried to forecast. Admittedly, estimating its marketing potential and desired production level for 1961 was a rather arbitrary undertaking. Since neither the sector nor the product existed in 1958, we had to alter the Leontief table by tabulating in the 1958 table a hypothetical value of robot production and the likely production growth rate. In fact, it remains very difficult for a "new product" to find a place within the French System of National Accounts.

5.3   Are technology coefficients really "technology"?

Another difficulty also appeared. What sort of meaning could be ascribed to technology coefficients? The so-called "technology coefficients" used in input-output tables were introduced to calculate the intermediate demand and, if final demand were added, the total production of the various sectors. These coefficients were supposed to indicate the technology achieved, or to be attained, by the various sectors at a given point in time.

Let us, to put it simply, take 1958 as the reference year in the development of the third Plan. We were required to describe the probable economic situation three years later in 1961, so it was compulsory to anticipate the evolution of the technology coefficients for every sector.

But did these coefficients really represent "technology"? In the steel industry, for instance, the "true" technology coefficients would specify the tonnage of both coke and iron ore required to produce a ton of pig iron. In this case, the "technology coefficients" are clearly defined, although across the many plants various qualities of coke and iron ore can contribute to the production of pig iron. Fifty years ago, a ton of coke was needed to produce a ton of pig iron. Nowadays, less than half a ton of coke is needed. In this case, input and output are measured in physical units: tons. When the technology coefficients are thus defined, it is quite easy to indicate the cause and amplitude of technological progress.

It is a completely different story, however, with the "coefficients" in a typical value-based input-output table. Here they are obtained by dividing a "value of shipments" by another "value of shipments." Thus, the value of each intermediate demand entry is divided by the total value of the sector's production requiring the material. Moreover, as mentioned before, the terms "commodities" and "sectors" are complex aggregates composed of elements so heterogeneous that the sectors and the commodities are rather abstract. On the other hand, such "technology coefficients" might change with technological progress. By measuring only the size of the change, one would not get detailed knowledge of the causes of the change. The change might not only be technological but also economic or political. In our case, such a coefficient need not have embodied only "technology." Indeed, it mostly represented nothing more than a "statistical quota." Hence we concluded that our value-based "technology coefficients" were unable to yield an authentic picture of the various production techniques and their evolution.

Other difficulties originated in the discrepancy between the definitions of processes used by industry experts and those assumed by national accounts specialists. Let us return to the previous example of the steel industry. The various steel products had early on been ranked in lists of items that remained in use. The products and their mix within the industry had not basically changed in nature. Whenever they did change, their name also changed. In addition to "ordinary" steel, there now existed specialty steels. As for statistics, they were continuously updated, calculated annually and quickly released to the public. They took into account tonnages – a physical unit.

On the contrary, the input-output table dealt only with values, i.e. physical units multiplied by prices (in French francs). Moreover, the list of products for steel was outmoded, and the products were too aggregate for use by the industry. Recall that we assumed at the outset of this discussion, for the sake of simplicity, that the input-output table (and, hence, the technology coefficients) had been available for the year 1958. But, as we are all painfully aware, statistics, even when available, are very often several years old. In our case, the official product classifications had been established many years earlier. Many categories were out of date by the time we applied them, such as the lists of industrial items that had been established during World War II and the years immediately following, in order to achieve a fair allocation of scarce raw materials to firms.

It seldom happens that official classifications or codes are modernized. Revising them often destroys a valuable inheritance. For any items where such changes arise, econometricians, for example, can lose the long time series they need to produce forecasts! But, if the lists of items stay unchanged, difficulties also occur. Although the names of the goods and services remain the same, the nature and main features of the sectors will, over time, become more and more different in character from how they were in the initial year that the classification scheme was developed. For instance, the automobile today is very different from an automobile of even ten years ago. It has become a machine packed with electronics regulating speed, fuel consumption, heating, gears, and even self-monitoring systems. Nonetheless, we still call it an automobile. Meanwhile, in economic terms it has changed rather radically. In particular, each of its intermediate inputs in an input-output table has changed in both volume and composition.

In fact, technological progress has dictated two forms of dynamism. On the one hand, it has improved the productivity of firms by modernizing the old goods and improving the management of machines, production lines, and the firms themselves. On the other hand, and at the same time, it has unceasingly created new processes and products, so that new terminology has to be invented to identify them. Obviously, statisticians ought to update their official classifications as often as needed.

We found that a sound economic forecast ought to be concerned with characterizing two aspects of an economy. One should forecast productivity change in sectors producing traditional goods using traditional processes. But it is no less important to anticipate the emergence of new processes and new products that may soon flood the market. The first of these aspects has received much attention through numerous papers and clever analyses. The second remains in search of a suitable formal approach.

5.4   The role of semantics

In the elaboration of the third Plan, the input-output model was an important forecasting tool. Its function was to match the desired level of demand with corresponding national production activities. The planning approach intended to draw on information supplied by the expert members of the Plan Committees. On the whole, the collected information was very rich. Nevertheless, it proved impossible (with a limited number of exceptions) to apply the knowledge obtained to the input-output table (Aujac, 1972a). Why was this so? Basically, because the working language of a firm is grounded on a far more detailed nomenclature of products and techniques – one sometimes covering several thousands of items.

The vocabulary of the French national accounts uses fewer than one hundred terms to describe the whole national production system. Its "technology coefficients," whether relating to capital or labor input per unit of output, are simple ratios of statistical aggregates. These coefficients do not represent what an engineer would consider technology. Managers of national accounts are able to forecast the type of reality depicted via an input-output table, but the methods at their disposal are rudimentary indeed. These include the forecasting of production, and of labor input coefficients, and the international comparison of input-output ratios. Our experience clearly demonstrated a collaborative failure between national accounts specialists and industry and business experts.

This first attempt at technological forecasting foundered because the experience of engineers could not easily be reconciled with the language of the system of national accounts. A dictionary should have been established to facilitate translation from one language to the other. Now it seems such a tool will never be created in France.

What is needed is a special language that is specific, concrete and fairly accurate at technical levels. (This means the language is likely to be vague in terms of its economic correspondence.) At the same time, this language needs to be synthesizing, global and abstract, and outwardly accurate because its objects are quantifiable. (This means it will have little real technological content, and that its economic content will become harder and harder to grasp as the forecast period is extended.) The first set of characteristics of this language relates to the technological, economic and social structures of the *future*; the second is firmly anchored to *current* technological and economic structures.

6.   New attempts to improve the efficiency of the input-output table

When the calculations for expected sectoral production levels were finished, we wrote a report about our travails when using the input-output table. Claude Gruson, with the help of François Bloch-Lainé, head of the Caisse des Dépôts et Consignations (a very old and important state bank), decided to open the Bureau d'Informations et de Prévisions Economiques (BIPE) as a private non-profit association. François Bloch-Lainé was president of the founding board; its vice-president was the standing

president of the CNPF (the national board of the French employers –
now known as MEDEF). The board also included the heads of the main
economic offices of the state and six managing directors of private firms.
Initially there were about forty members of the association; thirty-five
managing directors of big private firms and five managing directors of
nationalized firms. The financial resources were provided partly by the
Caisse des Dépôts et Consignations and partly by the private firms. As the
chair of this office, I had to direct its activities so that public and private
managers could have free and trustful relationships with one another.

6.1   First experiences

In order to reach this objective, the first condition was to discover a
common language able to facilitate interrelations. With this in mind, we
used the terminology selected by the industry association. A series of
diagrams was drawn, each diagram showing the successive transforma-
tions induced by the production process of a particular raw material. The
changes appearing in the diagrams were calculated from data the industry
associations collected from their member firms and expressed in physical
units. We next tried to evaluate these changes by multiplying the physical quantities by the corresponding prices. This research soon proved
disappointing. The diagrams were indeed rather attractive and allowed
the young researchers to deal directly with the real production processes.
But it was impossible to identify and quantify the intermediate inputs of
the products (particularly in the case of services) needed to bring about
the various changes in the demand for raw materials, for numbers, however necessary, could not be collected easily. In most cases, they were too
many and too small. More often than not, the corresponding prices were
unknown. On the other hand, when we used the lists of items drawn up
by the industry association, a few "technology coefficients" were able to
play a specific role, i.e. to indicate the characteristics of the processes in
use and to measure their productivity.

On the whole, it eventually appeared that this kind of research was
inadequate to establish an input-output table that could validly describe
the production system and all the production processes at work in a national economy. So we changed our objectives and looked for a method
that could allow us to anticipate the eventual appearance on the market
of new products and new processes.

6.2   A new approach to technological forecasting

In 1967 BIPE initiated a research program on the textile industries. We
wanted to know the nature and value of the technological progress that

could be expected in that sector during the ensuing twenty years. The research concerned both the materials and the fibers (Aujac, 1973). Thanks to her comprehensive knowledge of textile industries, a fellow researcher – Mme Guiriec – was clever enough to establish fruitful relationships with the experts in the research and development (R&D) office of the textile industries association. As a result she was able to draw up a list of the materials and fibers under development in France and elsewhere. Seven development stages were defined: (1) basic research; (2) pre-development research; (3) development research; (4) pilot plant production; (5) experimental marketing; (6) limited distribution; and (7) broad distribution. Of the thirty-two new textile machines and new textiles in the development stage, seven were in hosiery, three in power-loom weaving, five in new spinning mills, three in non-woven fabrics, six in whitening and dyeing techniques, three in new texture techniques, and five in new textile fibers. For each of these technologies, it was our job to anticipate both the successive stages of this development and their diffusion into the market.

Our research pointed out the nature of the progress that was expected and the likely schedule of the emergence of the new technologies on the market (Aujac, 1983). In order to get an idea of the probable entry into the market of the new materials and the new fibers, the woman in charge of the research accounted for not only the expected superiority of the techniques and fibres then under development, but also the vintage of machines already in use around the world. As it was rather easy to guess the average life of these older machines from loan information and depreciation schedules, it was possible to guess when the new ones would be purchased.

Table 5.1 contains the main results. It includes a list of the various likely innovations to come and the probable timetable for the technological and economic stages of their development. It was obvious from this table that the era characterized by an unceasing improvement of traditional techniques and products, in the years before about 1967, was nearly at an end. Instead, a period of deep technological transformation was afoot. The textile industries, which up to that point maintained a large labor force, would clearly very soon become a set of heavy industries, resting on chemistry and computer science. It was similarly clear that, if the French textile industries could not succeed in making good from this transformation, they would suffer considerable damage. So, the systematic synthesis of individual forecasts had the valuable result of permitting the anticipation of imminent technological transformation. Before the publication of that paper, neither corporate managers nor professional associations had been fully aware of the extent of the change to come.

This research on the influence of technological progress on the French textile industries had been initiated at the request of the Planning

Table 5.1 Time forecast for R&D and spreading of new techniques in the textile industries[a]

	1955	1960	1965	1970	1975	1980	1985	1990	1995
Assembly operations									
Knitting									
• Warp knitting machine			4	5	6	6	7		
• Flat knitting machine			4	5	7				
• Cotton knitting machine (automated)			4	5	6	7			
• Circular knitting machine (positive feed)	3	3	5	6	7				
• Cotton knitting machine (positive feed)			3	4	6	7			
• Jacquard knitting machine	3	3	4	5	6	7			
• Circular knitting machine (drive control)	3	3	3	3	4	5	6	7	
Weaving									
• Shuttleless loom	4	5	6	6	7				
• Waveline shed loom				2	3	5	5	6	7
• Process control weaving				2	3	4	5	6	7
Spinning									
• Turbine			4	5	6	6			
• Automated preparation				6	6	7	7		
• Electrostatic spinning				3		5	6	7	
• Electrostatic preparation				3	4	5	6	7	
• Fluid-controlled preparation and spinning				3		4			
Non-wovens									
• Dry process	5	5	6	6	6	6	7		
• Spun-bonded			4	5	6	6	7		
• Wet process		4	5	5	6	6	7		

Source: Adapted from Aujac (1972b).

Production and finishing operations

Bleaching, dyeing, printing and finishing

• Solvents bleaching, dyeing		2	3	4/5	6	7	
• Computerized dyeing				5	6	6	6
• Differential dyeing			4	5	5	6	6
• Transfer printing techniques			4/5	5	6	7	
• Fibers grafting (finishing)				2	6	6	7
• Modification of cotton fibrillar structure			1		3	4/5	

Texturizing

• Conventional (false twist)	5	7[b]		7[c]	7[d]	7	
• At the spinneret		3	4	5	6	6	7
• Chemical	3		4			5	

Man-made fibers

• Bi-component fibers	3	3			5	6	7
• Bi-constituent fibers		5	4			5	6
• Stereospecific polymerization				4	6	7	
• Interfacial polymerization			4/5		6	6	
• Solid-state polymerization		3		4/3	3		7

Note: The numbers in columns without headings refer to "mid-term" changes in technology.

a 1: fundamental research; 2: pre-development; 3: development; 4: industrial prototype; 5: experimental application only; 6: limited industrial application; 7: increasing industrial application.

b 200,000 tonnes.

c 600,000 tonnes.

d 1,000,000–3,000,000 tonnes.

Source: Adapted from Aujac (1972b).

Office. Unfortunately, it was cut short due to a lack of sufficient funding. Nonetheless, the Organisation for Economic Co-operation and Development (OECD) favorably mentioned this brief undertaking in its final report on *Technological Forecasting in Perspectives* (Jantsch, 1967). Erich Jantsch wrote: "At national level, technological forecasting is only gradually introduced into general planification. The two most impressive attempts in this field have been made by France and the United States" (p. 22).

7.   Final remarks

Soon after the end of the war, first nationalizing policy and then a National Development Plan were started in France. Within a few years the French economy enjoyed historically strong growth, thanks to an exceptionally high level of investment. More importantly, national unity was restored. Could anyone have anticipated such surprising events about twelve years in advance – say, in 1945? The only decent reply would be: "No, nobody could have expected them." But why?

Typically, when someone tries to develop a long-term forecast, he/she systematically neglects two factors that, under certain circumstances, are essential agents that guide history and set economic growth and social progress in motion. This certainly was the case in France after World War II. These two factors are sheer luck and outstanding leadership. Such leadership is sufficiently gifted to recognize and articulate the latent desires of the majority of the population. It is a pity to ignore these two factors, when a summary analysis of any historical period reveals their crucial influence. But, generally, we forecasters do not know how to incorporate such factors.

In France, the part played by chance had two sides: the bad luck of a ruined post-war economy with its risks of social disintegration; and the good fortune to nationalize core industries and to undertake national planning. The part played by humans was certainly exceptional. It is amazing that two men so different in their opinions and character as General De Gaulle and Jean Monnet were able to work together to restore both the economy and the social unity of France, and to start or actively support the Development Plan.

In this context, Leontief's input-output table had been, at first, a useful tool for giving a rough description of the French economy. However, its use was assisted by the nationalization policy and the existence of big firms with production targets that became the Plan objectives. It was much more difficult to apply this kind of forecasting to the other private firms, however. The language of the input-output table greatly restricted its usefulness. So, while Leontief's table was certainly helpful, it had its limits.

When a technological forecast is made, econometric techniques can only rehash a dead past. A method that can make concrete the practical conditions for mobilizing varied experience must induce its participants to join in a collective, self-educational, forecast-oriented system that will endow them gradually with a common language and modes of reasoning acceptable to all. The construction of a forecast should be a collective enterprise, mobilizing the full diversity of society's experience as efficiently as is humanly possible. Input-output techniques have proved too inflexible to make full allowance for technological evolution, or to appraise its consequences.

It is likely that other people, elsewhere, have had different experiences in the use of the input-output table; what I wanted to describe in this paper was the very first attempt made to use it in France, and the consequences arising from this, as I was intimately involved in it.

REFERENCES

Aujac, H. (1960) La hiérarchie des industries dans un tableau des échanges interindustriels et ses conséquences sur la mise en oeuvre d'un Plan National décentralisé, *Revue Economique*, 11, 169–238.
  (1972a) A French experiment in long- and very long-term national technological forecasting: the basic role of semantics, *Technological Forecasting and Social Change*, 4, 23–35.
  (1972b) New approaches in French national planning: input-output tables and technological forecasting, in A. Brody and A. P. Carter (eds.) *Input-Output Techniques* (Amsterdam, North-Holland), 406–417.
  (1973) A new approach to technological forecasting in French national planning, in B. R. Williams (ed.) *Science and Technology in Economic Growth* (London, Macmillan), 96–124.
  (1983) Une prévision technologique utile, *Futuribles*, 71, 101–109.
Jantsch, E. (1967) *Technological Forecasting in Perspectives* (Paris, Organisation for Economic Co-operation and Development).

6   Leontief and dynamic regional models

William H. Miernyk

1.   Dynamics of the input-output system

The original edition of *The Structure of American Economy, 1919–1929* did not mention economic dynamics (Leontief, 1941). A fairly complete exposition of dynamic economic theory, in an input-output framework, was presented to the American Economic Association (AEA) by Leontief in 1949, and later included as chapter D in the enlarged version of *The Structure of American Economy, 1919–1939* (Leontief, 1951).

Leontief and several of his associates continued to make major advances in input-output analysis, which were brought together in a major publication (see Leontief et al., 1953). In this volume Leontief described open and closed, static, comparative static, and dynamic models. He also summarized the work he had been doing in the development of spatial models.

The basis of any input-output system is a transactions table: a two-way ordering of all interindustry sales and purchases during a given time period (usually a year). To complete the system a column of sales to ultimate users (or final demand) is added on the right-hand side of the transactions table, and a corresponding row, called value added (or payments sectors), is included at the bottom of the table. This is the raw material of an input-output model, from which a number of coefficients are calculated and used for a variety of analytical purposes (for further details at an elementary level, see Miernyk, 1965, pp. 9 and 149). Constructing transactions tables is costly and time-consuming. National tables are assembled by central statistical agencies. All but a handful of regional tables, and only one multiregional table known to this writer, have been derived from national tables.

A static model does not include the stock requirements of an economic system. It represents only the flow of purchases and sales on current account. Purchases on capital account are assumed to be part of the system's final demand. The same is true of comparative static models, which require two (or more) transactions tables, but which still deal only with sales on current account. Once each sector's capital (or stock) requirements are recognized, however, we have the data needed to calculate the coefficients from the structural equations of a dynamic input-output system. A simple balance equation for such a model is:

$$x_i = \Sigma_j z_{ij} + \Sigma_j l_{ij} + f_i$$

where x_i represents total gross output in sector i, z_{ij} is the amount of purchases on current account from sector j, l_{ij} the amount of purchases from sector j on capital account, and f_i is final demand. For the equations used to construct a dynamic regional model, see Miernyk et al. (1970, pp. 52–59). The addition of capital coefficients to the structural equations in a dynamic model was a major development in input-output analysis. Details about their calculation and nature are given in a later section dealing with regional input-output. What is said there applies, *mutatis mutandis*, to any dynamic input-output system. Capital coefficients are also discussed when the issue of the stability of dynamic input-output models is considered.

Leontief was aware of the limiting nature of the assumption of constant technical coefficients, which early critics of input-output analysis were quick to point out. These critics seemed unaware, however, that this was far from a critical assumption for the viability of input-output analysis. They also appeared to forget that the assumption of *ceteris paribus* is central to neoclassical theory. Without that assumption there would be no basis for conventional microeconomic theory, while the far more realistic assumption of constant technical coefficients, in the short run, was obviated by the development of comparative static and dynamic input-output models.

Meanwhile, conventional micro-theorists must continue to examine the effects of a change in economic variables, one at a time, while assuming that everything else remains unchanged. This assumption is universally recognized as being at variance with actual economic conditions anywhere.

The comparative static model requires a new transactions table for a future period. It also requires calculation of new input coefficients. These, compared with the original set, show the extent of changes in the structure of the economic system under analysis. The detailed study by Carter (1970) of the coefficients of the first three US input-output tables (1939, 1947 and 1953) showed that interindustry requirements were relatively stable (see also Miller and Blair, 1985, pp. 266–269). The stability of input coefficients over relatively short periods is of more than historical interest. The construction of a transactions table is a difficult and lengthy process. Input-output tables are typically published only after a two- or three-year lag, particularly for large, complex economies such as that of the United States. This "supports the contention that input-output coefficients . . . may remain useful for a number of years, even though the year [for which they were calculated] may appear to make them out of date" (Miller and Blair, 1985, p. 269).

2.   Projecting technical and capital coefficients

If a dynamic input-output model is to be used for forecasting, simulation, or a combination of the two, it will be necessary to project the technical coefficients of the base-year **A** and **B** matrices. This is an entirely different approach from the one described in the last section. Only two methods will be discussed in any detail here, since they are generally applicable, i.e. to both national and regional models. These are the "best practice" approach and the RAS technique. For a more detailed discussion of these methods, including numerical examples, see Miller and Blair (1985, pp. 275–294). Their discussion is limited to technical coefficients (a_{ij}). The "best practice" approach can also be used to project capital coefficients (b_{ij}), since the initial matrix of the latter must be derived from survey data (see Miernyk and Sears, 1974, pp. 14–25). A third approach, the *ex ante* method, is mentioned briefly here. It is designed for more limited use than the others.

2.1   The "best practice" approach

This approach is limited to input-output systems based on survey data (for a regional example, see Miernyk et al., 1970). It was suggested by the method used by the Bureau of Labor Statistics to estimate changes in industrial productivity. Base-year coefficients are obtained by calculating the average coefficients (a_{ij}) for each sector. Target-year coefficients are calculated for a sample of establishments in each sector characterized by low labor/output and high profit/output ratios. The technical coefficients of these "best practice" establishments are assumed to be the average coefficients of the sector in the target year. There is no logical basis for this assumption, "but in its favor is the fact that it is a workable, feasible way of constructing technical coefficient matrices that are more likely to represent the future structure of production than would a table . . . constructed to represent the average structure in each sector today" (Miller and Blair, 1985, p. 275). It is also worth noting that this method does not assume uniform changes along each row or column of the projected matrix of coefficients. It is consistent with Carter's findings about the historical behavior of technical coefficients over time (for a summary of those findings, see Miller and Blair, 1985, pp. 268–269).

2.2 The RAS method

The RAS method is an attempt to project a new matrix of technical coefficients $(\mathbf{A}_1^{RAS})$, for a target year 1, from a known matrix $(\mathbf{A}_0)$ of coefficients for a base year 0. The elements in $\mathbf{A}_1^{RAS}$ are meant to be consistent with two vectors – $\mathbf{u}_1$, which represents total intermediate output, and $\mathbf{v}_1$, total intermediate input – of each sector in the target year 1. The procedure may be summarized as

$$\mathbf{A}_1^{RAS} = \hat{\mathbf{r}}\mathbf{A}_0\hat{\mathbf{s}} \tag{1}$$

$$\left(\mathbf{A}_1^{RAS}\hat{\mathbf{x}}_1\right)\mathbf{i} = \mathbf{T}_1^{RAS}\mathbf{i} = \mathbf{u}_1 \tag{2}$$

$$\mathbf{i}'\left(\mathbf{A}_1^{RAS}\hat{\mathbf{x}}_1\right) = \mathbf{i}'\mathbf{T}_1^{RAS} = \mathbf{v}_1' \tag{3}$$

where $\mathbf{x}_1$ is the vector of gross sector output in the target year, $\mathbf{A}_1^{RAS}\hat{\mathbf{x}}_1 = \mathbf{T}_1^{RAS}$ is the projected transactions matrix for the target year, and $\mathbf{i}$ is the unit summation vector. The circumflex above a vector (^) indicates the formation of a diagonal matrix with elements on the main diagonal and zeros elsewhere.

Richard Stone, who – with Brown and Bacharach – developed the RAS technique, hypothesized that input coefficients had a substitution effect and a fabrication effect. These were assumed to operate evenly along the columns and rows of the target-year matrix via substitution (r_i) and fabrication (s_j) multipliers (see Stone and Brown, 1965, and Bacharach, 1970).

Two advantages are claimed for the RAS technique. First is its computational simplicity, while preserving signs (i.e. no positive coefficient in the base year can be negative in the target year), and second is its minimal data requirement. As I have argued elsewhere, however, the technique "substitutes computational tractability for economic logic" (Miernyk, 1977, p. 30). Carter (1970) has shown that, while technical coefficients have changed slowly, on the average, there are marked differences when the coefficients are examined sector by sector (see also Miller and Blair, 1985, pp. 268–271). As Almon and his associates have noted, after studying changes in hundreds of coefficients, "coefficient change is by no means the same thing as technological change . . . They reflect changes in laws, preferences, prices and product mixes at least as much as they reflect changes in product technology. We refrain, therefore from the flashy term 'technological change' and stick with the unexciting but correct expression 'coefficient change'" (Almon et al., 1974, p. 164). This reinforces the view that it would be unrealistic, as the RAS method does, to assume uniform change along rows and columns. Moreover, when partial, exogenously-derived data are substituted for RAS projections, the percentage error in the coefficient matrix increases! For illustrations see Miernyk (1977, pp. 30–34). The original RAS technique is an interesting exercise in numerical analysis, but it serves no useful role in the projection of input-output coefficients.

The concluding sentence of the preceding paragraph would not necessarily apply to a substantially modified RAS technique. Van der Linden and Dietzenbacher (2000), for example, have developed a method for decomposing a set of input coefficients into their average fabrication, average substitution, and sector-specific substitution effects. If the residual sector-specific effects are large, relative to the fabrication and substitution effects, this modification could improve on the original RAS method of projecting input coefficients. Even a vast improvement in a modified RAS method would not alter my conclusion about its efficacy as a predictor of change in input coefficients, however. This is because, following Georgescu-Roegen (and – indirectly –Schumpeter), my objection to the RAS method is epistemological rather than mathematical.

Economic growth, or – more generally – economic change, is the result of qualitative rather than quantitative factors. And the economic process can only be described dialectically, rather than arithmomorphically, because mathematical models are unable to incorporate qualitative change (see Georgescu-Roegen, 1971). For a brief, non-technical discussion of dialectics versus analysis, see Miernyk (1999, pp. 69–70). The RAS method, including recent modifications, is an example of a simple economic model with rigid assumptions locked into its axiomatic basis.

As many of his followers have noted, Georgescu-Roegen was a thinker far ahead of his time. How was he viewed by Leontief? The answer is given in a volume of essays published in Georgescu's honor: "Professor Georgescu-Roegen, in contrast to many other mathematical economists, was interested in the problems of economic theory and not in demonstrating his command of mathematical methods. He made a significant contribution to the advancement of economics by using not only his good knowledge of economics but also his perfect command of mathematics" (Mayumi and Gowdy, 1999, dedication).

2.3   *The* ex ante *method*

The *ex ante* method of projecting coefficient changes was designed as a forecasting tool for specific sectors rather than as a method for projecting changes in input coefficients per se. Unlike the "best practice" and RAS techniques, which are attempts to generate new matrices of coefficients by statistical/mathematical methods, the *ex ante* approach is entirely judgmental. This is not meant to be pejorative. There are circumstances under which the estimates of experts are more reliable than those derived statistically, particularly when qualitative changes are involved.

Published input-output tables are expressed in sales and purchases. But Leontief considered these entries to be indexes of physical goods and services. That is, he thought in terms of engineering production functions. This is also true of the *ex ante* input-output tables produced at the Battelle Memorial Institute, in Columbus, Ohio (see Fisher and Chilton, 1975).

3. The stability of dynamic systems

3.1 Capital coefficients

The expansion capital coefficient b_{ij} is defined as the stock of capital requirements by sector j from sector i per unit increase in capacity in j. The row sums of capital sales by each sector are designated as $\Sigma_j l_{ij}$. Not all purchases on capital account are the result of expansion of capacity. Capital goods have widely varying "useful lives." A heavy machine tool – a lathe, for example – might run profitably for twenty years. But the chisels used to shape metal parts on the lathe might last only one year. Thus it is useful to distinguish between expansion and replacement capital. The former, designated as l_{ij}^e, depends upon anticipated changes in the capacity of sector j, and the latter (l_{ij}^r) upon the sector's output. For further details, and numerical examples, see Miernyk et al. (1970, pp. 59–70) as well as Miller and Blair (1985, pp. 341–351).

The capital coefficients are defined as follows. The replacement capital coefficients are given by $d_{ij} = l_{ij}^r/x_j$, and the expansion capital coefficients by $b_{ij} = l_{ij}^e/\Delta x_j$. Using matrix notation, the equation of a general dynamic model may be written as

$$(\mathbf{I} - \mathbf{A} - \mathbf{D} - \mathbf{B})\mathbf{x}_t + \mathbf{B}\mathbf{x}_{t-1} = \mathbf{f}_t \tag{4}$$

with $a_{ij} = z_{ij}/x_j$. Solving for $\mathbf{x}_t$ yields

$$\mathbf{x}_t = (\mathbf{I} - \mathbf{A} - \mathbf{D} - \mathbf{B})^{-1}(\mathbf{f}_t - \mathbf{B}\mathbf{x}_{t-1}) \tag{5}$$

This is a recursive system. Say that gross output is known for the year 2000 (i.e. $\mathbf{x}_{t-1}$) and final demand for the year 2001 (i.e. $\mathbf{f}_t$); equation (5) would give us total output $\mathbf{x}_t$ for 2001. The process can be repeated as long as the coefficients in matrices **A**, **D** and **B** adequately reflect conditions in the economy.

Is the dynamic model inherently unstable? It is a gross oversimplification to describe a system, economic or otherwise, as either "stable" or "unstable." As Samuelson noted long ago, "analysis of the concept of stability with the implied investigation of the *qualitative behavior* of generalized dynamical paths leads into some of the most difficult problems of higher mathematics" (Samuelson, 1963, p. 335, emphasis added). There are also semantic problems because of the ways "stability" can be defined, each correctly in its own context (Samuelson, 1963, pp. 333–334). Finally, as will be noted presently, economic models can be compared in terms of stability, as well as other characteristics, only if they have common taxonomic origins (Miernyk, 1999, pp. 72–74). All of the above remains true if the other side of the coin is examined, and attention is focused on "instability" or "unstable" models. In a broadside attack on the Leontief dynamic model, Sargan concluded: "In all the simple cases considered [in his paper] the Leontief dynamic equilibrium is unstable . . . [It] is not adapted to explaining the actual movements of the economic system . . . This conclusion is purely negative, and this is as far as we can go on a priori grounds" (Sargan, 1958, p. 392).

Replying in the same journal, Leontief argued that "the novel stability criterion which Sargan proposes to use in judging the empirical validity of dynamic systems makes it so weak as to render it practically useless" (Leontief, 1961a, p. 659). The essence of Sargan's criticism was that the Leontief model contains no lags (e.g. between sales to and purchases from sector i). He proposed an alternative (which Leontief called the "S-system") that does contain lags. If these are made infinitely small, but remain greater than zero, "the positive real part of one of its roots tends to become infinitely large . . . [and the system becomes] potentially explosive." Leontief concluded: "Sargan's special lagged system . . . obviously does not make a good dynamic general equilibrium model" (1961a, p. 663).

There is a further exchange in the same issue of the journal, but it is clear that Leontief and Sargan are talking about two different models; hence their differences are irreconcilable.[1] The fact remains that workable dynamic input-output models have been constructed and used for a number of analytical purposes (see, for example, Miernyk et al., 1970; Miernyk and Sears, 1974; and Miller and Blair, 1985, p. 341).

---

[1] See the reply by Sargan (1961) and the rejoinder by Leontief (1961b).

3.2   *The taxonomy of dynamic models*

Taxonomy refers to the principles governing the classification of objects. There is no reason, however, why these principles cannot be applied to ideas as well as objects, and there are good reasons why they should be.

Sargan began his critique of the Leontief dynamic model by asserting: "The idea that there is any point in calling any dynamic model 'unstable' was suggested by Harrod (1948)" (Sargan, 1958, p. 381). He went on to assert that "Leontief's can be regarded as a more complicated analogue of the simple Harrodian system" (p. 382). This is a major taxonomic error, about of the magnitude of making behavioral comparisons between a mouse and a moose because both happen to be mammals.

Harrod was one of the pioneers in what is now called "growth economics" – arguably the dominant topic of discussion among conventional economic theorists today. This branch of economics is a lineal descendant of Keynes's aggregate economic theory. An oversimplified version would state that

$$\Delta C + \Delta I = \Delta Y$$

where C denotes consumers' spending (including additions to or withdrawals from savings), I is total investment, and Y is national income. Changes in income depend upon changes in the behavior of consumers and investors.

Consider next a simplified static input-output system

$$\mathbf{x} = \mathbf{A}\mathbf{x} + \mathbf{f}$$

where $\mathbf{x}$ is a vector of total gross outputs, $\mathbf{A}$ a matrix of input requirements, and $\mathbf{f}$ is a vector of final demand. The latter is not determined by changes in $\mathbf{A}$; causation goes the other way. Future final demand is projected by a conventional statistical method, and changes in this vector will affect the entries in $\mathbf{A}$. For an illustrative example, see Miernyk (1965, pp. 34–38).

Clearly, the Leontief dynamic model is not a more complicated analogue of the simple Harrodian system. Thus it should not be expected to contain the same behavioral equations as does the latter. Moreover, the emphasis in input-output analysis is on disaggregation, while conventional growth theory continues to deal in broad aggregates. Attempts to generalize about the disparate behavioral characteristics of these two systems will inevitably lead to a taxonomic trap, as it did in Sargan's case.

The Harrodian system, as well as the numerous growth models engendered by it, and the virtually identical model developed independently by Domar are lineal descendants of the aggregated Keynesian system. The precursors of Leontief, however, are Quesnay and Walras, as well as others who proposed theoretical formulations of economic interdependence. "The fundamental discovery that distinguished Leontief's work from that of all his predecessors is that it was practical to calculate the input-output coefficients from recorded data" (Dorfman, 1973, p. 432). What is impressive about this discovery, Dorfman goes on to observe, is that it occurred a decade before the appearance of the first electronic computer.

4.   Leontief and regional input-output analysis

4.1   *Regional and interregional theory*

Two events led to the proliferation of regional input-output studies during the last three decades of the last century: the invention of the digital computer, and the emergence of a new multidisciplinary approach called Regional Science. An input-output bibliography compiled in 1975 included 276 entries, and this omitted studies that did not do "more than replicate techniques developed earlier" (see Giarratani et al., 1976). It did, however, include eight other bibliographies, which encompassed all types of regional studies ranging in size from rural counties and one small city to national interregional and multiregional tables (Giarratani et al., 1976, pp. 23–25; see also Richardson, 1972, especially pp. 261–283).

Leontief was not directly concerned with small-area studies. He did, however, publish a fully developed theory of interregional input-output analysis, but preferred the term "intranational" (Leontief et al., 1953, pp. 93–115). The same volume includes "Some Empirical Results and Problems of Regional Input-Output Analysis" by Walter Isard, generally regarded as the founder of Regional Science. In collaboration with Strout, Leontief also developed an interregional trade model using gravity constants, q_i^{gh}, in which i represents some arbitrary good, and g and h are regions. This innovation recognized cross-hauling in interregional trade (see Leontief, 1966, pp. 223–257). For further discussion that distinguishes between real and apparent cross-hauling, see Miernyk (1982, p. 19).

While not directly involved, Leontief had more than a passing interest in small-area studies, particularly if their objective was the empirical implementation of a phase of input-output not yet subjected to verification. In the early 1960s two such studies were under way at the Bureau of Economic Research of the University of Colorado. The first was a multiregional analysis of the Colorado river basin, involving other universities and government agencies. Survey-based input-output tables were constructed for each of the six sub-basins, linked together via import columns and export rows. The objective was to estimate the environmental impacts of expanding economic activity on each sub-basin of the Colorado river basin. The final report, which ran to thousands of mimeographed pages, was never published. The basic model is described in Miernyk (1969), and the aggregated Colorado river basin transactions table was published in Miernyk (1967).

At the same time, a survey of consumer spending was being conducted in Boulder, Colorado, as part of an input-output impact study. The results permitted the model to be closed with respect to households, and thus provided estimates of the direct, indirect, and induced impacts of a change in final demand (see Miernyk et al., 1967).

In spite of his busy schedule at Harvard, including direction of the Harvard Economic Research Project, Leontief arranged to visit Boulder. He suggested that the next time we conducted an input-output survey it should include data on capital and capacity changes. We could then construct a dynamic model. This was done at the Regional Research Institute, at West Virginia University, starting in 1965. Part of the results of that effort are reported in Miernyk et al. (1970) and Miernyk and Sears (1974).

When Leontief visited our research group in the late 1970s he was pleased that our model was being used for a number of analyses. He also mentioned specifically his satisfaction that the West Virginia dynamic model was stable, and reminded us of Sargan's taxonomically unsound, and now largely forgotten, attack on his theoretical dynamic model.

5. A final word

The best biographical sketch of Leontief is Robert Dorfman's, which opens with the assertion: "Whoever thinks of Wassily Leontief thinks of input-output, and vice versa" (Dorfman, 1973, p. 431). The extensive bibliography appended to Dorfman's paper shows that input-output is Leontief's outstanding achievement. More broadly, he should be remembered for his view that "the only valid test of economic research is its empirical significance and its practical implications" (Dorfman, 1973, p. 431).

There is one minor drawback to Dorfman's excellent survey of Leontief's life work. It was published in 1973, the year Leontief was awarded the Nobel Prize in Economics, and Dorfman wrote that "Leontief stands, near the end of his career, as the model of the scientific method in economics" (Dorfman, 1973, p. 441). My only quibble with this assessment is that it was written a quarter-century too soon.

In 1975 Leontief left Harvard, after forty-four years of teaching and research, to become Director of the Institute for Economic Analysis at New York University – a position he held until 1991. He continued to remain in touch with input-output researchers on a global basis. He died on February 5, 1999, to join the small handful of great men in economics, such as Adam Smith and John Maynard Keynes, who will be remembered as long as economics remains a viable discipline.

How will Leontief be remembered? What is his intellectual legacy? It is hard to improve on Dorfman's words. He saw him as the model of the scientific method in economics. "Herein lies his pre-eminence. The student of economics, of any age or stage, could do far worse than review Leontief's work on any topic to see scientific economics exemplified at its best. The discovery of input-output is a fitting capstone to his combination of scientific soundness and technical brilliance" (Dorfman, 1973, p. 441).

REFERENCES

Almon, C., M. M. Buckler, L. M. Horowitz and T. C. Reimbold (1974) *1985: Interindustry Forecasts of the American Economy* (Lexington, MA, D. C. Heath).
Bacharach, M. (1970) *Biproportional Matrices and Input-Output Change* (Cambridge, Cambridge University Press).
Carter, A. P. (1970) *Structural Change in the American Economy* (Cambridge, MA, Harvard University Press).
Dorfman, R. (1973) Wassily Leontief's contribution to economics, *Swedish Journal of Economics*, 75, 430–449.
Fisher, H. W., and C. H. Chilton (1975) Developing *ex ante* input-output flow and capital coefficients, in W. F. Gossling (ed.) *Capital Coefficients and Dynamic Input-Output Models* (London, Input-Output Publishing Company), 1–13.
Georgescu-Roegen, N. (1971) *The Entropy Law and the Economic Process* (Cambridge, MA, Harvard University Press).
Giarratani, F., J. D. Maddy and C. F. Socher (1976) *Regional and Interregional Input-Output Analysis: A Bibliography* (Morgantown, WV, West Virginia University Press).
Harrod, R. E. (1948) *Towards a Dynamic Economics* (London, Macmillan).
Leontief, W. W. (1941) *The Structure of American Economy, 1919–1929* (Cambridge, MA, Harvard University Press).
    (1951) *The Structure of American Economy, 1919–1939: An Empirical Application of Equilibrium Analysis* (New York, Oxford University Press).
    (1961a) Lags and the stability of dynamic systems, *Econometrica*, 29, 659–669.
    (1961b) Lags and the stability of dynamic systems: a rejoinder, *Econometrica*, 29, 674–675.
    (1966) *Input-Output Economics* (New York, Oxford University Press).

Leontief, W. W., et al. (1953) *Studies in the Structure of the American Economy* (New York, Oxford University Press).

van der Linden, J. A., and E. Dietzenbacher (2000) The determinants of structural change in the European Union: a new application of RAS, *Environment and Planning A*, 32, 2,205–2,229.

Mayumi, K., and J. M. Gowdy (eds.) (1999) *Bioeconomics and Sustainability: Essays in Honor of Nicholas Georgescu-Roegen* (Cheltenham, Edward Elgar Publishing).

Miernyk, W. H. (1965) *The Elements of Input-Output Analysis* (New York, Random House).

(1967) Simulazione di sviluppo regionale con un modello input-output, *Rivista Internazionale di Scienze Economiche e Commerciali*, 16, 741–753.

(1969) *An interindustry forecasting model with water quantity and quality constraints*, paper presented to the Fourth Symposium on Water Resource Research at the Ohio State University Water Resources Center.

(1977) A projection of technical coefficients for medium-term forecasting, in W. F. Gossling (ed.) *Medium-Term Dynamic Forecasting: The London Input-Output Conference* (London, Input-Output Publishing Company), 29–41.

(1982) *Regional Analysis and Regional Policy* (Cambridge, MA, Oelgeschlager, Gunn & Hain).

(1999) Economic growth theory and the Georgescu-Roegen paradigm, in K. Mayumi and J. M. Gowdy (eds.) *Bioeconomics and Sustainability: Essays in Honor of Nicholas Georgescu-Roegen* (Cheltenham, Edward Elgar Publishing), 69–81.

Miernyk, W. H., E. R. Bonner, J. A. Chapman, Jr., and K. L. Shellhammer (1967) *Impact of the Space Program on a Local Economy* (Morgantown, WV, West Virginia University Press).

Miernyk, W. H., and J. T. Sears (1974) *Air Pollution Abatement and Regional Economic Development* (Lexington, MA, D. C. Heath).

Miernyk, W. H., K. L. Shellhammer, D. M. Brown, R. L. Coccari, C. J. Gallagher and W. Wineman (1970) *Simulating Regional Economic Development* (Lexington, MA, D. C. Heath).

Miller, R. E., and P. D. Blair (1985) *Input-Output Analysis: Foundations and Extensions* (Englewood Cliffs, NJ, Prentice-Hall).

Richardson, H. W. (1972) *Input-Output and Regional Economics* (New York, John Wiley).

Samuelson, P. A. (1963) *Foundations of Economic Analysis* (Cambridge, MA, Harvard University Press).

Sargan, J. D. (1958) The instability of the Leontief dynamic model, *Econometrica*, 26, 381–392.

(1961) Lags and the stability of dynamic systems: a reply, *Econometrica*, 29, 670–673.

Stone, R., and A. Brown (1965) Behavioural and technical change in economic models, in E. A. G. Robinson (ed.) *Problems in Economic Development* (London, Macmillan), 428–443.

7 Experiences with input-output and isomorphic analytical tools in spatial economics

Jean H. P. Paelinck

1. Introduction

Concepts of input-output analysis pervade economics. In a study dedicated to Wassily Leontief, Varii Auctores (1966, epigraph) stated that "dependence and independence, hierarchy and circularity (or multiregional dependence) are the four basic concepts of structural analysis." Indeed, in this chapter I argue that input-output relationships may well be even more important at the level below that of a national geography. Thus, I do not dwell here upon non-spatial studies in which the input-output framework is encountered or general introductions to spatial input-output analysis (e.g. Paelinck and Nijkamp, 1975, chapter 5), nor do I dwell upon studies that are not directly relevant, although possibly related. Instead I present a personal reconnaissance in spatial analysis, focusing upon applications of input-output.

My work on spatial analysis began with a study on the workings of a regional economy based on metalworking and, to a lesser extent, on chemicals (Davin et al., 1959; see more below in section 2.1). Technology links between the activities studied were a central part of the analysis, although, due to a lack of regional input-output tables in the mid-1950s, the technology chains (henceforth referred to using the French term "filières") could only be analyzed qualitatively. This study was the primary foundation of my later thinking (see Paelinck, 1963) on the contents of a theory of polarized regional growth put forward by François Perroux, in which input-output concepts play a central role. Early reading of Sir Richard Stone's work (Stone, 1961) and subsequent contacts with the HERP team, led by Wassily Leontief, helped me to clarify certain fundamental issues.

As regional input-output tables became progressively more available, analytical concepts were applied to them. The possibility of the joint use of several such tables prompted the idea of modeling interregional flows of goods and services (Leontief and Strout, 1963). The practice of regional science, however, showed that specific *spatial* elements should be introduced; this took place progressively. Highlighting some of the most important of these elements is the main object of this chapter, which is organized in two parts.

The first part relates to applications of input-output analysis at the spatial – i.e. the regional and/or urban – level. The second part treats some applications further afield from input-output, namely isomorphic concepts, which can be seen as complementary to input-output analysis proper and, in fact, include its workings.

In the course of the first part I introduce fundamental spatial elements, which should complement traditional input-output analysis. It is my view that spatial components enrich general economic analysis, the primary principles of which remain untouched throughout this synthesis.

2.   Extending spatial input–output analysis

In this section I present a number of applications of regional input-output analysis. I progressively introduce spatial elements. For the sake of clarity, assume all parameters and coefficients are positive, unless otherwise stated.

2.1   Exploration, simulation, impact

In the 1960s regional development problems attracted great attention, especially so in France (Aujac, 2004). Different types of interregional inequalities were analyzed (e.g. declining, mostly old, industrial regions; traditionally stagnant regions; peripheral regions; and border regions). The focus tended to be on how to enhance or jump-start a region's economic growth.

One application of input-output analysis is that of exploring the economic impacts of certain, often new, economic activities or "filières" (Paelinck et al., 1965; compare also to Szyrmer, 1986, and 1992). The technique used was novel albeit simple: it consisted of removing a sector from an input-output table, essentially replacing its deliveries by imports, and letting the rest of the economy remain the same (though refinements, such as adapting local final demand, were also introduced). This approach revealed that Liège, an old industrial region in Belgium, had a lopsided industrial structure. Metalworking was directly and indirectly responsible for nearly 50 percent of the economy's value added, while chemicals contributed less than 8 percent. The main criticism raised against this type of exploration was its global character (I will return to this point later). Another criticism focused on the method's hypothesis

Table 7.1 *Decomposition of impacts of an industrial complex*

Entries	Percent
Intraregional final deliveries	1.27
Exports	82.62
Impact of final demand for other sectors' products	3.00
Effect of the complex's own multiplier matrix	9.00
Effect of its insertion in the rest of the economy	4.11
Total	100.00

that the supply of primary factors would be sufficiently elastic to adapt to a radically new situation, even in the long run.

A variant of this method consists of breaking out the impacts of a cluster of local activities, now conventionally called an industrial complex, upon the global workings of the local economy (Paelinck, 1970; see also Sonis and Hewings, 1999, and Miller and Lahr, 2001). In any case, the derivation of the general approach to the latter problem follows, 1 being the index of the complex (or industries of interest) and 2 that of all other activities. The vectors $\mathbf{x}$ and $\mathbf{y}$ are output and demand, respectively, and $\mathbf{A}$ is the direct requirements matrix, the usual symbols of input-output notation.

$$\begin{pmatrix} \mathbf{x}_1 \\ \mathbf{x}_2 \end{pmatrix} = \begin{bmatrix} \mathbf{A}_{11} & \mathbf{A}_{12} \\ \mathbf{A}_{21} & \mathbf{A}_{22} \end{bmatrix} \begin{pmatrix} \mathbf{x}_1 \\ \mathbf{x}_2 \end{pmatrix} + \begin{pmatrix} \mathbf{y}_1 \\ \mathbf{y}_2 \end{pmatrix}$$

Hence

$$\mathbf{x}_1 = [\mathbf{I} - \mathbf{A}_{11} - \mathbf{A}_{12}(\mathbf{I} - \mathbf{A}_{22})^{-1}\mathbf{A}_{21}]^{-1}[\mathbf{y}_1 + \mathbf{A}_{12}(\mathbf{I} - \mathbf{A}_{22})^{-1}\mathbf{y}_2]$$

An average decomposition of $\mathbf{x}_1$ is shown in table 7.1. The figures relate to a region in southern Belgium called Basse-Sambre; twelve "complex" sectors and ten others were distinguished. The first three entries correspond to terms in the second set of square brackets, $\mathbf{y}_1$ having been split up into intraregional final deliveries and exports; the fourth entry corresponds to $[(\mathbf{I} - \mathbf{A}_{11})^{-1} - \mathbf{I}]$ applied to the sum of the final demand terms, the last one to the residual. Again, lopsidedness (toward exports this time) is a remarkable outcome; given the relative smallness of multiplier effects only a "pseudo-complex" seems to be present.

A slight variation of the two approaches just described can be used to analyze the effects of changes in intermediate deliveries (see Paelinck, 1983a, pp. 199–208, in particular for techniques to derive matrix $\mathbf{C}_{ij}$ hereafter). The impact on the regional income r – defined as total value added at market prices – of an increase in regional deliveries x_{ij}, at the expense of imports, of activity i to activity j in this case is

$$\partial r / \partial x_{ij} = \frac{\mathbf{v}' \mathbf{C}_{ij} \mathbf{y}}{(\mathbf{1}'_j + a_{ij} \mathbf{c}'_{ij,j}) \mathbf{y}}$$

where $\mathbf{C}_{ij} = \partial \mathbf{L} / \partial a_{ij}$, $\mathbf{L} = (\mathbf{I} - \mathbf{A})^{-1}$, $\mathbf{1}'_j$ the jth row of $\mathbf{L}$, $\mathbf{c}'_{ij,j}$ the jth row of $\mathbf{C}_{ij}$, and $\mathbf{v}'$ the row vector of sectoral values added.

An application reveals that the multipliers of intermediate demand can reach much higher values than those for final demand, which have the maximum of 1 in this context. Such multipliers can be obtained, either from the observed (partial) input coefficients or from the maximum (technology coefficients proper) values. More research on locally promising activities is reported in Sonis et al. (2000).

In order to gain further insight into the linkages within an input-output economy, Paelinck (2003) first defined a "club" as a series of highly connected activities, e.g. of the input-output type. The general idea then is to extract clubs serially from an input-output table, each club having the maximal total interindustry linkages prior to its extraction. The mathematical program can be written as follows

$$\max_{\mathbf{u}} \varphi = [\text{vec}(\mathbf{A}'_-)]' \mathbf{u} \qquad (1)$$

$$\text{subject to } \mathbf{J} \mathbf{u} \leq \mathbf{i} \text{ and } \hat{\mathbf{u}} \mathbf{u} = \mathbf{u} \qquad (2)$$

where $\text{vec}(\mathbf{Z})$ is the vectorization of a matrix $\mathbf{Z}$, the $n \times (n - 1)$ matrix $\mathbf{A}_-$ is obtained from the $n \times n$ matrix $\mathbf{A}$ by omitting its diagonal elements, and $\mathbf{u}$ is an $n(n - 1)$ column vector of binary variables (as follows from the condition $\hat{\mathbf{u}} \mathbf{u} = \mathbf{u}$, where a "hat" is used to indicate the diagonal matrix corresponding to vector $\mathbf{u}$).

The conditions $\mathbf{J} \mathbf{u} \leq \mathbf{i}$ in (2) are the weakened assignment conditions, the $2n \times n(n - 1)$ matrix $\mathbf{J}$ – the so-called assignment matrix – being binary and $\mathbf{i}$ indicating the column summation vector. If the weak inequalities were replaced by equalities, exactly n *directed* relations would be selected, each sector appearing twice. This relaxation allows the creation of *incomplete* clubs.

Once the solution to the mathematical program is obtained, one has generated a first club with maximal internal cohesion (alternatively, maximum total mutual deliveries). One then cancels the corresponding entries of $\mathbf{A}$, leading up to a matrix $\mathbf{A}^*$ to be treated similarly, and so on until all the entries have been exhausted.

Results for this method applied to a 10×10 input-output table for the United Kingdom in 1950 (Stone and Croft-Murray, 1959, p. 33) are as follows. One round reproduces the food cycle, another round centers around chemical production, while a third round depicts the metalworking complex; further rounds refer to more involved technologies, but the level of aggregation is too high to allow the ready disentangling of them. Anyhow, the above-mentioned filières are clearly present. This would not necessarily be the case for an input-output table that describes the structure of a regional economy, especially in an aggregate fashion. This is because the absence of certain activities and/or the presence of important competitive imports could produce false filières.

It should be observed that very few if any spatial elements have been present in the exercises mentioned to this point. To be sure, the regions or complexes analyzed are located somewhere in geographical space, and, as a function of the definition of the input-output tables used, coefficients can depend on competitive imports; but the "spatiality" ends there. Hereafter some of the first typical spatial elements will be introduced.

2.2   Spatializing input-output-based models: economies of scale and scope; externalities; non-convexities; and supply effects

Focusing first on the planning aspect of the regional development problem, input-output relations can be used to set up mathematical programming models for deriving a minimal investment (k) viable industrial complex, in the sense that all the activities present are minimally profitable. One such model is specified as follows

$$\min k = \sum_i p_i^* \left(k_{i0}/x_{i0}^{a_i}\right) x_i^{a_i} u_i$$

subject to

$$p_i x_i u_i - \sum_{j \neq i} p_j a_{ji} \exp(-a_{ji} x_j u_j) x_i u_i - w_i \left(l_{i0}/x_{i0}^{b_i}\right) x_i^{b_i} u_i$$
$$+ r_i p_i^* \left(k_{i0}/x_{i0}^{a_i}\right) x_i^{a_i} u_i \geq \pi_i p_i^* \left(k_{i0}/x_{i0}^{a_i}\right) x_i^{a_i} u_i \text{ for all } i \qquad (3)$$
$$\text{and } x_i u_i \geq x_{i0}, \, u_i = u_i^2 \text{ for all } i, \text{ and } \sum_i u_i \geq 1$$

Here x_i is production level of plant i; k_i is investment in plant i; l_i is labor input into production of i; a_{ji} is the input coefficient of product j into production of i; p_i is the unit price of product i, net of intermediate products not considered for the industrial complex; p_i^* is the unit price of investment in plant i; w_i is the unit wage in production i; r_i is the unit period depreciation rate for investment i; π_i is the desired unit period profitability rate for activity i; and u_i is a binary (0-1) variable, representing the absence or presence of a plant of type i in the final solution of the problem.

The expressions $(k_{i0}/x_{i0}^{a_i})x_i^{a_i}$ and $(l_{i0}/x_{i0}^{b_i})x_i^{b_i}$, $0 \le a_i, b_i \ge 1$, are derived from production functions with the scale economies (parameters a_i and b_i), k_{i0}, l_{i0} and x_{i0} being the minimum feasible levels of the corresponding variables; the exponential function in equation (3) reflects local externalities, linked to overall scope economies. As such, the problem boils down to a continuous mixed-integer geometric program. A solution method for it is described in Paelinck (1972). This method can be used either to build up an industrial complex from scratch or to complement an already loosely integrated "pseudo-complex," as discussed above. It should finally be noted that, if public authorities start launching several of these programs, problems of consistency will creep in (Paelinck, 1971); I come back to this problem later.

The important point to be mentioned here is the explicit introduction of spatial elements. Two of them are clearly present: externalities and non-convexities. Location externalities appear in equation (3), as already mentioned (compare to the industrial complex analysis in Isard et al., 1959), as do non-convexities in the variables u_i. They crop up systematically in spatial economic analysis and cannot be ignored in the specification of such models. The following developments will add still another important spatial feature.

In Weberian location theory, localization economies are held (partly) responsible for the location decisions of potential investors. It is well known that input-output analysis is demand-oriented; in many spatial applications, however, supply effects should not be omitted from modeling exercises. Paelinck and Wagenaar's (1981) specification of this is systematized below.

The input-output ("pull") model for all sectors is

$$\mathbf{x} = \mathbf{Ax} + \mathbf{y} + \mathbf{e} \tag{4}$$

where $\mathbf{y}$ is regional final demand, and $\mathbf{e}$ net exports. A "push" equation can now be specified as

$$\mathbf{x} = \hat{\mathbf{b}}^{-1}\tilde{\mathbf{A}}'\mathbf{x} \tag{5}$$

where $\tilde{\mathbf{A}}$ is the matrix of intermediate allocation coefficients, "hats" denoting, once more, diagonal matrices. Vector $\mathbf{b}$ has to be estimated from a specific input-output table. Equations (4) and (5) can be combined linearly by a diagonal weighing matrix $\hat{\boldsymbol{\lambda}}$ to be applied to (5). A reasonable assumption is that $\boldsymbol{\lambda} = \tilde{\mathbf{A}}\mathbf{i}$, where $\mathbf{i}$ is the summation vector. If we now define $\hat{\boldsymbol{\mu}} = \mathbf{I} - \hat{\boldsymbol{\lambda}}$, it follows that

$$\hat{\mathbf{x}} = \hat{\boldsymbol{\mu}}\mathbf{Ax} + \hat{\boldsymbol{\mu}}\mathbf{y} + \hat{\boldsymbol{\mu}}\mathbf{e} + \hat{\boldsymbol{\lambda}}\hat{\mathbf{b}}^{-1}\tilde{\mathbf{A}}'\mathbf{x} \tag{6}$$

Now consider $\mathbf{y}$; in part it will be demand-pulled

$$\mathbf{y} = \alpha \mathbf{v}'\mathbf{x} \tag{7}$$

where α is a vector of consumption propensities and, as already defined above, $\mathbf{v}' = \mathbf{i}'(\mathbf{I} - \mathbf{A})$. The push effect can be specified as

$$\mathbf{y} = \hat{\varphi}\mathbf{x} \tag{8}$$

where $\hat{\varphi}$ is the diagonal matrix of the domestic final demand allocation coefficients. If one combines (7) and (8) linearly, the weights for (8) can be reasonably put equal to φ, and those for (7) to $\mathbf{i} - \varphi$. A similar argument applies to $\mathbf{e}$ with weighing vector ψ. Inserting these developments into (6) leads to $\mathbf{x} = \mathbf{Q}\mathbf{x}$, a system of homogeneous equations in $\mathbf{x}$.

Next, splitting up $\mathbf{x}$ into $\mathbf{x}_1$ and $\mathbf{x}_2$, and $\mathbf{Q}$ similarly into $\mathbf{Q}_{11}, \mathbf{Q}_{12}, \mathbf{Q}_{21}$ and $\mathbf{Q}_{22}$, one can express the effects symmetrically as

$$\mathbf{x}_1 = (\mathbf{I} - \mathbf{Q}_{11})^{-1}\mathbf{Q}_{12}\mathbf{x}_2^* \quad \text{and} \quad \mathbf{x}_2 = (\mathbf{I} - \mathbf{Q}_{22})^{-1}\mathbf{Q}_{21}\mathbf{x}_1^*$$

where $\mathbf{x}_2^*$ and $\mathbf{x}_1^*$ are assumed to be exogenous, so that mutual push-and-pull impacts can be computed. The relevant partial coefficients are, of course, those of the matrices $(\mathbf{I} - \mathbf{Q}_{11})^{-1}\mathbf{Q}_{12}$ and $(\mathbf{I} - \mathbf{Q}_{22})^{-1}\mathbf{Q}_{21}$. It should be noted that all the parameters can be derived from a standard input-output table. One possible application is the computation of economic effects of transportation sectors (Paelinck and Stough, 2000).

2.3   Combining input-output analysis and spatial econometrics: five more spatial elements

Input-output analysis can be conjoined with spatial econometrics, just as it has been with macroeconomic modeling (West, 1995). Recalling Paelinck and Klaassen (1979, chapter 1), Anselin (1988) and Anselin and Florax (1995), five features or principles characterize macroeconomic modeling: (1) spatial interdependence of endogenous variables; (2) spatial heterogeneity and asymmetry; (3) "allotopy" or the presence at a distance of spatially oriented exogenous explanatory variables; (4) *ex ante* non-linearity with possible *ex post* linearity; and (5) the presence of topological variables: pre-specified distances already mentioned, coordinates, densities, etc.

Ancot and Paelinck (1983) present the spatial econometrics of an interregional model, the so-called European "FLEUR" model (Factors of Location in EURope), obeying all five principles. To quote an important passage from that study (pp. 231–232):

Regions cannot be regarded as closed systems, nor is sectoral growth an isolated phenomenon; spatial interaction is not an intra-regional mechanism. Indeed, both input and output markets of most modern industrial sectors are spatially dispersed far beyond the frontiers of the region where the industries are settled, and industrial technologies are also interdependent beyond regional borders. Industries may settle in a given region not because that region itself is so attractive, but because it is next to an important market area for their products that is too congested to admit new firms. Or a region may be chosen as a spatial compromise between various contiguous regions of which one offers an output market, the second offers access to primary inputs, the third offers ancillary services, and so on. Obviously, such interregional effects are very important elements to include, at least implicitly, in the model.

On the basis of these elements, an estimable dynamic function was specified; input-output played an essential role in the estimation of the demand and supply variables that act as location factors. Applying principle (3) above, these estimates were "potentialized": they were "discounted" over space using an appropriate spatial decay function. Both specifications follow. In fact, if the equations of the model are put together, they lead up to a multiregional input-output model, but extended by supply effects and other location factors, all relevant demand and supply elements being duly spatially discounted.

The dynamic sectoral function was specified with a double error correction

$$\Delta' y_t = \alpha \left(y_t^0 - y_t \right) + \beta \left(\Delta' y_t^0 - \Delta' y_t \right)$$

where y_t is the natural logarithm of a non-linear transform of the activity indicator, y_t^0 a log-linear function of the equilibrium values of the location factors, all variables at time t; Δ' is the backward difference operator. The function y_t^0 includes potentialized values of relevant demand and supply variables, the flexible decay function being

$$f_{rs}(d_{rs}) = \exp(1 - \gamma^*)[\ln(1 + \gamma d_{rs}) + \gamma^*]/(1 + \gamma d_{rs})$$

with $\gamma^* = \gamma/(1 + \gamma)$, $\gamma \geq 0$, and where d_{rs} is the appropriate distance between regions r and s.

If both aspects, dynamic and spatial, have been mentioned explicitly, it is to insist on the fact that the specifications permitted the omission of the so-called "bogus calibration" problem (Wilson, 1974, p. 324; see also Bennett, 1979, for a general treatment) that has beset exercises in spatial modeling.

Apart from the usual projection exercises, the estimated equations were also applied in a way that deserves to be mentioned. It combined the econometric model, reduced to two sectors (industry and services), with a mathematical programming exercise (an early example where input-output analysis was straightforwardly combined with mathematical programming is Sandee, 1960). The general idea was to devise a minimal investment program (recall the industrial complex programming model of section 2.2) for less developed regions, so that all of them are guaranteed to reach at least a specified critical threshold level in terms of their endowment of location factors. The threshold was specified to separate the less developed regions from more developed ones. To that effect, over two long periods investment funds could be channeled to five types of policy instruments: infrastructure improvement; industry base enhancement; greater scope in service delivery; the use of financial stimuli; and the enhancement of urban externalities.

Using this approach, I found (see Paelinck 1983b, pp. 176–177) that the enhancement of accessibility by improving outbound infrastructure (inbound infrastructure was not considered explicitly in this exercise) during both periods (in concordance with its long-term character and relative expensiveness) was strategic for the take-off of practically all less developed regions. Increasing the local supply of industrial products and services was already more selective, between regions and periods, meaning that only a limited number of regions – different over the two periods concerned – were supposed to be stimulated in that way. From the programming results it also appeared that financial stimuli were to be applied only at rather low levels; they showed, in fact, a complementary character. Finally, urban externalities should be stimulated only in the second period; a logical result, as the ensuing (generally high-tech) activities need an existing concentrated, yet diverse, local economic base (Oerlemans et al., 2001).

A remarkable hierarchy presented itself through that first exploratory exercise in multiregional consistent planning, already hinted at in section 2.2. In fact, there is some spatial logic behind it: accessibility to demand, both intermediate and final, and to supply is an important mechanism in spatial markets and, hence, so is the structure of the local economic base. Once those elements are sufficiently strong, urban externalities (which favor high-tech developments), information and communication technologies, and the like come into play. Thus, looking jointly at space and time is an essential requirement for designing consistent, possibly optimal, multiregional policies.

Given the still aggregate character of the exercise reported here, nothing is said about some practical implications. Urban externalities or economies could indeed be realized in different ways: stimulating the location of research laboratories, of higher education facilities, or of appropriate services, e.g. in the sphere of information and communication technologies.

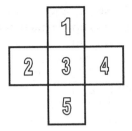

Figure 7.1   A Manhattan network with a radius of 1

2.4   General spatial economic equilibrium: introducing coordinates

Multiregional input-output applications implicitly consider locations of sectoral activities, as is clear in the Leontief-Strout model. The purpose of the present section, on the one hand, is to enable me to introduce another important spatial element explicitly: specific coordinates for production units. On the other hand, as will be said later, the method revealed here has definite links to the rationale for which Leontief introduced his analysis. Moreover, I would like to show that technological links are a critical element for determining the mutual interdependence of the locations of production units.

General spatial economic equilibrium is examined here from the perspective of an approach developed in the 1960s by Tinbergen (1961) and Bos (1964). Such an equilibrium was designed to operationalize Lösch's general spatial economic equilibrium model, in particular to derive propositions on economic "landscapes" in terms of clusters of activities ("centers"), a specific combination of clusters being called a "system."

Indeed, if in theory the system of equations characterizing a Löschian equilibrium allows for the estimation of establishment locations, quantities produced and their unit f.o.b. prices, market areas and boundaries, no specific "landscapes" can *theoretically* be derived. Moreover, the problem itself is – in principle – of a non-linear, mixed continuous-discrete nature and, thus, rather difficult to solve. The initial idea of Tinbergen-Bos systems was to simplify Lösch's model to a linear one without prices, locations and market areas, paralleling the manner in which Leontief operationalized Walras's aspatial equilibrium.

The original model was implicitly based on a discrete (0-1) metric. Kuiper et al. (1990) introduced a "Manhattan" metric defined by a network of orthogonal arcs of radius R^* (see figure 7.1 for an example with $R^* = 1$). Paelinck and Kulkarni (1999) discovered that, through such an exercise, Tinbergen-Bos systems became a special case of a location-allocation problem.

The equilibrium is computed by minimizing, for given unit prices, an objective function derived from consumption and production coefficients. The composition and location of centers – the "economic landscape" or "system" – are indeed determined by the minimization of global transport costs (though this may correspond to profit-maximization behavior by individual firms: see Paelinck, 2000), i.e. of a function

$$\phi = \mathbf{w}'\mathbf{x} \tag{9}$$

where $\mathbf{x}$ is a vector of the exports of goods and services, and $\mathbf{w}$ a vector that depends on the distances d_{ij} between all the possible locations i and j (whatever the metric used; in figure 7.1, $i, j = 1, \ldots, 5$; the locations are situated at the center of each "elementary square," and linked together by a Manhattan network), on unit transportation costs, and on relative quantities shipped – the latter depending on consumption propensities and technology coefficients as follows.

Define a_k as the propensity to consume product k; y^* as the total value of production (or value added in the absence of interindustry relations) of the system (exogenous); $a_k y^*$ as production of sector k. So, in the absence of interindustry relations, the value transported between sectors k and l equals $a_k a_l y^*$. If there are n_l^* plants of type l, each firm of sector l demands $a_k a_l y^* / n_l^*$ from sector k. The total weight for deliveries between k and l thus becomes $(t_k + t_l) a_k a_l y^*$, so that the *relative* weights (excluding distances) relating to the above-mentioned flows become

$$w_{kl} = (t_k + t_l) a_k a_l / n_l \tag{10}$$

where t_k and t_l are the unit transportation costs.

In the same vein, equation (10) can be generalized using input-output relations – Bos's approach systematized by Kuiper and Paelinck (1984). If a_{kl} is the input coefficient of k in sector l, and m_k the value added versus production multiplier of sector k, then for deliveries between sectors k and l total transportation costs become

$$t_{kl} = [t_k(a_k + a_{kl}m_l)a_l + t_l(a_l + a_{lk}m_k)a_k]y^* \tag{11}$$

How complex such interactions can be is shown by figure 7.2 (drawn by J. H. Kuiper), which pictures the potential flows between agriculture (sector 0) and two industrial sectors (sectors 1 and 2). The indices of the flows are based on the indices inside the squares, which refer to their spatial characteristics. These indices are as follows: agricultural activities 0, centers producing goods 1 or 2, and center 3 including both types of production.

Figure 7.3 (computed by J. H. Kuiper) shows how varying elements of function (9) can affect the economic landscape; the relative weights

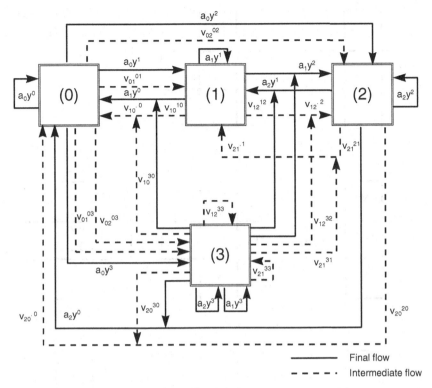

Figure 7.2   Spatial allocation relations

w_3/w_1 refer to deliveries between industries 1 and 2, on the one hand, and activities 1 and 0 (agriculture) on the other. As equation (11) shows, the causes of these changes may be multiple: changes in transportation costs, in consumption propensities, or in technological data. The "crosses" X refer to activity 1, "circlets" O to activity 2.

3.   Extensions of input-output analysis

In what follows, some isomorphic extensions to input-output analysis are treated; they center on the concept of location elasticity. At first sight it may look strange that a construct such as this should be given attention here; but there are several reasons to do so. In the first place it is shown that the fundamental treatment derives directly from input-output. But, apart from that formal aspect, dynamic spatial links are present; links that are based on technologies and their spatial (interregional) relations. Though representing a very specialized field of investigation, location

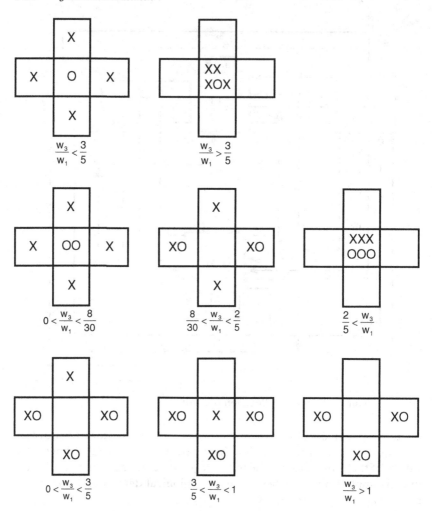

Figure 7.3   Different economic landscapes on a Manhattan network of radius 1

elasticities, for these reasons, deserve to be treated here in conjunction with more traditional input-output approaches.

3.1   *Location elasticities*

Location elasticities were first presented by Kuiper and Paelinck (1981). This subsequently led to a number of analyses, some of which will be revealed hereafter. The central notion of a location elasticity is that of a relative reaction of a spatialized (regionalized) variable to the rate of growth of that same variable measured over a reference area (e.g. a country). Formally

$$E_{ir} = \partial \ln x_{ir} / \partial \ln x_{i\cdot}.$$

where i denotes an activity, say; r a spatial unit (e.g. a region); and x a given variable (production, or value added, for instance). The "dot" notation in $x_{i\cdot}$ denotes the aggregation of the corresponding variable over all the values of the replaced index.

Generalizing, one can define a spatialized transverse or cross-location elasticity as

$$E_{ijrr} = \partial \ln x_{ir} / \partial \ln x_{jr}$$

and a matrix $\mathbf{E}_{rr}$ of those elasticities for region r. A generalized model can now be set up as

$$\boldsymbol{\rho}_r = \mathbf{E}_{rr} \boldsymbol{\rho}_r + \boldsymbol{\rho}_r^* \qquad (12)$$

where $\boldsymbol{\rho}_r$ is the column vector of the ρ_{ir}'s (the regional growth rates of activity i) and $\boldsymbol{\rho}_r^*$ a column vector of the locally autonomous ρ_{ir}^*'s, expanded upon below. Expression (12) leads to $\boldsymbol{\rho}_r = \mathbf{M}_{rr} \boldsymbol{\rho}_r^*$, where $\mathbf{M}_{rr}$ is now an elasticity matrix multiplier applicable to the elements of $\boldsymbol{\rho}_r^*$. The latter can be linked to national activity growth rates by

$$\boldsymbol{\rho}_r^* = \hat{\mathbf{e}}_r \boldsymbol{\rho}_i \qquad (13)$$

Further

$$\rho_{ir} = E_{ir} E_{i\cdot} \rho_{\cdot\cdot} \qquad (14)$$

So, in a sense, diagonal matrix $\hat{\mathbf{e}}_r$ is composed of "residual" elements E_{ir}. In its turn, $\boldsymbol{\rho}_i$ can be expressed as $\boldsymbol{\rho}_i = \mathbf{E}_i \boldsymbol{\rho}_i + \boldsymbol{\rho}_i^*$. Hence $\boldsymbol{\rho}_i = \mathbf{M}_i \boldsymbol{\rho}_i^*$ and, proceeding as in (13), one obtains

$$\boldsymbol{\rho}_r = \mathbf{M}_{rr} \hat{\mathbf{e}}_r \mathbf{M}_i \hat{\mathbf{e}}_i \rho_{\cdot\cdot} \qquad (15)$$

and from (15)

$$\boldsymbol{\rho}_{ir} = (\mathbf{m}_{ir}' \hat{\mathbf{e}}_r)(\mathbf{M}_i \hat{\mathbf{e}}_i) \rho_{\cdot\cdot} \qquad (16)$$

which should be compared with (14). In fact, the latter expression is a simplification of the multiplier-weighted expressions in the parentheses of (16), and E_{ir} and $E_{i\cdot}$ incorporate multiplier operations. This also suggests an immediate generalization of (14) to $\rho_{ir} = \Sigma_j E_{jr} E_{j\cdot} \rho_{\cdot\cdot}$.

A multiregional extension of (15) can be envisaged, leading to

$$\boldsymbol{\rho} = \mathbf{M}_{rs} \hat{\mathbf{e}}_s \widetilde{\mathbf{M}}_i \widetilde{\mathbf{e}}_i \rho_{\cdot\cdot} \qquad (17)$$

Table 7.2 *Optimal solutions*

Variables	Values
p	1.25
s	1.00 or 0
m	4.1875 or 4.6875
ψ	0.0685705

where $\widetilde{\mathbf{M}}_i\widetilde{\mathbf{e}}_i$ is a repetitive vector of $\mathbf{M}_i\mathbf{e}_i$ from (15) or (16). The vector of total regional growth rates, ρ^T, is finally given by

$$\rho^T = \Lambda\mathbf{M}_{rs}\hat{\mathbf{e}}_s\hat{\tilde{\mathbf{w}}}_i\widetilde{\mathbf{M}}_i\widetilde{\mathbf{e}}_i \tag{18}$$

where Λ is a matrix displaying the regional location quotients as row vectors in suitable positions, and $\hat{\tilde{\mathbf{w}}}_i$ a (repetitive) diagonal matrix of national activity shares.

The formal, isomorphic, relatedness of the analysis just presented can easily be seen from the equations. As a first example take (18), which obviously represents an open system. The set of equations (17), on the other hand, can be transformed into a closed system by expressing $\rho_{..}$ as $\rho_{..} = \mathbf{w}'\rho$, where $\mathbf{w}$ is a suitable weighting vector. Rewriting (17) as $\rho = \mathbf{m}\rho_{..}$ one obtains the closed system $(\mathbf{I} - \mathbf{mw}')\rho = 0$. Despite this quite formal presentation, one should not forget that the whole analysis is based on technology links between spatially differentiated activities.

The preceding analysis can, again, be used as a basis for setting up a mathematical program like that in section 2.2. Paelinck (1999) did so, where the objective function was the national rate of growth of employment, ψ, and the instruments were regional policy, p, sectoral policy, s, and macroeconomic policy, m. Table 7.2 reports the results of this exercise.

Notice the equivalence of two substitutable solutions in s and m. Clearly, this finding should get more attention in applied spatial policy design. The overall result is an increase by nearly seven percentage points in the growth rate of employment.

Location elasticities could be readily generalized introducing a price system, as the following developments show. Let x_r be a regional quantity variable, p_r its unit price, and the same for the referential totals x and p. The *nominal location elasticity* could then be expressed as

$$E_r^* = \mathrm{d}\ln p_r x_r/\mathrm{d}\ln px = (\mathrm{d}\ln p_r + \mathrm{d}\ln x_r)/(\mathrm{d}\ln p + \mathrm{d}\ln x)$$

whence $d \ln x_r = E_r^*(d \ln p + d \ln x) - d \ln p_r$. Since $d \ln x_r = E_r d \ln x$ it follows that $E_r d \ln x = E_r^*(d \ln p + d \ln x) - d \ln p_r$, or $E_r(1 + d \ln p_r / d \ln x_r) = E_r^*(1 + d \ln p / d \ln x)$. So, finally,

$$E_r^* = E_r[1 + (1/\varepsilon_r)]/[1 + (1/\varepsilon)]$$

where ε_r and ε are, respectively, the local and referential price elasticities, to be analyzed by an appropriate model.

3.2   Multiregional dynamics and growth

A number of models that use the notion of location elasticity have been developed (Girardi and Paelinck, 1994; Paelinck, 1986, and 1987). From the FLEUR model, presented in section 2.3, a remarkable expression can be derived for the equilibrium (shown by a circlet) share location elasticity for a sector and a region. (The sector index i will be omitted here for reasons of simplicity; only the regional index r will be used.)

$$E_{ar}^0 = 1 - (a_r^0 / b) \tag{19}$$

where a_r^0 is the regional equilibrium share of region r (for activity i, say), and where b is defined as

$$b = \sum_{s=1}^{R} (a_s^0)^2 \tag{20}$$

From (19) and (20), with – for the observed a_r – an error correction specification, one can set up the following dynamic model, ρ being equivalent to $\rho_{..}$ of equations (15) to (17), and η the error correction parameter, $0 < \eta < 1$

$$\dot{a}_r^0 = \rho a_r^0[1 - (a_r^0 / b)] \tag{21}$$

$$\dot{a}_r = \eta(a_r^0 - a_r) \tag{22}$$

$$\dot{b} = 2\rho \left[b^2 - \sum_s (a_s^0)^3 \right] \bigg/ b \tag{23}$$

The model has a singular point $a_r^0 = b$, $a_r = a_r^0$, $b = [\Sigma_s (a_s^0)^3]^{1/2}$. It converges to that point when $\rho > 0$; for $\rho = 0$ the shares converge to their initial equilibrium values, and when $\rho < 0$ the region (or regions) with the highest initial equilibrium share(s) has/have (a) share(s) that converge(s) to 1 (or $1/n$, n being that number of regions).

All this is true for constant location factors; adding a second-order differential correction factor to (22) would also not impair the conclusions. Reflecting anew on equations (21) through (23) leads to the following development. To the right-hand side of (22) add a term such as $-\theta[1 - (a_r^0/b)]$, which for small a_r^0 would be negative and for relatively large θ (i.e. when compared to η) would dominate the first term. For $\rho > 0$ the region concerned would decline initially, only to grow again in the long term; hence only short-term concerns obtain for that type of region. The new term represents preference for spatial externalities present in larger and/or denser areas that are (locationally) better endowed. Thus, complex but realistic multiregional dynamics can be encompassed in a simple model based on location elasticities; extensions to a multisectoral situation follow immediately.

4.   Conclusion

In the course of this overview of spatial input-output and related applications, the following important concepts emerged, quoted here in alphabetical order: asymmetry; economies of scale and scope; externalities; non-convexity; non-linearity; prices (f.o.b. versus delivered); spatial interdependence and allotopy; and topology (especially metrics). Each plays an important role in spatial economic modeling, where, as I said in the introduction, input-output analysis is an all-pervasive feature of it. In conclusion I would like to dwell on some important effects of all these factors on future input-output research work, whether input-output tables are used directly or integrated into more general models, such as the one commented on in section 2.3.

A first remark is that input-output tables inherently incorporate spatial elements; it would take a whole study to show how all the elements quoted above make their mark on specific – regional or national – versions of these tables. I will pick out a particular example to illustrate the assertion made.

The location of productive entities influences practically all the entries of a typical input-output table. Indeed, goods are not only produced, they are shipped from their production site to their places of intermediate or final consumption. Suppose now that the table values entered into each cell are valued at f.o.b. prices; this implies that each sector pays its transport costs in a separate entry from the transportation sector or sectors, and, as remarked above, these costs will be a function of the relative locations of suppliers and demanders.

One sees immediately the necessity to introduce explicitly both shipping patterns and intermodal competitive features into multiregional applications. The main idea goes back, in fact, to Lefeber (1958), but it should be taken up again in applied multiregional work; maybe this can help postpone the requiem for interregional input-output suggested by McGregor et al. (1999). Once more, and apart from the arguments advanced by the authors just quoted, spatial elements should be explicitly introduced. Paelinck (2001, section 5) has insisted on precisely defining the price system used (f.o.b. or c.i.f.) to convert quantities into values, especially given recent interest in input-output price formation (Schumann, 1990; Aroche-Reyes, 1993; Folloni and Miglierina, 1994; Tokutsu, 1994; and Cabrer et al., 1998), although we should remember that Sir Richard Stone (1961) had already devoted a chapter to prices in input-output models.

The end point would be a computable general multiregional equilibrium (or disequilibrium) model with endogenously located multimodal transportation systems, in which locations would in turn depend – partly, at least – on the different shipping facilities available, the latter defining the relative accessibility of each region studied. The mobility of production factors – an important spatial element referred to in section 2.1 – would complete the picture. A simple summary of this chapter is its underlying motto: *space matters*.

ACKNOWLEDGEMENTS

The author thanks Erik Dietzenbacher and Michael Lahr for valuable editing and editorial comments; all remaining imperfections are the author's sole responsibility.

REFERENCES

Ancot, J.-P., and J. H. P. Paelinck (1983) The spatial econometrics of the European FLEUR model, in D. A. Griffith and A. C. Lea (eds.) *Evolving Geographical Structures* (The Hague, Martinus Nijhoff Publishers), 229–246.

Anselin, L. (1988) *Spatial Econometrics: Methods and Models* (Dordrecht, Kluwer Academic Publishers).

Anselin, L., and R. J. G. M. Florax (eds.) (1995) *New Directions in Spatial Econometrics* (Berlin, Springer-Verlag).

Aroche-Reyes, F. (1993) Endogenous prices for input-output models: a note, *Economic Systems Research*, 5, 365–376.

Auctores, Varii (1966) *Etude Comparée des Tableaux d'Entrées et de Sorties des Communautés Européennes*, Collection "Econométrie Européenne", n° 1 (Namur, Faculté des Sciences Economiques et Sociales).

Aujac, H. (2004) Leontief's input-output table and the French Development Plan, chapter 5 in this volume.

Bennett, R. J. (1979) *Spatial Time Series* (London, Pion).

Bos, H. C. (1964) *The Spatial Dispersion of Economic Activity* (Rotterdam, Rotterdam University Press).

Cabrer, B., D. Contreras and A. Sanchez (1998) Prices revisited: their effects on industrial structure, *Economic Systems Research*, 10, 31–43.

Davin, L., L. Degeer and J. H. P. Paelinck (1959) *Dynamique Economique de la Région Liégeoise* (Paris, Presses Universitaires de France).

Folloni, G., and C. Miglierina (1994) Hypothesis of price formation in input-output tables, *Economic Systems Research*, 6, 249–264.

Girardi, R., and J. H. P. Paelinck (1994) A regional equilibrium growth model and its disequilibrium dynamics: a one-sector approach, *Regional Studies*, 28, 305–317.

Isard, W. E., E. W. Schooler and T. Vietorisz (1959) *Industrial Complex Analysis and Regional Development: A Case Study of Refinery-Petrochemical Synthetic Fiber Complexes and Puerto Rico* (Cambridge, MA, MIT Press).

Kuiper, J. H., and J. H. P. Paelinck (1981) Macro, sectoral, regional policies and regional growth, *Revue d'Economie Régionale et Urbaine*, 4, 517–534.

(1984) Tinbergen-Bos systems revisited, in J. M. Pillu and R. Guesnerie (eds.) *Modèles Economiques de la Localisation et des Transports* (Paris, Ecole Nationale des Ponts et Chaussées), 117–140.

Kuiper, J. H., J. H. P. Paelinck and K. E. Rosing (1990) Transport flows in Tinbergen-Bos systems, in K. Peschel (ed.) *Infrastructure and the Space-Economy* (Berlin, Springer-Verlag), 29–52.

Lefeber, L. (1958) *Allocation in Space* (Amsterdam, North-Holland).

Leontief, W. W., and A. Strout (1963) Multiregional input-output analysis, in T. Barna (ed.) *Structural Interdependence and Economic Development* (London, Macmillan), 119–150.

McGregor, P., K. J. Swales and Y. P. Yin (1999) Spillover and feedback effects in general equilibrium interregional models of the national economy: a requiem for interregional input-output, in G. J. D. Hewings, M. Sonis, M. Madden and Y. Kimura (eds.) *Understanding and Interpreting Economic Structure* (Berlin, Springer-Verlag), 167–190.

Miller, R. E., and M. L. Lahr (2001) A taxonomy of extractions, in M. L. Lahr and R. E. Miller (eds.) *Regional Science Perspectives in Economic Analysis* (Amsterdam, North-Holland), 407–441.

Oerlemans, L. A. G., M. H. T. Meeus and F. W. M. Boekema (2001) Firm clustering and innovation: determinants and effects, *Papers in Regional Science*, 80, 337–356.

Paelinck, J. H. P. (1963) La teoría del desarrollo regional polarizado, *Revista Latino-americana de Economía*, 9, 175–229.

(1970) De quelques aspects opératoires dans l'usage de techniques d'entrée et de sortie au niveau régional et interrégional, *Revue Juridique et Economique du Sud-Ouest*, Série Economique, 1, 1–11.

(1971) Techniques of regional plan formulation: problems of interregional consistency, in D. M. Dunham and J. G. M. Hilhorst (eds.) *Issues in Regional Planning* (Paris, Mouton), 184–194.

(1972) Selecting a minimum investment viable industrial complex, in N. Hansen (ed.) *Growth Centers in Regional Policy* (London, Macmillan), 139–159.

(1983a) (with the assistance of J.-P. Ancot and J. H. Kuiper) *Formal Spatial Economic Analysis* (Aldershot, Gower Press).

(1983b) Investment and the development of backward regions, in A. Heertje (ed.) *Investing in Europe's Future* (London, Basil Blackwell), 152–187.

(1986) A consistent model for sectoral regional dynamics, in J. H. P. Paelinck (ed.) *Human Behaviour in Geographical Space* (Aldershot, Gower Press), 91–110.

(1987) Some multisectoral multiregional dynamics, in B. Guesnier and J. H. P. Paelinck (eds.) *Modélisation Spatiale: Théorie et Applications* (Dijon, Collection de l'Institut de Mathématiques Economiques, Série d'Econométrie Appliquée), 87–94.

(1999) Location elasticities revisited, or employment and competition in regional growth, *Emprego e Desenvolvimento Regional*, 1, 15–26.

(2000) Quasi-dynamics of Tinbergen-Bos systems, *Region and Development*, 11, 119–132.

(2001) *Tinbergen-Bos Systems: A Compendium of Recent Results*, working paper.

(2003) Network analysis through linear assignment, *Journal of Geographical Systems*, 5, 1–13.

Paelinck, J. H. P, J. de Caevel and J. Degueldre (1965) Analyse quantitative de certains phénomènes du développement régional polarisé: essai de simulation statique d'itinéraires de propagation, *Problèmes de Conversion Economique: Analyses Théoriques et Etudes Appliquées,* Bibliothèque de l'Institut de Science Economique de l'Université de Liège, n° 7 (Paris, Génin), 341–387. [Reprinted in J. Boudeville (ed.) *L'Univers Rural et la Planification* (Paris, Presses Universitaires de France, 1968), 123–169.]

Paelinck, J. H. P., and L. H. Klaassen (1979) *Spatial Econometrics* (Farnborough, Saxon House).

Paelinck, J. H. P., and R. Kulkarni (1999) Location-allocation aspects of Tinbergen-Bos systems, *Annals of Regional Science*, 33, 573–580.

Paelinck, J. H. P., and P. Nijkamp (1975) *Operational Theory and Method in Regional Economics* (Farnborough, Saxon House).

Paelinck, J. H. P., and R. R. Stough (2000) *CRATON: Transportation Impact Analysis, a first theoretical exploration,* paper presented at the North American meetings of the Regional Science Association International, Chicago.

Paelinck, J. H. P., and S. Wagenaar (1981) Supply effects in regional modelling, *Canadian Journal of Regional Science*, 4, 145–168.

Sandee, J. (1960) *A Demonstration Planning Model for India*, Indian Statistical Series, No. 7 (London, Asia Publishing House).

Schumann, J. (1990) On some basic issues of input-output economics: technical structure, prices, imputations, structural decomposition, applied general equilibrium, *Economic Systems Research*, 2, 224–239.

Sonis, M., and G. J. D. Hewings (1999) Miyazawa's contributions to understanding economic structure: interpretation, evaluation and extension, in G. J. D. Hewings, M. Sonis, M. Madden and Y. Kimura (eds.) *Understanding and Interpreting Economic Structure* (Berlin, Springer-Verlag), 13–51.

Sonis, M., G. J. D. Hewings and J. Guo (2000) New image of classical key sector analysis: minimum information description of the Leontief inverse, *Economic Systems Research*, 12, 401–423.

Stone, R. (1961) *Input-Output and National Accounts* (Paris, Organisation for Economic Co-operation and Development).

Stone, R., and G. Croft-Murray (1959) *Social Accounting and Economic Models* (London, Bowes and Bowes).

Szyrmer, J. M. (1986) Measurement of connectedness of input-output models: 2. Total flow concept, *Environment and Planning A*, 18, 107–121.

(1992) Input-output coefficients and multipliers from a total flow perspective, *Environment and Planning A*, 24, 921–937.

Tinbergen, J. (1961) The spatial dispersion of production: a hypothesis, *Schweizerische Zeitschrift für Volkswirtschaft und Statistik*, 97, 412–419.

Tokutsu, I. (1994) Price-endogenized input-output model: a general equilibrium analysis of the production sector of the Japanese economy, *Economic Systems Research*, 6, 323–345.

West, G. R. (1995) Comparison of input-output, input-output + econometrics and computable general equilibrium impact models at the regional level, *Economic Systems Research*, 7, 209–227.

Wilson, A. G. (1974) *Urban and Regional Models in Geography and Planning* (London, John Wiley).

8   Leontief and Schumpeter: a joint heritage with surprises

Andrew Brody and Anne P. Carter

1.   Close but distant neighbors

Except for the dwindling band of us old-timers, there are few who associate Leontief with Schumpeter. Yet, in many ways, they were a pair. Schumpeter welcomed Leontief to the Harvard faculty in the mid-1930s and continued to respect and even envy Leontief's talents and accomplishments until his death in 1950. Their lives had a lot in common. Both were cultivated European intellectuals, wiry and compact in physical stature, who appreciated Russian caviar, French champagne, ballet, opera and well-informed cultural discussions on topics beyond the range of interest of the average American economist then, or now. Leontief taught the first-year graduate theory course; Schumpeter taught the second. Each had an office of modest size in Littauer Center, headquarters of the Harvard Department of Economics. They walked home across the Cambridge Common to their spacious clapboard houses in Cambridge, less than a block apart. Some twenty years after Schumpeter died Leontief settled into a summer residence in Lakeville, Connecticut, the next town to Taconic, where the Schumpeters had had their country retreat. When the Leontiefs decided to be buried in Connecticut, they approached the caretaker of the local cemetery. He steered them, unwittingly, to the area where "another economist" (guess who?) was buried. Thus Leontief and Schumpeter remain neighbors to this day.

Leontief focused on the interdependencies of the real growth process, though these were often obscured by the jagged contours of observed economic time series. Schumpeter focused on the fluctuations themselves. And, like other economists, they saw economic expansion as an exponential process where growth depends on the actual position of the economy. Such an exponential process may have a complex exponent: a real α, representing the rate of long-run growth; and an imaginary ω responsible for the frequency of returning cycles, with the wavelength of $2\pi/\omega$. Leontief sought the real and tangible α, while Schumpeter centered on the imaginary and ever-confusing ω.

While their works have deep common roots, they maintained a polite distance. Schumpeter praised Leontief's pioneering mathematical models but he himself relied entirely on words – lots of them – to express his own unique vision of the economic system. Schumpeter was a political conservative, a strong believer in capitalism, even while predicting its final demise. After the McCarthy period Leontief openly criticized the laissez-faire market system and actively advocated planning on a nationwide, even worldwide, scale.

Both departed radically from the dominant values of the profession. At a time when theoretical speculation was the hallmark of a successful economist, both stressed and engaged in painstaking and detailed empirical work. Both broke with the prevailing (and ever-growing) reliance on optimization as a crucial feature of economic analysis. Leontief did this by building a model that did not specify technological choice. Schumpeter singled out innovation, rather than optimal choice among given alternatives, as the prime focus of capitalism.

Finally, both recognized the central importance of technology, albeit with very different emphasis. For Leontief, technology dictated the fine-grained structure of the economy. Schumpeter stressed the dynamic functions of change. For him, technology was the engine driving economic activity and development. Both saw invention, the precursor of innovation, as exogenous to the economic system.

Despite these deep commonalities, they never collaborated during their lifetime. Schumpeter's and Leontief's separate unfinished – or, rather, open-ended – agendas became the respective foci of the International J. A. Schumpeter Society and the International Input-Output Association, which continue to encourage work in their respective traditions.[1] The evolution of computer technology, general knowledge and improved data have made it possible to extend and elaborate their original ideas in far greater detail and depth than either thought possible.

To appreciate fully the intellectual heritage of Schumpeter and Leontief, however, we must look beyond the literal testing and elaboration of their models. Great men cannot avoid collaboration, if not directly in their own time, then indirectly through the combinations and linkages of their concepts made by later generations. Some of these linkages continue to surface in the work of their direct intellectual heirs.

---

[1] There is already some overlap in their foci. This is demonstrated, for example, by the fact that issues 15(1) and 15(2) of *Economic Systems Research* (see ESR, 1997a, and 1997b) were devoted to invention and innovation in input-output analysis, and by two publications (Goodwin, 1990; Carter, 1992) in conference volumes of the Schumpeter Society. Also, the first Leontief Memorial Prize was awarded at the international conference (in Macerata) of the International Input-Output Association to Bart Los for a paper combining the ideas of the New Growth Theory with input-output (see Los, 2001).

Beyond the persistence of intellectual tradition intact, creative scholars have a way of selecting, modifying and rearranging elements of existing theories and combining them with others to advance in surprising new directions. Thus the ideas of Leontief and Schumpeter, reinterpreted and reshuffled, reawaken among strange bedfellows, some of whom would be agreeable, some unfamiliar, or even objectionable, to the originators.

This paper cites two such surprising combinations: the work of scholars at opposite ends of the spectra of professional background, work styles, and personal association with Leontief and Schumpeter. Richard Goodwin, a student and protégé of both, eschewed empirical work altogether and proved theoretically that a multisectoral system can, under plausible circumstances, generate cycles even in the absence of innovation. Eric Von Hippel, on the other hand, became acquainted with Leontief's and Schumpeter's work only after he had espoused their ideas "out of the air." His research has uncovered networks of competition and collaboration that are obscured by Leontief's reliance on published data and by Schumpeter's armchair impressions of technological diffusion.

2.   Richard Goodwin: cycles without innovation

By the early 1950s, inspired by Leontief's new work, statistical offices around the world had begun to compile input-output tables. At the same time, empirical research on innovation and the cyclic components in economic time series permitted economists to test and elaborate the promise of Schumpeter's metaphors. Instead of following either path, Goodwin went his own way. While Schumpeter saw innovation as the essential driving force of cycles, Goodwin's cycle model has fixed technology. According to Goodwin, cycles result from the market's attempts to reach equilibrium. They are generated by the very "invisible hand" of the market that both his mentors de-emphasized.

At the Second International Conference on Input-Output Techniques (held at Driebergen, the Netherlands), Goodwin (1953) posed an interesting question. What will happen to such a system if it becomes unbalanced, i.e. "out of equilibrium"? He referred to Adam Smith's description of the market, the cross-regulation of prices and quantities that became the central theme of economics in Ricardo, Walras and Marshall and into the present day. Differences between production and consumption act on prices, and differences between costs and prices act on quantities to "reconstitute equilibrium soon."

According to Goodwin, the process they described does not balance the system but produces self-repeating cycles. By connecting the closed static Leontief model for quantities with its dual, the closed static model of prices, Goodwin showed that the governing hypermatrix of the double and simultaneously ongoing process is strictly skew-symmetric. The excess demand is $\mathbf{Ax} - \mathbf{x}$. This difference is zero if – and only if – the system is in equilibrium. Similarly, prices will cover costs if – and only if – they are proportional to the equilibrium price system. Under real world conditions the prices (given by row vector $\mathbf{p}'$) will deviate from costs, computable as $\mathbf{p}'\mathbf{A}$. Thus some sectors will register monetary gains while others show losses. Every positive element of the vector $\mathbf{Ax} - \mathbf{x}$ represents some excess demand that, in turn, will augment the sectoral price. Similarly, a negative element – excess supply – will decrease it. Increases in price will motivate increases of production while decreases will motivate output reduction.

The adaptive process of each branch is governed by the discipline of financial constraints and inventories. Every positive element of the vector $\mathbf{p}' - \mathbf{p}'\mathbf{A}$ represents gain. This signals increases in production. The negative elements are losses, prompting decreases in production.

In sum, the differential equation governing this market process allows one equilibrium solution and various cyclic swings around this equilibrium path. Goodwin presents a strictly qualitative and formal proof. Cross-regulation leads to a skew-symmetric matrix, and such a structure must create cycles. No data are needed, no facts; just straight theoretical reasoning. Of course, continuous swings in prices and production can be observed in the market, but that fact doesn't enter his argument. Furthermore, Goodwin's system rests on static technology. It is not innovations and their bunching that drives these cycles; nor does the birth of cycles require any innovation at all. Innovation is neither a necessary nor a sufficient condition for Goodwin's cycles. While innovation could presumably be taken into account in some extension of his model, he made it clear that simple linear interdependence can yield cyclic fluctuations with theoretically computable frequencies.

Goodwin's linear system has other interesting properties. Since all the trajectories of such systems are always perpendicular to the equilibrium vector, there is no automatic convergence to equilibrium. This is true for the trajectories of both the price and the quantity vectors separately, in that they are orthogonal to their respective equilibrium vectors. Furthermore, because the system matrix is skew-symmetric, motion is also orthogonal to the vector of the system's momentary position.

Further research later demonstrated that this "closed static" Leontief system, investigated by Goodwin, is far from being simple and trivial. Piero Sraffa's neo-Ricardian restatement of a self-replacing system turned out to be strictly equivalent, in a mathematical sense, to this model. Later, Sir Richard Stone devised appropriate links to his system of Social Accounts and used the same form of model for his so-called "Demographic Accounting"; see e.g. Stone (1970). Clopper Almon's Inforum (Interindustry Forecasting at the University of Maryland) models may be brought to the same forms.[2] Maria Augusztinovics (1965) pointed out the parallel with her money flow (banking) accounts. She extended the model to depict transactions among co-existing generations, providing a rational foundation for addressing various pension fund questions.

In essence a very broad range of linear systems, whether closed or open, static or dynamic, may be mathematically reduced to the same neat and transparent form. If final demand (linked to its support) and expansion of capacities (linked to the production of investment goods) are properly specified in the system matrix, then – basically – all linear systems may be expressed in the form of this "simple" model.

Leontief himself pioneered many new applications for his system. His studies of military expenditures, pollution questions, and the United Nations world model may be considered as more or less elaborate extensions. In his last years he applied the same structure to describe knowledge flows among the sciences. It appears that the same simple form can be adapted to many aspects of human cooperation and interaction. It may be exploited to describe their interdependence, to compute their required or "equilibrium" proportions, and also to explore their cyclical properties.

Goodwin's surprising and consequential finding united two nonmainstream theories that challenge the optimistic core of classical and neoclassical beliefs. The mechanism of the market, believed to be automatic and self-correcting, does not converge toward an efficient equilibrium.

3.   Eric Von Hippel: the sectoral locus of innovation

In contrast to Goodwin, Von Hippel, an engineer by training, had no direct personal or professional association with Leontief or Schumpeter. His undergraduate education at Harvard included no formal economics training. Thus, he did not know about their work when he began his innovation studies in the 1970s. Nevertheless, his research embraced and integrated major concepts of both. Later, when looking for economic precursors, he did find and study them in some depth.

---

[2] Almon (1966) is the first of a long series of write-ups documenting his model. It was dubbed "Inforum" when Almon moved from Harvard to the University of Maryland. It remains a working model, having been elaborated, augmented and improved continually over the past thirty-five years.

Despite his relatively recent entrance into this intellectual territory, Von Hippel's work serves to illustrate the power of combining ideas from different scholars in novel ways. Economists familiar with the ideas of Leontief and Schumpeter will readily recognize their themes in Von Hippel's work. Von Hippel (1987) classified each invention in terms of its locus of origin in a vertical chain of "supplier," "manufacturer" and "user" – a categorization that fits closely into an input-output framework. He speculated that innovations would be sited so as to maximize entrepreneurial profits. Schumpeter would say that these loci afforded innovators the best chances to capture (temporary) rents of innovation.

Searching trade and technical journals and canvassing engineering personnel, Von Hippel traced the origins of more than a hundred inventions across the spectrum of manufacturing. (Von Hippel uses the term "innovation" to cover the whole sequence of invention and innovation in the Schumpeterian sense. Inventions that aren't adopted are not studied in his work.) He classifies each innovation according to where in the vertical structure of production the design originates. Thus each innovation is characterized by whether it was proposed by the "supplier," the "manufacturer" or the "user" of a particular good or service. If a physician suggests a design improvement in imaging equipment and his suggestion is implemented by an equipment manufacturer, the change is called "user innovation," since the physician, a user of the equipment, proposed it. Von Hippel hypothesized that suppliers, manufacturers and users specialize in designing different types of technological changes because of their loci in the productive chain. For the most part, users would know best what changes in the product would most benefit them. Hence they (the users) are most likely to make fruitful suggestions for product improvement. Manufacturers have the greatest expertise about process inventions (i.e. changes that will increase the efficiency of producing a given product rather than its utility to users). Suppliers are motivated to invent changes that increase the use of the input they produce. Studies of the origins of actual innovations in a range of manufacturing sectors gave strong confirmation to the thesis. Harhoff (1991) later transferred Von Hippel's ideas explicitly to the traditional input-output framework.

Von Hippel's team went on to examine the strategies that entrepreneurs employ to hide their new technologies from their competitors in order to protect their rents. To their surprise, they found that secrecy was far from ubiquitous. A study of steel mini-mills (relatively small enterprises for producing and delivering specialized steel products) showed that technical personnel cooperated regularly with their counterparts in other firms, trading technical information and/or exchanging solutions to problems they had already solved for other kinds of expertise that they needed. This practice of bartering technical knowledge is known as "knowhow trading."

Their analysis of information-sharing behavior calls into question the economist's implicit assumptions about homogeneity within sectors and the nature of competition. Even in an industry with a relatively homogeneous product such as steel, firms differ markedly in their specialization (the form of steel produced, their locations, and the location and specialization of their customers). The degree to which any given pair of firms see themselves as competitors depends on how similar they are with respect to market niche. Some are too close to permit cooperation; as competitive distance grows, the advantages of knowhow trading outweigh the dangers. Furthermore, groups of similar firms may cooperate against other groups to boost the reputation of a product against close substitutes or of domestic versus foreign suppliers.

Von Hippel's original study was extended to other manufacturing industries, where, again, a surprising amount of technical information is voluntarily pooled. His team now focuses on high-tech sectors. Currently they are studying the motivation behind open source software and the competitive circumstances (types of users; complexity of programs) under which this type of collaboration is particularly advantageous. Von Hippel's findings on competition and cooperation remain consistent with Schumpeter's thesis on the maximization of temporary rents, but they extend the concept of diffusion into the complex framework of information sharing. Innovation may create Schumpeter's temporary monopoly, but Von Hippel reveals a web of competitive and cooperative relationships that govern the cumulative process of technological transformation.

The challenge of this work to Leontief's fixed sectoral grid is more serious, although not entirely new. Innovations rarely have uniform effects across plants in a sector. The miniaturization of semiconductors, for example, will confer the greatest benefits in uses where size is crucial. Thus, a classification suited to a given set of input structures may cease to fit in the face of change. Early studies of the input structures of individual plants in two presumably homogeneous four-digit industries (tin cans and ball- and roller bearings) revealed enormous variance (Carter, 1957). Cans vary in size, shape and function, as do bearings. Their input structures – requirements for materials, labor, energy and equipment – can be significantly different.

Similarly, studies of capacity expansion at individual plants in most manufacturing sectors showed that, contrary to the first models, most expansions are "unbalanced"; they provide excess capacity in some respects, and take advantage of initial slack in others (Carter, 1960). The persistence of heterogeneity even at the most detailed sectoral level suggests a problem in fractal geometry. Leontief was of two minds on this problem. On the one hand, he saw the solution to this problem in simple disaggregation. On the other hand, he recognized that qualitative change compromised any attempt to make long-range comparisons over time. What constitutes a "long-range comparison" in the current environment?

4.   Intellectual specialization and loci of insight

Von Hippel's approach combines the theoretical concepts of Schumpeter and Leontief with methods of data gathering – primarily interviews and direct observation – that they did not use. These approaches to empirical research are much less common in economics than in other social sciences. Normally, economists test their models by implementing them with administrative or other published data. Economists' practice seems to be more efficient because it takes advantage of the enormous informational resources already in place and allows economists themselves to concentrate on modeling and econometric methodology. However, using published information has a significant disadvantage: it eliminates a range of potential surprises and learning that might have taken place at the information-gathering stage. Von Hippel's most important discoveries arose in the process of the data gathering, rather than in the model-testing stages of his research.

In some important respects, Von Hippel's work parallels that of those respected economists who followed Leontief's and Schumpeter's traditions more directly. Schmookler (1966, chapter 8) recommended the input-output framework for tracing the flow of new technology from industries engaged in R&D to sectoral adopters. He did not solve the empirical question of how to implement such a system before his untimely death. More recently, Scherer (1982), DeBresson (1996) and Evenson,[3] to name a few, have modeled invention and/or innovation by sector of origin and use. Scherer and Evenson rely on administrative data on R&D expenditures and patents as proxies for invention and innovation. DeBresson relies heavily on questionnaires – on primary rather than published data – to measure sectoral innovation.

Economists caution, quite rightly, that responses to questionnaires may not correspond to actual behavior. On the other hand, questionnaires can be targeted more directly than administrative data to the problem being

---

[3] See, for example, Evenson and Johnson (1997) with an introduction to ESR (1997b), which is devoted to invention input-output analysis. See also DeBresson (1997).

investigated. For example, patent records contain a vast store of technical and historical information covering every invention for which a patent has been granted. The Yale patent concordance makes it possible to associate inventions with their industries of origin. On the other hand, only a modest fraction of inventions is implemented – i.e. leads to innovations – and some innovations do not involve patented, or patentable, inventions at all. Questionnaires can cover innovations regardless of whether they're based on patented inventions. Of course, most government information systems do not even cover innovations. Direct questionnaires are labor-intensive and it is hard to guarantee that respondents share a uniform standard for judging what is or is not an innovation; patent data cover a very large universe of observations and the criteria for issuing a patent are explicit. Both have their place.

More to the point, gathering primary data for the problem at hand opens the door to "surprises" to be found along the way. Sometimes significant fresh insights emerge at the data-gathering stage. For most economists, empirical work consists primarily of testing the overall validity of a fully specified model or proposition, using published information. Such testing is, like motherhood, important and necessary. But "outsourcing" the collection of data limits the opportunity, considered essential by experimentalists, to examine the basic variables at very close range. Asking questions about the firms' actual behavior in sharing or hiding their special knowledge, Von Hippel's teams learned important lessons about how industry assigns values to information and also gained insights into the subtle structure of competition. Talking to decision-makers raises questions about Leontief's and Schumpeter's older perspectives on technological change. Von Hippel's observations reveal a world of shifting sectoral boundaries where the traditional "industry" concept, based on many firms producing the same outputs with similar input structures, is obsolete. Today's products come from firms with very different product mixes, different degrees of vertical integration, and different degrees of participation in shorter-term alliances.

Surprises, of course, can surface at many different stages in an investigation. No one knows for sure what Leontief expected to find in his first foreign trade computation. The study would have been worthwhile even if it had only confirmed empirically the generally accepted theoretical conclusions about the factor content of US trade. It turned out that the United States exports its labor-intensive rather than its capital-intensive products. This was a "counter-intuitive" result that triggered some very fruitful further research. It focused attention on the quality of labor, on the significance of human and intellectual capital, on natural resource endowments, and – of course – on the intricacies of foreign trade statistics.

An empirical finding that confirms an accepted theory may, of course, be useful. But it does not expand the scope of our knowledge; it only confirms what we already believe. An unexpected finding gives directions for further research, or suggestions for rethinking and extending existing ideas. Whatever his expectations, Leontief was willing – in fact, eager – to accept and build on an unorthodox finding.

There is no accepted algorithm for finding the unexpected, and nor can we presume to derive one from this brief study of Schumpeter and Leontief and their followers. Schumpeter's recognition of innovation as the driving force of capitalism and its cyclical properties was revolutionary and profound. Like his classical predecessors, he rooted his insights in broad general observation, not on the implementation and testing of formally stated hypotheses. One can guess that his ideas stem from his experiences as Austrian Finance Minister, but he does not cite the observations that inspired him. Goodwin's radically new perspective seems even further removed from observation of the economy. His connections to it are essentially second-hand, through the eyes of his mentors.

Leontief reframed the whole discipline of economics, extending its purview to quantitative empirical implementation. His focus on sectoral interdependence had deep intellectual roots in the perspectives of Quesnay, Marx and Walras. His synthesis of formal modeling and implementation with quantitative data was a radical departure. It challenged the prevailing methodological paradigm. The simultaneous evolution of the econometric movement suggests that pressures for a more rigorous scientific approach were "in the air."

In the early days Leontief looked to data collection as a fertile source of insights. Brainstorming sessions on secondary products, transportation and trade margins, and research and development activities engaged economists in designing their accounts and models to reflect stubborn features of the real economy. Structural change was more daunting. "Pilot studies" of technological layering, engineering production functions and the composition of real investment were promising, but, unfortunately, practical constraints on funding and on human energy prevailed. As in the rest of the profession, input-output data collection became "efficient," a specialized function, generally separate from applications and analysis. Some vital arteries connecting observation to modeling were blocked.

Von Hippel's work, as well as the recent input-output-based innovation surveys, remind us that gathering primary data can be a major source of insight. Economists' division of labor between brilliant theorists (who think) and data gatherers (who serve them) may well be dysfunctional. But, happily, human creativity thrives in a wide range of environments.

Fifty years ago Leontief and Schumpeter sat back to back, like Tweedle-dum and Tweedledee, peering stubbornly at different horizons. Never-theless, over time, their ideas have joined forces and marched off in new directions.

How would they have reacted to the two renegades who combined their basic concepts to produce radically different conclusions? Neither Schumpeter nor Leontief knew Von Hippel's work and Schumpeter died before Goodwin's was published. Leontief rarely referred to Goodwin's work, in spite of the fact that – or, perhaps, because – the Goodwins and Leontiefs were close friends. For Leontief, theoretical work with no refer-ence to data was suspect. But is it really worthless? Heisenberg's anecdote about his first meeting with Einstein captures the spirit of this ques-tion. In discussing Heisenberg's novel approach (which Einstein never entirely endorsed) Einstein suddenly asks: "But why are you writing that theories should be founded only on observable and measurable facts?" Heisenberg, red in the face, stutters that this was a guideline set down by the master, Einstein himself. To which Einstein responds: "Maybe when I was still very young I did voice such stupidities. But, pray tell me, if we base our theories only on known facts, how will we know what new facts to look for, and how will we be able to interpret them, once found?"

REFERENCES

Almon, C. (1966) *The American Economy to 1975* (New York, Harper & Row).
Augusztinovics, M. (1965) A model of money circulation, *Economics of Planning*, 5, 44–57.
Carter, A. P. (1957) Capital coefficients as economic parameters: the problem of instability, in *Problems of Capital Formation: Concepts, Measurement, and Controlling*, NBER Studies in Income and Wealth, no. 19 (Princeton, NJ, Princeton University Press).
    (1960) Investment, capacity utilization, and changes in input structure in the tin can industry, *Review of Economics and Statistics*, 42, 283–291.
    (1992) Appropriation and profits in a leaky system, in F. M. Scherer and M. Perlman (eds.) *Entrepreneurship, Technological Innovation, and Economic Growth: Studies in the Schumpeter Tradition* (Ann Arbor, MI, University of Michigan Press), 217–235.
DeBresson, C. (1996) *Economic Interdependence and Innovative Activity* (Chel-tenham, Edward Elgar Publishing).
    (1997) Foreword, *Economic Systems Research*, 9, 147.
Economic Systems Research (1997a) Special issue: intersectoral R&D spillovers, *Economic Systems Research*, 9, 3–142.
    (1997b) Special issue: invention input-output analysis, *Economic Systems Research*, 9, 147–230.
Evenson, R. E., and D. Johnson (1997) Introduction: invention input-output analysis, *Economic Systems Research*, 9, 149–160.

Goodwin, R. M. (1953) Static and dynamic linear equilibrium models, in Netherlands Economic Institute (ed.) *Input-Output Relations* (Leiden, Stenfert Kroese), 54–87.

—— (1990) Walras and Schumpeter: the vision reaffirmed, in A. Heertje and M. Perlman (eds.) *Evolving Technology and Market Structure: Studies in Schumpeterian Economics* (Ann Arbor, MI, University of Michigan Press), 39–49.

Harhoff, D. (1991) *Strategic Spillover Production, Vertical Organization, and Incentives for Research and Development*, Ph.D. thesis (Cambridge, MA, Massachusetts Institute of Technology, Sloan School of Management).

Los, B. (2001) Endogenous growth and structural change in a dynamic input-output model, *Economic Systems Research*, 13, 3–34.

Scherer, F. M. (1982) Industrial technology flows in the United States, *Research Policy*, 11, 227–245.

Schmookler, J. (1966) *Invention and Economic Growth* (Cambridge, MA, Harvard University Press).

Stone, R. (1970) Demographic input-output: an extension of social accounting, in A. P. Carter and A. Brody (eds.) *Contributions to Input-Output Analysis* (Amsterdam, North-Holland), 293–319.

Von Hippel, E. (1987) *The Sources of Innovation* (New York, Oxford University Press).

9　Some highlights in the life of Wassily Leontief – an interview with Estelle and Wassily Leontief

Christian DeBresson

1.　The context

There is as yet no biography of Wassily Leontief. Insights into his early childhood in St Petersburg, his Russian family, his relationship to his mother, and his own family in the United States can best be gleaned by reading a short book written by Estelle Leontief.[1] But the biography of this remarkable man and scientist – the only true genius I have had the privilege to meet in my life – remains to be written. Needless to say, this short piece has no such ambition.

I had been collecting and reading Leontief's writings in historical sequence, trying to make better sense of the work of the man who had served as my role model and motivated me to become a researcher. His meanings seemed always to remain opaque (you will probably find some of his statements below to be elliptical and abridged, if not cryptic). I knew the historical contexts and the economists before him and his contemporaries. Yet something was missing. Most interviews with him dealt with intellectual history and tried to locate his work in relation to other economists, but often in these interviews, made at different times, Leontief's comments would lead to different interpretations regarding his relationship with other economists. I felt something was eluding me in my attempt to understand the man: something about the link between his times, his own life and his attitudes.

As I was going away to China for a sabbatical year, I decided to ask the Leontiefs for an interview where we could discuss his personal life in retrospect. I had had the privilege of talking with him half a dozen times

---

[1] Estelle Leontief (1987) *Genia & Wassily – A Russian-American Memoir* (Somerville, MA, Zephyr Press). This memoir is a timeless account and reflection on the ambivalent relations between a spouse and in-laws. It reveals a compelling attraction to them but a simultaneous insistent need to keep those loving, invading in-laws at bay. This short book has a literary appeal far beyond the Leontiefs themselves. Even those who know nothing about or have no interest in the economist will glean precious insights by reading it. And, because it unveils the complexity of these human relationships, it brings the reader right into the Leontiefs' family living room as a trusted friend.

before, but then he was always asking me questions about *my* work. This time, I would ask him questions about himself. They accepted, and they chose the place and time: the Knickerbocker Bar & Grill, on University Place in their home town of New York City, on Saturday, April 5, 1997. Two days before he had slipped in his apartment and broken a rib, and he came, assisted by Estelle, walking into the Knickerbocker Bar & Grill – one of their favorite places – while leaning on a walking frame. I introduced them to Ina Drejer, who assisted me by taking notes, and we settled down at their favorite table in the far right corner. And a casual conversation started.

2.   The interview

Chris DeBresson (*CDB*): What do you remember of your student life in St Petersburg during the Russian Revolution?

Wassily Leontief (*WL*): As a very young student in university, I read systematically. I read practically all the economists from the beginning of the seventh century. I just read one after the other.

CDB: Were you not at the time also studying philosophy?

WL: Only for a short time.

CDB: Did you ever think of going into another field, of doing something else?

WL: No. I never had a problem in doing what I wanted. In that sense I was lucky.

CDB: Which of the authors do you remember best from that intense reading period?

WL: I could not say. My memory is very bad. But, of course, Karl Marx. I think he is possibly the greatest classical economist. He really understood how the capitalistic system works. He was no mathematician. His theory was a kind of labor theory. I think that somebody who comes entirely from outside would learn something about the present market capitalist economy from Marx because he is so very broad. *Das Kapital* is much better than typical textbooks. It is really rich.

CDB: In relationship to the events of the Russian Revolution were there some that positioned you emotionally?

WL: My family was a typical intellectual family. Part of it was in the textiles industry. My father was a professor in economics; not theoretical economics but labor economics and its social aspect. I was opposed to the Communists, and I was arrested for it when I was fifteen years old. I just expressed my opinion openly.

CDB: Do you remember what the opinion was?

WL: Probably my objection to the dictatorship. However, I must say I still had many friends who were Communist students and we discussed a lot.

Estelle Leontief (EL): The story you tell is a little different each time. I find there is a new twist in it each time you tell it.

WL: Possibly socialism was my idea at the time, but I must confess that my ideas about economic and social systems have changed somewhat. But I think the present capitalist system will definitely have to change; it will change. It is impossible that a system [does] not change.

CDB: When did you decide to leave Russia?

WL: I left in 1925.

EL: He had a good pretext. He'd had jaw surgery in the USSR – a replacement of the jaw. Tests were made of the jaw in Berlin.

WL: This made it easier for me to exit because they thought I would die anyway; but I didn't. At the time, under the Communists, it was not easy to get permission to leave. I went to Berlin. My father was educated in German. I knew German and French. I had read most prominent economists in German and French. This was very good preparation for me to speak in Germany. It was under the Weimar Republic. Very interesting times. I got my Ph.D. in Berlin.

CDB: Who was your adviser, Bortkiewicz or Sombart?

WL: Both. I had two advisers. Professor Sombart was very interesting. He was a real social scientist. I ran his seminars. His seminars were full of ideas.

CDB: Who did you learn most from, Bortkiewicz or Sombart?

WL: Bortkiewicz – there was an intelligent mathematician! He was complementary with Sombart, who was a real social scientist but did not know mathematics. I had made up my mind from the beginning that economic theory requires mathematics; mathematics is indispensable. This is why I worked simultaneously with Bortkiewicz and Sombart. I chose that right from the beginning.

CDB: Were you fascinated by the intellectual life in Berlin at the time?

WL: It was a beautiful time. The Weimar Republic and German society were terribly interesting to me. I took part as much as I could.

EL: You did not give me the impression that you sat in cafés and talked about intellectual things with other students; that you had a café life at all. He was very poor; very, very poor. And you did not have much money to spend in cafés. My impression of what he told me was that he led a very single, isolated life except for working with professors.

WL: I still had long discussions with students. We would chat. Then, of course, I began to work on my dissertation: the national economy as a circular process. I would say that this idea is neoclassical. But the vision of the economy as a whole system made me very unsatisfied with supply and demand equilibrium. So I attempted to provide an empirical framework for the study of interdependence of individual cells in the economy.

CDB: Many – for instance Joan Robinson – like to debate (which I find boring and irrelevant) whether you are Walrasian or classical.

WL: Not interesting. I have my own system.

CDB: So, the idea of input-output was already there at the time of your thesis?

WL: Yes. Then, of course, I had a very strong theoretical emphasis. But, on the other hand, although I considered with much interest different theoretical approaches, I always have felt that economists did not pay enough attention to empirical facts. I would say to myself, "I want to develop a theoretical framework that would enable detailed analysis of the operations of a national economy." This was most important to me.

CDB: Your focus at the time was the national economy, more than the international one?

WL: Oh yes, definitely. But it is hard to say exactly . . . My interests then were not so much in improving the operations of the economy; I was then just interested in understanding how it works. I had seen too many economists trying to improve it without trying to understand how it works. Only after 1936 did I focus on trying to improve the economic process.

CDB: Your first input-output tables gave you the tools?

WL: Right. We need cooperation between theoretical formulation and empirical analysis. Theory is the basis on which empirical analysis can be made. For instance, I never became a Keynesian. I criticized Keynes very early, because he was too pragmatic. Let me say it differently: he developed his theory for his political program. I myself, as a matter of fact, do not remember ever having pushed any particular economic policy.

CDB: But Keynes had extraordinary intuitions about theory, what to do, and how to get rich himself.

EL: And making King's College at Cambridge rich.

WL: No doubt: he was an extremely intelligent man . . . Theory is a question of attitude. I definitely feel that theory is terribly important. Empirical analysis is useless without theoretical analysis. As time went on, I became more and more cognizant of evolution, change, development, experiments . . . You can hardly understand the operations of an economy without knowing how it developed.

CDB: How does this fit with your ideas about equilibrium?

WL: Equilibrium is essentially a mathematical expression of interdependence. I prefer to use the term "interdependence." The economy cannot live in equilibrium. It is always getting out of equilibrium. This has been the main cause for economic development. And, here, of course, technology is crucial. I think Marx understood the role of technology. I think developments in technology always, but particularly now, are a driving force for economic change. And economic change is a driving force for social change.

CDB: For you, technological change is, then, largely exogenous to the economic system?

WL: It is closely related to scientific change.

CDB: Aside from Marx, were there any other encounters that convinced you of the importance of technology? Plant visits? Contacts with engineers?

WL: No. It is not easy for an economist to develop good contacts with engineers. My youth was really absorbed in a social scientist's research program. The importance of technology slowly became more essential.

CDB: But your production function, like Ragnar Frisch's, is very close to the engineer's production world.

WL: I met Ragnar Frisch only a few times. We were both early users of mathematics. We had our disagreements, but in retrospect our views are quite close; our production functions are quite close and complementary to each other.

CDB: Coming back to the sequence of your life: if you had wanted it, you could easily have obtained a position in Germany. What made you decide to leave?

WL: The success of National Socialism was quite clear at the time. In 1929 I went to spend a year in China, traveling extensively, helping to plan their railways. It was very interesting. I took the slowest way from Europe to China – the slow boat; through Arabia and India. It gave me some knowledge of less developed countries. This was my first exposure. Russia, when I left it, already had industry, essentially textiles. After, I went back to Kiel, as a staff member for the Institute of World Economics – the same job as before I left for China. Then I went to the United States.

CDB: Let me switch to a more personal question. Until then you were very much just a single man, a lone scholar.

WL: That is true. Very much so. I met Estelle soon after I came to the United States.

EL: Although he rode horseback, sailed, and thoroughly enjoyed himself in Kiel. And in New York, one of the first things we did together was to get dressed up – he in tails, I in evening dress – and go to Cab Calloway's Cotton Club. In New York, those days, I could safely walk up Seventh Avenue and not worry.

CDB: What made you decide all of a sudden to stop being a single man?

WL: Just talking to her. I met her at International House.

EL: Students from all over the world came to live at International House. They did not stay for long; just until they found more permanent places to stay. He did not stay long either. I had come to visit there with some friends. He just stared at me . . . until I invited him over to have some chocolate. Then he joined me, and we went all over the globe, and he showed me all the places he had been to in the world. He was working for the National Bureau of Economic Research [NBER] in New York.

WL: It was Simon Kuznets who came and got me off the boat, and we went directly to the National Bureau. At the time it was very empirically driven. Mitchell; Burns; Mills – those are the ones I remember. I, on the other hand, was then always interested in theory and I conducted a series of theoretical seminars.

CDB: Their attention to economic facts pleased you, though, did it not?

WL: Yes. But I did not like the lack of any theory.

CDB: In relation to the use of economic data, you do not seem to use probability theory. Yet, through your studies with Bortkiewicz, you know this field.

WL: No. It is not so easy to use probability theory. It is too general. It applies to everything. I do not know any economist who really bases himself on probability theory – because it is too general.

CDB: A lot of contemporary econometricians since the so-called "Haavelmo revolution" claim to. But this does not seem to have affected you.

WL: No. But, you know, I am not your typical econometrician. I understand mathematics and probability. I think I am, perhaps, one of the founding members of the Econometric Society, but I do not think that mathematics solves problems. It is very useful, but it does not solve a problem. I am now ninety-one years old, and the more I observe, in economics – like all social sciences – Darwin's ideas are the intellectual driving force. Darwin was one of the greatest scientists of the nineteenth century. He was full of ideas. Darwin's ideas are very important. And economics, as a theory of competition, is Darwinist.

After all, if I am not mistaken, Darwin took some of his ideas from classical economists.

CDB: Malthus; who got them from Smith. Darwin's is partly an economic argument. An economist at Aalborg, in Denmark, is trying to reconcile the analysis of the structure of an interdependent economic system with that of evolution.

WL: I am completely in agreement with such an objective. The structure of a system is terribly important. This is why I proposed input-output economics. It was a move to force economists to really study facts not in isolation, but in their economic interdependence. But not without theory. For input-output analysis I developed a mathematical theory, and I also pushed empirical analysis by constructing myself the first input-output tables based on observed facts.

CDB: Was there any time during the building of these first matrices when you considered giving up?

WL: No. I was very lucky. The first big input-output matrix for the United States was built by the US Air Force for war production planning. I also worked with the first computer. Bernard Cohen says I am the first social scientist to use computers. The first practical computer, the one at Harvard – there were two: one at Harvard, one at MIT – was built by a professor who was not a great mathematician but an engineer. At the time, electronics had not been invented. It was a big mechanical and electrical machinery and looked like a printing machine. And I am the first person, perhaps the only one, to use that computer.

CDB: You therefore must have been paying close attention to the most recent technological developments. One of the few other scientists then who also was paying attention to the emergence of computers was von Neumann. Did your paths cross at the time?

WL: Oh yes. I met him. I remember, I had an interesting experience with him. We had a controversy. He published an article in which he advanced a proposition to try to solve simultaneous equations with many different variables. It did not make any sense. It was really a big mess. I could not agree with it. As an economist, I had already worked at solving a system of many simultaneous equations. If you choose any set of constraints or constants, it is true that, as von Neumann said, a system of simultaneous equations can be very difficult to solve. An economic system is a particular type of system where a certain type of, not equilibrium, but temporary balance is necessary. At the American Philosophical Society meetings in the Academy of Sciences (we were both members), in Philadelphia or Boston, I challenged him. I said he was wrong. I could show it; I had an empirical example. He did not object, he did not contradict me. Not every such system can be solved, but my economic system could. He did not disagree.

CDB: Let us shift focus for a while. Estelle, how did family life interact with Wassily's far-fetched intellectual projects?

EL: It hardly touched our family life at all. We never had students come to the house, and we did not have colleagues who were close personal friends. There was very little interaction between the two. I think that is, for instance, one reason why our daughter never became interested in mathematics or economics. Wassily and his daughter had a very good relationship, but until she was twelve and learned mathematics they did not become interested together in the same things.

WL: She was an intellectual thinker. She became a very well-known art historian.

CDB: Were Wassily's projects constraining for the family?

EL: For about five years I worked very hard at learning something about economics, and I think I gained some understanding about what he does.

WL: Estelle is a writer.

CDB: You write novels?

EL: No; memoirs. One is about his family. Our main friends were not amongst Wassily's colleagues or students.

WL: I have few friends among colleagues. I think it is my character not to.

EL: By the way, do you know Frank Scott? They had a house in Massawapi, just north of the border. We had a house in northern Vermont (when we came to New York, we sold it). He was dean at a law school and member of the Socialist Party in Canada. His wife was a major painter. They were very good friends of ours.

WL: They were very great friends of ours.

EL: My daughter's godfather, Pitimin Sorokin, also had a place in Canada, just above the border, on Lake Memphremagog. There was also a French-Canadian poet. They were very hostile to the British. They did not want to sell their properties to them. And Marian had a studio nearby that she rented from a French-Canadian; only rented.

CDB: This region of Quebec – the Eastern Townships – is a British enclave populated by a lot of British Empire loyalists who left the United States after American independence, or even after the Civil War.

EL: Not only there, but Baltimore Bay was inhabited by Southerners who did not want to go to New England, so they went and established themselves in Canada. So there were a lot of Americans there, but they were a very British kind of group by their habits: drinking, dinner parties, shops . . . We, in northern Vermont, knew a lot of French people – for instance the Lapierres, who had a marvelous property on the other side of Brompton Lake.

CDB: Was getting a place in Vermont in the late 1930s an important part of your lives?

EL: Oh, very important. The first year we rented a place on the east side of Lake Willoughby up the hill. The property had a lovely view – spectacular. We had a babysitter that summer. While we were there Wassily – that was his plan – went to an auction in Barton and bought a place on the west side of the lake.

WL: One of my favorite sports is trout fishing. Fly-fishing. I learned it as a boy in Finland. My family had a place in Finland. I learned fly-fishing from my father at the beginning of the century.

EL: That was another high point for me. He used to go out at two in the afternoon and come home around nine. And I was left with whatever babysitter we had with us at the time and my daughter – and then just try to get some work done!

WL: But you did not mind it.

EL: I did not mind you going off three or four times a week for five or six hours. But you had me worried sometimes when you would come home so late. How would I have found you in the midst of northern Vermont? When his parents came over we set them up there in Vermont. We tried to get them over to the United States after what happened in Germany. They had followed Wassily to Berlin. His father worked in the Russian embassy. When he was asked to come back to Moscow to stand trial for something he never did, they stayed in Germany on their own. Wassily's mother was Jewish, both were non-communist, and there they were alone in Germany under Hitler. Finally they left. But, before leaving, they decided they had to walk miles in Yugoslavia and Italy. After that they came to Cambridge, and then went up to Vermont and stayed there to live in the country. Only Russians will do it. Only upper-class Russians are capable of this. No car. The nearest town, many miles away, is Brompton. The place had no running water. They would just go up about five hundred yards and carried their water in pails. They just stayed there. They made do. They had a wood furnace. The father chopped wood. They got friendly with a neighbor who had a car and helped them out. Finally we had to get them out, so we rented a cottage for them on Crystal Lake near Barton.

CDB: Do you see his parents coming to the United States as a turning point in both your lives? Did it mean you now had all the pieces of your respective lives in one place together?

EL: No. They were terrible. It is all in the memoir. She was a Freudian-type mother, totally possessive of her son. To give you just one example: papa, just when dinner was announced, would always think of something he had to do. He would go and do it and say, "I'll be right there." Wassily did this too. But, at the time, I did not know papa that well and had not noticed, so I say to my mother-in-law, "Does your Wassily do this sort of thing that my Wassily does?" "Your Wassily is my Wassily," she replied. That gives you some indication of what she was like. Their arrival started with a bang. They arrived on Thanksgiving Day 1939, the year Roosevelt made two Thanksgiving holidays. They went down to Washington to visit friends, and there they had another Thanksgiving. I remember mama said to me, "They are vegetarians, and we had a vegetarian turkey."

CDB: Were there any other big family events that changed your lives?

EL: I think Wassily's going to Washington during the war was difficult.

WL: We did not move. I never lived there. I always commuted; just stayed over nights.

CDB: Which bureau in Washington did you work for during the war?

WL: The OSS: the Office of Strategic Services. Intelligence.

CDB: Did you volunteer or did they ask you?

WL: They asked me.

EL: I think Wassily was surprised, later, when he was suddenly accused by the CIA and FBI. Wassily wanted to find out why. The CIA and FBI spent a large part of the next two years tracking down all our connections.

WL: I did not accept the charges. Other people accepted. I went to see the president of Harvard. He was helpful and recommended a lawyer.

EL: Proctor was his name. I remember him. It was very interesting. I had been a member of the League of Women Shoppers. I left it when I realized it was a communist lobby organization. We were both members of the Russia War Research. All Russians were. But after the Russians became enemies, that became a problem. We did a lot of research ourselves on why they accused us, and, partly because of that, they did not charge us.

WL: But we won.

EL: Yes: we won the day, didn't we? The day we came down to New York for the big trial in court, there were nine [judges]. We both

were placed in separate rooms. It was 1956, '57, or even later – '59.
I don't remember. But, anyway, they all had wonderful witnesses. It
was a terrible waste of time. Half of our witnesses could not come.
They questioned us separately. I will tell you an interesting story in
relationship to this questioning: Elizabeth Schumpeter was quoted
at the hearings. She was a bit of a fascist and pro-Japanese. And
her husband was pro-German. They were very close friends. The
FBI interrogated her about me. And she told them, "Estelle told
me that she would rather live under the Communists in Romania
than under the fascists. And she named her daughter after Stalin's
daughter." This is stupid. I just liked the name Svetlana, so I chose
that name. I had just realized I was pregnant when, on a bus out
to California (we had sold our car), I read an article about Stalin
having a daughter, and I told Wassily, "Oh, if we have a daughter, let
us name her Svetlana. That is a lovely name; not Nadia or Vera or
another common name." But she told them I named my daughter
after Stalin's. They questioned Wassily separately. Tell them what
happened.

WL: Secret services are very often extremely inefficient . . .

CDB: You must know something about that, having worked in one your-
self during the war.

WL: When they interrogated me, they finally asked, "How come you, an
American economist, a famous American economist, publish books
in Moscow under the name A. A. Leontief?" I, of course, am W.
They were just confused.

EL: And that was the whole story. They were absolutely mistaken. The
whole prosecution was ridiculous. Two years, a lot of money, and a
lot of agitation on our part. And it turned out to be nothing.

WL: Just a mix-up.

CDB: From what you mentioned, Joseph and Elizabeth Schumpeter were
difficult people.

EL: Oh, very.

WL: Very difficult, but very interesting.

EL: She said she had remained a socialist, but only the times had changed.
This is how she put it. He was outrageous. He always took the non-
conformist view. It did not matter on what topic. So he would say
something like "Roosevelt is black and Hitler white" just to exasper-
ate people.

WL: Just to annoy Estelle.

EL: Not just with Americans; with Europeans too. He particularly liked
to do that type of thing: *épater les bourgeois*. He called us "bourgeois."
I should have replied: "How nice!" Now I would; but then I did not.

He would have the Irish mayor of Boston over for dinner; and he had his problems, this mayor – because he was anti-British. And Joseph was actually pro-Nazi; Elizabeth, pro-Japanese. He admired Stalin. He admired power. Typically Austrian, to admire power.

CDB: I would not make such a blanket statement!

EL: I always do.

CDB: I gather you were no friends of Joseph Schumpeter, then; right?

EL: Oh, we were very good friends. We were very close.

WL: It was kind of paradoxical. Interesting.

EL: He was fascinating. He carried Homer, in Greek, in his coat pocket. He read Greek. He traveled all over, saw all the Romanesque cathedrals in France. Wassily is not a letter writer. He had friends in the faculty who wrote a lot of letters. I have a couple of Schumpeter's letters. Schumpeter had a very gentle side.

WL: Oh yes, definitely.

EL: Very good friends were, and still are, the Solows. They both were students of Wassily's. And they are very close. They are almost like nephew and niece; something like that. In 1948 we went to Salzburg together. We are very close, very good friends.

WL: But we are from different generations. Anne Carter, of course, is also a very good friend. I consider she understands my attitude and approach toward economics better than anybody else.

CDB: Of these colleagues and friends you interacted with, which of them did you find influenced you most?

WL: I think very separately from my friends and colleagues.

EL: When Wassily's mind is at work, he puts a wall around himself.

3.   Epilogue

The lunch was then over. Estelle invited me over to their apartment on the other side of Washington Square so that she could give me copy of her book, *Genia & Wassily – A Russian-American Memoir*. I got to see the rug that Joseph Schumpeter had given them for their wedding – on which Wassily had slipped two days beforehand. "It is going to have to go, Wassily," Estelle told him. "No! Please!" he responded, a bit like a child attached to a favorite plaything. "I hope, with time, she will change her mind," he said to me. On the coffee table were a few of the latest issues of *Nature*. In the living room was Estelle's beloved piano. It was a simple, comfortable room, no doubt full of memories.

The next time I went to New York was April 8, 1999, for a memorial gathering for Wassily Leontief at New York University. I had lost my second father.

ACKNOWLEDGEMENTS

This interview was transcribed by Ina Drejer, and edited by Ina Drejer and Chris DeBresson. It was checked in the fall of 1997 by Wassily and Estelle Leontief. We benefited from further suggestions from Michael Lahr and Erik Dietzenbacher, although they cannot be held responsible for the shortcomings of the above.

Part II

Perspectives of input-output economics

10   A neoclassical analysis of total factor productivity using input-output prices

Thijs ten Raa

1.   Introduction

During one of our very last discussions Wassily Leontief asked me: "What are you doing these days?" I replied that I reconcile input-output analysis and neoclassical economics. He leant back, thought, looked me straight in the eyes, and said: "Should be easy."

Yet input-output analysis and neoclassical economics seem hard to mix. The resentment between the two schools of economics is a two-way affair. Neoclassical economists consider input-output analysis a futile exercise in central planning. The relationship between the delivery of a bill of final goods and its requirements in terms of gross output and factor inputs is considered mechanical, with little or no attention paid to the role of the price mechanism in the choice of techniques (Leontief, 1941). True, input-output analysis is used to relate prices to factor costs, but here too the analysis is considered mechanical as input-output coefficients are presumed to be fixed. To make things worse, the quantity and value analyses are perceived to be disjunct, with no interaction between supply and demand.

Conversely, input-output economists consider neoclassical economics a futile exercise in marginal analysis that fails to grasp the underlying structure of the economy. Firms supply up to the point that marginal revenue equals marginal cost and set the price accordingly. But does not marginal cost depend on all prices in the system, including the one of the product under consideration? And if the answer is yes, should not we take into account the interindustry relations, i.e. apply input-output analysis?

Many, including me, have been held captive by these perceptions. Yet they are misleading. Instead of criticizing the critiques – a meta-analysis that is doomed to have little input – I provide some shock therapy that turns the perceptions upside down by analyzing a concrete issue, namely productivity measurement. Why productivity? Well, the standard, neo-classical measure of productivity growth, the so-called "Solow residual"

151

between output growth and input growth, employs market values of labor and capital to compute a weighted average of their input growth rates. Now, it can be shown that the Solow residual is equal to a weighted average of the growth rates of the real wage and the real rental rate of capital. (In other words, total factor productivity (TFP) growth is the sum of labor productivity growth and capital productivity growth.) By taking the wage rate and rental rate at market values in computing the Solow residual, neoclassical economists accept at face value what they are supposed to measure.

In this paper I adopt the methodological position of neoclassical economics, by which productivity is defined as the marginal contribution of factor inputs, but apply input-output analysis to determine its value. The analysis is framed in the orthodox general equilibrium model, which subsequently will be specified to accommodate growth accounting. I will recover the neoclassical formulas, such as the Solow residual, but the structure of the economy will be exploited to determine the values.

2.   Earlier work

My first attempt to reconcile input-output and neoclassical economics is in the sequel papers ten Raa (1994) and ten Raa and Mohnen (1994). We maximized the value of final demand at world prices. Final demand for non-tradable commodities was simply fixed at the observed level. In short, we expanded final demand for tradable commodities, but not for non-tradable commodities. The model lacks a utility foundation. We rectified this in ten Raa (1995) and Mohnen et al. (1997), where we maximized the level of the entire domestic final demand vector, given its proportions. In ten Raa and Mohnen (2002) we investigated not only the frontier of the economy, but also the fluctuations of the observed economy about its frontier. All the aforementioned papers are about small, open economies with exogenous prices for the tradable commodities. The main contribution of this paper is that it lays out the theory for a closed economy. In other words, we make the step from partial to general equilibrium analysis.

Subsidiarily, I now present the theory from an orthodox mathematical economic perspective, say Debreu (1959). First and foremost, the two "practical" approaches of input-output analysis and growth accounting are clearly embedded in a unifying framework. Second, the general equilibrium framework endogenizes the value shares used in growth accounting exercises (such as Jorgenson and Griliches, 1967). Third, the exposition makes Debreu's framework accessible to applied economists.

3.   Growth accounting

There are two sources of growth. The first is that economies produce more output simply because they use more input, such as labor. Of course, this is a mere size effect; there is no increase in the standard of living. The second source of growth is more interesting. Economies produce more output per unit of input because of technological progress. The classical exposition of these two sources of growth is Solow (1957). He demonstrates that the residual between output and input growth measures the second source of growth; that is, the shift of the production possibility frontier. In his analysis Solow makes two assumptions. First, the production function is macroeconomic, hence transforming labor and capital into a single output. Second, the economy must be perfectly competitive, so that factor inputs are priced according to their marginal productivities. By the first assumption, the output has a well-defined growth rate. The input growth rate, however, must be some weighted average of the labor growth and capital growth rates; the appropriate weights are shown to be the value shares of labor and capital in national income. The two assumptions are quite restrictive. The use of a single output requires aggregation of commodities and makes it difficult to compare sectors in terms of productivity performance. The notion of perfect competition is a far cry from most observed economies.

I will show how growth accounting can be freed from these assumptions. Basically, I will work in a multidimensional commodity model and calculate productivities without using observed value shares. The analysis is self-contained and serves as a nice refresher of mathematical economics. The main concepts of this branch of economics are equilibrium, efficiency, and the welfare theorems that interrelate equilibrium and efficiency. I will review all this in the next section. To make the theory operational I will then consider the linear case of the model, with constant returns to scale and non-substitutability in both production and household consumption. Efficiency is then the outcome of a linear program, and the Lagrange multipliers of the factor input constraints measure their productivities. Summing over endowments I obtain total factor productivities. The analysis is shown to be consistent with the aforementioned Solow residual. Moreover, input-output analysis will enable us to reduce TFP growth rates to sectoral productivity, and thus to pinpoint the strong and the weak sectors.

4.   Equilibrium and efficiency

Denote the number of commodities in an economy by integer n. The commodity space is the n-dimensional Euclidian space, $\mathbb{R}^n$. A commodity bundle is a point in this space, say $\mathbf{y} \in \mathbb{R}^n$. Negative components represent inputs and positive components outputs. For example, in a Robinson Crusoe economy, where (labor) time is transformed into food, $(-1, 1)'$ is the bundle representing one hour of work and an ounce of food. A prime is used to indicate transposition. Denote the collection of all technically feasible commodity bundles by Y. Y is a subset of $\mathbb{R}^n$. It represents the production possibilities of the economy. I make two assumptions on Y. First, Y is convex. This means that, if $\mathbf{y}$ and $\mathbf{z}$ belong to Y, then so does $\lambda\mathbf{y} + (1 - \lambda)\mathbf{z}$ for any λ between 0 and 1. Although the assumption is always made in general equilibrium analysis, it is not innocent; it rules out increasing returns to scale. Second, Y is compact. In the context of our Euclidian commodity space this means that Y is bounded and closed. In the literature this assumption – namely the boundedness – is relaxed, but at the expense of uninteresting complications.

In a perfectly competitive economy producers pick the production plan that maximizes profit given the prices. Denote the commodity prices by vector $\mathbf{p}$ and let a prime denote transposition. The profit of any production plan $\mathbf{y}$ is then given by $\mathbf{p}'\mathbf{y}$ since inputs have negative signs in $\mathbf{y}$. $\mathbf{p}'\mathbf{y}$ is the inner product of $\mathbf{p}$ and $\mathbf{y}$: $\Sigma_{i=1}^{n} p_i y_i$. Here the positive terms represent revenue and the negative terms cost. Now maximize $\mathbf{p}'\mathbf{y}$ by choosing $\mathbf{y}$. The solution will depend on $\mathbf{p}$ and, therefore, is denoted $\mathbf{y}(\mathbf{p})$. Formally,

$$\mathbf{y}(\mathbf{p}) = \operatorname*{argmax}_{\mathbf{y} \in Y} \mathbf{p}'\mathbf{y}$$

Given $\mathbf{p}$, producers "supply" $\mathbf{y}(\mathbf{p})$. Strictly speaking, only the positive components represent supply, while the negative components represent business demand, as for labor. I define "supply" as the mapping $\mathbf{y}(\bullet)$. This constitutes one side of equilibrium analysis.

Turn to consumers. For simplicity I assume there is only one utility function, u, so consumers have the same preferences. For a commodity bundle $\mathbf{y}$, the real number $u(\mathbf{y})$ represents the utility it yields to the consumers. Utility is essentially ordinal. Comparing commodity bundles $\mathbf{y}$ and $\mathbf{z}$, what matters is if $u(\mathbf{y}) > u(\mathbf{z})$, $u(\mathbf{y}) < u(\mathbf{z})$, or $u(\mathbf{y}) = u(\mathbf{z})$, but the absolute difference between the utility levels is immaterial. In fact, the entire analysis will be unaffected by a monotonic transformation of the utility function. I make three assumptions on u. First, u is continuous. This is an innocent, technical assumption, that can be shown to be implied by the other assumptions, using a monotonic transformation. The second assumption is that u is increasing. This means that more is preferred. Third, u is quasi-concave. This is defined by the condition that the preferred set, $\{\mathbf{y} \mid u(\mathbf{y}) \geq \text{constant}\}$, is convex. It means that consumers prefer convex combinations.

In a perfectly competitive economy consumers pick the commodity bundle that maximizes utility, subject to the budget constraint and given the prices. What is the budget constraint? For the moment ignore dividends, so that all income stems from labor. In the framework of Robinson Crusoe's economy, the question is when $\mathbf{y} = (-h, f)'$ is financially feasible. (Here h is hours worked and f is amount of food.) If p_2 is the price of the good and p_1 the price of labor time, then the answer is $p_2 f \leq p_1 h$, which can be written succinctly as $\mathbf{p}'\mathbf{y} \leq 0$. The budget constraint is basically zero, because the commodity bundle has a negative component that generates (labor) income. In a private enterprise economy, profit, $\mathbf{p}'\mathbf{y}(\mathbf{p})$, supplements the budget constraint and consumers solve the following optimization problem

$$\max_{\mathbf{y}} u(\mathbf{y}) \text{ subject to } \mathbf{p}'\mathbf{y} \leq \mathbf{p}'\mathbf{y}(\mathbf{p})$$

The commodity bundle that comes out of this is what consumers "demand." (The positive components represent demand, the negative components household supply, as of labor.) I define "demand" as the mapping from prices $\mathbf{p}$ to the commodity bundle that solves the consumers' problem.

Now we have all the building blocks and can proceed to define the main concepts of mathematical economics, namely equilibrium and efficiency. Conceptually, they are very different. Equilibrium requires a price system; it is defined by the equality between demand and supply. Since the latter are both mappings from prices to commodity bundles, "equilibrium" is defined formally as a price vector, $\mathbf{p}^*$, such that supply and demand assume a common value. Equilibrium is a positive concept, to describe what actually happens in market economies, without saying it is good or bad. Statements on the performance of an economy, however, are normative and require no price mechanism. Suppose we want to compare a centrally planned economy to a decentralized market economy. The centrally planned economy may have no price system at all. Still, we want to evaluate which one performs better. This is a matter of utility. We say one economy is better than another if it attains a higher utility level for the consumers. An economy is efficient if it obtains the maximum utility level that is technologically feasible. Since utility is defined on commodity bundles, "efficiency" is defined formally by a commodity bundle, $\mathbf{y}^*$, such that utility is maximized over Y

$$\mathbf{y}^* = \underset{\mathbf{y} \in Y}{\operatorname{argmax}} \, u(\mathbf{y})$$

Notice the conceptual difference between equilibrium and efficiency. The former is given by a price vector, the latter by a commodity bundle. An equilibrium equates supply and demand, but makes no statement on the level of utility. Efficiency promotes utility, but requires no price system.

Although the concepts are very different, there is a deep, close relationship for perfectly competitive economies. By definition, an economy is perfectly competitive if no producer or consumer can manipulate the prices, but considers them as given. It can be claimed that the commodity bundle generated by the equilibrium price vector is efficient. In short, an equilibrium is efficient. This statement is called the "first welfare theorem". I also claim that an efficient commodity bundle can be generated by an equilibrium price vector. In short, an efficient allocation is an equilibrium. This statement is called the "second welfare theorem". The two welfare theorems are deep and must be proved.

The proof of the first welfare theorem is relatively easy. We must show that an equilibrium, say $\mathbf{p}^*$, generates an efficient allocation, $\mathbf{y}(\mathbf{p}^*)$. The proof is by contradiction. Suppose $\mathbf{y}(\mathbf{p}^*)$ is not efficient. By definition of efficiency there exists $\mathbf{y} \in Y$ such that $u(\mathbf{y}) > u(\mathbf{y}(\mathbf{p}^*))$. By definition of demand it must be that $\mathbf{y}$ is too expensive: $\mathbf{p}^{*\prime}\mathbf{y} > \mathbf{p}^{*\prime}\mathbf{y}(\mathbf{p}^*)$. By definition of supply it must be that $\mathbf{y}$ is not feasible: $\mathbf{y} \notin Y$. This contradicts the definition of $\mathbf{y}$. The supposition that $\mathbf{y}(\mathbf{p}^*)$ is not efficient is therefore not tenable. This completes the proof that an equilibrium is efficient.

The proof of the second welfare theorem proceeds as follows. Let $\mathbf{y}^*$ be efficient, hence maximize $u(\mathbf{y})$ over Y. Then we must construct an equilibrium price system that generates it. Consider the feasible set, Y, and the preferred set, $\{\mathbf{y} \in \mathbb{R}^n \mid u(\mathbf{y}) > u(\mathbf{y}^*)\}$. By efficiency of $\mathbf{y}^*$, the sets do not intersect. By assumptions on production and utility, the two sets are convex. Now we invoke Minkowski's separating hyperplane theorem, by which two convex sets that do not intersect can be separated by a hyperplane. (See, for example, Rockafellar, 1970.) Hence there exists a row vector, say $\mathbf{p}^*$, such that

$$\mathbf{p}^{*\prime}\mathbf{y}_1 > \mathbf{p}^{*\prime}\mathbf{y}_2$$

holds for all $\mathbf{y}_1 \in \{\mathbf{y} \in \mathbb{R}^n \mid u(\mathbf{y}) > u(\mathbf{y}^*)\}$ and $\mathbf{y}_2 \in Y$. I claim $\mathbf{p}^*$ is an equilibrium. For this we must show that, given $\mathbf{p}^*$, $\mathbf{y}^*$ is supplied and demanded. First consider supply. Since utility is increasing, the above inequality yields for any $\varepsilon > 0$ (in $\mathbb{R}^n$)

$$\mathbf{p}^{*\prime}(\mathbf{y}^* + \varepsilon) > \mathbf{p}^{*\prime}\mathbf{y}, \mathbf{y} \in Y$$

Hence $\mathbf{p}^{*\prime}\mathbf{y}^* \geq \mathbf{p}^{*\prime}\mathbf{y}$, hence $\mathbf{y}^*$ maximizes profit and, therefore, is supplied: $\mathbf{y}^* = \mathbf{y}(\mathbf{p}^*)$. Next consider demand. If $\mathbf{y}$ is superior to $\mathbf{y}^*$, $u(\mathbf{y}) > u(\mathbf{y}^*)$, then it is out of the budget, $\mathbf{p}^{*\prime}\mathbf{y} > \mathbf{p}^{*\prime}\mathbf{y}^* = \mathbf{p}^{*\prime}\mathbf{y}(\mathbf{p}^*)$. Hence $\mathbf{y}^*$ maximizes utility subject to the budget constraint and, therefore, is demanded. This completes the proof that an efficient allocation is an equilibrium.

So far, I have remained silent about existence. Does an equilibrium exist? The usual analysis to find an intersection point of supply and demand is by means of a so-called "fixed point theorem". This is difficult. We take a short cut. It is easy to see that an efficient allocation exists. All we have to do is maximize utility, u, over the feasible set, Y. Since u is continuous and Y is compact, a maximum exists, say $\mathbf{y}^*$. By the second welfare theorem it is an equilibrium, say $\mathbf{p}^*$. Hence an equilibrium exists.

In the literature all sorts of variations on the above analysis are found. More commodities, more products, more consumers – you name it. The basic structure, however, remains the same. Equilibrium is defined by the equality of supply and demand, efficiency by the impossibility of raising the utility level further, and the two are related by the first and second welfare theorems, provided convexity assumptions hold and agents are price takers. Then competitive prices can be analyzed by studying the efficiency problem, where utility is maximized over the feasible set. For example, the well-known statement that competitive economies reward factor inputs according to their productivities can be demonstrated. This will be done in the next section for linear economies.

5.   Efficiency and productivity

The model of the last section is quite general, at least in terms of functional forms. I now add the flesh and blood of linear economics, including input-output analysis. Let there be m activities. Denote an $m \times n$-dimensional matrix of outputs by $\mathbf{V}$ and an $n \times m$-dimensional matrix of inputs by $\mathbf{U}$. Add an m-dimensional vector of capital inputs, $\mathbf{k} \geq 0$, and similarly for labor, $\mathbf{l} \geq 0$. Let the economy be endowed with a capital stock k and labor force l. Assume every activity i requires positive factor input (k_i and l_i not both zero). Let

$$Y = \{\mathbf{y} \in \mathbb{R}^n \mid \mathbf{y} \leq (\mathbf{V}' - \mathbf{U})\mathbf{s}, \mathbf{k}'\mathbf{s} \leq k, \mathbf{l}'\mathbf{s} \leq l, \mathbf{s} \geq 0\}$$

where $\mathbf{s} \in \mathbb{R}^m$ is the vector listing m activity levels. Then Y is an example of a production possibility set as we defined it in section 3. Y is the intersection of a number of half-spaces, which is obviously convex. The assumption that every activity requires factor input ensures that Y is compact.

The modeling of household consumption is similar. Denote an n-dimensional vector of consumption coefficients by $\mathbf{a} > 0$. Then, for $\mathbf{y} \geq 0$,

$$u(\mathbf{y}) = \min y_i / a_i$$

is the Leontief utility function. (I choose this utility function because it enables us to substitute observed consumption values in the TFP growth expression of the next section.) Basically, consumers want their bundle in the proportions of $\mathbf{a}$, say $c\mathbf{a}$, where c is a scalar. It is easy to see that

$$u(\mathbf{y}) = \max_{c\mathbf{a} \leq \mathbf{y}} c$$

Proof. First we prove $u(\mathbf{y}) \geq \max_{c\mathbf{a} \leq \mathbf{y}} c$. For all $\mathbf{y} \geq c\mathbf{a}$, $u(\mathbf{y}) \geq u(c\mathbf{a}) = c$. Hence also $u(\mathbf{y}) \geq \max_{c\mathbf{a} \leq \mathbf{y}} c$. Next we prove the converse. At least one constraint in $\max_{c\mathbf{a} \leq \mathbf{y}} c$ is binding: $a_j c^* = y_j$ for some j, where c^* is the constrained maximum. Now $u(\mathbf{y}) = \min y_i/a_i \leq y_j/a_j = c^* = \max_{c\mathbf{a} \leq \mathbf{y}} c$. This completes the proof.

We have production and utility, so we can set up the efficiency problem,

$$\max_{\mathbf{y} \in Y} u(\mathbf{y})$$

Using the alternative formulation of the utility function, we can rewrite the efficiency problem as

$$\max_{\mathbf{s},\mathbf{y},c} c \text{ subject to } c\mathbf{a} \leq \mathbf{y} \text{ and } \mathbf{y} \in Y.$$

Notice that both the objective and the constraints are linear in the variables. The efficiency problem of a linear economy is a linear program. The linear program can be simplified slightly by eliminating one of the variables, $\mathbf{y}$

$$\max_{\mathbf{s},c} c \text{ subject to } c\mathbf{a} \leq (\mathbf{V}' - \mathbf{U})\mathbf{s}, \mathbf{k}'\mathbf{s} \leq k, \mathbf{l}'\mathbf{s} \leq l, \mathbf{s} \geq 0$$

This linear program maximizes the level of final consumption subject to the material balance, the capital and labor constraints, and a nonnegativity constraint. Another, succinct formulation of the linear program is

$$\max(\mathbf{0}' \ 1) \begin{pmatrix} \mathbf{s} \\ c \end{pmatrix} \text{ subject to } \begin{bmatrix} \mathbf{U} - \mathbf{V}' & \mathbf{a} \\ \mathbf{k}' & 0 \\ \mathbf{l}' & 0 \\ -\mathbf{I} & 0 \end{bmatrix} \begin{bmatrix} \mathbf{s} \\ c \end{bmatrix} \leq \begin{bmatrix} \mathbf{0} \\ k \\ l \\ \mathbf{0} \end{bmatrix}$$

In general, when we $\max f(\mathbf{x})$ subject to $g(\mathbf{x}) \leq b$, the first-order conditions are $\mathbf{f}' = \lambda \mathbf{g}'$, $\lambda \geq 0$. Here $\mathbf{f}'$ is the (row) vector of partial derivatives $\partial f/\partial x_i$ of f. If g is scalar valued, $\mathbf{g}'$ is also the row vector of partial derivatives $\partial g/\partial x_i$. If the constraints are given by $G(\mathbf{x}) \leq \mathbf{b}$, with G vector valued,

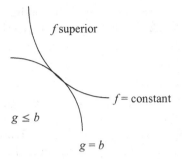

f superior

f = constant

$g \leq b$

$g = b$

Figure 10.1   Isoquants of the objective and constraint functions

the first-order conditions are $\mathbf{f}' = \boldsymbol{\lambda}'\mathbf{G}$, $\boldsymbol{\lambda} \geq \mathbf{0}$, where $\mathbf{G}$ is the Jacobian matrix of partial derivatives (i.e. element g_{ij} of matrix $\mathbf{G} = \partial g_i(\mathbf{x})/\partial x_j$).

The first-order conditions reflect the tangency of the isoquants to the objective and constraint functions. In figure 10.1 f and g grow in the same direction (the north-east), hence $\lambda \geq 0$. If λ were negative, then f and g would grow in opposite directions and one could simply increase f by wandering into the feasible region (g would be reduced). λ is called the Lagrange multiplier. Because $\mathbf{f}' = \lambda \mathbf{g}'$, and $g(\mathbf{x}) \leq b$, λ measures the rate of change of the objective function with respect to the constraint. If b is relaxed by one unit, then f goes up by λ units. If G is vector valued, then each constraint has a Lagrange multiplier and $\boldsymbol{\lambda}$ is a vector of Lagrange multipliers.

In our linear program, $f\binom{\mathbf{s}}{c} = (\mathbf{0}'\ 1)\binom{\mathbf{s}}{c}$ and $\mathbf{f}' = (\mathbf{0}'\ 1)$. Also,

$$G\binom{\mathbf{s}}{c} = \begin{bmatrix} \mathbf{U} - \mathbf{V}' & \mathbf{a} \\ \mathbf{k}' & 0 \\ \mathbf{l}' & 0 \\ -\mathbf{I} & \mathbf{0} \end{bmatrix}\binom{\mathbf{s}}{c} \quad \text{and} \quad \mathbf{G} = \begin{bmatrix} \mathbf{U} - \mathbf{V}' & \mathbf{a} \\ \mathbf{k}' & 0 \\ \mathbf{l}' & 0 \\ -\mathbf{I} & \mathbf{0} \end{bmatrix}$$

The constraints are the material balance, the capital constraint, the labor constraint, and the non-negativity constraint. It is customary to denote the Lagrange multipliers by $\mathbf{p}$, r, w and $\boldsymbol{\sigma}$ respectively. The first-order conditions, $\mathbf{f}' = \boldsymbol{\lambda}'\mathbf{G}$, $\boldsymbol{\lambda} \geq \mathbf{0}$, read

$$(\mathbf{0}'\ 1) = (\mathbf{p}', r, w, \boldsymbol{\sigma}') \begin{bmatrix} \mathbf{U} - \mathbf{V}' & \mathbf{a} \\ \mathbf{k}' & 0 \\ \mathbf{l}' & 0 \\ -\mathbf{I} & \mathbf{0} \end{bmatrix}, \quad (\mathbf{p}', r, w, \boldsymbol{\sigma}') \geq \mathbf{0}'$$

The second component, $\mathbf{p}'\mathbf{a} = 1$, is a price normalization condition. The first component, $\mathbf{0}' = \mathbf{p}'(\mathbf{U} - \mathbf{V}') + r\mathbf{k}' + w\mathbf{l}' - \boldsymbol{\sigma}'$, can be rewritten as $\mathbf{p}'(\mathbf{V}' - \mathbf{U}) = r\mathbf{k}' + w\mathbf{l}' - \boldsymbol{\sigma}', \boldsymbol{\sigma} \geq \mathbf{0}$, or

$$\mathbf{p}'(\mathbf{V}' - \mathbf{U}) \leq r\mathbf{k}' + w\mathbf{l}'$$

On the left-hand side we find value added and on the right-hand side factor costs for the respective activities.

$\mathbf{p}$, r and w are the perfectly competitive equilibrium prices. I am going to demonstrate this by means of the so-called "phenomenon of complementary slackness". Let me explain this phenomenon in terms of $\max f(\mathbf{x})$ subject to $G(\mathbf{x}) \leq \mathbf{b}$. The first-order conditions are $\mathbf{f}' = \boldsymbol{\lambda}'G, \boldsymbol{\lambda} \geq \mathbf{0}$. The phenomenon says that, if a constraint is non-binding, $g_i(\mathbf{x}) < b_i$, then the Lagrange multiplier is zero, $\lambda_i = 0$. Hence g_i plays no role in the first-order condition. The phenomenon also says that, if a Lagrange multiplier is strictly positive, $\lambda_i > 0$, then the constraint is binding, $g_i(\mathbf{x}) = b_i$. A nice way to write the phenomenon of complementary slackness is

$$\boldsymbol{\lambda}'[G(\mathbf{x}) - \mathbf{b}] = 0$$

The left-hand side is the inner product of two non-negative vectors. It is zero if – and only if – each term of the inner product is zero: $\lambda_i[g_i(\mathbf{x}) - b_i] = 0$. This, indeed, is a short way of writing $g_i(\mathbf{x}) < b_i \Rightarrow \lambda_i = 0$ and $\lambda_i > 0 \Rightarrow g_i(\mathbf{x}) = b_i$.

Now I explain why the Lagrange multipliers are competitive prices. Suppose that, for some activity, value added is strictly less than factor costs. Then $\sigma_i > 0$. By the phenomenon of complementary slackness, $s_i = 0$. Hence the price system is such that negative profits signal activities that are inactive in the coefficient allocation. If the economy had this price system and producers were profit maximizers, they would undertake precisely those activities that we want them to do. Notice that profits would be zero. The unprofitable activities are inactive, and value added is everywhere less than or equal to factor costs.

There is another interesting consequence of the phenomenon of complementary slackness, namely the identity between national product and national income. If G is linear, $G(\mathbf{x}) = \mathbf{Gx}$ and the last equation becomes

$$\boldsymbol{\lambda}'\mathbf{Gx} = \boldsymbol{\lambda}'\mathbf{b}$$

By the first-order condition $\mathbf{f}' = \boldsymbol{\lambda}'G$,

$$\mathbf{f}'\mathbf{x} = \boldsymbol{\lambda}'\mathbf{b}$$

If f is also linear, this reads

$$f(\mathbf{x}) = \boldsymbol{\lambda}'\mathbf{b}$$

In our linear program,

$$(\mathbf{0}' \ 1)\begin{pmatrix} \mathbf{s} \\ c \end{pmatrix} = (\mathbf{p}', r, w, \boldsymbol{\sigma}')\begin{bmatrix} \mathbf{0} \\ k \\ l \\ \mathbf{0} \end{bmatrix}$$

or

$$c = rk + wl$$

This is the famous macroeconomic identity of the national product and national income. It confirms that Lagrange multipliers measure the rate of change of the objective function (consumption level c) with respect to the constraints (capital k and labor l). If the stock of capital is increased by a unit, then the contribution to the objective is r. Hence r measures the productivity of capital. Similarly, w measures the productivity of labor. r and w need not be the observed prices of capital and labor, but are the Lagrange multipliers of the efficiency program, also called shadow prices. For perfectly competitive economies, however, there is agreement.

6. Total factor productivity

Capital productivity is r and labor productivity is w, where r and w are the shadow prices of the linear program that maximizes consumption, subject to the material balance, the capital constraint, the labor constraint and the non-negativity constraint. Now let time elapse. Everything changes; not only the output levels, but also the technical coefficients and the consumption coefficients. The linear program changes; r and w change. Hence there is capital productivity growth, $\dot{r} = dr/dt$, and labor productivity growth, $\dot{w} = dw/dt$. All this is per unit of capital or labor. Total capital productivity growth is $\dot{r}k$ and total labor productivity growth is $\dot{w}l$. Adding and normalizing by the level, we obtain the nominal total factor productivity growth rate, $(\dot{r}k + \dot{w}l)/(rk + wl)$. To obtain it in real terms we must subtract the price increase of the consumption bundle, $\dot{p}_{j(i)} - \mathbf{p}'\dot{\mathbf{a}}$. The real "total factor productivity growth rate" is

$$TFP = (\dot{r}k + \dot{w}l)/(rk + wl)$$

Here k and l are the factor constraints, and r and w their Lagrange multipliers. Although this productivity growth concept is grounded in the theory of mathematical programming (where Lagrange multipliers measure productivities of constraints), there is perfect consistency with the traditional Solow residual. By total differentiation of the macroeconomic identity of the national product and national income, $\dot{r}k + \dot{w}l = \dot{c} - r\dot{k} - w\dot{l}$, and dividing through by the identity itself we obtain

$$TFP = \dot{c}/c - r\dot{k}/p_{j(i)} - \mathbf{p}'\dot{\mathbf{a}}/(rk+wl) - w\dot{l}/(rk+wl)$$

If we use shorthand $\hat{c} = \dot{c}/c$ for a relative growth rate, we obtain

$$TFP = \hat{c} - \alpha_k\hat{k} - \alpha_l\hat{l}/p_{j(i)} - \mathbf{p}'\dot{\mathbf{a}}$$

where $\alpha_k = rk/(rk + wl)$, the competitive value share of capital, and $\alpha_l = wl/(rk + wl)$, the competitive value share of labor. The right-hand side of the last equation is precisely the Solow residual. Notice, however, that the competitive value shares are not necessarily the observed ones. For non-competitive economies, they must be calculated by means of the linear program of section 4; for an application see ten Raa and Mohnen (2002).

7.   Input-output analysis of total factor productivity

By definition, positive TFP growth means that output grows at a faster rate than input and, therefore, that the output/input ratio or standard of living goes up. In this section I will explain the phenomenon in terms of technical change at the sectoral level.

The linear program selects activities to produce the required net output of the economy. In continuous time we may consider infinitesimal changes, and the pattern of activities that are actually used is locally constant (except in degenerate points where the linear program has multiple solutions). In this section we ignore the activities that are not used. Hence, activity vector $\mathbf{s}$ is and remains positive.

From the last section, recall that the numerator of the Solow residual is $\dot{c}/p_{j(i)} - \mathbf{p}'\dot{\mathbf{a}}c - r\dot{k} - w\dot{l}$. We are going to express c, k and l in terms of $\mathbf{s}$. By complementary slackness between $c\mathbf{a} \le (\mathbf{V}' - \mathbf{U})\mathbf{s}$ and $\mathbf{p} \ge \mathbf{0}$ we have $c\mathbf{p}'\mathbf{a} = \mathbf{p}'(\mathbf{V}' - \mathbf{U})\mathbf{s}$, or, using the price normalization condition,

$$c = \mathbf{p}'(\mathbf{V}' - \mathbf{U})\mathbf{s}$$

Assume that capital and labor have positive productivity. Then, also by complementary slackness,

$$k = \mathbf{k}'\mathbf{s}, \quad l = \mathbf{l}'\mathbf{s}$$

Substitute in $\dot{c} - r\dot{k} - w\dot{l}$, and use $[x]^*$ for the rate of change $\dot{x}$ if x is the product of variables, then we obtain

$$\{[\mathbf{p}'(\mathbf{V}' - \mathbf{U})]^* - r\dot{\mathbf{k}}' - w\dot{\mathbf{l}}'\}\mathbf{s}/p_{j(i)} - \mathbf{p}'\dot{\mathbf{a}}c[\mathbf{p}'(\mathbf{V}' - \mathbf{U}) - r\mathbf{k}' - w\mathbf{l}']\dot{\mathbf{s}}$$

Since $\mathbf{s}$ remains positive, by complementary slackness, $\mathbf{p}'(\mathbf{V}' - \mathbf{U}) = r\mathbf{k}' - w\mathbf{l}'$, and the second term vanishes. It is customary to define TFP growth of sector i as output growth minus input growth, normalized by output

$$TFP_i = \frac{[\mathbf{p}'(\mathbf{V}' - \mathbf{U})]_i^* - r\dot{k}_i - w\dot{l}_i}{(\mathbf{p}'\mathbf{V}')_i}$$

It then follows that

$$TFP = \sum_i (\mathbf{p}'\mathbf{V}')_i TFP_i s_i / [c + \dot{\mathbf{p}}'(\mathbf{V}' - \mathbf{U})\mathbf{s}/p_{j(i)} - \mathbf{p}'\dot{\mathbf{a}}c]/c$$

$$= \sum_i d_i TFP_i$$

where $d_i = (\mathbf{p}'\mathbf{V}')_i s_i / \mathbf{p}'(\mathbf{V}' - \mathbf{U})\mathbf{s}$. These weights are called Domar weights and sum to the gross/net output ratio of the economy, which is greater than one. The last step assumes that the material balance is binding.

To see the reduction of TFP growth as the reduction of input-output coefficients in the traditional sense, consider the case where sectors produce single outputs. Then

$$TFP_i = \left(p_i \dot{v}_{ij(i)} - \sum_j p_j \dot{u}_{ji} - r\dot{k}_i - w\dot{l}_i \right) \bigg/ \left(p_i v_{j(i)} \right)$$

In this case input coefficients are defined by $a_{ji} = u_{ji}/v_{ij(i)}$, $\kappa_i = k_i/v_{ij(i)}$ and $\mu_i = l_i/v_{ij(i)}$. Substitution yields

$$TFP_i = \left(p_i \dot{v}_{ij(i)} - \sum_j p_j [a_{ji} v_{ij(i)}]^{\cdot} \right.$$

$$\left. - r[\kappa_i v_{ij(i)}]^{\cdot} - w[\mu_i v_{ij(i)}]^{\cdot} \right) \bigg/ \left(p_{j(i)} v_{ij(i)} \right)$$

By complementary slackness, $p_i v_{ij(i)} = \sum_j p_j a_{ji} v_{ij(i)} - r\kappa_i v_{ij(i)} - w\mu_i v_{ij(i)}$ and we obtain

$$TFP_i = \left(-\sum_j p_j \dot{a}_{ji} - r\dot{\kappa}_i - w\dot{\mu}_i \right) \bigg/ p_{j(i)}$$

that is, sectoral cost reductions. With obvious matrix notation,

$$TFP = -\sum_i d_i (\mathbf{p}'\dot{\mathbf{a}}_i - r\dot{\boldsymbol{\kappa}} - w\dot{\boldsymbol{\mu}})$$

is reduced to a reduction in input-output coefficients. If there is only one sector producing each commodity, then $j(i) = i$. If sectors produce multiple outputs, then the result basically holds, but input-output coefficients are no longer obtained by simple scalar divisions.

8.   Conclusion

For perfectly competitive economies there is an intimate relationship between efficiency and equilibrium. The marginal productivities of capital and labor that are the Lagrange multipliers to the efficiency program coincide with perfectly competitive equilibrium prices. For such economies one can measure TFP growth by means of the Solow residual, using the observed value share of the factor inputs. Most economies, however, are not perfectly competitive. Then, to measure productivities, one must find the shadow prices of the factor inputs by solving a linear program. In this paper I have proposed the linear program that maximizes Leontief utility subject to resource constraints. We have thus obtained a Solow residual measure for TFP without assuming that the economy is on its frontier. The flip side of the coin is that the numerical values we use in the residual reflect shadow prices instead of observed prices. The data required for the determination of TFP are input-output coefficients and constraints on capital and labor. These data capture the structure of the economy and are real rather than nominal. Our measure of TFP growth, firmly grounded in the theory of mathematical programming, admits a decomposition in sectoral contributions, allowing us to pinpoint the strong and the weak sectors of the economy.

We have freed neoclassical growth accounting from its use of market values of factor inputs in the evaluation of the Solow residual and, therefore, some circularity in its methodology. Perhaps surprisingly, we accomplished this by using input-output analysis to determine the values of factor inputs. Input-output analysis and neoclassical economics can be used fruitfully to fill gaps in each other. Contrary to perception, the gap in input-output analysis is not the interaction between prices and quantities but the concept of marginal productivity, and the gap in neoclassical economics is not the structure of the economy but the determination of value shares of factor inputs.

REFERENCES

Debreu, G. (1959) *Theory of Value* (New Haven, CT, Yale University Press).
Jorgenson, D., and Z. Griliches (1967) The explanation of productivity change, *Review of Economic Studies*, 34, 308–350.

Leontief, W. W. (1941) *The Structure of American Economy, 1919–1929* (Cambridge, MA, Harvard University Press).

Mohnen, P., T. ten Raa and G. Bourque (1997) Mesures de la croissance de la productivité dans un cadre d'équilibre général: l'économie du Québec entre 1978 et 1984, *Canadian Journal of Economics*, 30, 295–307.

ten Raa, T. (1994) On the methodology of input-output analysis, *Regional Science and Urban Economics*, 24, 3–25.

(1995) *Linear Analysis of Competitive Economies* (New York, Harvester Wheatsheaf).

ten Raa, T., and P. Mohnen (1994) Neoclassical input-output analysis, *Regional Science and Urban Economics*, 24, 135–158.

(2002) Neoclassical growth accounting and frontier analysis: a synthesis, *Journal of Productivity Analysis*, 18, 111–128.

Rockafellar, R. T. (1970) *Convex Analysis* (Princeton, NJ, Princeton University Press).

Solow, R. M. (1957) Technical change and the aggregate production function, *Review of Economics and Statistics*, 39, 312–320.

11 What has happened to the Leontief Paradox?

Edward N. Wolff

1. Introduction

Standard trade theory predicts that a country will export products that intensively use endowments in which a country is favored relative to the other countries and will import products that are intensive in endowments scarce in that country. It was generally believed, for example, that the United States exported capital-intensive goods and imported labor-intensive ones, but empirical work showed that US exports tended to be human-capital intensive and imports capital intensive – the so-called "Leontief Paradox."

In this paper, I investigate the Leontief Paradox in the United States for the period from 1947 to 1996. Does the Leontief Paradox continue to hold? Does it hold when we consider only equipment and machinery, and, in particular, only office and computing equipment?

A related issue regards the R&D intensity of US trade. During the 1960s and 1970s the major export strength of the United States lay in industries where research was heavily subsidized by the US government (particularly the Department of Defense), including aircraft, armaments, mainframe computers, and medical equipment (Dollar and Wolff, 1993). Is it still the case?

This paper presents statistics on the capital content of both US exports and imports from 1947 to 1996. It also contains a discussion of the relative labor costs and productivity performance of US exports and imports. Both the direct and indirect content of trade are then computed using input-output data.

The results show that imports are more capital- and equipment-intensive than are exports, but the difference in intensity between the two has fallen over time. Moreover, by 1987 exports were more intensive in office, computing, and accounting equipment (OCA) than imports were. In contrast, while in 1958 the R&D intensity of US exports was much greater than that of imports, by 1996 the R&D intensity of imports was slightly greater than that of exports. I also find that labor productivity rose more rapidly in export than in import industries and that the unit labor cost of export industries relative to import industries declined almost steadily over time.

Section 2 of this paper reviews the literature on the capital content of trade. Section 3 develops the accounting framework used in the analysis. Section 4 presents the results for the United States from 1947 to 1996. Concluding remarks are made in the last section.

2.   Review of previous literature

The most common framework used to explain why different countries will specialize in different industries with regard to trade patterns derives from the Heckscher-Ohlin model with factor-price equalization (see Heckscher, 1919; Ohlin, 1933). The key assumption in the model is that all countries face the same technology but differ in the relative abundance of factors of production, from which it can be shown that factor prices will be equalized across countries. In the original Heckscher-Ohlin formulation, the proof is based on a two-good, two-factor model. Vanek (1968) extended the model to the multi-good, multi-factor case. The model is now referred to as the Heckscher-Ohlin-Vanek model. Deardorff (1982) generalized the model further. The main implication of this model is that trade specialization is dictated by relative factor abundance. In particular, a country will export products that use intensively those factors in which a country is relatively abundant and import products that use intensively those factors that are relatively scarce.

This prediction has been subject to a long series of studies. These studies can be categorized into two types. The first compares the resource content of exports with that of the domestic substitutes for imported products in a single country. This is legitimate, since, by the assumptions of the HOV model, the technology used to produce a given product is the same in every country that produces the product. Moreover, the factor prices faced in the countries are the same, so that relative costs are identical.

The most widely known tests of the effects of relative factor endowments on trade patterns were conducted by Leontief (1956, and 1964) using input-output data for the United States. The main finding is that, despite the fact that the United States was then the most capital-intensive country in the world, it exported goods that were relatively labor-intensive and imported goods that were relatively capital-intensive. This phenomenon became known as the Leontief Paradox. Many explanations were offered for the Leontief Paradox. These include: (1) R&D differences among countries; (2) skill differentials between countries;

(3) differences in educational attainment and other human capital attributes; and (4) relative abundance of land and other natural resources (see Caves, 1960, for more discussion). The first of these factors is examined in the next section.

The second type of study compares trade patterns between two or more countries, and relates these patterns to differences in factor abundance. One of the earliest was by MacDougall (1951, and 1952), who compared British and American exports. He was interested in seeing whether the British share of capital-intensive exports was smaller than the American share, as the HOV model would predict due to the higher capital-labor ratio in the United States. He did not find any systematic evidence to support this prediction.

In a more comprehensive study, Leamer (1984) examined trade patterns for over a hundred economies and found that actual patterns could be explained fairly well by an endowment-based model with ten factors, including capital, several types of natural resources and land, and three skill classes of labor. Nonetheless, Leamer did not test for correspondence between the factor content of trade and the relative abundance of these factors within a country. In a later study, Bowen et al. (1987) computed the amount of each of twelve factors of production embodied in the net exports of twenty-seven countries in 1967 on the basis of the US input-output matrix of total input requirements for that year. These factor contents were then compared to the relative factor abundance of the twenty-seven countries. Using regression tests, they failed to find any correspondence between the two, contradicting the HOV model.

Like Bowen et al. (1987), Trefler (1993, and 1995) first computed both the labor and capital requirements of the net exports of a set of countries on the basis of the technology matrix of a single country (the United States). He then compared the labor and capital requirements with the national endowments of both labor and capital to determine whether the Leontief Paradox held. This was generally confirmed. He then relaxed the assumption of factor-price equalization and showed that cross-country differences in factor prices could account for the fact that more capital-abundant countries had net exports that were labor-intensive and that less capital-abundant countries had net exports that were capital-intensive.

Several studies of the Leontief Paradox have also been conducted on the interregional level. In one of the most recent papers on the subject, He and Polenske (2001) used regional input-output data for Japan in 1985. Using pairs of regions as the basis of their test, they found confirmation of the Leontief Paradox for some pairs but confirmation of the HOV theorem for other sets of pairs.

3. Accounting framework and skill measures

The input-output model can be introduced as follows, where all vectors and matrices are 45-order and in constant (1992) dollars, unless otherwise indicated (see section 6, the data appendix, for sources and methods). We have

$$x = (I - A)^{-1}y \tag{1}$$

with

$$y = d + e - m \tag{2}$$

where x is the vector of gross output by sector, y the vector showing the final output by sector, e the vector of exports by sector, m the vector of imports by sector,[1] d the vector of domestic consumption by sector (household consumption, investment, and government expenditures), A the square matrix of interindustry input-output coefficients, and I the identity matrix. Vectors are column vectors; row vectors are obtained by transposition, indicated by a prime.

Also, let 1 be the summation vector consisting of ones; ε the vector of export shares, where $\varepsilon_i = e_i / 1'e$; μ the vector of import shares, where $\mu_i = m_i / 1'm$; n' the row vector of labor coefficients, showing employment per unit of gross output; $\lambda' = n'(I - A)^{-1}$, showing the direct plus indirect labor requirements per unit of final output; k' the row vector of capital coefficients, showing total capital per unit of gross output; $\gamma' = k'(I - A)^{-1}$, showing the direct plus indirect capital requirements per unit of final output; r' the row vector showing R&D expenditures per unit of gross output; $\rho' = r'(I - A)^{-1}$, showing the direct plus indirect R&D requirements per unit of final output; and w' the row vector showing average employee compensation in 1992 dollars by industry.

---

[1] Technically, there are two types of imports recorded within the US input-output framework. The first, called "competitive" or "comparable" imports, are ones for which there are direct domestic substitutes, such as Japanese steel. These are recorded in the row in which there are domestic substitutes (the "steel" row, for example). The intermediate deliveries recorded in the steel row, for example, include both domestic and imported flows. The domestically produced steel and the imported steel cannot be distinguished, however. It is also not possible to identify the destination of these imports by industry or final user. The row sum of all imported deliveries is known and enters final demand as a negative (the import column). Because of this subtraction, the sum of the entire row equals the industry's gross domestic output.

The second type of import, called "non-competitive," "transferred," or "non-comparable" imports, are ones for which there are no direct domestic substitutes, such as rubber. These are recorded in a separate row in the interindustry matrix by sector of destination. The calculations of labor or capital embodied in imports are performed only for competitive imports.

4.   Results

4.1   *The changing make-up of US exports and imports*

Let us first look at the changing composition of US trade. The composition of exports in current dollars is shown in table 11.4, in the data appendix. I use current prices rather than constant prices because this is the conventional measure for both export and import composition. For example, the determination of the "most important" export is usually in terms of current value, rather than constant prices.[2]

In 1996 the most important US export was (non-electrical) Industrial machinery, which made up 12.6 percent of all exports. This category includes OCA, which by itself comprised 5.1 percent of all exports. Other important exports were Electrical and electronic equipment, Motor vehicles, and Chemicals. Altogether, Industrial machinery, Electrical and electronic equipment, the transportation equipment industries and Chemicals made up almost 40 percent of all exports.

There have been some very striking changes in export composition over the half-century. In 1947 the most important US exports included Food and kindred products; Agriculture, forestry and fishing products; Industrial machinery; Primary metal products such as steel; Motor vehicles and equipment; and Textile mill products such as fabrics. Since 1947 agriculture and food exports have steadily declined in relative importance, from 20.3 percent to 7.2 percent in 1996, as have exports of Primary metal products (from 9.0 to 1.9 percent) and Textiles (from 5.5 to 0.8 percent). The biggest gains were made by Electrical and electronic equipment, which rose from 3.2 to 9.3 percent of exports.

As shown in table 11.5, in the data appendix, the three leading imports in 1996 were Motor vehicles and equipment, Industrial machinery, and Electrical and electronic equipment. Together, this group comprised 41.5 percent of all imports. It is notable that these three industries were also among the leading four industries in terms of exports.

Changes in the composition of imports have been even more dramatic than those for exports. In 1947 the leading import sector by far was Food and kindred products, accounting for 29.0 percent of all imports. Also important were Agriculture, forestry and fishing products; Paper and paper products; and Primary metal products. Agriculture, food

[2] Another problem with the use of constant prices is that the computation of export composition is sensitive to the choice of base year. However, it should be noted that changes in the composition of exports in current prices over time reflects both changes in the composition of exports in real terms and changes in relative prices.

products, and Primary metal products were also among the leading four exports in 1947.

Between 1947 and 1996 Food and kindred products declined steadily from 29.0 to 3.4 percent of all imports, Agriculture, forestry and fishing products from 15.4 to 2.6 percent, and Paper and paper products from 14.5 to 2.0 percent. The share of Primary metal products in total imports, after doubling from 10.3 to 20.5 percent between 1947 and 1967, plummeted to 4.3 percent in 1996. In contrast, the import share of Industrial machinery rose steadily between 1947 and 1996, from 1.2 to 14.1 percent, as did that of Electrical and electronic equipment, from almost zero to 13.2 percent. Imports of Motor vehicles and equipment were volatile, first increasing from virtually zero in 1947 to 6.0 percent in 1958, dropping to 3.3 percent in 1967, expanding to 18.9 percent by 1987 (a reflection of the surge in Japanese car imports), and then tailing off to 14.2 percent in 1996. The other notable change is that oil imports swelled from 5.1 percent of all imports in 1947 to 23.8 percent in 1977, reflecting the steep oil price increases of the mid-1970s, and then abated to 8.4 percent in 1996.

Overall, import composition changed much more than export composition. The correlation in import shares between 1947 and 1996 is a meager 0.13. The correlation in import shares between 1958 and 1996 reaches only 0.38; that between 1967 and 1996 is 0.49; that between 1977 and 1996 is 0.70; and, finally, that between 1987 and 1996 is 0.96. In contrast, the correlation in export shares between 1947 and 1996 is a fairly high 0.64, and the correlation coefficient between 1996 export shares and those of other years rises to 0.83 with 1958 export shares, 0.89 with 1967 export shares, 0.91 with 1977 export shares, and 0.97 with 1987 export shares. In sum, while the composition of US exports has remained fairly constant since the mid-1960s, import composition has stabilized only since the late 1980s.

4.2   The factor content of US exports and imports

I next turn to the factor content of US exports and imports. The calculations are based on the total (direct plus indirect) factor requirements of exports and of the domestic substitutes for imports. These are sometimes referred to as "total factor content." The scalars $\lambda'e$ and $\lambda'm$ give the total (direct plus indirect) labor requirements to produce the exports and the same array of domestic goods that correspond to the imports of a given year, respectively. The total labor content is based on employment both in the actual export (import) industries as well as in the industries that supply the exports (imports).

It should be stressed that, as in previous studies, the subsequent analysis of comparative advantage is based on a comparison of the factors of production needed to produce exports with those needed to produce the domestic equivalent of imports. As discussed in section 1, however, the technique receives theoretical justification in the HOV model by the assumption that technology is the same among countries that trade with one another. Needless to say, this is a strong assumption of the model and is hard to verify empirically (see Dollar and Wolff, 1993, for more discussion).

Another limitation of this kind of analysis is that a large part of trade is intra-industry. With the available data we cannot distinguish between low-end and high-end imports or exports – that is, to distinguish products that require less sophisticated technology and skills from those that require more sophisticated technology and skills. With the data at hand it is necessary to assume that the skill (and other factor input) content of exports from an industry is the same as the skill (and other factor input) content of the domestic substitutes of the imports.[3]

Both the export and import vectors include retail and wholesale trade margins and transportation margins.[4] The former represents the value added of domestic wholesale and retail activities involved in the sales of the exports; and the latter represents the shipping costs borne by American-based shippers. Since retail, wholesale and shipping inputs will accompany any set of exports (and imports), they are not really indicative of comparative advantage. It makes sense to exclude these margins when analyzing comparative advantage, which I do in the tables that follow. Calculations were also performed for total exports and imports, and for exports and imports excluding retail and wholesale trade margins only, but they are not shown here. The pattern of results are, by and large, very similar to those shown in the text tables.

Panel A of table 11.1 shows the capital intensity of exports and imports. This comparison forms the basis of the Leontief Paradox. Capital is measured as the stock of net capital, where capital in year $t + 1$ equals capital in year t less depreciation in year t plus investment in year t (see

---

[3] A further limitation, as noted in footnote 1, is that non-competitive imports cannot be included in the analysis, since, by definition, such imports do not have domestic substitutes. However, this is a relatively small share of total imports – only 12 percent in 1996.

[4] Technically, the wholesale and retail margins also include insurance margins, as well as the value added of the "Rest of the World" sector. In the case of imports, these margins appear as negative entries, since imports generally generate domestic value added in American retailing, wholesaling, insurance and transport industries.

Table 11.1 *Capital and R&D intensity of US exports and imports: direct plus indirect capital, labor and R&D input, 1947–1996*

	1947	1958	1967	1977	1987	1996	Ratio of 1996 to 1947
A. Ratio of total net capital (1,000s of 1992 dollars) to employment							
Exports	29.4	51.0	63.5	87.2	93.7	103.8	3.53
Imports	34.6	71.0	81.7	129.2	102.1	114.1	3.29
Ratio	0.85	0.72	0.78	0.67	0.92	0.91	
Total Economy	54.7	65.8	76.9	83.5	87.7	95.6	1.75
B. Ratio of net equipment (1,000s of 1992 dollars) to employment							
Exports	9.4	17.5	23.1	34.7	38.9	46.2	4.91
Imports	10.5	20.3	26.4	39.0	40.7	47.5	4.51
Ratio	0.89	0.86	0.87	0.89	0.96	0.97	
Total Economy	14.7	16.5	19.9	22.2	25.2	29.5	2.01
C. Ratio of OCA (100s of 1992 dollars) to employment[a]							
Exports	0.5	0.9	0.9	1.7	10.8	40.5	78.26
Imports	0.9	1.1	0.8	1.7	9.0	34.6	37.98
Ratio	0.57	0.87	1.01	1.01	1.20	1.17	
Total Economy	0.9	1.2	1.1	1.6	9.2	33.9	39.64
D. Ratio of R&D expenditures to net sales (percent)[b]							
Exports	–	1.77	1.91	1.51	2.61	2.15	1.21
Imports	–	0.89	1.18	1.37	2.55	2.17	2.44
Ratio		1.99	1.62	1.10	1.02	0.99	
Total Manufacturing	–	2.70	2.92	2.27	3.40	3.03	1.12

Note: Exports and imports exclude wholesale and retail trade and transportation margins. The total employment and capital generated by exports is given by $\lambda'e$ and $\gamma'e$ respectively. The total employment and capital generated by imports is given by $\lambda'm$ and $\gamma'm$ respectively.

a The government sector is not included.

b R&D data are available only for manufacturing. The total (direct plus indirect) R&D intensity of exports and imports is given by $\rho'e$ and $\rho'm$ respectively. The ratios are 1996 to 1958.

Katz and Herman, 1997, for details). Total capital includes both structures and equipment and machinery. Total net capital (in thousands of 1992 dollars) per worker of exports and imports is given by $\gamma'e/\lambda'e$ and $\gamma'm/\lambda'm$ respectively. The results show a pronounced and continuous rise in the capital intensity of exports from 1947 to 1996. In contrast, the capital intensity of imports rose steeply between 1947 and 1977 and then slipped from 1977 to 1997. The reason is the tremendous increase in the importation of oil, a very capital-intensive industry, during the 1970s and its subsequent decline in relative terms (see table 11.5 in the data appendix). Another important finding is that the capital intensity of both exports and imports was below the overall capital-labor ratio of the economy in 1947 but equal to or above overall capital intensity by 1996. Imports, in fact, exceeded the overall capital-labor ratio by 1958 and remained above average through 1996. This indicates a shifting of both exports and imports toward more capital-intensive industries (primarily durable manufacturing).

The results show that, in fact, imports have been more capital-intensive than have exports – the Leontief Paradox. What is more telling, however, is that the capital intensity of exports relative to imports, after falling between 1947 and 1977, climbed from 1977 to 1996. The capital intensity of exports rose by a factor of 3.5 between 1947 and 1996, compared to a 3.3-fold increase for imports. The capital intensity of exports relative to imports increased from a ratio of 0.85 in 1947 to 0.91 in 1996. These results thus indicate a gradual shifting of US comparative advantage back toward capital-intensive goods, particularly since 1977.

Panel B shows results for total net stocks of equipment and machinery per worker. Again, we find a continuous rise in the equipment intensity of both exports and imports between 1947 and 1996. In 1947 both exports and imports were less equipment-intensive than was the overall economy, but by 1958 imports had exceeded and by 1967 exports had exceeded the economy-wide equipment-per-worker ratio. The results also show the equipment intensity of exports rising more rapidly than that of imports over the years 1947 to 1996. Equipment per worker in export industries increased by a factor of 4.9 over this period, compared to a factor of 4.5 for imports. As a result, the equipment intensity of exports relative to imports grew from a ratio of 0.89 in 1947 to 0.97 in 1996, with most of the gain occurring after 1977. Thus, while imports have continued to remain more equipment-intensive than exports, comparative advantage is clearly shifting back toward industries with a high equipment-to-worker ratio.

The results are even more dramatic for OCA per worker (see panel C). The OCA intensity of exports has grown much more rapidly than that of imports between 1947 and 1996 – a 78-fold increase compared to a 38-fold increase. Most of the growth occurred between 1977 and 1987 and again between 1987 and 1996, reflecting the widespread diffusion of information technology in the US economy over these two periods. Moreover, while imports were more intensive in OCA than exports in 1947, the situation has reversed since 1967. The OCA intensity of exports relative to imports climbed from a ratio of 0.57 in 1947 to 1.01 in 1967, 1.20 in 1987, and 1.17 in 1996. US comparative

Table 11.2 *Decomposition of the change in capital and R&D intensity into a trade composition effect and a technology effect, 1947–1996*

	Decomposition			Percentage decomposition		
	Trade composition effect	Technology effect	Total change	Trade composition effect	Technology effect	Total change
A. Ratio of total net capital (1,000s of 1992 dollars) to employment						
Exports	−9.5	83.9	74.4	−13	113	100
Imports	−42.9	122.4	79.5	−54	154	100
Ratio	0.12	−0.06	0.06	207	−107	100
B. Ratio of net equipment (1,000s of 1992 dollars) to employment						
Exports	−6.3	43.1	36.8	−17	117	100
Imports	−16.8	53.8	37.0	−45	145	100
Ratio	0.18	−0.10	0.08	228	−128	100
C. Ratio of OCA (100s of 1992 dollars) to employment						
Exports	5.6	34.4	40.0	14	86	100
Imports	17.1	16.6	33.7	51	49	100
Ratio	−1.81	2.41	0.60	−301	401	100
D. Ratio of R&D expenditures to net sales (percentage points)[a]						
Exports	0.50	−0.12	0.38	132	−32	100
Imports	1.26	0.02	1.28	98	2	100
Ratio	−0.84	−0.15	−0.99	85	15	100

Note: Exports and imports exclude wholesale and retail trade and transportation margins. The decompositions are based on total factor requirements; see equations (3) and (4).

a R&D data are available only for manufacturing. The decomposition covers years 1958 to 1996 only.

advantage now lies in industries that intensively use office and computing equipment.

The decompositions in table 11.2 highlight some of the reasons for this remarkable turnaround in the capital intensity of exports relative to imports. The change in the capital-labor ratio generated by exports is given by

$$
(\gamma_2' \varepsilon_2 / \lambda_2' \varepsilon_2) - (\gamma_1' \varepsilon_1 / \lambda_1' \varepsilon_1)
$$
$$
= \tfrac{1}{2} [(\gamma_1' \varepsilon_2 / \lambda_1' \varepsilon_2 - \gamma_1' \varepsilon_1 / \lambda_1' \varepsilon_1) + (\gamma_2' \varepsilon_2 / \lambda_2' \varepsilon_2 - \gamma_2' \varepsilon_1 / \lambda_2' \varepsilon_1)]
$$
$$
+ \tfrac{1}{2} [(\gamma_2' \varepsilon_1 / \lambda_2' \varepsilon_1 - \gamma_1' \varepsilon_1 / \lambda_1' \varepsilon_1) + (\gamma_2' \varepsilon_2 / \lambda_2' \varepsilon_2 - \gamma_1' \varepsilon_2 / \lambda_1' \varepsilon_2)]
$$
$$
(3)
$$

where vector subscripts 1 and 2 indicate years 1 and 2.[5] The first term (the "trade composition" effect) measures how much the capital intensity of exports would have grown from the change in the composition of exports over the period (the difference between ε_1 and ε_2) while holding technology constant. The second term (the "technology" effect) measures how much the capital intensity of exports would have increased from changes in labor and capital coefficients in export industries while holding export composition constant.[6] A similar decomposition can be used for the change in the capital-labor ratio of imports.[7]

As shown in panel A, the ratio of total net capital per worker generated by exports increased by $74,400 (in 1992 dollars) between 1947 and 1977. Of this, $83,900 (or 113 percent) was accounted for by the rising capital intensity of export industries. Changes in export composition favored labor-intensive industries but the effect was small. Change in technical coefficients in import industries had an even stronger effect on the increase in the capital-labor ratio generated by imports in this period, accounting for $122,400 (or 154 percent) of the total gain of $79,500. However, imports shifted away from capital-intensive industries (mainly agriculture and primary metal products) toward low-capital-intensive ones (primarily industrial machinery, electrical equipment, and motor vehicles), accounting for a $42,900 decline in the capital-labor ratio of import industries. As a result, the growth in the capital intensity of exports relative to imports was entirely due to changes in export and import composition (mainly the latter), which was partially offset by changes of technology in export and import industries and their suppliers.

Results are even stronger for the equipment per worker (panel B). In this case, the ratio of the equipment intensity of exports relative to imports rose from 0.89 in 1947 to 0.97 in 1996. The change in the equipment to employment ratio generated by exports of $36,800 was due to the rising capital intensity of export industries, which was offset in part by shifts in export composition toward low-equipment-intensive industries. Likewise, the rising equipment intensity of imports, amounting to $37,000, was due to both the rising capital intensity of import industries and the negative effects of changing import composition. As with total

---

[5] The derivation is straightforward since the cross-terms, such as $\gamma'_1 \varepsilon_2 / \lambda'_1 \varepsilon_2$, cancel out.

[6] The technology effect can, likewise, be separated into two effects: one reflecting changes in labor coefficients, and the other changes in capital coefficients. This further decomposition is not used here.

[7] I use average weights to measure the two effects in order to provide an exact decomposition.

capital intensity, the growth of the ratio in equipment intensity between exports and imports over this period emanated entirely from the trade effect (mainly changes in import composition), counterbalanced, in part, by the technology effect.

The pattern is different for OCA per worker. The ratio of OCA intensity of exports relative to imports increased from 0.57 in 1947 to 1.17 in 1996. The evidence here indicates that the composition of exports shifted toward industries that were intensive in their use of computers and office machinery, accounting for 14 percent of the total growth of OCA per worker of $4,000 over the 1947–1996 period. The other 86 percent was due to the rising investment in OCA per worker in export industries and their suppliers. Imports likewise shifted toward computer-intensive industries, particularly after 1977. Over the full 1947–1996 period, 51 percent of the overall gain of $3,370 in OCA per worker among import industries was attributable to changes in import composition and the other 49 percent to increases in OCA intensity in import industries and their suppliers. Over the half-century, imports shifted more strongly toward computer-intensive industries than exports, while computer intensity rose much more rapidly in export industries than import industries. As a result, the rise in the ratio of OCA intensity in exports relative to imports over this period was due to the faster growth of OCA per worker in export industries than in import industries, which was partly offset by shifts in export and import composition.

4.3   R&D intensity of exports and imports

Panel D of table 11.1 shows R&D expenditures generated by both exports and imports as a percentage of total output. Total (direct plus indirect) R&D expenditures as a percentage of total output generated by exports are given by $\rho'e/q'e$; and total R&D expenditures as a percentage of total output generated by imports are given by $\rho'm/q'm$, where $q' = 1'(I - A)^{-1}$.

The results are surprising. The total R&D intensity of US exports in 1958 was almost twice as great as that of imports. The R&D intensity of both exports and imports increased between 1958 and 1987 and then fell off somewhat in 1996. However, over the 1958–1996 period, R&D intensity rose much more rapidly for imports than exports – a factor of 2.4 versus 1.2. As a result, by 1996 the R&D intensity of imports was slightly greater than that of exports. Interestingly, neither exports nor imports were as R&D intensive as overall manufacturing.

The decomposition shown in panel D of table 11.2 indicates some of the reasons behind the falling R&D intensity of export industries relative to import industries. The decomposition of the change in the total (direct plus indirect) R&D expenditures generated by exports as a ratio to total output generated by exports is given by

$$(\rho_2' \varepsilon_2 / q_2' \varepsilon_2) - (\rho_1' \varepsilon_1 / q_1' \varepsilon_1)$$

$$= \tfrac{1}{2}[(\rho_1' \varepsilon_2 / q_1' \varepsilon_2 - \rho_1' \varepsilon_1 / q_1' \varepsilon_1) + (\rho_2' \varepsilon_2 / q_2' \varepsilon_2 - \rho_2' \varepsilon_1 / q_2' \varepsilon_1)]$$

$$+ \tfrac{1}{2}[(\rho_2' \varepsilon_1 / q_2' \varepsilon_1 - \rho_1' \varepsilon_1 / q_1' \varepsilon_1) + (\rho_2' \varepsilon_2 / q_2' \varepsilon_2 - \rho_1' \varepsilon_2 / q_1' \varepsilon_2)]$$

$$(4)$$

The first term is the trade composition effect, and the second term (the technology effect) shows the average effect of changes in industry R&D coefficients on overall R&D intensity. A similar decomposition can be applied to the R&D intensity of output generated by imports.

The effect of the changing composition of exports and imports explains almost the entirety of the decline in the R&D intensity of exports relative to imports. Between 1958 and 1996 both exports and imports shifted toward more R&D-intensive industries, but the shift effect was more than twice as great for imports. Export growth was particularly strong in Electrical and electronic equipment and Instruments and related products, while imports gained share in Motor vehicles and equipment, Electrical and electronic equipment, Chemicals, Instruments and related products, and – especially – Industrial machinery. Moreover, overall R&D expenditures in manufacturing, after declining from 2.70 percent of net sales in 1958 to 2.27 percent in 1977, increased to 3.03 percent in 1996. On net, the change in R&D coefficients (the technology effect) essentially washed out between the two periods. The fact that the trade effect was much stronger for imports than exports accounts for 85 percent of the elimination of the gap in R&D intensity between exports and imports.

4.4   Labor costs and labor productivity of exports and imports

The final part of the analysis considers the average labor costs of both exports and imports. According to the Trefler variant of HOV trade theory, a country will export those products where the cost is relatively low and import those products where the cost is relatively high. Though the relevant comparison is with other trading countries, it may still be expected that a country will export the products of those industries that pay relatively low wages and import the products of industries with high wages.

Table 11.3 *Labor costs of US exports and imports: direct plus indirect labor input, 1947–1996*

	1947	1958	1967	1977	1987	1996	Ratio of 1996 to 1947
A. Employee compensation per FTEE (1,000s of 1992 dollars)							
Exports	15.6	21.4	27.8	35.5	38.4	39.4	2.53
Imports	14.3	20.8	27.9	36.2	37.9	37.8	2.65
Ratio	1.09	1.03	1.00	0.98	1.01	1.04	
Total Economy	15.8	21.5	27.0	32.6	34.7	34.8	2.20
B. Employee compensation plus half proprietors' income per PEP (1,000s of 1992 dollars)							
Exports	15.8	21.5	27.6	35.4	37.9	39.2	2.48
Imports	14.7	20.8	27.7	36.3	37.4	37.2	2.53
Ratio	1.08	1.03	1.00	0.98	1.01	1.05	
Total Economy	15.0	20.4	26.3	31.7	33.1	33.7	2.25
C. Output (GDP) per FTEE (1,000s of 1992 dollars)							
Exports	24.1	31.8	41.7	48.1	59.4	70.7	2.94
Imports	25.6	33.2	42.1	51.9	55.6	67.2	2.62
Ratio	0.94	0.96	0.99	0.93	1.07	1.05	
Total Economy	30.1	38.1	46.3	53.1	57.5	61.1	2.03
D. Unit labor cost[a]							
Exports	0.65	0.67	0.67	0.74	0.65	0.56	0.86
Imports	0.56	0.63	0.66	0.70	0.68	0.56	1.01
Difference	0.09	0.05	0.00	0.04	−0.04	−0.01	
Total Economy	0.53	0.56	0.58	0.61	0.60	0.57	1.08

Note: Exports and imports exclude wholesale and retail trade and transportation margins. Average wages generated directly and indirectly by exports are given by $w'(I - A)^{-1}e/\lambda'e$. Average wages generated directly, and indirectly by imports are given by $w'(I - A)^{-1}m/\lambda'm$.

The average unit labor cost generated directly and indirectly by exports is given by $w'(I - A)^{-1}e/q'e$.

The average unit labor cost generated directly and indirectly by imports is given by $w'(I - A)^{-1}m/q'm$.

a The export row in panel D is calculated as the ratio of the export row in panel A to the export row in panel C. Likewise, the import row in panel D is calculated as the ratio of the import row in panel A to the import row in panel C.

The results are shown in table 11.3. Average wages generated both directly and indirectly by exports are given by $w'(I - A)^{-1}e/\lambda'e$, where w is a vector showing average employee compensation per full-time equivalent employee (FTEE) in 1992 dollars by industry. Average wages generated directly and indirectly by imports are given by $w'(I - A)^{-1}m/\lambda'm$. The unit labor cost of industry i is defined here as the ratio of employee compensation (in 1992 dollars) in industry i to total output (in 1992 dollars) in industry i. The average unit labor cost generated directly and indirectly by exports is given by $\mathbf{w}'(\mathbf{I} - \mathbf{A})^{-1}\mathbf{e}/\mathbf{q}'\mathbf{e}$; and the average unit labor cost generated directly and indirectly by imports is given by $\mathbf{w}'(\mathbf{I} - \mathbf{A})^{-1}\mathbf{m}/\mathbf{q}'\mathbf{m}$.

Panel A in table 11.3 shows employee compensation per FTEE. Export industries and their suppliers were paying 9 percent more than import industries and their suppliers in 1947 but 2 percent less by 1977. Between 1977 and 1996 the situation reversed and average wages among exporters rose relative to import industries. By 1996 export industries were paying 4 percent more than import industries. It is also of note that both export and import industries paid wages lower than the economy-wide average wage in 1947. However, average compensation in both import and export industries grew more rapidly than overall wages, so that by 1996 exporting and importing industries were both paying higher than the overall average wage.

Panel B uses another measure of labor costs: employee compensation plus half of proprietors' income per person engaged in production (PEP).[8] Results are almost identical. By this measure, exporters paid 8 percent higher wages than import industries in 1947 and 5 percent higher wages in 1996.[9]

Between 1947 and 1996 labor productivity grew more rapidly in export than import industries: 2.2 versus 2.0 percent per year (panel C). In 1947 output per FTEE was 6 percent higher in import industries than in export industries, but in 1996 it was 5 percent higher for exporters. Labor productivity also grew more rapidly among both exports and imports than in the total economy over the 49-year stretch, because of the heavy concentration of manufactured goods in trade. In 1947 output per worker for both exports and imports was lower than the economy-wide average; but, by 1996, the situation had completely reversed.

Changes in unit labor cost reflect both changes in worker compensation and labor productivity. In 1947 export industries had higher unit labor cost than import industries (panel D) – a reflection of their higher wages. However, in this case, we see an almost continuous decline in the unit labor cost of export industries relative to import industries between 1947 and 1996. The reason is the higher productivity growth of export

[8] Proprietors' income includes compensation for time worked as well as a return on the capital invested in unincorporated businesses. Since we do not know what the correct proportions between these two types of income are, I have assumed that half of proprietors' income represents remuneration for time worked.

[9] A third measure – wages and salaries per FTEE – also shows almost exactly the same pattern (results not shown).

industries relative to import industries, not the declining relative wages of export industries. By 1996 unit labor costs of exports were slightly below those of import industries.

5.   Conclusion

The compositions of both exports and imports have changed considerably over the post-war period. In 1947 the most important US exports in rank order (excluding Wholesale trade, Retail trade and Transportation services) were Food and kindred products, Agriculture, forestry and fishing products, Industrial machinery, Primary metal products, Motor vehicles and equipment and Textile mill products. Of this group, only Industrial machinery could be considered high-tech and only Motor vehicles medium-tech. By 1996 Industrial machinery exports ranked first, followed by Electrical and electronic equipment, Motor vehicles, Chemicals, and Other transportation equipment such as aircraft. These are all high-tech or medium-tech industries.

In 1947 the leading import was, by far, Food and kindred products, followed by Agriculture, forestry and fishing products, Paper and paper products, Primary metal products and Metal mining. These were all low-tech industries. In 1996 the three leading imports were Motor vehicles, Industrial machinery, and Electrical and electronic equipment – all medium- or high-tech. So, while US exports shifted over time away from low-tech industries and toward medium- and high-tech ones, the shift was even more pronounced for US imports.

The results here provide new confirmation that imports are more capital-intensive than are exports. However, the capital intensity of exports relative to imports has been climbing since 1977. The results also show that imports are more equipment-intensive than exports and that the equipment intensity of exports rose more rapidly than that of imports over these years. The OCA intensity of exports has also grown much more rapidly than that of imports, and by 1987 exports were considerably more OCA-intensive than were imports. These results thus indicate a gradual shifting of US comparative advantage back toward capital-intensive goods since 1977, and particularly toward industries with a high equipment and OCA intensity.

The decomposition analysis indicates that almost all the growth in the total capital and equipment intensity of exports relative to imports over the years 1947 to 1996 was due to changes in export and import composition (mainly the latter), partially offset by the greater rise in capital intensity among import industries. In contrast, the increase in the OCA intensity of exports relative to imports over this period was due entirely to the faster growth of OCA per worker in export industries than in import industries, while shifts in export and import composition had a negative effect on the ratio.

While the (total) R&D intensity of US exports was almost twice as great as that of imports in 1958, it was slightly higher in import industries in 1996. The decompositions show that almost the entirety of the growth in R&D intensity in imports relative to exports is explained by changes in trade composition – particularly growing imports of Motor vehicles, Industrial machinery, Electrical and electronic equipment, Chemicals and Instruments and related products over these years.

There is no indication that average wages or employee compensation grew more rapidly in import than in export industries. However, labor productivity rose more rapidly in export than import industries between 1947 and 1996. As a result, the unit labor cost of export industries declined almost steadily relative to import industries over this period, as the Trefler version of the HOV model would predict.

In sum, with regard to the gradual loss of comparative advantage in R&D-intensive products, this also reflects a catch-up in R&D by other OECD countries. Indeed, by 1995 Japan had overtaken the United States in R&D intensity. According to the National Science Board (1998), Japan's R&D intensity (the ratio of R&D expenditures to GDP) has steadily grown since 1980, and by 1995 Japan had the highest R&D intensity in the G7 (2.78 percent, compared to 2.52 percent in the United States, 2.28 percent in Germany, 2.34 percent in France, and 2.05 percent in the United Kingdom).

While the United States no longer has the edge in R&D, it has taken the lead in another aspect of high-tech production – computer intensity – and is gradually reclaiming its advantage in total capital and equipment intensity. This is likely a reflection of the gradual erosion in the human capital advantage of the United States vis-à-vis other OECD countries. For the moment, complementarities between OCA and both cognitive skills and knowledge worker jobs (see Wolff, 1996) may account for the lower capital intensity of exports than imports. Nevertheless, the trends also suggest that the Leontief Paradox may be overturned in the near future. This may create a new paradox, however, since the United States is no longer the most capital-abundant country in the world; according to the OECD's *International Sectoral Database*, in 1995 the United States ranked behind Germany, the Netherlands and Belgium in overall capital intensity.

The results on productivity and labor costs are consistent with my earlier studies (Dollar and Wolff, 1993; Wolff, 1995, 1997, and 1999), which found on the basis of cross-national evidence that changes in industry net exports were positively related to industry productivity growth and negatively related to changes in unit labor cost. On the other hand, these results, together with the findings on capital and R&D intensity, are hard to reconcile with the standard (and static) HOV model. Nonetheless, they do appear potentially consistent with the Trefler variant of the HOV model, which allows for factor price and unit labor cost differences across countries.

6.   Data appendix

1. NIPA employee compensation: figures are from the National Income and Product Accounts, available on the Internet. Employee compensation includes wages and salaries and employee benefits. Proprietors' income is net income to self-employed persons, including partners in businesses and owners of unincorporated businesses.
2. NIPA employment data: the number of FTEEs equals the number of employees on full-time schedules plus the number of employees on part-time schedules converted to a full-time basis. The number of FTEEs in each industry is the product of the total number of employees and the ratio of average weekly hours per employee for all employees to average weekly hours per employee on full-time schedules. The number of PEPs equals the number of full-time and part-time employees plus the number of self-employed persons. Unpaid family workers are not included.
3. Capital stock figures are based on chain-type quantity indexes for net stock of fixed capital in 1992 dollars, year-end estimates. These series are available for fifty-three sectors. Source: US Bureau of Economic Analysis, CD-ROM NCN-0229, "Fixed Reproducible Tangible Wealth of the United States, 1925–97."
4. Research and development expenditures performed by industry, including company, federal, and other sources of funds. Company-financed R&D performed outside the company is excluded. Industry series run from 1957 to 1997. Source: National Science Foundation, Internet. For technical details, see National Science Foundation (1996).
5. The input-output data are 85-sector US input-output tables for the years 1947, 1958, 1963, 1967, 1972, 1977, 1982, 1987, 1992 and 1996 (see, for example, Lawson, 1997, for details on the sectoring). The 1947, 1958 and 1963 tables are available only in single-table format. The 1967, 1972, 1977, 1982, 1987, 1992 and 1996 data are available in separate make and use tables. Sectoral price deflators are available on the 85-sector level. The data source is the Bureau of Labor Statistics' Historical Output Data Series (obtained on computer

Table 11.4 *Percentage composition of US exports, with industries ranked by 1996 exports*

Industry	1947	1958	1967	1977	1987	1996
Industrial machinery exc. electrical	9.2	12.7	14.3	12.8	10.9	12.6
Electrical and electronic equipment	3.2	4.5	5.4	6.5	7.4	9.3
Shipping and other transport services	13.0	12.0	10.6	6.7	8.8	8.2
Motor vehicles and equipment	5.7	4.8	5.5	7.9	7.6	6.9
Chemicals and allied products	3.8	5.3	6.0	5.3	5.9	5.6
Other transportation equipment	2.4	4.5	5.5	5.8	7.4	5.4
Retail trade	2.9	3.7	3.6	4.4	4.4	4.8
Wholesale trade	2.9	3.7	3.6	4.4	4.2	4.6
Real estate	0.3	1.3	1.6	2.6	3.4	4.6
Instruments and related products	1.1	1.4	2.4	2.4	4.0	4.1
Agriculture, forestry and fishing products	9.5	9.8	9.0	9.2	4.5	3.7
Food and kindred products	10.9	6.7	5.2	5.1	3.8	3.5
Rubber and plastic products	1.6	2.9	2.7	2.2	2.6	3.0
Fabricated metal products	2.2	2.9	3.6	4.0	3.4	2.4
Insurance	0.2	0.1	0.1	0.2	2.4	2.1
Banking, credit and investment companies	0.2	0.1	0.1	0.2	2.4	2.1
Primary metal products	9.0	5.0	4.4	2.6	1.7	1.9
Paper and allied products	1.7	1.6	2.0	1.8	2.1	1.8
Petroleum and coal products	3.1	3.4	2.1	2.3	2.1	1.5
Business and repair services, except auto	0.2	0.7	0.6	1.0	0.7	1.1
Professional services & non-profits	0.2	0.6	0.6	1.0	0.7	1.1
Apparel and other textile products	1.8	0.8	0.7	0.7	0.5	1.1
Lumber and wood products	1.0	0.6	1.0	1.4	1.2	0.9
Tobacco products	1.3	2.3	1.6	1.2	0.8	0.9
Amusement and recreation services	0.7	1.3	0.9	0.3	0.4	0.8
Textile mill products	5.5	1.3	0.9	1.2	0.8	0.8
Printing and publishing	0.4	0.5	0.7	1.0	0.7	0.7
Miscellaneous manufactures	1.0	0.6	0.9	0.9	0.9	0.7
Stone, clay and glass products	1.0	0.9	0.9	0.8	0.6	0.6
Telephone and telegraph	0.2	0.3	0.4	0.7	1.1	0.6
Oil and gas extraction	1.2	0.2	0.3	0.2	0.5	0.6
Coal mining	2.1	1.7	0.8	1.5	0.8	0.3
Correlation with 1996 export composition:	0.64	0.83	0.89	0.91	0.97	1.00

Note: Exports are in current dollars. Industries are classified according to a 45-sector aggregation. Only industries that account for 1 percent or more of exports in any year are listed.

diskette) in current and constant dollars. The flow matrices in current dollars were first deflated to constant dollars on the 85-sector level. These tables were then aggregated to forty-five sectors for conformity with the other data sources (particularly the capital stock data, which are available for only fifty-three sectors).

Table 11.5 *Percentage composition of US imports, with industries ranked by 1996 imports*

Industry	1947	1958	1967	1977	1987	1996
Motor vehicles and equipment	0.2	6.0	3.3	12.2	18.9	14.2
Industrial machinery exc. electrical	1.2	2.9	7.6	5.2	10.9	14.1
Electrical and electronic equipment	0.1	1.3	6.7	7.6	11.5	13.2
Oil and gas extraction	5.1	11.4	6.0	23.8	7.2	8.4
Apparel and other textile products	0.4	0.4	0.3	4.1	6.5	6.7
Chemicals and allied products	3.1	3.7	4.3	3.6	4.9	5.8
Primary metal products	10.3	12.8	20.5	8.1	4.5	4.3
Instruments and related products	1.8	1.8	2.0	2.0	4.0	3.9
Miscellaneous manufactures	2.2	2.4	3.2	2.5	3.8	3.5
Food and kindred products	29.0	12.4	7.5	5.5	4.5	3.4
Rubber and plastic products	0.4	0.7	1.9	2.1	2.9	3.2
Agriculture, forestry and fishing products	15.4	8.4	5.7	1.9	1.7	2.6
Fabricated metal products	0.3	1.7	3.1	2.0	2.8	2.5
Other transportation equipment	0.3	1.2	1.8	1.5	2.4	2.1
Leather and leather products	0.5	0.5	0.5	1.8	2.3	2.0
Paper and allied products	14.5	9.6	7.2	2.6	2.5	2.0
Petroleum and coal products	2.7	6.2	5.5	7.6	3.3	1.8
Lumber and wood products	4.5	4.9	4.6	2.4	1.6	1.6
Transportation services	0.3	0.1	0.6	0.2	0.6	1.3
Stone, clay and glass products	0.9	1.6	1.6	1.2	1.6	1.3
Furniture and fixtures	0.0	0.0	0.2	0.5	1.3	1.2
Textile mill products	3.4	5.5	4.8	1.1	1.2	0.9
Banking, credit and investment companies	1.1	0.2	0.2	0.2	0.4	0.3
Insurance	1.0	0.2	0.2	0.2	0.4	0.3
Mining of non-metallic minerals	2.9	1.9	1.1	0.4	0.2	0.2
Tobacco products	2.9	0.3	0.1	0.2	0.2	0.1
Metal mining	7.1	7.0	4.9	1.3	0.3	0.0
Correlation with 1996 import composition:	0.13	0.38	0.49	0.70	0.96	1.00

Note: Imports are in current dollars. Industries are classified according to a 45-sector aggregation. Only industries that account for 1 percent or more of imports in any year are listed.

6. Imports and exports. Sources for the industry-level data are US input-output data for years 1947, 1958, 1963, 1967, 1972, 1977, 1982, 1987, 1992 and 1996.

REFERENCES

Bowen, H. P., E. E. Leamer and L. Sveikauskas (1987) Multicountry, multifactor tests of the factor abundance theory, *American Economic Review*, 77, 791–809.

Caves, R. E. (1960) *Trade and Economic Structure: Models and Methods* (Cambridge, MA, Harvard University Press).

Deardorff, A. V. (1982) The general validity of the Heckscher-Ohlin theorem, *American Economic Review*, 72, 683–694.

Dollar, D., and E. N. Wolff (1993) *Competitiveness, Convergence, and International Specialization* (Cambridge, MA, MIT Press).

He, S., and K. R. Polenske (2001) Interregional trade, the Heckscher-Ohlin-Vanek theorem and the Leontief Paradox, in M. L. Lahr and E. Dietzenbacher (eds.) *Input-Output Analysis: Frontiers and Extensions* (Basingstoke, Palgrave), 161–186.

Heckscher, E. (1919) The effect of foreign trade on the distribution of income, *Ekonomisk Tidskrift*, 21, 497–512. [Reprinted in abridged form in H. S. Ellis and L. A. Metzler (eds.) *Readings in the Theory of International Trade* (Homewood, IL, Irwin, 1949), 272–300.]

Katz, A. J., and S. W. Herman (1997) Improved estimates of fixed reproducible tangible wealth, 1929–95, *Survey of Current Business*, 77 (5), 69–92.

Lawson, A. M. (1997) Benchmark input-output accounts for the US economy, 1992, *Survey of Current Business*, 77 (11), 36–83.

Leamer, E. E. (1984) *Sources of International Comparative Advantage* (Cambridge, MA, MIT Press).

Leontief, W. W. (1956) Factor proportions and the structure of American trade: further theoretical and empirical analysis, *Review of Economics and Statistics*, 38, 386–407.

(1964) International comparisons of factor cost and factor use, *American Economic Review*, 54, 335–345.

MacDougall, G. D. A. (1951) British and American exports: a study suggested by the theory of comparative costs, Part I, *Economic Journal*, 61, 697–724.

(1952) British and American exports: a study suggested by the theory of comparative costs, Part II, *Economic Journal*, 62, 487–521.

National Science Board (1998) Science & engineering indicators – 1998, *Bulletin NSB 98-1* (Arlington, VA, National Science Foundation).

National Science Foundation (1996) Research and development in industry, *NSF 96-304* (Arlington, VA, National Science Foundation).

Ohlin, B. (1933) *Interregional and International Trade* (Cambridge, MA, Harvard University Press).

Trefler, D. (1993) International factor price differences: Leontief was right!, *Journal of Political Economy*, 101, 961–987.

(1995) The case of missing trade and other mysteries, *American Economic Review*, 85, 1,029–1,046.

Vanek, J. (1968) The factor proportions theory: the N-factor case, *Kyklos*, 21, 749–756.

Wolff, E. N. (1995) Technological change, capital accumulation, and changing trade patterns over the long term, *Structural Change and Economic Dynamics*, 6, 43–70.

(1996) Technology and the demand for skills, *OECD Science, Technology and Industry Review*, 18, 96–123.

(1997) Productivity growth and shifting comparative advantage on the industry level, in J. Fagerberg, P. Hansson, L. Lundberg and A. Melchior (eds.) *Technology and International Trade* (Cheltenham, Edward Elgar Publishing), 1–19.

(1999) Specialization and productivity performance in low-, medium-, and high-tech manufacturing industries, in A. Heston and R. E. Lipsey (eds.) *International and Interarea Comparisons of Prices, Income, and Output*, Studies of Income and Wealth, Vol. 61 (Chicago, Chicago University Press [National Bureau of Economic Research]), 419–452.

12 The decline in labor compensation's share of GDP: a structural decomposition analysis for the United States, 1982 to 1997

Erik Dietzenbacher, Michael L. Lahr and Bart Los

1. Introduction

A book in memory of Wassily Leontief would hardly be complete without some piece on the structure of the American economy. After all, Professor Leontief had developed his first input-output table using US data and subsequently published his first three books with the purpose of examining the structure of the American economy (Leontief, 1941, and 1951; Leontief et al., 1953).[1] In this contribution we study the decline of labor compensation's share of US GDP in the 1980s and early 1990s. According to data on gross domestic product constructed by the Bureau of Economic Analysis (BEA) in the US Department of Commerce, this share steadily decreased from 59.1 to 56.0 percent between 1982 and 1997. This 3.1 percentage point drop may not seem notable. But it contrasts strongly against its steady rise of 6.6 percentage points from 1950 to 1970 (from 52.8 to 59.4 percent), when productivity rose rapidly. Moreover, it is clear that wage rates did not increase at the same pace as labor productivity during this period.

Recent literature suggests many potential causes for this phenomenon. Some of the causes pertain to almost all industries of the American economy (shift effects), whereas others strongly relate to structural changes (share effects). We propose a multiplicative structural decomposition analysis (SDA) inspired by Dietzenbacher et al. (2000) to get insight into the relative empirical importance of these two categories of causes. The US dataset that we study in our decomposition analysis covers the period 1982 to 1997 and recognizes 175 different industries. It is constructed on the basis of input-output and labor data available from the BEA and the Bureau of Labor Statistics.

The chapter is organized as follows. In section 2 we review the literature on the declining share of labor compensation in US GDP. Section 3

---

[1] The well-known Leontief Paradox also stemmed from his examination of the structure of the American economy, namely trade (Leontief, 1953, and 1956). See also Leontief (1965).

discusses multiplicative SDA methods in general, including aspects that are also paramount in index number theory. In section 4 we propose a specific multiplicative decomposition to analyze compensation's share of value added. It enables us to study, over time, the contributions of changes in compensation per hour worked; changes in value added per hour worked; structural changes in the technology (i.e. labor input coefficients and intermediate input coefficients); and final demand changes, all at the 175-industry level. We propose a Fisher-type index for our empirical analysis. In section 5 we describe the data we used and how they were prepared for our application. Section 6 is devoted to the presentation and the discussion of the results. The final section summarizes our main findings.

2.   Potential causes of declining labor shares in income

In a dynamic, innovative economy such as that of the United States, changes in labor compensation's share of income are essentially the net result of two countervailing forces. The diffusion of innovations generally leads either to ever more capital-intensive modes of production, the labor requirements per physical unit of output of which are declining steadily, or ever-increasing quality levels of products, which allows for higher profit margins. *Ceteris paribus*, labor compensation shares should decline in both cases. Generally, however, workers are able to negotiate higher real wages that reflect their increased productivity. This implies an upward tendency in labor compensation's share of value added. Productivity growth and changes in compensation per worker have been studied extensively, both at the national and industry level. Comparatively little research has investigated them jointly.[2] This is despite a series of attention-grabbing publications on the relative stagnancy of average real compensation per worker during the 1980s – a period during which productivity itself remained on the rise.[3] The lack of research on this topic is even more surprising since the apparent flat real returns to labor observed in the US economy were not paralleled in other G7 nations, notwithstanding rather similar patterns in productivity growth (Sparks and Greiner, 1997; Cobet and Wilson, 2002).[4]

---

[2] Most of the exceptions are published in the *Monthly Labor Review* by US Bureau of Labor Statistics (BLS) employees, and deal exclusively with cross-country comparisons in manufacturing (see, e.g., Neef et al., 1993; Sparks and Greiner, 1997).

[3] Some oft-cited pieces dealing with this material are Levy and Murnane (1992); Blank (1997); and Katz and Autor (1999).

[4] It may well be that Bosworth and Perry (1994) stymied further work by discounting some of the BLS findings by pointing out some measurement error.

With the objectives of this chapter in mind, we find it useful to classify the forces behind US trends in productivity and compensation per worker from 1982 to 1997 into shift and share effects. Shift effects are changes (rising or falling "tides") that affect most, if not all, industries. Share effects stem from changes in industry mix.

With regard to the US productivity growth slowdown in the 1980s and early 1990s (in comparison to the 1970s), the following shift effects have been put forward:[5] (1) the reluctance of firms to shed labor when output growth slows down, as was the case in the 1990s (Gordon, 1979); (2) a weaker contribution of the Verdoorn-Kaldor effect, which is a positive feedback effect between output growth and productivity growth, often attributed to learning-by-doing processes and increasing opportunities for division of tasks (Wolff, 1996); (3) a negative endogenous vintage effect, which occurs if investment is a function of the change in the rate of output growth (Hulten, 1992); and (4) the time that firms and workers need to get accustomed to innovations (such as the computer) that change the modes of production to a considerable extent (David, 1990).

Regardless of the relevance of these shift effect explanations for the productivity slowdown during the early 1990s, it was clear that so-called "Baumol's disease" – the pre-existing proclivity of the US economy for shifting out of manufacturing and into lower-productivity services (Baumol, 1967) – was another partial cause of relatively low productivity growth. Saturation of consumer demand for an increasing number of manufactured goods and increased competition from low-wage countries may be regarded as the most important determinants of these share effects. Interestingly, the increasing shares of output in the less productive sectors were exacerbated by their own declining productivity growth during much of this period (Triplett and Bosworth, 2001).

Turning our attention to the causes of stagnant real wage growth, the literature also offers shift and share effects. Shift effects include: (1) the deceleration of the growth of college-educated workers as part of the entire workforce (Blackburn et al., 1990); (2) the declining role of union membership in the workforce (Blackburn et al., 1990); (3) a declining real minimum wage rate (DiNardo et al., 1996); (4) the revitalization of immigration, which may have depressed wages in key regions of the United States (Borjas, 1995); (5) a strengthened mandate to get return to stockholders; and (6) the increasing proportion of US households holding equities.[6] According to recent finance research, there may be a

---

[5] For explanations of post-1995 changes, see, e.g., Jorgenson and Stiroh (2000) and Oliner and Sichel (2000).

[6] During this period of stagnant worker income the share of US households holding stock rose from 19 percent in 1983 (New York Stock Exchange, 1985) to a full 49 percent in 1998 (Kennickell et al., 2000).

negative relationship between stock ownership and wage income (Davis and Willen, 2000; Viceira, 2001).

While they do not play down these shift effects, many authors cite Baumol's disease also as a primary cause of stagnant labor compensation per worker. One of the most prominent explanations of Baumol's disease in this regard is trade (Brauer and Hickok, 1995). The trade effect is induced by increased exports from developing countries, which compete with manufacturing jobs held by less skilled domestic labor, depressing its wages.[7] Indeed, since the 1980s there has been a wholesale shift of employment into services. BEA data show that in 1980, manufacturing jobs comprised 14.1 percent of the workforce. In contrast, by 2000 manufacturing's share of employment had reduced to 11.4 percent. At the same time, the service industries took up even more than the slack in the economy left by manufacturing's decline, growing from a share of 70.2 percent of the U.S. economy in 1980 to 79.2 percent in 2000. Although some of the service jobs created were in high-paying services, evidence suggests that the many low-paying, part-time retail jobs likely dominated the share effects.

In an interview (Foley, 1998), Leontief stated that, when the demand for labor approaches the economy's "minimum tolerable limit," household-level social problems crop up with greater frequency within that economy. Hence, according to Leontief, "it would be very interesting to see how modern technological change has affected the demand for labor" (Foley, 1998, p. 127). In this contribution we will follow up this suggestion, although our primary interest concerns trends in compensation for labor and its relation to productivity growth rather than demand for labor per se. Leontief's analytical input-output framework seems a natural choice to analyze the relative contributions of shift effects and share effects as put forward as potential causes of changes in the main determinants of labor compensation's share in GDP (labor productivity growth and wage rate dynamics).

So, did shareholders and capital benefit from enhanced productivity at the expense of US workers during the 1990s? Or is it simply that the US economy is divesting into industries that are more laden with property-type income than labor compensation? Did technological change (in terms of changes in the labor input and intermediate input coefficients) continue to play a role, as Leontief might suppose? Could a major change in the structure of US final demand be a cause?

---

[7] Brauer and Hickok (1995) also contend that the shift to services may well have played a part in decelerating the demand for college-educated workers and in the decline in union membership, thus making it difficult to disentangle them from the symptoms of Baumol's disease.

3.   Methodological aspects of structural decompositions

Structural decompositions aim at breaking up the change in a variable into changes in its constituent parts, with the object of making the variable more readily understood. In input-output economics, decomposition formulae typically have an additive form. The simplest example of such a decomposition is where the change in the value of a basket of goods is split into the effect of price changes of the goods and the effect of quantity changes of the goods in the basket. If we denote the value at time 0 as $v(0)$ and the price and quantity of the goods as $p_i(0)$ and $q_i(0)$, we have $v(0) = \Sigma_i\, p_i(0)q_i(0)$, or in matrix terms $v(0) = \mathbf{p}(0)'\mathbf{q}(0)$. Vectors are columns by definition and a prime is used to indicate transposition. The additive decomposition forms would be given by

$$v(1) - v(0) = [\mathbf{p}(1)'\mathbf{q}(1) - \mathbf{p}(0)'\mathbf{q}(1)] + [\mathbf{p}(0)'\mathbf{q}(1) - \mathbf{p}(0)'\mathbf{q}(0)]$$
$$(1)$$

$$= [\mathbf{p}(1)'\mathbf{q}(0) - \mathbf{p}(0)'\mathbf{q}(0)] + [\mathbf{p}(1)'\mathbf{q}(1) - \mathbf{p}(1)'\mathbf{q}(0)]$$
$$(2)$$

The term between the first brackets indicates the value change due to price changes, using the quantities in period 1 as weights in (1) and those of period 0 in (2). Similarly, the term between the second brackets gives the value change caused by quantity changes with prices of period 0 as weights in (1) and those of period 1 in (2). Because there is, a priori, no reason why one form should be preferred to the other, typically the arithmetic average is used. That is,

$$v(1) - v(0) = 0.5[\mathbf{p}(1) - \mathbf{p}(0)]'[\mathbf{q}(0) + \mathbf{q}(1)]$$
$$+ 0.5[\mathbf{p}(0) + \mathbf{p}(1)]'[\mathbf{q}(1) - \mathbf{q}(0)]$$
$$= 0.5(\Delta\mathbf{p})'[\mathbf{q}(0) + \mathbf{q}(1)] + 0.5[\mathbf{p}(0) + \mathbf{p}(1)]'(\Delta\mathbf{q})$$
$$(3)$$

In the present paper we use multiplicative decomposition forms (see Dietzenbacher et al., 2000) that are more in line with the theory of index numbers. In the example above, instead of decomposing the absolute difference in the values, the relative change in the values is examined. Similar to equations (1) and (2), we now have

$$\frac{v(1)}{v(0)} = \frac{\mathbf{p}(1)'\mathbf{q}(1)}{\mathbf{p}(0)'\mathbf{q}(1)}\frac{\mathbf{p}(0)'\mathbf{q}(1)}{\mathbf{p}(0)'\mathbf{q}(0)}$$
$$(4)$$

$$= \frac{\mathbf{p}(1)'\mathbf{q}(0)}{\mathbf{p}(0)'\mathbf{q}(0)}\frac{\mathbf{p}(1)'\mathbf{q}(1)}{\mathbf{p}(1)'\mathbf{q}(0)}$$
$$(5)$$

Note that the first factor on the right-hand side of equation (4) equals the Paasche price index, while the second factor gives the Laspeyres quantity index. Similarly, the first factor in (5) is the Laspeyres price index and the second factor is the Paasche quantity index. As in (3), we take the average of the two decompositions. For additive cases the arithmetic average is commonly used; its equivalent for multiplicative cases is the geometric average. This yields

$$\frac{v(1)}{v(0)} = \left(\frac{\mathbf{p}(1)'\mathbf{q}(1)}{\mathbf{p}(0)'\mathbf{q}(1)}\frac{\mathbf{p}(1)'\mathbf{q}(0)}{\mathbf{p}(0)'\mathbf{q}(0)}\right)^{0.5} \left(\frac{\mathbf{p}(0)'\mathbf{q}(1)}{\mathbf{p}(0)'\mathbf{q}(0)}\frac{\mathbf{p}(1)'\mathbf{q}(1)}{\mathbf{p}(1)'\mathbf{q}(0)}\right)^{0.5}$$

(6)

The first factor on the right-hand side is the Fisher price index, and the second factor is the Fisher quantity index.

As is well known, Fisher indexes satisfy certain desirable properties, of which we discuss three. First, the factor reversal test requires that, if the price index is multiplied by the quantity index, the value index – i.e. $v(1)/v(0)$ – is obtained. Equation (6) immediately shows that this holds for the Fisher indexes – in contrast to the Laspeyres or the Paasche indexes, for example. Second, the time reversal test requires that the index for period 1 with period 0 as its base multiplied with its reverse (i.e. the same index for period 0 with period 1 as its base) equals one. If we take the Fisher price index – i.e. the first factor in (6) – as an example, we have to multiply it with the index that is obtained by replacing all 0s by 1s (and vice versa). It is easily seen that this yields 1. Again, in contrast to the Fisher indexes, the Laspeyres and the Paasche indexes do not satisfy the time reversal test. Third, the test for symmetry requires that the price index becomes the corresponding quantity index, once $\mathbf{p}(1)$ and $\mathbf{p}(0)$ are replaced by $\mathbf{q}(1)$ and $\mathbf{q}(0)$ respectively, and vice versa. The Laspeyres, the Paasche and the Fisher indexes all satisfy this test for symmetry.

The discussion above, where the value change has been decomposed into a component reflecting the effect of price changes and another component indicative of the quantity changes, presents an example of the simplest possible decomposition. That is, it is a decomposition where the variable under consideration (i.e. the value of a basket of goods) is determined by just two underlying factors (namely prices and quantities of the goods). In most structural decomposition studies in input-output economics, the variable under consideration is determined by a much larger number of factors. This also increases the number of possible decomposition forms tremendously. The forms that have been used the most are the so-called "polar" decompositions (see Dietzenbacher and Los, 1998). For the ease of exposition, suppose the change in the scalar z is to be decomposed into its three constituent parts, based on $z = \mathbf{a}'\mathbf{Bc}$, where $\mathbf{a}$ and $\mathbf{c}$ are vectors and $\mathbf{B}$ is a matrix. The two polar decompositions in a multiplicative format are as follows.

$$\frac{z(1)}{z(0)} = \frac{\mathbf{a}(1)'\mathbf{B}(1)\mathbf{c}(1)}{\mathbf{a}(0)'\mathbf{B}(1)\mathbf{c}(1)} \frac{\mathbf{a}(0)'\mathbf{B}(1)\mathbf{c}(1)}{\mathbf{a}(0)'\mathbf{B}(0)\mathbf{c}(1)} \frac{\mathbf{a}(0)'\mathbf{B}(0)\mathbf{c}(1)}{\mathbf{a}(0)'\mathbf{B}(0)\mathbf{c}(0)} \tag{7}$$

$$= \frac{\mathbf{a}(1)'\mathbf{B}(0)\mathbf{c}(0)}{\mathbf{a}(0)'\mathbf{B}(0)\mathbf{c}(0)} \frac{\mathbf{a}(1)'\mathbf{B}(1)\mathbf{c}(0)}{\mathbf{a}(1)'\mathbf{B}(0)\mathbf{c}(0)} \frac{\mathbf{a}(1)'\mathbf{B}(1)\mathbf{c}(1)}{\mathbf{a}(1)'\mathbf{B}(1)\mathbf{c}(0)} \tag{8}$$

Note that the polar decomposition in equation (7) can be viewed as an approach "from left to right". That is, starting from $z(1) = \mathbf{a}(1)'\mathbf{B}(1)\mathbf{c}(1)$, first change $\mathbf{a}(1)'$ into $\mathbf{a}(0)'$, next change $\mathbf{B}(1)$ into $\mathbf{B}(0)$, and finally change $\mathbf{c}(1)$ into $\mathbf{c}(0)$. The decomposition in (8) reflects an approach "from right to left", where first $\mathbf{c}$ is changed, then $\mathbf{B}$ and finally $\mathbf{a}'$.

Just as we did with the forms in (4) and (5), we again take the geometric average, which yields the Fisher type of indexes.

$$\frac{z(1)}{z(0)} = \left(\frac{\mathbf{a}(1)'\mathbf{B}(1)\mathbf{c}(1)}{\mathbf{a}(0)'\mathbf{B}(1)\mathbf{c}(1)} \frac{\mathbf{a}(1)'\mathbf{B}(0)\mathbf{c}(0)}{\mathbf{a}(0)'\mathbf{B}(0)\mathbf{c}(0)} \right)^{0.5}$$

$$\times \left(\frac{\mathbf{a}(0)'\mathbf{B}(1)\mathbf{c}(1)}{\mathbf{a}(0)'\mathbf{B}(0)\mathbf{c}(1)} \frac{\mathbf{a}(1)'\mathbf{B}(1)\mathbf{c}(0)}{\mathbf{a}(1)'\mathbf{B}(0)\mathbf{c}(0)} \right)^{0.5}$$

$$\times \left(\frac{\mathbf{a}(0)'\mathbf{B}(0)\mathbf{c}(1)}{\mathbf{a}(0)'\mathbf{B}(0)\mathbf{c}(0)} \frac{\mathbf{a}(1)'\mathbf{B}(1)\mathbf{c}(1)}{\mathbf{a}(1)'\mathbf{B}(1)\mathbf{c}(0)} \right)^{0.5} \tag{9}$$

The first factor on the right-hand side, which we call the $\mathbf{a}$-index, reflects the change in z brought about by the change in the vector $\mathbf{a}$. Similarly, the second and third factors indicate the change in z due to the change in the matrix $\mathbf{B}$ and vector $\mathbf{c}$ respectively. They will be termed the $\mathbf{B}$-index and the $\mathbf{c}$-index.

Note that these indexes satisfy the factor reversal and the time reversal test. The factor reversal test requires that the $\mathbf{a}$-index multiplied by the $\mathbf{B}$-index and by the $\mathbf{c}$-index equals $z(1)/z(0)$, which is exactly what equation (9) expresses. The $\mathbf{a}$-index above is the index for period 1 with period 0 as its base. Replacing the 0s by 1s, and vice versa, yields the $\mathbf{a}$-index for period 0 with period 1 as its base. The time reversal test requires that if these two different $\mathbf{a}$-indexes are multiplied the answer should be equal to 1, which is easily seen to hold. The test for symmetry needs to be extended first. For example, we say that the $\mathbf{a}$-index is symmetric to the $\mathbf{B}$-index if replacing $\mathbf{a}(1)'$ and $\mathbf{a}(0)'$ by $\mathbf{B}(1)$ and $\mathbf{B}(0)$ respectively, and vice versa, turns the $\mathbf{a}$-index into the $\mathbf{B}$-index (and vice versa). It readily follows that the **B**-index is not symmetric to another index. The **a**- and **c**-indexes, however, are symmetric.

In the general case, the variable z is considered to be the multiplication of k parts. That is $z = \mathbf{x}_1\mathbf{x}_2 \ldots \mathbf{x}_k$, where each of the components may be a scalar, vector or matrix. The $\mathbf{x}_i$-index (with $i = 1, \ldots, k$) obtained from taking the geometric average of the two polar decompositions yields in this case

$$\left(\frac{\mathbf{x}_1(1)\ldots\mathbf{x}_{i-1}(1)\mathbf{x}_i(1)\mathbf{x}_{i+1}(0)\ldots\mathbf{x}_k(0)\ \mathbf{x}_1(0)\ldots\mathbf{x}_{i-1}(0)\mathbf{x}_i(1)\mathbf{x}_{i+1}(1)\ldots\mathbf{x}_k(1)}{\mathbf{x}_1(1)\ldots\mathbf{x}_{i-1}(1)\mathbf{x}_i(0)\mathbf{x}_{i+1}(0)\ldots\mathbf{x}_k(0)\ \mathbf{x}_1(0)\ldots\mathbf{x}_{i-1}(0)\mathbf{x}_i(0)\mathbf{x}_{i+1}(1)\ldots\mathbf{x}_k(1)} \right)^{0.5}$$

(10)

Again, the $\mathbf{x}_i$-indexes satisfy the factor reversal and time reversal tests, while the $\mathbf{x}_1$-index and the $\mathbf{x}_k$-index are also symmetric.

The discussion above provides some theoretical foundation for using the Fisher type of indexes in a decomposition study. An empirical motivation for using this type of index is given by Dietzenbacher and Los (1998). The Fisher type of index is derived from averaging the two polar decompositions, obtained from the "left to right" and the "right to left" approach. There is no a priori reason, however, why the sequence of changes need to be ordered in this way. For example, it is also possible that first **B** is changed, after which **c** is changed, while **a**' is changed last. This ordering would yield

$$\frac{z(1)}{z(0)} = \frac{\mathbf{a}(1)'\mathbf{B}(0)\mathbf{c}(0)}{\mathbf{a}(0)'\mathbf{B}(0)\mathbf{c}(0)} \frac{\mathbf{a}(1)'\mathbf{B}(1)\mathbf{c}(1)}{\mathbf{a}(1)'\mathbf{B}(0)\mathbf{c}(1)} \frac{\mathbf{a}(1)'\mathbf{B}(0)\mathbf{c}(1)}{\mathbf{a}(1)'\mathbf{B}(0)\mathbf{c}(0)}$$

Hence, in the case of k determinants this would lead to $k!$ equally plausible decomposition forms. Dietzenbacher and Los (1998) examined all these forms for an additive decomposition and found that the arithmetic average of the two additive polar decomposition forms was extremely close to the average of all $k!$ decomposition forms. In empirical studies, it thus seems justified to consider the average of the two polar decompositions, instead of the average of all $k!$ decompositions.

4.   Decomposing labor compensation's share of value added

This section presents the decomposition forms that will be applied later to US input-output tables. The definitions, all for industry i, are:

v_i = value added (in 1996 dollars);

w_i = labor compensation (in 1996 dollars);

l_i = labor inputs (in hours worked);

$\pi_i = v_i/l_i$ = labor productivity;

$\alpha_i = w_i/l_i$ = compensation per hour worked;

$\lambda_i = l_i/x_i$ = hours worked per 1996 dollar of gross output;

$\sigma_i = w_i/v_i$ = labor compensation's share of value added.

The totals are obtained by summation, i.e. $v = \Sigma_i v_i$, $w = \Sigma_i w_i$ and $l = \Sigma_i l_i$, while the economy-wide ratios are obtained as the ratios of the totals, i.e. $\pi = v/l$, $\alpha = w/l$ and $\sigma = w/v$. Our aim is to decompose the overall labor compensation's share of value added. That is,

$$\sigma = \frac{w}{v} = \frac{w/l}{v/l} = \frac{\alpha}{\pi} \tag{11}$$

The numerator gives the overall compensation per hour worked and can be written as

$$\alpha = \frac{w}{l} = \frac{\alpha'\hat{\lambda}\mathbf{x}}{\lambda'\mathbf{x}} = \alpha's$$

so that the overall ratio α is the weighted average of the industry ratios α_i. The vector of weights is given by $\mathbf{s} = (\hat{\lambda}\mathbf{x})/(\lambda'\mathbf{x})$, where s_i denotes the industry's labor input as a share of the total labor inputs (i.e. $s_i = \lambda_i x_i/\Sigma_i \lambda_i x_i = l_i/\Sigma_i l_i$) and where a circumflex or hat, $\hat{}$, over a variable denotes a diagonal matrix, in this case with the vector λ on the diagonal and zeros elsewhere. Further, $\mathbf{x} = (\mathbf{I} - \mathbf{A})^{-1}\mathbf{f} \equiv \mathbf{Lf}$, where $\mathbf{A}$ denotes the matrix of input coefficients, $\mathbf{f}$ the final demand vector, and $\mathbf{L} = (\mathbf{I} - \mathbf{A})^{-1}$ – the Leontief inverse. Substitution yields

$$\alpha = \frac{\alpha'\hat{\lambda}\mathbf{Lf}}{e'\hat{\lambda}\mathbf{Lf}}$$

where e' denotes the row summation vector, i.e. $(1, \ldots, 1)$. In the same way we find that the denominator in (11) – i.e. the overall labor productivity – can be written as

$$\pi = \frac{v}{l} = \frac{\pi'\hat{\lambda}\mathbf{x}}{\lambda'\mathbf{x}} = \pi's = \frac{\pi'\hat{\lambda}\mathbf{Lf}}{e'\hat{\lambda}\mathbf{Lf}}$$

The overall labor productivity is the weighted average of industry labor productivities, again using industry labor input shares (in total labor inputs) as weights. This implies for the ratio of aggregate labor compensation to value added

$$\sigma = \frac{w}{v} = \frac{\alpha'\hat{\lambda}\mathbf{Lf}}{\pi'\hat{\lambda}\mathbf{Lf}}$$

The two polar decompositions now yield that σ_1/σ_0 equals

$$
\left(\frac{\alpha_1'\hat{\lambda}_1 L_1 f_1}{\alpha_0'\hat{\lambda}_1 L_1 f_1}\right)\left(\frac{\pi_0'\hat{\lambda}_1 L_1 f_1}{\pi_1'\hat{\lambda}_1 L_1 f_1}\right)\left(\frac{\alpha_0'\hat{\lambda}_1 L_1 f_1}{\alpha_0'\hat{\lambda}_0 L_1 f_1}\,\frac{\pi_0'\hat{\lambda}_0 L_1 f_1}{\pi_0'\hat{\lambda}_1 L_1 f_1}\right)
$$

$$
\times\left(\frac{\alpha_0'\hat{\lambda}_0 L_1 f_1}{\alpha_0'\hat{\lambda}_0 L_0 f_1}\,\frac{\pi_0'\hat{\lambda}_0 L_0 f_1}{\pi_0'\hat{\lambda}_0 L_1 f_1}\right)\left(\frac{\alpha_0'\hat{\lambda}_0 L_0 f_1}{\alpha_0'\hat{\lambda}_0 L_0 f_0}\,\frac{\pi_0'\hat{\lambda}_0 L_0 f_0}{\pi_0'\hat{\lambda}_0 L_0 f_1}\right)\qquad(12a)
$$

and

$$
\left(\frac{\alpha_1'\hat{\lambda}_0 L_0 f_0}{\alpha_0'\hat{\lambda}_0 L_0 f_0}\right)\left(\frac{\pi_0'\hat{\lambda}_0 L_0 f_0}{\pi_1'\hat{\lambda}_0 L_0 f_0}\right)\left(\frac{\alpha_1'\hat{\lambda}_1 L_0 f_0}{\alpha_1'\hat{\lambda}_0 L_0 f_0}\,\frac{\pi_1'\hat{\lambda}_0 L_0 f_0}{\pi_1'\hat{\lambda}_1 L_0 f_0}\right)
$$

$$
\times\left(\frac{\alpha_1'\hat{\lambda}_1 L_1 f_0}{\alpha_1'\hat{\lambda}_1 L_0 f_0}\,\frac{\pi_1'\hat{\lambda}_1 L_0 f_0}{\pi_1'\hat{\lambda}_1 L_1 f_0}\right)\left(\frac{\alpha_1'\hat{\lambda}_1 L_1 f_1}{\alpha_1'\hat{\lambda}_1 L_1 f_0}\,\frac{\pi_1'\hat{\lambda}_1 L_1 f_0}{\pi_1'\hat{\lambda}_1 L_1 f_1}\right)\qquad(12b)
$$

Each of the two polar decompositions breaks down the changes in the aggregate labor share into five effects. The five Fisher-type indexes are obtained by taking the geometric average of the two corresponding effects. Note that, in the polar decompositions, the first factor relates to changes in the real compensation per hour worked. The second factor indicates how labor productivity changes affect the aggregate labor share. The first two factors together are the shift effects, as discussed in section 2. The other three factors relate to changes in economic structure and together form the share effects. These three factors are: changes in the labor input coefficients; changes in the intermediate input coefficients; and changes in the final demands. The third and fourth factors reflect technological changes in the production structure. The fifth factor covers changes in the preferences of consumers. Note that the last two terms are common determinants in SDAs.

An important and frequently neglected aspect in structural decompositions is that it is (often only implicitly) assumed that the determinants are independent of each other. For example, the first factor in the polar decompositions above measures what the effects would have been of the industry changes in the real compensation per hour worked had all other variables (i.e. λ, π, L and f) remained constant. In a study of the effects of such dependencies, Dietzenbacher and Los (2000) distinguish between "full" and "general" dependency. Full dependency occurs when some determinants are restricted by identities; as a consequence, it is for such a determinant impossible to change its value without changing the value of another determinant. A much weaker form is general dependency, where a binding constraint holds for the set of determinants plus some additional variables.

In the present case there are no binding definitions between the determinants, so full dependency does not apply. General dependency, however, does apply for the present decomposition. Note that the real rate of labor compensation $\alpha_i = w_i/l_i$ is included in labor productivity $\pi_i = v_i/l_i$, the difference between v_i and w_i being all unearned income in industry i. So, an increase in labor productivity will induce an increase in the real rate of labor compensation and/or unearned income per hour worked. The relationship between the variables is that $\lambda_i(\pi_i - \alpha_i)$ equals the share of unearned income in the gross output value. This implies that it is possible to change, for example, λ_i, whereas π_i and α_i remain constant. Implicitly it is then assumed that an increase in λ_i is accompanied by an increase in the unearned income. So, there is a binding constraint between the determinants λ_i, π_i and α_i, and the variable unearned income per unit of gross output. Another constraint is that $1 - (\lambda_i\pi_i)$ equals imports per unit of gross output.

Dietzenbacher and Los (2000) provide suggestions for tackling problems of full and general dependencies. Using a relatively simple decomposition, they show how dependencies can be taken into account by making an explicit assumption about how a change in some determinant changes another determinant. The present decomposition is much more complex, however, and applying this approach would involve too many such "behavioral" assumptions, some probably disputable. Since the more serious case of full dependency does not occur in the present decomposition, we have chosen not to correct for the existing general dependency. Indeed, the remedy may well be worse.

So far we have examined the decomposition of the share of value added claimed by labor compensation economy-wide. Similar results are obtained when we are interested in the contributions to labor share changes for a group of aggregated industries (say all manufacturing industries taken together, or all service industries consolidated). To this end, we define the following aggregation vector $\mathbf{g}' = (1, \ldots, 1, 0, \ldots, 0)$, or

$$g_i = \begin{cases} 1 & \text{if } i \text{ is part of the aggregate industry} \\ 0 & \text{if } i \text{ is not part of the aggregate industry} \end{cases}$$

For the compensation per hour worked in the aggregate industry I, we then obtain

$$\alpha_I = \frac{\mathbf{g}'\hat{\alpha}\hat{\lambda}\mathbf{Lf}}{\mathbf{g}'\hat{\lambda}\mathbf{Lf}} = \mathbf{g}'\hat{\alpha}\mathbf{s}$$

where $\mathbf{s} = \hat{\lambda}\mathbf{x}/(\mathbf{g}'\hat{\lambda}\mathbf{x})$. Similarly, for the labor productivity

$$\pi_I = \frac{\mathbf{g}'\hat{\pi}\hat{\lambda}\mathbf{Lf}}{\mathbf{g}'\hat{\lambda}\mathbf{Lf}} = \mathbf{g}'\hat{\pi}\mathbf{s}$$

and $\sigma_I = \alpha_I / \pi_I$. The rest of the analysis is parallel to the analysis for the changes in the overall labor share in value added.

5.   Description of the data used

To pursue the approach described in the previous section we elected to use a recent series of US national input-output tables. In particular, we decided to analyze the falling share of labor compensation in national income with the benchmark tables for 1982, 1987 and 1992, produced by the BEA. We also opted to use the BEA's 1997 annual table to this series in lieu of the impending benchmark table for that same year. We aggregated the BEA's benchmark and annual tables to the same set of 498 industries. While other US interindustry tables exist for intermediate years, the benchmark tables alone are based upon technology gathered from industry census data.[8]

A problem with performing decomposition analyses using interindustry tables is that their cell values are in terms of the nominal value of shipments. It is a problem because changes in interindustry coefficients can reflect price changes, quantity changes, or both. Therefore, in order to isolate quantity changes, we ought to have values in the interindustry tables in constant value terms.

Fortunately, the BLS has a series of annual input-output accounts in constant value terms (at present in 1996 dollars) for the years 1983 to 1998. The problem with using these BLS accounts alone is that the technology inherent in the interindustry portion of them is strictly that from the 1992 BEA benchmark table. That is, the annual real margins of the BLS tables (the final demands, imports, value added and output accounts) along with the 1992 BEA Make and Use tables were employed by the BLS to produce their constant dollar series of industry-by-industry input-output accounts (Chentrens and Andreassean, 2001). In any case, we used the annual real margins of the BLS tables as inputs in a procedure to obtain constant price tables that reflect changes in the interindustry structure as derived from the census-based BEA tables.

Before we could start an aggregation procedure to make the BEA and BLS tables as similar as possible concerning their industry classifications, both sets of tables had to be domesticated. That is, the tables needed to be adapted so that the interindustry deliveries only included deliveries from domestic suppliers. Such a domestication procedure is required because one of our aims was to identify the extent to which changes in the intermediate input mixes and the composition of final demand affected labor

---

[8] Planting and Guo (2004) discuss in more detail how the BEA annual tables are constructed.

compensation's share in US GDP between 1982 and 1997. These effects should be measured properly, i.e. changes in the employment levels of foreign sectors should not be taken into account. Implicitly, our decomposition results would have reflected such changes in foreign economies if we had not domesticated the US tables.

The domesticated industry-by-industry accounts were produced using techniques described in Jackson (1998) and Lahr (2001).[9] That is, the industry-by-industry transactions matrix, $\mathbf{Z}$, was produced as follows.

$$\mathbf{Z} = \mathbf{D}\hat{\rho}\mathbf{U}$$

where $\mathbf{D}$ is the Make technology matrix; $\mathbf{U}$ is the Use matrix; and ρ is the domestication vector. Its typical element is given by $\rho_i = (q_i - t_i)/(q_i - t_i + m_i)$, where q_i is the gross output of commodity i; t_i are the exports of commodity i; and m_i are the imports of commodity i. The Make technology matrix is defined by

$$\mathbf{D} = \mathbf{V}\hat{\mathbf{q}}^{-1}$$

where $\mathbf{V}$ is the Make matrix.

Next we adapted both sets of domesticated tables to arrive at a common industry classification. Our starting point was the set of BLS input-output accounts, which are (in comparison to our 498-industry consolidation of BEA accounts) rather aggregated. They distinguish 192 industries, including government. We reduced the 192 industries to 180 by eliminating (1) four industries not included in the BEA tables,[10] (2) six non-enterprise government industries, and (3) two industries (Royalties and Owner-occupied dwellings) that had no labor, making them invalid for this exercise. Some BLS industries were aggregated only because they were more detailed than those in the BEA table.[11] We further reduced the number of industries because of an incompatibility between the utility industries in the two sets of tables. Because of this, we

---

[9] In the United States, comparable imports are available only by commodity discharged. In other countries where more information may be available on imports alternative approaches to domestication should be undertaken. For example, some countries publish a vector of imports by using industry as well as the vector of commodities imported. Others provide a full matrix of imports that indicates what commodity is imported and what industry used it.

[10] The four industries not in the BEA tables are Non-comparable imports; Scrap, used and second-hand goods; Rest of the world industry; and Inventory valuation adjustment.

[11] The BEA table contains only two government enterprise industries: one for local and state governments and one for the federal government. From this action, five BLS industries became two.

aggregated three more BLS industries to make one in the final table.[12] By this set of procedures we wound up with 175 industries for our analysis.

We subsequently aggregated the BEA tables so that they were compatible with the BLS tables, to be able to employ the latter's (constant dollar) margin accounts to produce BEA tables in real terms. These BLS industry-based margins were obtained by calculating the respective industry-by-industry transactions matrix for each set of BLS tables that we opted to use. We then summed across the rows and columns of each to obtain total intermediate industry-based inputs and outputs. Like Dietzenbacher and Hoen (1998, and 1999), we used the RAS technique to "deflate" the aggregated BEA tables into the constant 1996 US dollars used in the BLS tables.[13]

After applying RAS we calculated final demand by industry as the difference between the BLS-provided industry-based output and the intermediate outputs in the inflation-adjusted BEA matrices. Real value added for these tables was estimated as the difference between the BLS-provided industry-based output and the sum of intermediate inputs that resulted from the inflation-adjusted BEA tables and imports by using industry (μ), which we derived from the real BLS tables as follows

$$\mu' = (e - \rho)'U$$

For our decomposition analysis we required additional data for employment and labor income, at the same 175-industry level. The BLS accounts also include estimates of employment (in terms of hours worked) by industry for each year. The only account that we used that was not provided within the context of the BLS's or BEA's input-output accounts were those for labor income. We produced them using techniques similar to those described by Lahr (2001) for regions. That is, for a given year, estimates of detailed industry payrolls were obtained from the Bureau of Labor Statistics *ES202* data for unemployment-insurance-covered employment. These were then enhanced using nominal data on the compensation of employees by industry from more aggregate gross product accounts as follows

$$\left(\mathbf{w}_{earn}^{n}\right)' = \left(\mathbf{w}_{w\&s}^{n}\right)' * \left\{\left[\left(\mathbf{w}_{earn}^{p}\right)' \div \left[\left(\mathbf{w}_{w\&s}^{n}\right)'\mathbf{S}\right]\right]\mathbf{S}'\right\}$$

where $\mathbf{w}_{w\&s}^{n}$ is an n-vector of industry payroll; $\mathbf{w}_{earn}^{p}$ is the p-vector of labor compensation ($p < n$); and $\mathbf{S}$ is an n-by-p aggregation matrix

---

[12] Also we aggregated Combined utilities, Gas utilities and Electric utilities into a single Utilities industry, since no equivalent to Combined utilities existed in the BEA tables.

[13] In the case of the 1982 BEA table we applied 1983 BLS margins, understanding that this adjustment, while imprecise, was the best that could be done given the available data.

composed of 1s and 0s that appropriately maps the n industries into the p industries for which labor compensation is known. The symbols $*$ and $\div$ express element-by-element (i.e. Hadamard) multiplication and division respectively. We followed this by calculating labor compensation/output ratios in nominal terms. These same ratios were assumed to hold in real terms and were checked to make sure that they did not exceed BLS value added/output ratios except where expected (for example, in the public transit industry).

6.   Causes of labor's declining share of value added

6.1   *Decomposition of the aggregate economy*

Table 12.1 shows the aggregate results of our decomposition. The figures in the row labeled "Total" show that, by 1997, labor's share of value added for *non-government* sectors (which was 55.1 percent that year) had fallen to 88.7 percent of its 1982 share (which was 62.1 percent). This compares to BEA's measured modest decline from 59.1 to 56.0 percent (a decline in share of 3.1 percentage points) for *all* sectors, including government, for the same years. Further, since the value of "Total" is less than one for each successive period, we can gather that the decrease was a rather steady one over the entire study period, although the decline may have leveled off somewhat between 1987 and 1992 – a period when US wages were rising somewhat more steeply compared to other portions of the last two decades.

On the whole, the components of the two polar decompositions provide similar findings. That is, the effects obtained from using equation (12a) – indicated by subscript a in table 12.1 – point in the same direction as those obtained from using equation (12b) – with subscript b in table 12.1. Notable exceptions are found for the effects of the final demand changes that conflict with regard to the general direction of the effect. They concur that final demand changes (which include changes in consumers' preferences and real consumption growth) provided little impetus for change in labor compensation's share of value added. Because of the conflicting directions, the Fisher index shows that final demand changes have a negligible effect when the whole period is considered.

The remaining components demonstrate stronger similarities across the two decompositions in equations (12a) and (12b). Because of this, we confine the balance of the discussion of our results for the entire economy to the Fisher index only.

Did changes in input coefficients influence labor compensation's share in value added? It seems that the intermediate input coefficient changes

Table 12.1 *Decomposition of labor compensation's share of value added for the aggregate US economy, 1982–1997*

	1982–1997	1982–1987	1987–1992	1992–1997
Total	88.69	94.86	98.94	94.50
Indexes				
α_a	104.81	99.31	106.09	101.08
π_a	81.71	94.53	92.38	91.61
λ_a	101.10	99.83	101.08	101.12
L_a	101.58	100.79	100.08	100.77
f_a	100.84	100.44	99.79	100.15
α_b	111.55	100.88	106.78	102.07
π_b	75.48	92.64	91.72	90.86
λ_b	104.15	100.17	101.38	101.70
L_b	102.05	101.13	100.13	100.69
f_b	99.11	100.20	99.52	99.50
Fisher indexes				
α	108.13	100.09	106.43	101.57
π	78.54	93.58	92.05	91.24
λ	102.61	100.00	101.23	101.41
L	101.81	100.96	100.10	100.73
f	99.97	100.32	99.66	99.82

Note: Indexes with subscript *a* are obtained from equation (12a) and those with subscript *b* from equation (12b), and the Fisher indexes are obtained as their geometric average.

consistently had a positive effect on the labor share of value added over the period of study. Its influence seems to have been not so strong, however – on the order of only 0.1 percent annually – over the entire study period. This influence was somewhat larger in the beginning and at the end, but was virtually non-existent between 1987 and 1992. The effects of the changes in the labor input coefficients are somewhat larger than those for the intermediate input coefficients; almost 0.2 percent annually over the whole period. The effects are absent in the first subperiod, and increase to an annual 0.3 percent in the last subperiod. Yet the effects of changes in the input coefficients (often referred to as technical changes) are only very modest. This finding might have disappointed Professor Leontief.

It is clear that changes in the final demands and changes in the input coefficients have had relatively little effect. On average, the share effects – i.e. the three components together – caused labor's share in value added to grow by 0.3 percent annually over the whole period. At first glance this finding may seem to be somewhat surprising, because in many structural decomposition analyses the final demand effects in particular are typically found to be dominant. Most SDAs, however, deal with changes in levels of a single variable instead of changes in ratios of two variables. To our knowledge, the decomposition of changes in labor productivity (i.e. the ratio of value added to employment) by Dietzenbacher et al. (2000) is the only other decomposition study of changes in ratios so far. In their paper, they also found very limited contributions from share effects. Apparently, employment shares of industries with low labor compensation shares in value added did not systematically grow at the cost of employment shares of high labor compensation industries, or the other way round. This result is not overturned by the steady decline of manufacturing's employment share and the corresponding rise of services' employment share. Manufacturing and, in particular, services are very heterogeneous aggregates with respect to labor compensation's shares in value added.

For all industries together, enhanced industry labor productivities (i.e. the second term) have exerted considerable downward pressure on compensation's share of value added, at an average annual rate of 1.4 percent from 1982 to 1997. Indeed, labor productivity's negative influence accelerated during each successive subperiod: from 1982 to 1987 it exerted a downward influence on the order of 1.3 percent annually; from 1987 to 1992 the influence was 1.6 percent annually; and from 1992 to 1997 it was 1.8 percent annually. This term's influence is negative because labor productivity π forms the denominator of the ratio represented by compensation's share of value added (i.e. α/π).

The numerator of that ratio is real compensation per hour worked, α. Hence, it should not be surprising that, after labor productivity changes, changes in real hourly compensation is the next most influential variable on compensation's share of value added. The influence of changes in hourly compensation on the change in compensation's share of value added rose at a rate of 0.5 percent annually. Most of its influence was wielded during a period of wage inflation, just prior to the recession of the early 1990s (i.e. between 1987 and 1992), when it rose at a rate of 1.3 percent annually. During the five years immediately prior to that period there was no measurable effect from the hourly rate of compensation on compensation's share of value added. In the five years following 1992 it returned to a state of effective stagnation, growing at an annual 0.3 percent.

It is evident from the figures in table 12.1 that the labor productivity increases have only partially been translated into higher real compensation per hour worked. The negative effects of the increases in the industry labor productivities are clearly larger than the positive effects of increases in real hourly compensation by industry. If we multiply (and divide by 100) the indexes for α and π in table 12.1, we obtain the indexes for the shift effects. They are 84.93 for the whole period and 93.66, 97.97 and 92.67 respectively for the consecutive subperiods. Over the whole period, the positive effects of improvements in real hourly compensation on labor compensation's share in value added offset only 38 percent of the negative effects of labor productivity increases.

Our results clearly show that the shift effects have been dominant, whereas the share effects played only a minor role. This also follows from the findings for the separate polar decompositions. Comparing the results for equation (12a) – indicated by subscript a in table 12.1 – with those obtained from equation (12b) – with subscript b – yields the following. Applying 1997 industry shares to the changes in real hourly compensation by industry induced a larger increase in labor compensation's share of value added than did 1982 industry shares. In other words, the biggest changes in real hourly compensation tended to occur in industries that grew the most between 1982 and 1997. The same is true for labor productivity by industry, except that it effectively lowered labor compensation's share of value added. That is, using the 1997 shares as weights for the labor productivity changes generated larger effects on labor compensation's share of value added than did 1982 shares. So, the larger changes in both hourly compensation by industry and labor productivities took place in industries that became more important to the US economy during the study period. Importance in this respect is measured by the industry's share in total labor income.

6.2   Decomposition by major sector

The decompositions of the changes by major sectors (primary, manufacturing and service industries) were generally quite similar to the decomposition of the aggregate economy. There were some differences, however. If we compare the results in tables 12.2 to 12.4 for the three major sectors with those in table 12.1 for the aggregate economy, it follows that the effects are generally more pronounced. Considering the separate effects, this indicates that the three sectors did not affect labor compensation's share in the same direction. Some canceling out of effects took place, as the findings for the aggregate economy are an average. For example, in the period 1982 to 1997 final demand changes had a negative effect (i.e. an index smaller than 100) for primary and service industries, but a positive effect for manufacturing industries, so that there was a zero net effect for the aggregate economy.

Table 12.2 gives the results for primary industries. The behavior of these industries is quite erratic because it is motivated (dampened)

Table 12.2 *Decomposition of labor compensation's share of value added for US primary industries (including construction), 1982–1997*

	1982–1997	1982–1987	1987–1992	1992–1997
Total	117.53	121.79	98.94	97.53
Indexes				
α_a	233.01	175.58	115.76	116.15
π_a	50.49	73.60	86.19	79.92
λ_a	93.38	95.99	100.62	98.49
L_a	109.41	105.06	101.33	102.00
f_a	97.79	93.46	97.27	104.57
α_b	243.68	188.51	116.07	118.89
π_b	49.88	72.65	86.03	79.55
λ_b	95.97	97.66	99.89	98.81
L_b	106.10	102.64	101.56	101.27
f_b	94.96	88.73	97.66	103.07
Fisher indexes				
α	238.28	181.93	115.92	117.51
π	50.18	73.12	86.11	79.73
λ	94.66	96.82	100.26	98.65
L	107.74	103.84	101.44	101.63
f	96.36	91.07	97.47	103.82

Note: Indexes with subscript a are obtained from equation (12a) and those with subscript b from equation (12b), and the Fisher indexes are obtained as their geometric average.

by weather (agriculture) and labor disturbance (mining). The primary industries, therefore, are characterized by heavy cyclicity, which may not be well captured by an analysis undertaken at five-year intervals. In any event, table 12.2 shows that labor compensation actually improved its share of value added by 21.8 percent in primary industries between 1982 and 1987. Note that in our analysis it is the only sector in any subperiod to show any improvement. This sector's labor compensation's share of value added edged downward, however, during each subsequent five-year period.

Perhaps more significant is that structural components had a relatively strong effect on compensation's share in the primary industries. Final demand change had a particularly heavy negative effect upon compensation's share between 1982 and 1987. Its negative effect moderated somewhat between 1987 and 1992 and then actually gave a lift to compensation's share of value added between 1992 and 1997, essentially

Table 12.3 *Decomposition of labor compensation's share of value added for US manufacturing industries, 1982–1997*

	1982–1997	1982–1987	1987–1992	1992–1997
Total	76.36	87.43	97.88	89.23
Indexes				
α_a	118.06	101.59	109.22	107.10
π_a	63.81	85.05	90.25	82.62
λ_a	99.33	100.23	99.66	100.04
L_a	100.07	99.83	99.94	100.14
f_a	101.96	101.13	99.69	100.66
α_b	122.73	102.43	109.62	108.07
π_b	62.12	83.99	89.84	82.78
λ_b	100.73	100.37	100.10	100.31
L_b	99.04	100.10	99.86	99.58
f_b	100.39	101.14	99.43	99.85
Fisher indexes				
α	120.37	102.01	109.42	107.58
π	62.96	84.52	90.05	82.70
λ	100.03	100.30	99.88	100.17
L	99.56	99.97	99.90	99.86
f	101.17	101.14	99.56	100.26

Note: Indexes with subscript a are obtained from equation (12a) and those with subscript b from equation (12b), and the Fisher indexes are obtained as their geometric average.

compensating for the losses it caused during the preceding five years. Over the whole period the changes in labor input and in intermediate input coefficients also had quite substantial effects. Note, however, that the combined effects of these three structural changes – i.e. the share effects – were very modest (−0.1 percent annually between 1982 and 1997), just as they were for the aggregate economy (0.3 percent).

Hourly compensation and productivity generally had much stronger effects (−6.6 percent and 9.2 percent respectively on an annual basis) in the primary industries than in either of the other two major sectors. This phenomenon could be due to the retirement of marginally productive mines and agricultural land as the nation's less developed trade partners made some headway in the US market. In contrast to the other sectors, we find for the primary industries that labor productivity increases are more than compensated for by increases in real hourly compensation.

The results for the manufacturing and services industries (tables 12.3 and 12.4 respectively) had far fewer unique trends worth reporting. For

Table 12.4 *Decomposition of labor compensation's share of value added for US service industries, 1982–1997*

	1982–1997	1982–1987	1987–1992	1992–1997
Total	90.67	96.98	97.98	95.43
Indexes				
α_a	100.78	98.86	104.23	99.29
π_a	87.23	98.15	92.58	94.51
λ_a	101.09	99.14	101.31	100.99
L_a	101.82	100.89	100.05	100.87
f_a	100.21	99.92	100.16	99.83
α_b	105.47	99.61	104.83	100.05
π_b	82.19	96.94	91.76	93.84
λ_b	102.93	99.21	101.47	101.43
L_b	102.60	101.29	100.22	100.88
f_b	99.04	99.94	100.16	99.33
Fisher indexes				
α	103.10	99.24	104.53	99.67
π	84.67	97.54	92.17	94.18
λ	102.01	99.18	101.39	101.21
L	102.21	101.09	100.14	100.87
f	99.62	99.93	100.16	99.58

Note: Indexes with subscript a are obtained from equation (12a) and those with subscript b from equation (12b), and the Fisher indexes are obtained as their geometric average.

manufacturing, the most interesting new thing to be said is that the structural change components had even less influence on compensation's share of value added than they did for the aggregate economy. Indeed, they were all almost negligible. Another interesting aspect is that its labor productivity increases are the least compensated by increases in real hourly compensation. The combined annual effect on compensation's share of labor productivity and real hourly compensation changes (i.e. the shift effect) was −1.6 percent for manufacturing industries, −0.8 percent for service industries, 1.3 percent for primary industries and −1.0 percent for the aggregate economy.

In the case of the service industries, the productivity and hourly compensation components were the smallest of the three major sectors examined. Indeed, the share deteriorated by only 9.3 percent during the study period, compared to a fall of 23.6 percent for manufacturing industries and a net rise of 17.5 percent for the primary industries. Observe that the results for the service industries were by far the closest to the results for the aggregate economy. To a large extent this was because the services sector is the largest of the three and weighs heavily in the process of aggregation. This importance of the service industries held as early as 1982, but had become even stronger by 1997 due to a continued shift from manufacturing to services.

7.   Conclusion

Our major finding is that the share of unearned income in value added has been outpacing the share held by labor's compensation across more industries. The shift effects were found to be dominant, and the share effects were only very modest. The share effects, i.e. the combined effects of changes in the final demands (covering changes in the consumption and export patterns), changes in the intermediate input coefficients (which also includes changes in the industry mix) and changes in the labor input coefficients, have affected labor compensation's share in value added only slightly. So, structural changes and changes in industry mix were not the main causes for the decline in labor compensation's share in value added.

It was shift effects that primarily caused the decline. We probed these effects a bit further and observed that the industry labor productivity increases only partially translated into increases in real hourly compensation by industry. While our analysis cannot identify why this is so, we naturally can hypothesize that it can be any one or a combination of a number of factors. Examples of such factors are a decline of union membership, a strengthened mandate to get return to stockholders, and a recent trend toward the co-option of labor in the ownership of capital through retirement and mutual funds.

From prior decomposition analyses we might have expected the effects of intermediate input coefficient changes to be limited. Changes in labor input coefficients and, in particular, changes in the final demands, on the other hand, have frequently been found to be important determinants. Clearly, final demands and (labor and intermediate) input coefficients determine the weights that are used to obtain the aggregate share of labor compensation in value added from the industries' shares. Because the US economy continued to shift significantly from manufacturing to services during the study period, we were somewhat surprised by the very small share effects, and the effects of industry mix changes in particular, across all three major sectors of the economy.

REFERENCES

Baumol, W. J. (1967) Macroeconomics of unbalanced growth: the anatomy of urban crisis, *American Economic Review*, 57, 415–426.

Blackburn, M. L., D. E. Bloom and R. B. Freeman (1990) The declining economic position of less skilled American men, in G. Burtless (ed.) *A Future of Lousy Jobs* (Washington, DC, Brookings Institution), 31–67.

Blank, R. M. (1997) *It Takes a Nation: A New Agenda to Fight Poverty* (Princeton, NJ, Princeton University Press).

Borjas, G. J. (1995) The internationalization of the US labor market and the wage structure, *Federal Reserve Board of New York Economic Policy Review*, 1 (1), 3–8.

Bosworth, B. P., and G. L. Perry (1994) Productivity and real wages: is there a puzzle?, *Brookings Papers on Economic Activity 1*, 317–335.

Brauer, D. A., and S. Hickok (1995) Explaining the growing inequality in wages across skill levels, *Federal Reserve Board of New York Economic Policy Review*, 1 (1), 61–75.

Chentrens, C., and A. Andreassean (2001) *Employment Outlook 2000–2010: Layout and Description for 192-order Input-Output Tables – 1983–2000 Historical and Projected 2010*, unpublished document (Washington, DC, Office of Occupational Statistics and Employment Projections, Bureau of Labor Statistics). [Available on-line at www.bls.gov/emp/empind3.htm.]

Cobet, A. E., and G. A. Wilson (2002) Comparing 50 years of labor productivity in U.S. and foreign manufacturing, *Monthly Labor Review*, 125 (6), 51–65.

David, P. (1990) The dynamo and the computer: an historical perspective on the modern productivity paradox, *American Economic Review, Papers and Proceedings*, 80, 355–361.

Davis, S. J., and P. Willen (2000) *Occupation-level Income Shocks and Asset Return: Their Covariance and Implications for Portfolio Choice*, NBER Working Paper W7905 (Cambridge, MA, National Bureau of Economic Research).

Dietzenbacher, E., and A. R. Hoen (1998) Deflation of input-output tables from the user's point of view: a heuristic approach, *Review of Income and Wealth*, 44, 111–122.

(1999) Double deflation and aggregation, *Environment and Planning A*, 31, 1,695–1,704.

Dietzenbacher, E., A. R. Hoen and B. Los (2000) Labor productivity in Western Europe 1975–1985: an intercountry, interindustry comparison, *Journal of Regional Science*, 40, 425–452.

Dietzenbacher, E., and B. Los (1998) Structural decomposition techniques: sense and sensitivity, *Economic Systems Research*, 10, 307–323.

(2000) Structural decomposition with dependent determinants, *Economic Systems Research*, 12, 498–514.

DiNardo, J., N. M. Fortin and T. Lemieux (1996) Labor market institutions and the distribution of wages, 1973–1992: a semiparametric approach, *Econometrica*, 64, 1,001–1,044.

Foley, D. K. (1998) MD interview: an interview with Wassily Leontief, *Macro-economic Dynamics*, 2, 116–140.

Gordon, R. J. (1979) The end of expansion phenomenon in short-run productivity behavior, *Brookings Papers on Economic Activity 2*, 447–461.

Hulten, C. R. (1992) Growth accounting when technological change is embodied in capital, *American Economic Review*, 82, 964–980.

Jackson, R. W. (1998) Regionalizing national commodity-by-industry accounts, *Economic Systems Research*, 10, 223–238.

Jorgenson, D. W., and K. J. Stiroh (2000) Raising the speed limit: US economic growth in the information age, *Brookings Papers on Economic Activity 1*, 125–136.

Katz, L. F., and D. H. Autor (1999) Changes in the wage structure and earnings inequality, in O. Ashenfelter and D. Card (eds.) *Handbook of Labor Economics*, Vol. 3A (Amsterdam, North Holland), 1,463–1,555.

Kennickell, A. B., M. Starr-McCluer and B. J. Surrette (2000) Recent changes in U.S. family finances: results from the 1998 survey of consumer finances, *Federal Reserve Bulletin*, 83, 1–29.

Lahr, M. L. (2001) Reconciling domestication techniques, the notion of re-exports, and some comments on regional accounting, *Economic Systems Research*, 13, 165–179.

Leontief, W. W. (1941) *The Structure of American Economy, 1919–1929* (Cambridge, MA, Harvard University Press).

(1951) *The Structure of American Economy, 1919–1939: An Empirical Application of Equilibrium Analysis* (New York, Oxford University Press).

(1953) Domestic production and foreign trade: the American capital position re-examined, *Proceedings of the American Philosophical Society*, 97, 332–349.

(1956) Factor proportions and the structure of American trade: further theoretical and applied analysis, *Review of Economics and Statistics*, 38, 386–407.

(1965) Structure of the US economy, *Scientific American*, 212, 25–35.

Leontief, W. W., et al. (1953) *Studies in the Structure of the American Economy* (New York, Oxford University Press).

Levy, F., and R. J. Murnane (1992) US earnings levels and earnings inequality: a review of recent trends and proposed explanations, *Journal of Economic Literature*, 30, 1,333–1,381.

Neef, A., C. Kask and C. Sparks (1993) International comparisons of manufacturing unit labor costs, *Monthly Labor Review*, 116 (12), 47–58.

New York Stock Exchange (1985) *Shareownership 1985* (New York, New York Stock Exchange).

Oliner, S. D., and D. E. Sichel (2000) The resurgence of growth in the late 1990s: is information technology the story?, *Journal of Economic Perspectives*, 14 (4), 3–22.

Planting, M. A., and J. Guo (2004) Increasing the timeliness of US input-output accounts, *Economic Systems Research*, to be published.

Sparks, C., and M. Greiner (1997) US and foreign productivity and unit labor costs, *Monthly Labor Review*, 120 (2), 26–49.

Triplett, J. E., and B. P. Bosworth (2001) Productivity in the services sector, in R. M. Stern (ed.) *Services in the International Economy* (Ann Arbor, MI, University of Michigan Press), 23–52.

Viceira, L. (2001) Optimal portfolio choice for long-horizon investors with non-tradable labor income, *Journal of Finance*, 56, 433–470.

Wolff, E. N. (1996) The productivity slowdown: the culprit at last? A follow-up on Hulten and Wolff, *American Economic Review*, 86, 1,239–1,252.

13 An oligopoly model in a Leontief framework

Robert E. Kuenne

1. Introduction

The price dual in the Leontief input-output system has played the Cinderella role in practical applications of the model. This results largely from the necessity of using the US dollar as the homogeneous unit of aggregation for inputs and outputs of sectors containing quite diverse products. Prices are assumed fixed and are used, therefore, to convert naturally calibrated input coefficients to cents' worth of input per dollar's worth of output, effectively neutralizing the price dual as an analytical tool. The "dollar's worth" is a homogeneous physical unit for all goods as long as prices do not change. Of course, the choice of this unit masks the heterogeneity of the natural physical units of the sectoral outputs, given the wide variety of products aggregated in the sectors of even the largest input-output models. Constant prices are "virtual" prices of a conglomerate of disparate sectoral products. But, in empirical and theoretical applications of the output primal, the values of outputs and inputs are meaningful units in short-run periods of stable prices and product mixes. They are operationally interpretable.

This analytical device can be used only if the gross output primal model is independent of the price dual. Constant returns to scale, perfect complementarity of inputs in infinitely elastic supply, and exogenization of the bill of final goods achieve this prerequisite. Gross output vectors cannot affect prices and the "dollar's worth" metric of the output primal is defensible.

When we turn to effective usage of the price model, however, we must employ natural units of sectoral outputs, and aggregation effects become daunting. In empirical and theoretical work we must estimate the "virtual" output numbers from the empirically derived values of gross products, bills of goods and production coefficients. We cannot logically assume the existence of unambiguous natural units in the face of heterogeneous products in the sectors.

At a deeper level, however, we may identify another deficiency in the potential usage of the price dual to cope with the determination of market prices. Even were each sector to possess reasonably homogeneous outputs, the oligopolistic interactions among firms within each sector are eliminated by the effective assumption of short-run perfect competition. Leontief, like Walras before him, chose the industry as the unit of analysis, rather than the firm, or – more realistically – the dominant firms. Perfect competition was an aggregative tool in the production segment of their models. Of course, given the analytical ambition of their models and the necessity to focus on intersectoral interdependence, the simplification was a necessity, and their choices cannot be faulted. But, nonetheless, it does effectively eliminate the oligopoly-inspired interplay between prices, outputs and profits within the sectors, with concomitant deficiencies in the output solutions of the model as well as prices.

2.   The rivalrous consonance approach to oligopolistic decision-making

This paper will use the input-output framework to illustrate in a simplified way one form of oligopolistic decision-making that I have termed "rivalrous consonance" in previous publications.[1] In brief, this framework applies to mature oligopolies that have formed relatively stable communities with relations that are a mixture of the competitive and the cooperative. They have developed a power structure reflecting patterns of dominance and deference, leadership and followership, self-interest and group interest. In short, as in all human communities they have formed a group of tacit mores or a rivalrous consonance of interests, incorporating both competitive and cooperative behavior. The proactive and reactive patterns of conduct result in industry decision-making as a mixture of the harshly competitive and the tacitly collusive, and my hypothesis is that its structure can be at least partially captured in a set of consonance coefficients, which I will discuss below.

Within the last ten years or so economists have become increasingly interested in such ambivalent relations among oligopolistic rivals. The term "co-opetition" has been used to signify such relations,[2] which are formalized in agreements short of outright merger. These include: joint ventures; licensing technologies to rivals; alliances; risk-sharing partnerships in such areas as research and development; outsourcing; and joint

---

[1] See, most recently, Kuenne (1999) and the bibliography cited there.
[2] Brandenburger and Nalebuff (1996).The term was coined by Ray Noorda, founder of Novell.

sales of rivals' competing products with one's own. The pressures of globalization, the drive to concentrate on core competencies, the need to enhance flexibility in production and marketing, and the large amount of funds required in many industries to engage in research are driving forces behind these developments. Antitrust authorities have been permissive – and, indeed, encouraging – to such arrangements when they perceive them to be advantageous to consumers and to competition; they have frowned on them consistently when such joint ventures include marketing apparatus and agreements.

These arrangements may be viewed as recent extensions of rivalrous consonance, but I have used that term more narrowly to denote the tacit cooperation in price and non-price competition that tempers the former, as described above. It is the implications of these more informal but realistically pervasive arrangements that I seek to model within the limitations of the Leontief price dual in this paper. The more direct price implications of such behavior may be illustrated thereby, as well as the impacts of an endogenous bill of goods (final demand) on gross output.

3.   The rivalrous consonance model in the Leontief price dual context

I will make a primary distinction between industries that are oligopolistic in structure and those that may be treated as effectively workably competitive. In the former case, the dominant firms will be identified and each will be treated as a Leontief sector with input-output coefficients. Once prices are determined we will introduce them into demand functions for the output model's bill of final goods and determine the implied gross outputs for the sectors from that model. Of course, there is no causative feedback from the primal solutions to the price dual, given its independence after endogenizing the bill of goods. It follows, therefore, that in our treatment of rivalrous consonance we are accepting the Leontief elimination of output as a determinant of price, and hence limiting the general equilibrium aspects of the model. Moreover, such acceptance also means that we must sacrifice profit maximization behavior by the rival firms in the oligopoly.

In our presentation of the model we will assume one oligopolistic industry and aggregate all "competitive" industries into a single sector. The oligopolistic industry is assumed to have three dominant firms that warrant identification as sectors 1, 2 and 3, with the "all other" sector denoted as 4. Ideally we would like to assume the availability of the Leontief input-output matrix in natural (i.e. physical) units

$$
\mathbf{A}^* =
\begin{bmatrix}
a_{11}^* & a_{12}^* & a_{13}^* & a_{14}^* \\
a_{21}^* & a_{22}^* & a_{23}^* & a_{24}^* \\
a_{31}^* & a_{32}^* & a_{33}^* & a_{34}^* \\
a_{41}^* & a_{42}^* & a_{43}^* & a_{44}^*
\end{bmatrix}
$$

Of course, the practical problem is that we do not have this matrix, but rather must deal with the value-based matrix of input-output coefficients. Indeed, given the rather heterogeneous product mixes of the typical Leontief sector, it would be difficult to interpret $\mathbf{A}^*$ in other than index terms. For the present sectors, however (other than the "all other goods" sector 4), we have reasonably homogeneous units for products, and so would be able to escape the indexing problem, were the $\mathbf{A}^*$ elements available.

Because we need $\mathbf{A}^*$ for our treatment of oligopoly pricing, it will be necessary to estimate it from the value-based coefficients. The customary value basis is the matrix $\mathbf{A}$, which may be represented in a form that indicates its manner of estimation in the modeling to follow.

$$
\begin{aligned}
\mathbf{A} &=
\begin{bmatrix}
a_{11} & a_{12} & a_{13} & a_{14} \\
a_{21} & a_{22} & a_{23} & a_{24} \\
a_{31} & a_{32} & a_{33} & a_{34} \\
a_{41} & a_{42} & a_{43} & a_{44}
\end{bmatrix} \\
&=
\begin{bmatrix}
p_1 a_{11}^*/p_1 & p_1 a_{12}^*/p_2 & p_1 a_{13}^*/p_3 & p_1 a_{14}^*/p_4 \\
p_2 a_{21}^*/p_1 & p_2 a_{22}^*/p_2 & p_2 a_{23}^*/p_3 & p_2 a_{24}^*/p_4 \\
p_3 a_{31}^*/p_1 & p_3 a_{32}^*/p_2 & p_3 a_{33}^*/p_3 & p_3 a_{34}^*/p_4 \\
p_4 a_{41}^*/p_1 & p_4 a_{42}^*/p_2 & p_4 a_{43}^*/p_3 & p_4 a_{44}^*/p_4
\end{bmatrix}
\end{aligned}
\tag{1}
$$

The coefficients $a_{ij} = p_i a_{ij}^*/p_j$ meld price and quantities in dissoluble aggregates. The elusive prices that convert the natural units to the homogeneous dollar unit cannot be expected to be equilibrium prices, and in our modeling they will have to be converted to the sectoral solution prices of the model. That is, the a_{ij}^* will have to be estimated from the a_{ij} by multiplication by the ratios p_j/p_i deriving from our pricing algorithm. Hence, the impact of oligopolistic pricing policies will be effected in three paths of causation: by changing the estimated values of the a_{ij}^*; via the direct impacts of tacit collusion on prices; and by determining the quantities of the bill of goods and thereby the gross outputs in value units. Matrix $\mathbf{A}^{**}$ is the result of the estimation process

$$\mathbf{A}^{**} = \begin{bmatrix} a_{11}^{**} & a_{12}^{**} & a_{13}^{**} & a_{14}^{**} \\ a_{21}^{**} & a_{22}^{**} & a_{23}^{**} & a_{24}^{**} \\ a_{31}^{**} & a_{32}^{**} & a_{33}^{**} & a_{34}^{**} \\ a_{41}^{**} & a_{42}^{**} & a_{43}^{**} & a_{44}^{**} \end{bmatrix}$$

$$= \begin{bmatrix} p_1 a_{11}/p_1 & p_2 a_{12}/p_1 & p_3 a_{13}/p_1 & p_4 a_{14}/p_1 \\ p_1 a_{21}/p_2 & p_2 a_{22}/p_2 & p_3 a_{23}/p_2 & p_4 a_{24}/p_2 \\ p_1 a_{31}/p_3 & p_2 a_{32}/p_3 & p_3 a_{33}/p_3 & p_4 a_{34}/p_3 \\ p_1 a_{41}/p_4 & p_2 a_{42}/p_4 & p_3 a_{43}/p_4 & p_4 a_{44}/p_4 \end{bmatrix} \approx \mathbf{A}^* \quad (2)$$

We now make the Leontief assumptions that wage ($\mathbf{w}$) and capital costs ($\mathbf{k}$) per gross unit of output are constant, and that gross profit margins ($\mathbf{m}$) are fixed proportions of price, varying among sectors. The profit margins are the "normal" profit proportions of price that must be recovered as a component of costs.

$$\mathbf{w} = \begin{bmatrix} w_1 \\ w_2 \\ w_3 \\ w_4 \end{bmatrix}$$

$$\mathbf{k} = \begin{bmatrix} k_1 \\ k_2 \\ k_3 \\ k_4 \end{bmatrix}$$

$$\mathbf{m} = \begin{bmatrix} m_1 \\ m_2 \\ m_3 \\ m_4 \end{bmatrix}$$

Then, treating prices $\mathbf{p}$ as a column vector, we obtain the straightforward Leontief price dual

$$\mathbf{p}'[\mathbf{I} - \mathbf{A}^{**} - \hat{\mathbf{m}}] = \mathbf{w}' + \mathbf{k}' \quad (3)$$

where $\hat{\mathbf{m}}$ denotes a diagonal matrix with the elements of the indicated vector on the main diagonal and where a prime is used to indicate transposition.

To build in the oligopolistic price interdependence we now determine the power structure of the oligopoly by defining a matrix of consonance coefficients, the significance of which will be made clear below.

$$
\mathbf{C} = \begin{bmatrix}
c_{11} & c_{12} & c_{13} & c_{14} \\
c_{21} & c_{22} & c_{23} & c_{24} \\
c_{31} & c_{32} & c_{33} & c_{34} \\
c_{41} & c_{42} & c_{43} & c_{44}
\end{bmatrix}
$$

In accordance with the rivalrous consonance approach to oligopoly as outlined in section 2, the power structure within an industry is a complicated web of subtle bilateral relations among incumbents that manifests itself in patterns of deference and leadership, proactive and reactive roles in price and non-price policy decisions, personal relationships among managements, and tacit or explicit cooperative ventures. In a mature oligopoly these relationships are immanent in a historically established body of cultural mores, which evolve over time as competitive successes or failures dictate, but which in any short-run period may be taken as given. Such an industry, like any other community, establishes rules of conduct and role expectations governing competitive and cooperative behavior, with effective sanctions for trespass. In the corporate area, of course, one expects the rivalrous relations to dominate the cooperative; but economists tend to overlook the latter in stressing the former. Successful new entrants into the industry are absorbed in the culture and taught the mores tacitly or explicitly, and over time they assume their position in the power structure. In some industries there develops a real sense of community pride that reinforces the tacit limitations on selfish behavior – whether at the club, on the golf course or through the market.

It is, admittedly, difficult – nay, impossible – to capture all the subtlety of this ethos in its implications for corporate policy in any scalar encapsulation. What I have done is to attempt to capture a portion of it in the form of the deference that firms display by taking into account in their price setting their impact on the profits of rivals. In this scheme of consonance coefficients, $\mathbf{C}$, each c_{ij} is the proportion of firm j's profit margin that firm i treats as a cost coordinate with its own profit margin. Such phantom costs raise the price that firm i charges and hence reduce its own bill of goods sales and increase those of firm j. If c_{ij} is 0.10, firm i will consider firm j's loss (gain) of \$1 in firm j's normal profit $(m_j p_j)$ as the equivalent of a loss (gain) of \$0.10 in its own profit, and make its price decision as if its expected profits are lowered (raised) by that amount. The size of c_{ij} will vary in largest part, of course, with firm i's view of the power of firm j to retaliate to its price decrease and thereby to reduce the attractiveness of such a policy initiation. But it will also be affected by the mores of the industry, as discussed above.

These consonance costs that firms introduce into their pricing decisions are phantom costs. They are not actually coordinate with labor and capital costs, although they enter the firms' calculations as such, but they may be suffered as reduced profits if outputs $\mathbf{x}$ are reduced by effects on final demand. We do not, of course, assert that firms actually calculate the consonance coefficients; rather they are analytical constructs meant to capture the pricing decision implications of industry structure and mores. Note also that $\mathbf{C}$ is not a symmetrical matrix: c_{ji} is generally not equal to c_{ij}. We set $c_{ii} \equiv 1$ although it is possible to imagine cases where the weakness of a firm leads to self-abasement that implies discounting its own profits.

We also set boundaries on the values of c_{ij} such that $0 \leq c_{ij} \leq 1$. When $c_{ij} = 1$, firm i values firm j's losses or profits as equal to its own – an extreme form of deference we should not expect to find in isolation. However, if the mores lead all firms to discount all rivals' profits at this value, we should have the case of near-joint-profit maximization.[3] This would be a case of perfect tacit collusion in price setting. If $c_{ij} = 0$, firm i would act in total disregard of its impacts on firm j's outputs and profits – an aggressive act that may well be engendered by its dominant position, but which would violate any competition-tempering tenets in the industry ethos. If all firms set their consonance coefficients to zero, we would have the "Cournot myopia" solution (albeit with respect to prices, not quantities), in which all firms ignore their impacts on their rivals' profits and losses. In a social welfare sense this "Cournot price solution" is the most socially desirable pricing state that it is possible to contemplate in oligopoly, where firms are acting at the lower limit of rationality by ignoring the welfare of their rivals (and their joint potential pricing power). Finally, if $c_{ij} < 0$, firm i is willing to sustain losses to inflict losses upon rival j and we have the makings of a price war. In the brackets set above we avoid such short-run rivalrous actions, which are not consistent with long-run behavior in a mature industry.

To begin the introduction of the consonance coefficients into the model, I define the following

$$
\mathbf{s} = \begin{bmatrix}
1 - a_{11}^{**} - c_{11}m_1 & -a_{12}^{**} & -a_{13}^{**} & -a_{14}^{**} \\
-a_{21}^{**} & 1 - a_{22}^{**} - c_{22}m_2 & -a_{23}^{**} & -a_{24}^{**} \\
-a_{31}^{**} & -a_{32}^{**} & 1 - a_{33}^{**} - c_{33}m_3 & -a_{34}^{**} \\
-a_{41}^{**} & -a_{42}^{**} & -a_{43}^{**} & 1 - a_{44}^{**} - c_{44}m_4
\end{bmatrix}
$$

$$(4)$$

---

[3] Perfect joint-profit maximization would involve each firm including its rivals' profits in its objective function and differentiating those profits with respect to its price.

which is simply $[\mathbf{I} - \mathbf{A}^{**}]$ enhanced along the main diagonal by subtracting $c_{ii}(\equiv 1)$ times the profit margin of the row and column sectors.

The remaining costs (both real and phantom), other than the own-profit margins, are defined as the vector $\mathbf{v}$[4]

$$\mathbf{v} = \begin{bmatrix} w_1 + k_1 + c_{12}m_2 p_2 + c_{13}m_3 p_3 + c_{14}m_4 p_4 \\ w_2 + k_2 + c_{21}m_1 p_1 + c_{23}m_3 p_3 + c_{24}m_4 p_4 \\ w_3 + k_3 + c_{31}m_1 p_1 + c_{32}m_2 p_2 + c_{34}m_4 p_4 \\ w_4 + k_4 + c_{41}m_1 p_1 + c_{42}m_2 p_2 + c_{43}m_3 p_3 \end{bmatrix} \tag{5}$$

In our example we assume that the oligopolistic firms have no regard for sector 4's fate and set $c_{i4} = 0$ for $i = 1, 2, 3$. In a larger model, however, some of the sectors external to the oligopoly may be suppliers to the oligopolistic firms, and the latter may exhibit concerns for the formers' profits by discounting them and lowering prices below what they would set in the absence of such concerns.

Consider, now, the limitations that the Leontief system exercises on our model. Most importantly, the impacts of rivals' consonance decisions on their own and their competitors' profits play no feedback role in their price decisions. In more sophisticated models we introduce profit maximization constrained by the consonance coefficients into the model. Prices may be raised or lowered by rivals on the basis of the effects on their profits via their total demand functions. In the Leontief model, however, the consonance decisions must generally raise prices as determined by the price dual, with gross output outcomes that will not reflect back upon their own-price choices. The gross outputs may rise or fall, via price impacts on the bill of goods, with consequent increases or decreases in their actual profits (i.e. "normal" profits plus rents occurring through rivalrous consonance). This is, of course, a serious deficiency in the attempt to study general equilibrium results of tacit collusion. Nonetheless, there are valuable insights to be gained from the simplicity of the model.

First, we may study the absolute and relative behavior of oligopolistic prices as the consonance parameters are varied. Most particularly of interest are the ranges of prices determined between a base case, when all $c_{ij} = 0, j \neq i$, and those resulting from extreme tacit collusion and all $c_{ij} = 1$. Second, it is interesting to note the behavior of prices in sectors external to the oligopolistic sectors, which are only indirectly affected by tacit collusion via the oligopolistic firms' intermediate goods requirements. Third, it is a valuable exercise, quite apart from the oligopoly price

---

[4] Placing the phantom costs with the "real" costs serves to emphasize their nature as price enhancements. For solution purposes, of course, they may be moved into the matrix $\mathbf{S}$.

and output implications, to study the degree to which estimates of the natural unit coefficients underlying our analysis differ as the consonance coefficients change and affect prices of oligopoly products.

In section 4 we present the model formally before performing simulations with it to derive insights that cast light on the questions raised above.

4. The model

We are given the matrix $\mathbf{A}$, defined in equation (1) as the production coefficients' dollar value form. From it we derive estimates of the production coefficients in natural units, as depicted in (2) by $\mathbf{A}^{**}$. From $\mathbf{S}$ in equation (4) and $\mathbf{v}$ in (5) the price system is defined as

$$\mathbf{p}' = \mathbf{v}'\mathbf{S}^{-1} \tag{6}$$

If $\mathbf{v}$ is defined as it is in (5), the system (6) must be iterated until $\mathbf{p}$ converges. Substitution of the price solution into the bill of goods equations yields for $\mathbf{y}$, the bill of goods,

$$\mathbf{y} = \begin{bmatrix} g_1 - f_{11}p_1 + f_{12}p_2 + f_{13}p_3 + f_{14}p_4 \\ g_2 + f_{21}p_1 - f_{22}p_2 + f_{23}p_3 + f_{24}p_4 \\ g_3 + f_{31}p_1 + f_{32}p_2 - f_{33}p_3 + f_{34}p_4 \\ g_4 + f_{41}p_1 + f_{42}p_2 + f_{43}p_3 - f_{44}p_4 \end{bmatrix} \tag{7}$$

where the vector $\mathbf{g}$ and matrix $\mathbf{F}$ are parameters.

Finally, gross outputs in natural units are then calculated as

$$\mathbf{x} = (\mathbf{I} - \mathbf{A}^{**})^{-1}\mathbf{y} \tag{8}$$

Profits may then be obtained by multiplying $\mathbf{x}$ by $\mathbf{p}$ and subtracting "real" costs from revenue. Oligopoly rents may then be estimated by comparing such profits with "normal" profits, which would be obtained from the mark-ups in $\mathbf{m}$ and gross outputs $\mathbf{x}$. These operations are interactions of the output model and the price dual, but do not constitute "causative" feedbacks.

5. Some illustrative simulations

Table 13.1 lists the parameter values for the four cases we will solve as illustrations and to gain insights into the impacts of tacit collusion within the Leontief context. The four cases are: (1) a base case with no rivalrous consonance; (2) low rivalrous consonance; (3) high rivalrous consonance; and (4) extreme rivalrous consonance. The only case-specific parameters

Table 13.1 *Parameter values for the simulations*

1. Common parameter values

$$A = \begin{bmatrix} 0.03 & 0.03 & 0.01 & 0.10 \\ 0.02 & 0.02 & 0.01 & 0.06 \\ 0.04 & 0.03 & 0.04 & 0.07 \\ 0.25 & 0.30 & 0.28 & 0.28 \end{bmatrix}, \quad w = \begin{bmatrix} 50 \\ 60 \\ 65 \\ 47 \end{bmatrix}, \quad k = \begin{bmatrix} 2.7 \\ 4.0 \\ 3.4 \\ 2.8 \end{bmatrix}, \quad m = \begin{bmatrix} 0.10 \\ 0.08 \\ 0.09 \\ 0.09 \end{bmatrix},$$

$$F = \begin{bmatrix} 10 & 4 & 5 & 0.5 \\ 3 & 12 & 13 & 0.3 \\ 7 & 12 & 18 & 0.4 \\ 0.05 & 0.06 & 0.04 & 10 \end{bmatrix}, \quad g = \begin{bmatrix} 250 \\ 300 \\ 500 \\ 2,000 \end{bmatrix}$$

2. Case-specific parameter values

Case 1: Zero rivalrous consonance

$$C = \begin{bmatrix} 1 & 0 & 0 & 0 \\ 0 & 1 & 0 & 0 \\ 0 & 0 & 1 & 0 \\ 0 & 0 & 0 & 1 \end{bmatrix}$$

Case 3: High rivalrous consonance

$$C = \begin{bmatrix} 1 & 0.15 & 0.10 & 0 \\ 0.25 & 1 & 0.15 & 0 \\ 0.30 & 0.20 & 1 & 0 \\ 0 & 0 & 0 & 1 \end{bmatrix}$$

Case 2: Low rivalrous consonance

$$C = \begin{bmatrix} 1 & 0.05 & 0.10 & 0 \\ 0.06 & 1 & 0.15 & 0 \\ 0.05 & 0.05 & 1 & 0 \\ 0 & 0 & 0 & 1 \end{bmatrix}$$

Case 4: Extreme rivalrous consonance

$$C = \begin{bmatrix} 1 & 1 & 1 & 0 \\ 1 & 1 & 1 & 0 \\ 1 & 1 & 1 & 0 \\ 0 & 0 & 0 & 1 \end{bmatrix}$$

are the elements of C, the matrix of consonance coefficients. Other parameters are common to all four runs.

5.1   Sector profiles

Firm 1 has a low basic demand parameter (g_1) and a high own-price coefficient (f_{11}), as well as low other-price coefficients, in its final demand equation. It is, therefore, sensitive to situations where firms 2 and 3 do not raise prices much (i.e. low c_{2j} and c_{3j}) and it has a high c_{11}. On the other hand, its primary factor costs are the lowest of the three rivals and its imports of inputs from sector 4 are also the lowest. Its input coefficients for imports from rivals are the highest among them, but their relatively small values do not materially offset its advantages from low sector 4 imports. Finally, as the largest exporter of industry products to sector 4, it benefits more than its rivals from increases in that sector's gross outputs. It is, therefore, the low-cost producer among the rivals, which counteracts to some degree its disadvantages on the demand side.

Firm 2 is also a low basic demand producer with high final demand sensitivity to rival prices (especially to p_3), somewhat offset by a high own-price coefficient. Rises in p_1 benefit its final demand only slightly, but high values of p_3 (caused by large c_{31} and c_{32}) benefit it greatly. On the cost side, its intermediate good costs are the highest among the rivals and its primary factor costs are intermediate among the rivals. Given the narrow variance of intermediate good costs among the rivals we must rank it as a medium-cost firm on the basis of its primary factor costs.

Firm 3 has high own-price and other-price coefficients and high basic demand in its final demand equation, so that willingness to participate in tacit collusion raises its own price significantly and lowers its final demand, tempered slightly by its high basic demand. At the same time it puts itself at the mercy of its rivals' willingness to reciprocate, or – alternatively – it benefits from their willingness to defer to it. Its primary factor costs are the highest of the rivals. It is not a great exporter of inputs to sector 4, and therefore does not benefit greatly from output expansion from the latter, although this is true for the other rivals as well.

Sector 4 does not participate in the tacit collusion of the oligopolistic industry and therefore does not actively change prices. It is wholly passive on price account and its gross output is affected by the rival firms' price changes and the imports of its product induced by their gross output changes. As a large aggregate sector its inputs into the three firms are large, as is its own absorption of product. Its basic final demand is large and its own-price coefficient large, but imports from the oligopolistic sectors are small. It is a low-cost producer on primary factor account, although its intermediate account costs are on the larger side. In short, it is a reactive sector the primary stimuli of which are the gross outputs of the rival firms.

5.2   Case solutions

Table 13.2 lists the values of the state variables in each of the four case solutions.

5.2.1   Case 1: the base case   Without any rivalrous consonance this case solution conforms well to the sector profiles. Firm 1 has the lowest price, and its bill of goods or final demand sensitivities, as well as its low basic demand, penalize its sales to final users. Although it is the lowest-cost rival, its large sector 4 input per unit reduces its actual profit margin below its "normal" margin. On the other hand, its high ratio of gross output to final demand (1.71) occurs because of its high value of exports to sector 4.

Firm 2's performance is initially something of a surprise. It is intermediate in its cost structure and its price reflects that, and it benefits

Table 13.2 *State variable solutions to models (with percentage changes from base-case values in parentheses)*

Model description	Sectors	Prices	Gross output	Final demand	Actual profits per unit	Total profits	Estimated natural unit production coefficients matrix A**			
1. Base case: zero rivalrous consonance	1.	$94.11	762	445	$9.34	$7,117	0.030	0.038	0.013	0.132
	2.	$118.52	914	757	$9.29	$8,491	0.016	0.020	0.010	0.063
	3.	$120.00	687	471	$10.86	$7,461	0.031	0.030	0.040	0.073
	4.	$124.50	1,891	772	$11.01	$20,820	0.189	0.286	0.270	0.280
2. Low rivalrous consonance	1.	$96.94 (3.0)	754 (−1.1)	442 (−0.7)	$11.10	$8,369 (17.6)	0.030	0.038	0.013	0.128
	2.	$122.64 (3.5)	893 (−2.3)	739 (−2.4)	$11.92	$10,640 (25.3)	0.016	0.020	0.010	0.061
	3.	$121.71 (1.4)	727 (5.8)	509 (8.1)	$11.75	$8,542 (14.5)	0.032	0.030	0.040	0.072
	4.	$124.50 (0)	1,919 (1.5)	772 (0)	$11.34	$21,760 (4.5)	0.195	0.296	0.274	0.280
3. High rivalrous consonance	1.	$98.88 (5.1)	786 (3.2)	472 (6.1)	$12.33	$9,691 (36.2)	0.030	0.038	0.013	0.126
	2.	$126.32 (6.6)	945 (3.4)	792 (4.6)	$14.37	$13,580 (59.9)	0.016	0.020	0.010	0.059
	3.	$128.75 (7.3)	650 (−5.4)	440 (−6.6)	$16.46	$10,700 (43.4)	0.031	0.029	0.040	0.068
	4.	$124.50 (0)	1,951 (3.2)	773 (0.1)	$11.08	$21,620 (3.8)	0.199	0.304	0.290	0.280
4. Extreme rivalrous consonance	1.	$146.29 (55.5)	666 (−12.6)	396 (−11.0)	$43.76	$29,140 (309.4)	0.030	0.036	0.012	0.085
	2.	$173.96 (46.8)	1,042 (14.0)	900 (18.9)	$43.70	$45,540 (436.3)	0.017	0.020	0.010	0.043
	3.	$170.08 (41.8)	810 (17.9)	600 (27.4)	$43.61	$35,320 (373.4)	0.034	0.031	0.040	0.051
	4.	$124.50 (0)	2,391 (26.4)	780 (1.0)	$11.16	$26,680 (28.1)	0.294	0.419	0.383	0.280

output-wise somewhat from firm 3's higher price. But its exports to sector 4 are the least of the rivals', so its gross output is only 21 percent above its final demand, and its profits suffer accordingly. The surprising aspect of its solution is its high market share and resulting profit, both of which are the highest of the three rivals. The latter occurs despite the shortfall of its actual profit margin from its "normal" value, the high input coefficient for sector 4's product in the production of firm 2's output being the largest cause of this. This large absolute value of profits nonetheless must be attributed to its large final demand, in turn the result of the high other-demand coefficient for firm 3 and the latter's high price.

Firm 3 has the lowest sales of the industry, although relatively high exports to its rivals and to sector 4 raise gross output 46 percent above its final demand. But its profits are only slightly above firm 1's. Its high own-price final demand coefficient and the low prices of firm 1 are the culprits causing its low final demand, and its high primary factor costs contribute to its disappointing profit performance. This occurred despite the fact that its actual profit margin was $0.06 above its "normal" margin – the only positive difference of the four sectors.

For a sector with high basic final demand sector 4's total final demand is relatively small, because it benefits only slightly from the rivals' prices. However, it does enjoy large enhancements from intermediate good contributions to the oligopolistic industry, so its ratio of gross output to final demand is 2.45 – the highest of the four sectors. Its low primary factor costs are largely offset by the cost of its inputs from the three rivals and from itself, so although its profit margin is the highest of the sectors it is about $0.20 below its normal profit margin, about matching the shortfall of firm 2 for the largest value of the four sectors.

5.2.2   Case 2: low rivalrous consonance   In this case firm 3 is the recipient of the largest deference, with $c_{13} + c_{23} = 0.25$, whereas firms 1 and 2 receive a total consonance deference of 0.11 and 0.10 respectively from their rivals. Firm 3, however, grants only a miserly 0.05 to each of its rivals. The result is that p_3 rises by a small amount, whereas p_1 and p_2 raise their prices most because of their more generous consonance coefficients. The net result is a fall in both final and gross outputs for firms 1 and 2, whereas firm 3 gains on both accounts. On the other hand, firm 3 raises price only 1.4 percent above the base case, and sees its final demand rise 8.1 percent and its gross output 5.8 percent. Its profits rise 14.5 percent over case 1 levels, but the greatest benefit accrues to the most deferential rivals. Firm 1's price rise of 3.0 percent and firm 2's of 3.5 percent more than offset sales declines, and their profits rise fully 17.6 percent and 25.3 percent respectively. With zero consonance coefficients in its **C** row sector 4's price does not change, but its total sales rise from its increased sales to firm 3, offset by losses from the fall in sales of the other two rivals.

Also note that the estimated quantities of sector 4's export coefficients rise by virtue of the rises in prices of the three firms, and that by the same token its import coefficients in the fourth column of $\mathbf{A}^{**}$ fall from their base case values – see the definition of $\mathbf{A}^{**}$ in equation (2) above. The result of these occurrences is to boost the sector's actual profit margins over their normal values on its increased sales, and its total profits rise by a modest 4.5 percent over the base case. This last result is suspect, of course, because, if we had the actual coefficients in natural units, sector 4's import and export coefficients would remain constant. So would the value of export coefficients with unchanged p_4, while the higher prices of its imports on intermediate account would raise their value. Hence its costs would rise, and with constant price in the Leontief model its profit margin would fall, so that sales would have to rise more than in case 2 to obtain higher profits. Note that the small proportional rises in p_1, p_2 and p_3 result in negligible differences in the intra-industry coefficients in $\mathbf{A}^{**}$ for the rivals compared with base-case levels.

In this Leontief framework, rises in consonance coefficients benefit all sectors, including those that suffer reduced sales as a consequence. This need not happen in a richer model in which firms maximize profits facing downward-sloping total demand functions. However, this universal profit gain frequently happens in such richer models, so the results are not unusual. The tide of tacit collusion can raise all ships through higher profits – even non-participating sectors that are constrained from raising prices.

5.2.3   Case 3: high rivalrous consonance   In this case the three rivals institute high levels of tacit price collusion, which we would expect to see in a mature oligopoly with developed cooperative institutions. Firm 1 in this case becomes the rival other firms defer to, while it nonetheless increases the sum of its coefficients to 0.25. Firm 2 raises its sum, when compared with case 2, to 0.40, most of it in deference to firm 1, while firm 3 increases the sum of the coefficients c_{3j} to 0.50, again with most of it favoring firm 1. As would be expected, price rises among the rivals are higher increases over the base case than those experienced in case 2. Firm 3 suffers from its large price increase by a reduction in final demand below its base case level and the induced gross output. Nonetheless, the 7.3 percent rise in price outweighs the 5.4 percent fall in final output, and its profits rise 43.4 percent over the base case level.

Firm 1 is led to increase price by 5.1 percent over the base case level, but this is a relatively small increase over case 2. Its small other-price coefficients in its final demand equation relative to its substantial own-price coefficient is to blame for its failure to increase its final demand and gross output by much, while its price increase is held back by its moderate coefficients c_{1j}. Nonetheless, its profit increase (from base-case levels) doubles over the case 2 figure, rising by 36.2 percent, though this is the smallest of both percentage rises among the rivals.

Firm 2 continues its record established in the base and low consonance case as the highest profit earner among the rivals. Its final demand is enhanced by firm 3's large price increase, and its gross output rises by 3.4 percent over the base case level. With the 6.6 percent price rise over the base case, profits jump almost 60 percent over the base case – the best performance of the rivals once more.

Finally, sector 4 continues its reactive record, with no increase in price and negligible increase in final demand from the price rises of the rivals. The increases in the gross outputs of firms 1 and 2 offset the decline in that of firm 3 to permit sector 4's sales to rise 3.2 percent over base case levels, and profits to rise 3.8 percent over the base case – far less than for the oligopolistic firms. Its actual profit margin also rises slightly over the base-case value, for reasons discussed in our discussion of case 2. It remains a reactive beneficiary from rivalrous consonance.

5.2.4   *Case 4: extreme rivalrous consonance*   This last case carries us into what we have defined as "extreme rivalrous consonance" or near-joint-profit maximization, in which each rival counts its rivals' profits on a par with its own. The results are dramatic instances of tacit price collusion.

Each rival's profits rise between 309 and 436 percent over the base case levels, firm 2 once more leading the pack, while even sector 4 profits rise 28 percent over base case levels. Prices rise between 42 and 56 percent in the oligopoly sectors, but remain constant in sector 4, even though the estimated natural unit values of its intermediate goods fall significantly below base case levels. Note that all of the oligopolistic firms are harmed a bit by the rise in the estimated amounts of sector 4's exports to them, but in line with our conclusion above actual profit margins are between 28 and 30 percent above the built-in values m_i for all rivals. One of the comforting results of this body of simulations is that the estimates of the coefficients a_{ij}^{**} do not materially affect the broad results with respect to prices and profits.

The large rise in p_1, given firm 1's large own-price sensitivity and relatively low other-price sensitivities, lowers its final demand below case 1 levels, and sales to other sectors do not prevent a fall in total sales below that benchmark. But a 13 percent drop in gross output is well neutralized by a 56 percent rise in prices to bring about the firm's profit rise.

Firm 2 retains its record as the rival that profits most from the extreme case as the intermediate-cost firm with favorable coefficients in its final demand equation. Its final demand expands by 19 percent above the base case level, and its total output by 14 percent. With a 47 percent rise in price and its moderate cost structure, its profits rise by 436 percent over base case levels, continuing a theme that emerged in the base case and was accentuated with all three cases of rivalrous consonance.

Despite its punishing own-price sensitivity in its final demand equation, firm 3 shows a dramatic increase in final demand from base case levels because of the large price increases of its rivals – especially firm 2. Enhanced by sales to sector 4, total output expands by 18 percent above the base case value, and, with an increase of 42 percent in its price, profits rise by 373 percent over base case levels.

Even plodding sector 4 benefits from the expanded sales of firms 2 and 3, as well as the larger estimated values of its export coefficients. Total output rises 26 percent above the base case value and profits rise 28 percent above that level. Its final demand rises by a negligible 1 percent, and its price is constant, so all of its good fortune must spring from the two causes noted above.

5.2.5   Summary Not surprisingly, all firms (including the non-oligopolistic sector) benefit from tacit price collusion of the rivalrous consonance variety, with their welfares rising monotonically with increasing collusion. It must be said that sector 4's welfare is innocently enhanced by the induced exports that rises in overall production of oligopolistic brands bring about. In the four cases, taken respectively, total outputs summed over the three rival brands are: 2,363; 2,374; 2,381 and 2,518 – a near-stationary performance. But the welfare consequences of tacit price collusion are gleaned from the lackluster performance over the four cases of final demand: 1,673; 1,690; 1,704 and 1,896. These must be compared against price rises in the cases to gauge the decline in welfare of final users.

6.   The ease of comparative statics calculations

One of the advantages of the simple forms of interdependence in the Leontief model, even after endogenizing final demand, is the ease with which parametric ranging and sensitivity analysis can be conducted with the model. Moreover, since the model is linear in all equations, our results are global rather than flowing from local linearizations of non-linear functions. To illustrate, I have arbitrarily chosen the model with high rivalrous consonance and firm 1's behavior within it to illustrate the points. The results are tabulated in table 13.3. The default parameter results are

Table 13.3 *Comparative statics operations on parameters of firm 1 (high rivalrous consonance case)*

Model description	Sectors	Default parameters	$c_{12} = 0.16\ (0.15)$	$c_{13} = 0.11\ (0.1)$	$f_{11} = 11\ (10)$	$f_{12} = 5\ (4)$	$f_{13} = 6\ (5)$	$f_{14} = 0.6\ (0.5)$
Prices	1.	$98.88	$99.06	$99.09	No Change From Default	No Change From Default	No Change From Default	No Change From Default
	2.	$126.32	$126.32 (+)	$126.33				
	3.	$128.75	$128.76	$128.76				
	4.	$124.50	$124.50 (+)	$124.50				
Final demand	1.	472	471	470	374	599	601	485
	2.	792	793	793	792	792	792	792
	3.	440	441	442	440	440	440	440
	4.	773	773 (+)	773 (+)	772	773	773	773
Gross output	1.	786	784	784	680	922	925	800
	2.	945	946	946	941	950	950	946
	3.	650	652	652	644	658	658	651
	4.	1,951	1,952	1,952	1,918	1,994	1,995	1,955

those for the original solution to the model, with the parameters listed in table 13.1. I have boosted these parameters singly by one unit or less from their default values (listed in parentheses in the column headings) and derived prices, final demands and gross outputs in each of the new solutions for comparison with the default parameter case. Figures have been rounded to two decimal places for prices and to the last digit for production values. Where a change from the default value was too small to register after rounding I have placed a sign to indicate the direction of the variable's movement above that value.

Increasing the consonance coefficients for firm 1 lifted the prices of the rivals as well as p_1. It lowered the final demand of firm 1, by virtue of the rise in p_1, and raised the final demands of rivals 2 and 3 by small amounts in reflection of the small rises in their prices offsetting the positive effects of the change in p_1. Gross output for firm 1 fell in both cases and rose for the rivals. Sector 4 revealed no change in price or final demand at the two-decimal level in both cases, but did gain one unit in gross output from the rise in rivals' gross outputs.

Changes in the final demand coefficients yielded some rather surprising sensitivities in final demand and gross outputs. Of course, given the lack of feedback from such quantities to prices, the latter retained their default parameter values. The unit change in own-price sensitivity for firm 1 resulted in almost a 20 percent fall in final demand, with – of course – no changes in final demands by its rivals. Firm 1's gross output fell about 13 percent from default level, and by its reduction in intermediate demand caused noticeable reductions in the gross outputs of its rivals. Most severely affected, however, was sector 4's gross output, which fell 12 percent. Such impacts emphasize the importance in such modeling of gaining accurate estimates of own-price coefficients in final demand equations.

Upward unit changes in f_{12} and f_{13} also resulted in dramatic increases in both final demand and gross output for firm 1. There were no changes in final demand for firms 2 and 3 but large increases in these amounts for the two rivals, and small increases in gross output benefited these two rivals from intermediate good absorption increases by firm 1. Finally, the rise in f_{14} led to a modest but non-ignorable increase in final demand for firm 1. Final outputs for the remaining three firms rose by four or five units. The impact on sector 4 was negligible, therefore.

7.   Conclusion

Economists and policy-makers are becoming increasingly sensitive to the strength of cooperative urges among competing industrial and services units, and their real and potential tempering of competition. Increasingly, formal institutions are arising in the fields of research and development, purchasing, product design and manufacture and even marketing to facilitate such cooperation without the extremity of merger or acquisition. Less formally, the rationality among oligopolistic rivals of tacit collusion in pricing and forms of non-price competition such as new brand introduction is being accepted increasingly by economists whose professional bias is to emphasize competition.

To illustrate one manner of incorporating parameters that permit mixtures of competition and cooperation in oligopolistic pricing, this article discusses the concept of rivalrous consonance and demonstrates some of its implications for the firms involved and for external industries. The Leontief price dual and its independent output primary model permit us to present such modeling in its simplest form, abstracting from profit maximization with defined total demand functions and rising marginal costs. We have discussed the limitations of the model above, but, nonetheless, have illustrated through simulations some of the impacts it has on prices and outputs throughout the economy. Our results must be presented with numerous caveats because of the restricted interdependence of the Leontief system, but at least the fundamental ideas have been illustrated.

ACKNOWLEDGEMENTS

I am indebted to Professor Erik Dietzenbacher, whose careful and perceptive editing has resulted in the elimination of a number of ambiguities and gaucheries, and the correction of some errors.

REFERENCES

Brandenburger, A. M., and B. J. Nalebuff (1996) *Co-opetition* (New York, Doubleday).
Kuenne, R. E. (1999) *Price and NonPrice Rivalry in Oligopoly: The Integrated Battleground* (London, Macmillan).

14   Economies of plant scale and structural change

Iwao Ozaki

1.   Introduction

This paper has two objectives. The first is to examine the effectiveness and usefulness of the establishment base production function for analyzing production structure. The second is to investigate how the expansion of plant capacity affects structural change, based on the parameter estimates of production functions.

The process of economic development is characterized by structural change. Sustained economic growth can be achieved only via a select subset of potential paths for structural change. We hope to illuminate at least one path that has led to sustained economic growth by analyzing rigorously the development process of the post-war Japanese economy.

By structural change we mean technological change (see Leontief et al., 1953; Carter, 1970). We use these terms interchangeably and adopt the normal input-output definition of technological change as changes in capital coefficients and intermediate input coefficients. In our model, changes in capital coefficients depend upon the magnitude of plant capacity. In a large subset of industries, changes in plant capacity are determined endogenously through the unit cost minimization behavior of corporations.

This endogeneity of changes in capital coefficients derives from our production function parameter estimates. Rather than assuming the standard homogeneous production function, we specify a function that allows limited substitutability among factors of production. We call this a non-homothetic, factor-limited production function; see, e.g., Komiya (1962), Komiya and Uchida (1963), Lau and Tamura (1972) and Nakamura (1990). Its specification and estimation are another contribution of this paper.

A "plant" is a compound commodity of durable goods (capital stock) that is used in the production process during a fixed period. In this sense, each plant is a "lump of capital goods" that has its own capacity, X_{j_i}, which is measured by the quantity of the final goods produced. Each plant is characterized by a technology that is described by the set of relationships between plant capacity, labor input and capital stock. In other words, a plant with capacity X_{j_i} is assumed to embody a specific technology that is characterized by plant capacity, labor and capital inputs.

Section 3 begins with observations about production technology relationships at the plant level using data from the *Census of Manufactures* published by MITI (now the Ministry of Economy, Trade and Industry – METI). This survey covers every manufacturer in Japan by establishment (factory), where an "establishment" is equivalent to a plant. These observations motivate our adoption of the factor-limited production function at the establishment level. Our production function parameter estimates, which are derived from establishment data, do not vary much over time and reveal three stable technological properties (section 3.2). First, the expansion of plant capacity produces a labor-saving effect in all sectors as a consequence of plant-level technology. Second, technologies can be divided into two groups: capital-using or capital-saving. Third, the rate of labor productivity enhancement caused by plant capacity expansion is greater than the rate at which capital productivity improves.

Our parameter estimates serve to divide Japanese industries into two basic groups, one of which is characterized by economies of plant scale (sections 3.3 and 3.4). After confirming the temporal stability of technology parameters, we conclude section 3 by introducing a unit cost minimization model to determine endogenously optimum plant capacity, $X_{j_i}^*$.

Our analysis of the impact on structural change of enlarging plant capacity uses time-series data at a more aggregated sector level. The resulting parameter estimates can be used to classify industries into five different technological categories. If technological properties are characterized by parameters of the factor-limited production functions, changes in capital coefficients depend on changes in plant capacity. Furthermore, for industries characterized as capital-using, changes in plant capacity are related to changes in relative factor prices.

Changes in plant capacity determine changes in the capital coefficient matrix proposed in the "dynamic inverse" model (see Leontief, 1970). In particular, we show that the effect on structural change of increasing capacity at each plant is significant in capital-intensive sectors. Interestingly, in industries with scale economies, our results reveal a surprising stability in the number of firms present over a fifteen-year period. This is suggestive of both barriers to entry and collusion amongst firms.

2.   Data

In Japan, from the 1960s through the 1980s, capital coefficients increased rapidly for almost all industrial sectors as well as for the whole economy. Enhanced labor productivity and rapid changes in the relative price of factor inputs – namely labor and capital – also characterized this period. Simultaneously, both aggregate capital accumulation and the plant capacity of establishments expanded rapidly. These various structural changes in the Japanese economy accompanied rapid economic growth.

Two sets of basic data for this period were used to estimate the properties of technology. One was a set of individual establishment data from the *Census of Manufactures*. The *Census* includes total samples of about 690,000 establishments in 1980. All establishments are classified into about six hundred four-digit sectors (industries) and about a hundred and fifty three-digit sectors using Japan Standard Industry Classification (JSIC) codes. In the *Census* data, annual gross output X_{j_i}, required labor L_{j_i} and fixed capital stock at the end of the period K_{j_i} are available to estimate production function parameters for establishments. Here, the subscript j denotes the j-th industry, which consists of various plants producing the same commodity. Also, i (=1, . . . , $n(j)$) denotes plant-based variables, and $n(j)$ denotes the number of establishments in sector j.

The other data set was comprised of aggregate time-series data for sectoral gross output X_j, labor input L_j and real capital stock K_j. Also, deflators for gross output and labor input at the sector level for the period 1951–1968 were estimated by Japan's Center for Economic Data Development and Research.[1]

3.   Measurement using a cross-section approach

3.1   Observations

Let us begin with observations of scatter diagrams between plant capacity X_{j_i} and the required labor for operating plant L_{j_i} or the capital stock K_{j_i}. Since results cannot be described for all industries because of limited space, we focus on a few: paper production, aluminum refining, copper smelting and zinc refining. Figures 14.1 and 14.2 show the distribution of samples in the paper industry for 1980 and 1985, with logarithmic

---

[1] The Center for Economic Data Development and Research was established in April 1970. It helps contribute to the advancement of economic theory and its practical application by developing an efficient high-quality data system for economic analysis and forecasting. During the period 1970–1972 its activity was concentrated on the reconstruction and development of the set of input-output time-series data.

values of X_{j_i} and L_{j_i}. For the paper industry, figure 14.3 shows the 1985 relationship between tangible fixed assets (capital stock) K_{j_i} and plant capacity X_{j_i}. Each sample point represents the logarithmic values of these variables at the individual establishment level. From the figures we can observe that stable linear relationships appear to exist between plant capacity X_{j_i} and the labor required for operating the plant L_{j_i}, and between plant capacity X_{j_i} and tangible fixed assets (capital stock) K_{j_i}. These observations motivate our adoption of the factor-limited production function presented in the following section.

3.2 Estimation

Based on the findings in the preceding section, we hypothesize that the technological relationships at the plant level are given by the following factor-limited production function

$$L_{j_i} = \alpha_{L_j} X_{j_i}^{\beta_{L_j}} \quad \text{or} \quad \ln L_{j_i} = \ln \alpha_{L_j} + \beta_{L_j} \ln X_{j_i} \tag{1}$$

$$K_{j_i} = \alpha_{K_j} X_{j_i}^{\beta_{K_j}} \quad \text{or} \quad \ln K_{j_i} = \ln \alpha_{K_j} + \beta_{K_j} \ln X_{j_i} \tag{2}$$

where X_{j_i} represents gross output for each establishment, a proxy for plant capacity. L_{j_i} is annual labor input (in terms of man-years) required to operate the plant, and K_{j_i} is the value of the fixed capital stock needed to realize plant capacity X_{j_i}. We call equation system (1) and (2) a "factor-limited production function" in which labor-capital substitution can occur only through the expansion of the production scale X_{j_i}. The statistical estimates of the technology parameters of the production function at the establishment base are shown in figures 14.1 to 14.6.

From equations (1) and (2), we obtain the following relationships between X_{j_i}, L_{j_i} and K_{j_i}.

$$\lambda_{L_j} = \frac{1}{\alpha_{L_j}} X_{j_i}^{1-\beta_{L_j}}$$

$$\lambda_{K_j} = \frac{1}{\alpha_{K_j}} X_{j_i}^{1-\beta_{K_j}}$$

$$\frac{K_{j_i}}{L_{j_i}} = \frac{\alpha_{K_j}}{\alpha_{L_j}} X_{j_i}^{\beta_{K_j}-\beta_{L_j}}$$

where λ_{L_j} and λ_{K_j} are labor and capital productivity, X_{j_i}/L_{j_i} and X_{j_i}/K_{j_i} respectively. From these formulations we can deduce the following three implications: (1) $(1 - \beta_{L_j})$ is a measure of the elasticity of labor productivity λ_{L_j} to plant scale X_{j_i}; (2) $(1 - \beta_{K_j})$ is a measure of the elasticity of capital productivity λ_{K_j} to plant scale X_{j_i}; and (3) $(\beta_{K_j} - \beta_{L_j})$ shows the

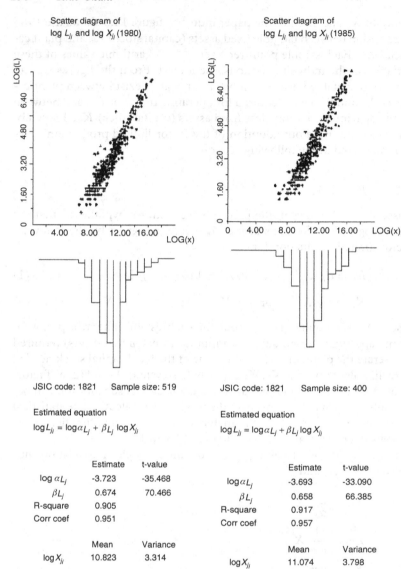

Figure 14.1 Distribution of establishments in the Paper industry, 1980

Figure 14.2 Distribution of establishments in the Paper industry, 1985

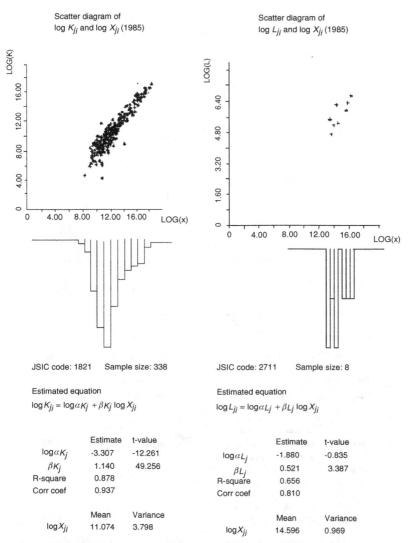

Figure 14.3   Distribution of establishments in the Paper industry, 1985

Figure 14.4   Distribution of establishments in the Copper smelting
industry (oligopoly case), 1985

238　　*Iwao Ozaki*

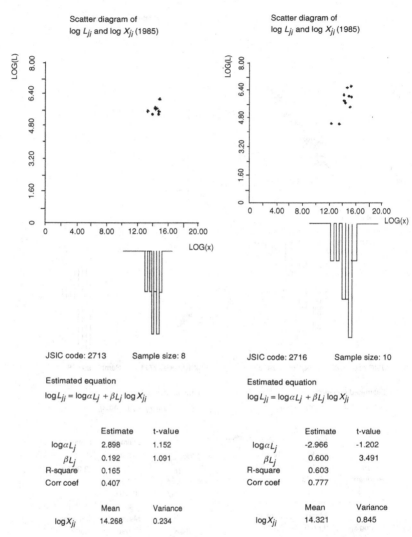

Scatter diagram of
log L_{ji} and log X_{ji} (1985)

Scatter diagram of
log L_{ji} and log X_{ji} (1985)

JSIC code: 2713　　Sample size: 8

Estimated equation

$\log L_{ji} = \log \alpha L_j + \beta L_j \log X_{ji}$

	Estimate	t-value
$\log \alpha L_j$	2.898	1.152
βL_j	0.192	1.091
R-square	0.165	
Corr coef	0.407	

	Mean	Variance
$\log X_{ji}$	14.268	0.234

JSIC code: 2716　　Sample size: 10

Estimated equation

$\log L_{ji} = \log \alpha L_j + \beta L_j \log X_{ji}$

	Estimate	t-value
$\log \alpha L_j$	-2.966	-1.202
βL_j	0.600	3.491
R-square	0.603	
Corr coef	0.777	

	Mean	Variance
$\log X_{ji}$	14.321	0.845

Figure 14.5　Distribution of establishments in the Zinc refining industry (oligopoly case), 1985

Figure 14.6　Distribution of establishments in the Aluminum refining industry (oligopoly case), 1985 rate of labor-capital substitution, measured as the elasticity of K_{j_i}/L_{j_i} with respect to X_{j_i}, accompanying the expansion of plant scale.

Figures 14.1 to 14.6 suggest that we can expect to obtain fairly stable estimates for equations (1) and (2). Using individual establishment data from the *Census of Manufactures*, we obtained estimates $\hat{\alpha}_{L_j}$, $\hat{\beta}_{L_j}$, $\hat{\alpha}_{K_j}$ and $\hat{\beta}_{K_j}$ for all four-digit industries. These results are summarized as follows. First, for almost all four-digit industries $\hat{\beta}_{L_j} < 1$. This means that plant capacity expansion causes labor saving in all sectors. Second, for $\hat{\beta}_{K_j}$ we obtained estimates of either $\hat{\beta}_{K_j} > 1$ or $\hat{\beta}_{K_j} \leq 1$, for various industries, implying that sectors can be divided into two groups: capital-using sectors with the technological property $\hat{\beta}_{K_j} > 1$ and capital-saving sectors with $\hat{\beta}_{K_j} \leq 1$. Third, we obtained the result that $\hat{\beta}_{K_j} - \hat{\beta}_{L_j} > 0$ for all sectors. This means that the rate of labor productivity growth caused by the expansion of plant scale is greater than the rate of improvement in capital productivity.

3.3   Capital-using sectors

Figures 14.1 and 14.2 show that estimates of $\hat{\beta}_{L_j}$ are fairly stable, in the range of 0.66 to 0.67, in the paper industry for 1980 and 1985 with a coefficient of determination greater than 0.90. Figure 14.3 shows the sample plots of X_{j_i} and K_{j_i} in this industry for 1985. The estimated parameter $\hat{\beta}_{K_j}$ is 1.14 with a coefficient of determination of 0.88.

3.4   Capital-saving sectors

From the equation system (1) and (2) the concept of "economies of plant scale" can be defined for capital-saving sectors (i.e. where $\hat{\beta}_{L_j} < 1$ and $\hat{\beta}_{K_j} < 1$). Economies of plant scale mean that enlarging plant capacity causes labor and capital saving at the same time. Since $\hat{\beta}_{K_j} - \hat{\beta}_{L_j} > 0$, we would expect that the number of establishments would tend to converge at a certain point because of oligopolistic competition. Establishments may well compete to pursue economies of plant scale. Figures 14.4 to 14.6 show the sample plots of X_{j_i} and L_{j_i} in Copper smelting, Zinc refining and Aluminum refining in 1985. In these industries the number of establishments declined because of oligopolistic competition induced by economies of plant scale. However, it is difficult to estimate parameters in cross-section data in industries with such small sample sizes. Hence, in section 4 we try to estimate parameters for these sectors using time-series data. It is assumed that oligopolistic competition in such sectors will result from the characteristics of production technologies.

3.5   Stability over time of the technology parameters

Table 14.1 shows parameter estimates for fifty-three three-digit industries. (Some sectors are excluded from this table because of changes in classification in 1985.) From this table we confirm the properties of technology that we observed at the four-digit level using establishment cross-section data. Also, we can confirm the temporal stability of the estimated parameters. We summarize our findings as follows.

First, the whole economic system can be divided into two parts. One is the capital-using industrial group characterized by $\hat{\beta}_{L_j} < 1$ and $\hat{\beta}_{K_j} \geq 1$. The other is the capital-saving group with the property of $\hat{\beta}_{L_j} < 1$ and $\hat{\beta}_{K_j} < 1$. As mentioned above, we refer to this latter property as "economies of plant scale." Second, for all industries we obtained the result that $\hat{\beta}_{K_j} - \hat{\beta}_{L_j} > 0$. This means that the expansion of plant capacity causes a limited substitution of capital for labor input. Third, for both groups the estimated values of the technology parameters $\hat{\beta}_{L_j}$ and $\hat{\beta}_{K_j}$ were generally stable from 1980 to 1985.

3.6   Technology embodied in plants

We can illustrate the relationship between plant capacity, labor and capital graphically. Figure 14.7 presents the parameters for the Paper industry ($\hat{\beta}_{L_j} < 1$ and $\hat{\beta}_{K_j} > 1$) while figure 14.8 presents the parameters for the industry comprised of Generators, electric motors and other rotating electric machinery ($\hat{\beta}_{L_j} < 1$ and $\hat{\beta}_{K_j} < 1$). Each figure is divided into four quadrants. In the first quadrant we plot the relationship between l_{j_i} and X_{j_i}, $l_{j_i} = L_{j_i}/X_{j_i} = \alpha_{L_j} X_{j_i}^{\beta_{L_j}-1}$, l_{j_i} being the labor coefficient. In the third quadrant the line represents the relationship between k_{j_i} and X_{j_i}, $k_{j_i} = K_{j_i}/X_{j_i} = \alpha_{K_j} X_{j_i}^{\beta_{K_j}-1}$, where k_{j_i} is the capital coefficient. Finally, the relationship between the capital and labor coefficients, k_{j_i}, and l_{j_i} corresponding to the scale of gross output X_{j_i} is shown in the second quadrant. This labor productivity/capital productivity line corresponds to a given level of gross output. This relationship is as follows

$$l_{j_i} = \alpha_{L_j} \alpha_{K_j}^{\frac{1-\beta_{L_j}}{\beta_{K_j}-1}} k_{j_i}^{\frac{\beta_{L_j}-1}{\beta_{K_j}-1}}$$

Figures 14.7 and 14.8 represent the technological structures of a plant, which are characterized by labor and capital inputs. In figure 14.7 the relationship between labor productivity and capital productivity depicted in the second quadrant implies that there exists a substitutable relationship between labor and capital with the expansion of the plant's capacity.

Table 14.1 *Stability over time of the parameters by cross-section analysis*

Sector	three-digit code	β_{L_j} 1980	β_{L_j} 1985	β_{K_j} 1980	β_{K_j} 1985	Number of establishments 1980	Number of establishments 1985	R^2 (equation (1)) 1980	R^2 (equation (1)) 1985	R^2 (equation (2)) 1980	R^2 (equation (2)) 1985	Mean of ($\log X_{ji}$) 1980	Mean of ($\log X_{ji}$) 1985
Silk reeling plants	141	0.62	0.63	0.93	0.98	266	160	0.81	0.81	0.78	0.71	9.99	9.98
Twisting and bulky yarns	143	0.52	0.52	0.62	0.66	3,295	2,757	0.59	0.58	0.33	0.35	7.62	7.82
Woven fabric mills	144	0.50	0.50	0.71	0.74	12,974	9,933	0.59	0.59	0.38	0.38	8.26	8.37
Knit fabric mills	145	0.53	0.52	0.74	0.74	8,589	9,270	0.56	0.55	0.43	0.42	8.49	8.65
Dyed and finished textiles	146	0.65	0.65	0.97	1.00	5,628	5,054	0.79	0.81	0.56	0.59	8.65	8.82
Rope and netting	147	0.58	0.53	0.85	0.94	757	705	0.75	0.66	0.48	0.50	8.63	8.76
Lace and other textile goods	148	0.55	0.56	0.82	0.79	1,497	1,403	0.55	0.58	0.41	0.33	8.45	8.70
Outer garments	151	0.60	0.60	0.65	0.68	17,183	18,499	0.57	0.58	0.36	0.35	8.08	8.21
Shirts and underwear	152	0.58	0.59	0.62	0.68	2,797	2,669	0.57	0.57	0.36	0.36	8.14	8.36
Hats	153	0.44	0.42	0.62	0.69	385	342	0.48	0.45	0.27	0.22	8.11	8.21
Fur apparel and apparel accessories	154	0.41	0.44	0.68	0.68	137	189	0.47	0.47	0.23	0.45	8.81	8.68
Other textile apparel	155	0.46	0.46	0.60	0.75	1,917	1,924	0.42	0.43	0.26	0.34	8.27	8.46
Sawing, planing mills and wood products	161	0.50	0.50	0.63	0.66	17,979	14,266	0.60	0.59	0.28	0.27	9.01	8.94
Millwork, plywood and prefabricated structural wood products	162	0.61	0.62	0.82	0.85	2,534	2,429	0.78	0.77	0.55	0.52	9.52	9.45
Wooden containers	163	0.56	0.55	0.62	0.62	2,445	2,047	0.67	0.66	0.25	0.22	8.43	8.55
Wooden footwear	164	0.47	0.53	0.73	1.26	135	77	0.49	0.57	0.23	0.52	7.78	7.99
Chemical fertilizer	201	0.59	0.53	1.05	1.12	183	192	0.78	0.72	0.69	0.66	11.12	11.16
Industrial inorganic chemicals	202	0.64	0.60	1.10	1.11	615	690	0.76	0.75	0.68	0.63	10.88	10.85

(cont.)

Table 14.1 (*cont.*)

Sector	three-digit code	β_{L_j} 1980	β_{L_j} 1985	β_{K_j} 1980	β_{K_j} 1985	Number of establishments 1980	Number of establishments 1985	R^2 (equation (1)) 1980	R^2 (equation (1)) 1985	R^2 (equation (2)) 1980	R^2 (equation (2)) 1985	Mean of (log X_{ji}) 1980	Mean of (log X_{ji}) 1985
Industrial organic chemicals	203	0.62	0.62	1.08	1.02	691	695	0.79	0.80	0.80	0.76	12.16	12.25
Chemical fiber	204	0.76	0.78	1.17	1.18	86	82	0.92	0.92	0.86	0.88	12.69	12.68
Oil and fat products, soaps	205	0.59	0.57	0.97	0.97	1,081	1,084	0.77	0.75	0.71	0.68	10.25	10.52
Drugs and medicines	206	0.62	0.60	0.89	0.90	1,087	1,175	0.86	0.85	0.72	0.71	10.34	10.54
Tires and inner tubes	231	0.68	0.66	1.03	1.03	63	62	0.95	0.94	0.91	0.94	12.15	12.20
Rubber and plastic footwear	232	0.50	0.50	0.78	0.72	2,148	2,262	0.57	0.58	0.47	0.39	8.43	8.50
Rubber belts, hoses and industrial rubber products	233	0.66	0.65	0.93	0.98	2,169	2,607	0.77	0.76	0.68	0.68	8.95	9.11
Glass products	251	0.69	0.67	1.06	1.05	1,309	1,338	0.85	0.84	0.72	0.70	9.26	9.51
Cement	252	0.49	0.49	0.76	0.81	8,846	8,317	0.65	0.64	0.42	0.39	9.69	9.87
Structural clay products	253	0.76	0.72	1.01	0.95	1,747	1,259	0.78	0.75	0.65	0.57	8.30	8.44
Pottery and related products	254	0.70	0.69	0.88	0.94	4,806	4,439	0.75	0.76	0.56	0.58	8.25	8.40
Clay refractories	255	0.69	0.68	0.97	0.99	284	271	0.85	0.86	0.76	0.67	10.16	10.25
Carbon and graphite products	256	0.63	0.63	1.17	1.17	135	158	0.81	0.80	0.85	0.77	10.04	10.11
Abrasive products	257	0.67	0.64	1.03	1.17	357	341	0.82	0.83	0.65	0.69	9.22	9.36
Aggregate and stone products	258	0.59	0.58	0.92	0.85	3,047	3,267	0.68	0.68	0.48	0.37	9.01	9.09
Electrical generating, transmission, distribution and industrial apparatus	301	0.62	0.58	0.86	0.86	8,422	10,294	0.73	0.69	0.58	0.57	9.06	9.18

Industry	Code												
Household electric appliances	302	0.59	0.58	0.83	0.85	2,363	2,688	0.77	0.76	0.64	0.62	8.95	9.25
Electric bulbs and lighting fixtures	303	0.60	0.60	0.82	0.80	1,508	1,390	0.72	0.74	0.54	0.61	9.02	9.21
Communication equipment	304	0.58	0.58	0.84	0.87	4,976	4,850	0.72	0.73	0.64	0.66	9.07	9.35
Digital and analog computer	305	0.64	0.60	0.93	0.91	769	1,717	0.78	0.75	0.69	0.63	9.09	9.40
Applied electronic equipment	306	0.62	0.59	0.86	0.84	773	2,708	0.74	0.69	0.64	0.61	9.34	9.26
Electric measuring instruments	307	0.66	0.63	0.88	0.87	1,042	1,200	0.77	0.77	0.62	0.59	9.10	9.36
Electronic parts and devices	308	0.61	0.62	0.91	0.99	6,347	8,031	0.71	0.86	0.63	0.67	8.95	9.35
Motor vehicles, parts and accessories	311	0.65	0.64	0.88	0.91	9,700	10,715	0.86	0.85	0.72	0.72	9.11	9.35
Railroad equipment and parts	312	0.72	0.70	0.83	0.77	423	398	0.86	0.85	0.55	0.42	8.98	9.18
Bicycles and parts	313	0.56	0.56	0.80	0.89	816	753	0.75	0.76	0.61	0.66	8.96	8.92
Shipbuilding and repairing	314	0.68	0.66	1.01	1.03	3,054	2,679	0.80	0.79	0.65	0.61	9.05	9.19
Aircraft and parts	315	0.79	0.76	0.93	0.86	133	151	0.93	0.92	0.76	0.78	9.57	9.92
Measuring instruments	321	0.66	0.64	0.87	0.86	1,703	2,003	0.80	0.78	0.55	0.52	9.02	9.23
Surveying instruments	322	0.64	0.61	0.94	1.00	128	117	0.76	0.73	0.60	0.58	8.65	8.86
Medical instruments	323	0.66	0.63	0.85	0.97	1,278	1,385	0.77	0.75	0.54	0.64	8.76	8.93
Physical and chemical instruments	324	0.63	0.61	0.82	0.78	252	263	0.76	0.78	0.42	0.41	8.94	9.23
Optical instruments and lenses	325	0.64	0.62	0.86	0.87	2,906	2,717	0.75	0.73	0.60	0.58	8.61	8.77
Spectacles	326	0.71	0.71	0.84	0.86	606	514	0.72	0.76	0.51	0.48	8.64	9.06
Watches and clocks	327	0.62	0.63	0.89	0.95	855	1,034	0.77	0.72	0.66	0.66	9.28	9.08

244   *Iwao Ozaki*

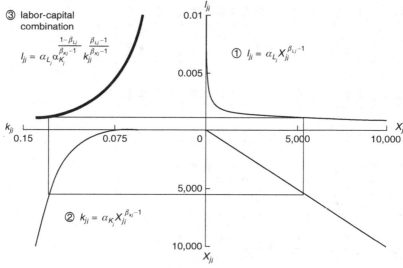

JSIC code: 1821 Paper producing industry (1985)

$\alpha_{K_j} = 0.037$ $\beta_{K_j} = 1.141$ $\bar{X}_{ji} = 5,198$ (millions of yen)
$\alpha_{L_j} = 0.025$ $\beta_{L_j} = 0.659$ $N = 400$

X_{ji}: plant capacity
l_{ji}: required labor for producing unit of products
k_{ji}: capital coefficient

Figure 14.7   Illustration of plant-embodied technology

On the other hand, in figure 14.8 both labor and capital productivity have a tendency to improve with plant capacity expansion. In this case of a capital-saving industry, optimal plant scale cannot be determined endogenously from the supply side since production costs decline with output. In the following section we present a model to determine optimal plant scale for industries like the one depicted in figure 14.7.

3.7   Unit cost minimization: the determination of optimum plant scale

In this system of technology we need to determine the optimum plant scale when $\hat{\beta}_{L_j} < 1$ and $\hat{\beta}_{K_j} > 1$ (as in figure 14.7) in order to evaluate the efficiency of production at each plant with a different scale of capacity X_{ji}. In the following framework of unit cost minimization by the producer, the producer determines the optimum scale of plant capacity and

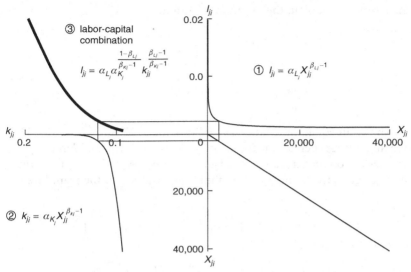

JSIC code: 3011 Generators, electric motors and other rotating electric machinery

$\alpha_{K_j} = 0.265$ $\beta_{K_j} = 0.912$ $\bar{X}_{ji} = 773$ (millions of yen)

$\alpha_{L_j} = 0.053$ $\beta_{L_j} = 0.615$ $N = 1,610$

X_{ji}: plant capacity

l_{ji}: required labor for producing unit of products

k_{ji}: capital coefficient

Figure 14.8   Illustration of plant-embodied technology

the corresponding labor and capital coefficients for given factor prices. Assuming the factor-limited production function in equation system (1) and (2), unit cost at the plant level is defined as follows

$$UC_{j_i} = \frac{C_{j_i}}{X_{j_i}} = w_{j_i}\alpha_{L_j}X_{j_i}^{\beta_{L_j}-1} + r_{j_i}\alpha_{K_j}X_{j_i}^{\beta_{K_j}-1} \tag{3}$$

where w_{j_i} and r_{j_i} stand for factor prices of labor and capital. A necessary condition for a minimum unit cost is

$$\frac{\partial UC_{j_i}}{\partial X_{j_i}} = (\beta_{L_j} - 1)w_{j_i}\alpha_{L_j}X_{j_i}^{\beta_{L_j}-2} + (\beta_{K_j} - 1)r_{j_i}\alpha_{K_j}X_{j_i}^{\beta_{K_j}-2} = 0 \tag{4}$$

As a result, we obtain the optimum solution, $X_{j_i}^*$.

$$
\begin{aligned}
X_{j_i}^* &= \left\{ \frac{(1 - \beta_{L_j})\alpha_{L_j}}{(\beta_{K_j} - 1)\alpha_{K_j}} \right\}^{\frac{1}{\beta_{K_j} - \beta_{L_j}}} \left(\frac{w_{j_i}}{r_{j_i}} \right)^{\frac{1}{\beta_{K_j} - \beta_{L_j}}} \\
&= A_j \left(\frac{w_{j_i}}{r_{j_i}} \right)^{\frac{1}{\beta_{K_j} - \beta_{L_j}}}
\end{aligned}
\tag{5}
$$

As shown in equation (5), it easily follows that $\partial X_{j_i}^* / \partial(w_{j_i}/r_{j_i}) > 0$. This means that an increase in the relative factor price w_{j_i}/r_{j_i} definitely increases the optimum plant capacity. Substituting equation (5) into equation (3) gives the following minimum unit cost $UC_{j_i}^*$ at the plant level

$$
\begin{aligned}
UC_{j_i}^* &= w_{j_i}\alpha_{L_j} A_j^{\beta_{L_j}-1} \left(\frac{w_{j_i}}{r_{j_i}} \right)^{\frac{\beta_{L_j}-1}{\beta_{K_j}-\beta_{L_j}}} + r_{j_i}\alpha_{K_j} A_j^{\beta_{K_j}-1} \left(\frac{w_{j_i}}{r_{j_i}} \right)^{\frac{\beta_{K_j}-1}{\beta_{K_j}-\beta_{L_j}}} \\
&= r_{j_i} \left(\alpha_{L_j} A_j^{\beta_{L_j}-1} + \alpha_{K_j} A_j^{\beta_{K_j}-1} \right) \left(\frac{w_{j_i}}{r_{j_i}} \right)^{\frac{\beta_{K_j}-1}{\beta_{K_j}-\beta_{L_j}}} \\
&= \left(\alpha_{L_j} A_j^{\beta_{L_j}-1} + \alpha_{K_j} A_j^{\beta_{K_j}-1} \right) r_{j_i}^{\left(\frac{1-\beta_{L_j}}{\beta_{K_j}-\beta_{L_j}} \right)} w_{j_i}^{\left(\frac{\beta_{K_j}-1}{\beta_{K_j}-\beta_{L_j}} \right)}
\end{aligned}
\tag{6}
$$

4.   Measurement using a time-series analysis

In Ozaki (1970) the following factor-limited type of production function in the j-th sector was estimated using time-series data. In that paper we used aggregated sector data over time. The variables used in the time-series analysis to estimate technology parameters are sector variables aggregated from the plant level as represented by the following equations

$$
X_j = \sum_i X_{j_i}
$$

$$
L_j = \sum_i L_{j_i}
$$

$$
K_j = \sum_i K_{j_i}
$$

Plant-level labor L_{j_i} and capital K_{j_i} are determined by the technological properties of each plant, where the technology is characterized by a factor-limited production function, as discussed in section 3. We can formulate the aggregate relationships for each sector as

$$L_j = \alpha_{L_j} X_j^{\beta_{L_j}} \tag{7}$$

$$K_j = \alpha_{K_j} X_j^{\beta_{K_j}} \tag{8}$$

where L_j and K_j represent, respectively, labor and the capital stock required for the production level X_j in sector j with data aggregated across plants by sector.

When we estimate the above functions using aggregate time-series data, we can identify the technology type for each sector using the parameters of the production function in equations (7) and (8). The results are summarized in table 14.2. All sectors were grouped into the following five technology types:[2]

(i) Type K(I-B) technology: large-quantity processing technology;

(ii) Type K(I-M) technology: large-scale assembly production technology;

(iii) Type K(II) technology: capital-using technology;

(iv) Type L technology: labor-using technology;

(v) Type (L-K) technology: traditional technology.

As shown in table 14.2, industries categorized as type K(I-B) are characterized as having the highest capital-labor ratio, where both $\hat{\beta}_{L_j}$ and $\hat{\beta}_{K_j}$ are also less than unity. Although industries categorized in type K(I-M) have the same properties in terms of the estimated parameters, values of the capital-labor ratio are not quite so high. Table 14.2 reveals that the K(I-B)-type technology sectors include (1) Electric power supply, (2) Petroleum refinery products, (3) Basic organic chemicals, (4) Synthetic fiber materials, (5) Iron and steel and (6) Primary non-ferrous products; while K(I-M)-type technology sectors include (7) Shipbuilding and ship repair, (8) Motor vehicles, (9) General machinery, (10) Electrical machinery, (11) Precision instruments, (12) Spinning mills and (13) Soft drinks and alcoholic beverages. Because of the technological properties of these industries, the optimum plant scale cannot be determined by a unit cost minimization procedure outlined in section 3.7, the application of which requires that $\hat{\beta}_{K_j} > 1$. Although the determination of plant capacity depends on the size of total demand in the market, the technology is predominantly characterized by the economies of plant scale.

On the other hand, industries categorized as type K(II) are characterized by $\hat{\beta}_{L_j} < 1$ and $\hat{\beta}_{K_j} > 1$. Capital-using technology distinguishes type

---

[2] This classification of technology type is slightly different from the classification in Ozaki (1970). This is because we focus here on the values of the estimated parameters instead of capital intensities.

Table 14.2 *Parameter characteristics of production functions in various industries, time-series approach*

Sector	Type of technology	Production function parameters		$(\overline{K}_j/\overline{L}_j)$	$\Delta(X_j/\Sigma X_j)$ $\dfrac{1965}{1955}$	$\Delta(L_j/\Sigma L_j)$ $\dfrac{1965}{1955}$
		β_{L_j}	β_{K_j}			
Large-quantity processing technology						
(1) Electric power supply	K(I-B)	0.12	0.80	17.43	1.14	0.94
(2) Petroleum refinery products	K(I-B)	0.27	0.65	14.76	2.21	1.52
(3) Basic organic chemicals	K(I-B)	0.33	0.72	5.70	3.44	2.05
(4) Synthetic fiber materials	K(I-B)	0.10	0.84	3.89	1.79	1.10
(5) Iron and steel	K(I-B)	0.30	0.80	3.86	1.44	1.44
(6) Primary non-ferrous products	K(I-B)	0.38	0.73	3.84	1.22	1.45
Large-scale assembly production technology						
(7) Shipbuilding and ship repair	K(I-M)	0.07	0.80	1.19	1.57	1.04
(8) Motor vehicles	K(I-M)	0.46	0.70	2.12	3.95	2.66
(9) General machinery	K(I-M)	0.52	0.88	0.62	1.48	1.95
(10) Electrical machinery	K(I-M)	0.55	0.91	1.00	2.74	2.86
(11) Precision instruments	K(I-M)	0.53	0.97	0.59	1.61	1.96
(12) Spinning mills	K(I-M)	0.26	0.59	2.07	0.72	1.19
(13) Soft drinks and alcoholic beverages	K(I-M)	0.33	0.79	2.26	0.88	1.18

Capital-using technology

(14) Paper	K(II)	0.13	1.03	3.07	1.08	1.03
(15) Cement	K(II)	0.08	1.03	9.07	1.06	0.94
(16) Basic inorganic chemicals	K(II)	0.04	1.01	2.71	1.01	0.95
(17) Building and construction	K(II)	0.53	1.32	0.25	1.32	1.64
(18) Seafood, preserved	K(II)	0.46	1.13	0.59	0.63	1.07
(19) Paints	K(II)	0.35	1.09	1.51	1.21	1.35
(20) Other transport equipment	K(II)	0.28	1.05	1.01	0.87	1.18
(21) Metal products	K(II)	0.51	1.01	0.49	1.74	2.05
(22) Printing and publishing	K(II)	0.47	1.15	0.57	1.08	1.42
(23) Other food, prepared	K(II)	0.42	1.36	0.65	0.67	1.10
(24) Finance and insurance	K(II)	0.45	1.22	0.70	1.40	1.66
(25) Communication services	K(II)	0.25	1.46	0.17	1.03	1.12

Note: The figures of $\overline{K}$ and $\overline{L}$ represent the annual average for the years 1955 through 1970. $\Delta(X_j/\Sigma X_j)$ and $\Delta(L_j/\Sigma L_j)$ represent the indexes of the changes in composition ratios of gross output gross output X_j and labor force L_j between 1955 and 1965, which is defined as the ratio of the amount of each variable for industry j to the total amount for all industries.

Source: Ozaki (1976, table 5–1).

K(II) industries from industries classified as type L and type (L-K). Unit cost minimization determines optimum plant scale for type K(II) industries. Given a change in relative factor prices, producers determine the optimum plant scale. When increases in labor input prices were relatively large compared with increases in capital input prices, the optimum plant capacity increased and producers expanded plant scale for the sake of economic efficiency.

Industries categorized as K(I-B), K(I-M) and K(II) are characterized by high capital intensity and benefit from economies of scale at the plant level. These industries are intimately involved in economic growth; it is these industries that have capital coefficients that change over time. On the other hand, type L industries are characterized by small-scale plants and low capital intensity and include such sectors as Wood products and apparel. Finally, type (L-K) includes traditional sectors such as Agriculture and Mining. These two types of industries change little in the course of economic development. Hence we exclude them from our discussion in this paper.

In the development of the Japanese economy, industries categorized as type K(I-B) and type K(I-M) played leading roles. As shown in table 14.2, we find that all composition ratios $\Delta(X_j / \Sigma X_j)$ and $\Delta(L_j / \Sigma L_j)$ for these industries have increased very rapidly, with the exception of the indexes for (12) Spinning mills and (13) Soft drinks and alcoholic beverages. In industries categorized as type K(I-B) and type K(I-M), the larger the plant scale the more unit costs will decrease. Hence an optimum solution for plant scale cannot be obtained. Nonetheless, table 14.3 reveals that there is a definite "preferred" plant scale in each industry. For instance, machinery sectors (type K(I-M)) and raw material processing sectors (type K(I-B)) have different average plant capacities. We can deduce from this that other factors preclude the limitless expansion of plant scale. We should incorporate other variables in the analysis, such as total demand, in order to ascertain the endogenous determination mechanism for plant capacity.

5.   Enlargement of plant scale and structural change

The previous two sections using both cross-section and time-series data provide a consistent summary of the characteristics of technology. Cross-section establishment data were used to estimate the properties of technology at the plant level. As already noted, these properties of technology at the plant level can be linked to the technological properties at the aggregate sector level through the distribution of plants in each period. Changes in factor prices over time would produce endogenous adjustments in the

Table 14.3 *Pattern of competition in the case of $\beta_{L_j} < 1$, $\beta_{K_j} < 1$*

JSIC code	Sector	Number of establishment $n(j)$				Average size of capacity (1985) $\bar{X}_{ji} = X_j/n_j$	Total demand size of sector (1985) X_j
		1970	1975	1980	1985		
Type K(I-B): basic material processing							
2641	Hot rolling	87	64	57	43	8,213	353,150
2642	Cold rolling	51	53	57	50	13,691	684,568
2643	Cold rolled steel shapes	40	39	38	34	3,185	108,304
2644	Steel pipes and tubes	76	98	84	78	8,968	699,484
2645	Re-rolled steel products	180	149	96	50	894	44,680
2647	Pipes and tubes drawing	64	60	59	48	1,640	78,729
2711	Primary smelting and refining of copper	13	11	8	8	34,875	279,001
2713	Primary smelting and refining of zinc	12	11	8	8	17,384	139,071
2716	Primary smelting and refining of aluminium	12	14	14	10	22,374	223,738
2719	Miscellaneous primary smelting and refining of non-ferrous metals	25	28	15	28	15,977	447,360
Type K(I-M): machinery							
2971	Pumps and pumping equipment	828	1,023	962	506	898	454,302
2972	Air compressors, gas compressors and blowers	631	666	640	417	564	235,000
2973	Elevators and escalators	220	330	351	250	932	232,906
2974	Conveyors and conveying equipment	1,804	2,298	2,300	1,713	496	850,048
2975	Mechanical power transmission equipment, except ball- and roller bearings	1,422	1,894	1,871	1,138	449	510,599
2976	Industrial furnaces and ovens	208	235	236	178	422	75,086
2977	Oil hydraulic equipment	1,019	1,591	2,023	1,267	472	598,352
2978	Chemical machinery and its equipment	1,310	2,078	1,826	1,590	723	1,149,933
2979	Miscellaneous general industry machinery and equipment	1,822	2,709	2,366	1,696	392	664,522
3011	Generators, electric motors and other rotating electric machinery	1,596	1,859	1,805	1,610	754	1,213,689
3012	Power and distribution transformers, except electronic appliances transformers	674	1,054	1,152	856	415	355,599
3013	Relay switches, switchboards and electrical control equipment	2,355	3,595	3,997	3,722	637	2,372,438
3014	Wiring devices and supplies	1,154	1,467	1,674	1,397	499	696,488
3015	Electrical welding equipment	207	252	278	197	510	100,568
3016	Auxiliary equipment for internal combustion engines	342	630	1,088	1,717	680	1,168,346

distribution of plant scale as the optimum scale of plants changed. Even when the distribution of optimum plant scale shifted in the time-series data because of changes in factor prices, at the aggregate level we still observe stable technological properties from parameters of factor-limited production functions. As shown in figures 14.1 and 14.2, the distributions of optimum plant scales were fairly stable during the economy's development. Therefore, in the aggregate, changes in the capital coefficients in Leontief's dynamic model can be determined endogenously by changes in optimum plant size, which is determined in turn by unit cost minimization at each plant. Hence, changes in capital coefficients at the aggregate level are dominated by the endogenous determination of optimum plant scale and the distribution of optimum plant scale.

The growth rate in the optimum scale of plant capacity for each establishment under unit cost minimization can be formulated from equation (5) as follows

$$\frac{\dot{X}_{j_i}}{X_{j_i}} = \frac{1}{\beta_{K_j} - \beta_{L_j}} \frac{\left(\dfrac{\dot{w}_{j_i}}{r_{j_i}}\right)}{\left(\dfrac{w_{j_i}}{r_{j_i}}\right)} \tag{9}$$

where the relative factor price for each establishment w_{j_i}/r_{j_i} is exogenously specified in each period. Changes in factor prices over time would change the optimum scale of plant capacity under unit cost minimization. Equation (9) represents the growth rate of the optimum scale of plant capacity for each individual establishment consistent with changes in relative factor prices.

On the other hand, we can obtain the growth rate of aggregate sector plant capacity consistent with changes in plant capacity at each individual establishment as follows

$$\frac{\dot{X}_j}{X_j} = \sum_i \frac{\dot{X}_{j_i}}{X_{j_i}} \frac{X_{j_i}}{X_j} = \frac{1}{\beta_{K_j} - \beta_{L_j}} \sum_i \frac{X_{j_i}}{X_j} \frac{\left(\dfrac{\dot{w}_{j_i}}{r_{j_i}}\right)}{\left(\dfrac{w_{j_i}}{r_{j_i}}\right)} \tag{10}$$

We define the aggregate sector capital coefficient as follows

$$B_j = \frac{K_j}{X_j} = \frac{\sum_i K_{j_i}}{\sum_i X_{j_i}} = \frac{\sum_i \alpha_{K_j} X_{j_i}^{\beta_{K_j}}}{\sum_i X_{j_i}}$$

Consequently, when we introduce a factor-limited production function, we can derive the following growth rate for the aggregate sector capital coefficient as a function of the optimum scale of plant capacity for each establishment

$$\frac{\dot{B}_j}{B_j} = \frac{\dot{K}_j}{K_j} - \frac{\dot{X}_j}{X_j} = \sum_i \frac{\dot{K}_{j_i}}{K_{j_i}} \frac{K_{j_i}}{K_j} - \sum_i \frac{\dot{X}_{j_i}}{X_{j_i}} \frac{X_{j_i}}{X_j} = \sum_i \beta_{K_j} \frac{\dot{X}_{j_i}}{X_{j_i}} \frac{K_{j_i}}{K_j} - \sum_i \frac{\dot{X}_{j_i}}{X_{j_i}} \frac{X_{j_i}}{X_j}$$

$$= \sum_i \left(\beta_{K_j} \frac{K_{j_i}}{K_j} - \frac{X_{j_i}}{X_j} \right) \frac{\dot{X}_{j_i}}{X_{j_i}} = \sum_i \left(\beta_{K_j} \frac{X_{j_i}^{\beta_{K_j}}}{\sum_i X_{j_i}^{\beta_{K_j}}} - \frac{X_{j_i}}{\sum_i X_{j_i}} \right) \frac{\dot{X}_{j_i}}{X_{j_i}}$$

$$= \sum_i \left(\beta_{K_j} \frac{X_{j_i}^{\beta_{K_j}}}{\sum_i X_{j_i}^{\beta_{K_j}}} - \frac{X_{j_i}}{\sum_i X_{j_i}} \right) \frac{1}{\beta_{K_j} - \beta_{L_j}} \frac{\left(\dfrac{w_{j_i}}{r_{j_i}} \right)^{\!\bullet}}{\left(\dfrac{w_{j_i}}{r_{j_i}} \right)} \tag{11}$$

This implies that changes in the capital coefficient for aggregate sectors depend upon the technological parameters of the production function and the distribution of the optimum scale of plant capacity for establishments – an optimum consistent with given changes of factor prices over time. Next we assume that changes in relative factor prices are the same for individual plants

$$\frac{\left(\dfrac{w_{j_i}}{r_{j_i}} \right)^{\!\bullet}}{\left(\dfrac{w_{j_i}}{r_{j_i}} \right)} = \frac{\left(\dfrac{w_j}{r_j} \right)^{\!\bullet}}{\left(\dfrac{w_j}{r_j} \right)}, \quad \text{for all } i \tag{12}$$

Substituting equation (12) into equation (10), and rearranging equations (10) and (11), we obtain the following two equations

$$\frac{\dot{X}_j}{X_j} = \frac{1}{\beta_{K_j} - \beta_{L_j}} \frac{\left(\dfrac{w_j}{r_j} \right)^{\!\bullet}}{\left(\dfrac{w_j}{r_j} \right)}$$

$$\frac{\dot{B}_j}{B_j} = \frac{\beta_{K_j} - 1}{\beta_{K_j} - \beta_{L_j}} \frac{\left(\dfrac{w_j}{r_j} \right)^{\!\bullet}}{\left(\dfrac{w_j}{r_j} \right)}$$

Hence, the change in the capital coefficient at the aggregate sector level is represented by the following equation

$$\frac{\dot{B}_j}{B_j} = (\beta_{K_j} - 1) \frac{\dot{X}_j}{X_j} \tag{13}$$

Finally, changes in the capital coefficients at the aggregate level in equation (13) depend upon the technological parameter β_{K_j} and the growth rate of plant capacity for aggregate sectors. Needless to say, the growth rate of plant capacity for aggregate sectors is a function of the optimum scale of plant capacity for each establishment. As previously mentioned, in the case in which the technological properties are $\beta_{K_j} > 1$ and $\beta_{K_j} > \beta_{L_j}$, typically plant capacity for aggregate sectors increases with the expansion of optimum plant scale at the establishment level (this expansion being the result of increases in relative factor prices). At the same time, the capital coefficient for aggregate sectors also increases. This implies that capital coefficients in the Leontief dynamic model can be determined endogenously, consistent with the properties of technological relationships at the plant level.

6.   Concluding remarks

The results obtained in this study may be summarized as follows. First, we showed the usefulness and effectiveness of the factor-limited production function in the analysis of structural change. Dynamic changes in the parameters in Leontief's dynamic models are determined endogenously.

In order to determine the optimum plant scale X_{ji}^*, two hypotheses were established. One was the "technology embodied in plant" hypothesis, and the other was the unit cost minimization principle. For all industries, we obtained $\hat{\beta}_{L_j} < 1$. And all industries are divided into either the case of $\hat{\beta}_{K_j} < 1$ or the case of $\hat{\beta}_{K_j} > 1$, which could be determined empirically. For the former case we defined the concept of "economies of plant scale" in terms of physical units. This means that enlargement of plant capacity causes the simultaneous saving of both labor and capital. It was, in fact, the concentration of resources into industries with the technology $\hat{\beta}_{K_j} < 1$ that resulted in the so-called "heavy" industrial structure during the period 1955 to 1985 in Japan (see Ozaki, 1976).

For the latter case, where $\hat{\beta}_{L_j} < 1$ and $\hat{\beta}_{K_j} > 1$, the optimum scale of plant capacity can be determined by unit cost minimization. We showed that there is a tendency toward the expansion of plant capacity X_{ji} in a process of economic growth with an increase in the relative factor price w_{ji}/r_{ji}.

As mentioned in section 3.2, we obtained the results $\hat{\beta}_{K_j} - \hat{\beta}_{L_j} > 0$ for all industries. This means that the limited substitution of capital for labor accompanied by the expansion of plant capacity would promote capital accumulation under the conditions of the factor-limited production function.

We further showed that changes over time in aggregate sector capital coefficients B_j depend on the expansion of optimum plant scale X_{ji}^*. These changes over time in the structural capital coefficients are the single most important factor causing structural change in Leontief's dynamic model.

Finally, we conclude that, in the following Leontief dynamic model,

$$A_t x_t + B_{t+1} \Delta x_t + c_t = x_t$$

capital coefficients b_{ij} shift endogenously with changes in the optimum scale of plant. Hence, our approach implies that a Leontief dynamic model with structural changes should be formulated as follows

$$A_t x_t + [B_{t+1}(X_{j_i})] \Delta x_t + c_t = x_t$$

where $B_{t+1}(X_{j_i})$ denotes the capital matrix with coefficients that depend on X_{j_i}. Needless to say, our analysis is confined to a supply-side study. Our work suggests that production function parameters have real implications for the structure of the market and are, therefore, key to development.

ACKNOWLEDGEMENTS

The author is indebted to Professors M. Kuroda and K. Nomura, both of Keio University, for their valuable discussions and for carrying out statistical operations.

REFERENCES

Carter, A. P. (1970) *Structural Change in the American Economy* (Cambridge, MA, Harvard University Press).
Komiya, R. (1962) Technological progress and production function in the United States steam power industry, *Review of Economics and Statistics*, 44, 156–166.
Komiya, R., and T. Uchida (1963) The labor coefficient and the size of establishment in two Japanese industries, in T. Barna (ed.) *Structural Interdependence and Economic Development* (New York, St Martin's Press), 265–276.
Lau, L., and S. Tamura (1972), Economies of scale, technical progress and the nonhomothetic Leontief production function, *Journal of Political Economy*, 80, 1,167–1,187.
Leontief, W. W. (1970) The dynamic inverse, in A. P. Carter and A. Brody (eds.) *Contributions to Input-Output Analysis* (Amsterdam, North-Holland), 17–46.
Leontief, W. W., et al. (1953) *Studies in the Structure of the American Economy* (New York, Oxford University Press).
Nakamura, S. (1990) A nonhomothetic generalized Leontief cost function based on pooled data, *Review of Economics and Statistics*, 72, 649–656.
Ozaki, I. (1970) Economies of scale and input-output coefficients, in A. P. Carter and A. Brody (eds.) *Applications of Input-Output Analysis* (Amsterdam, North-Holland), 261–279.
(1976) The effects of technological changes on the economic growth of Japan, 1955–1970, in K. R. Polenske and J. V. Skolka (eds.) *Advances in Input-Output Analysis* (Cambridge, MA, Ballinger Publishing Company), 93–111.

15 Technological change and accumulated capital: a dynamic decomposition of Japan's growth

Masahiro Kuroda and Koji Nomura

1. Introduction

In this paper we evaluate technological progress using static and dynamic production linkages. Technologies of an activity are mutually interdependent through the market transactions of all the "produced" inputs.[1] This implies that the production of one commodity is linked to that of all other commodities, both directly and indirectly, through intermediate transactions. Because of this, the change in a commodity's technological efficiency should be measured as the change in the economy's productivity induced by technology change in all linked activities. But production linkages between the commodity and the rest of the economy should not be evaluated simply through the static interdependent relationships among sectors. The dynamic interrelationship among sectors through the process of accumulating capital as produced factors of production should also be included.

The productivity of a sector in a specific period depends on its use of primary factors, such as labor and capital, as well as of intermediate inputs. The capital a sector uses is extracted from the capital accumulated through past investments. Prior investment is characterized by properties of technology during the periods when the accumulated capital was produced and invested. This means that past capital investment affects present production efficiency. In the traditional growth accounting framework, however, capital investments are measured as direct contributions to gross product with no direct link to technological progress. Hence, it would be interesting to isolate technological progress through the accumulation of these capital contributions, so that we could measure its effect on productivity.

The possibility of both static and dynamic technological linkages lends us to bifurcate traditional total factor productivity measurement into

---

[1] By "activity" we mean the set of direct inputs required to produce a specific commodity, as articulated in an input vector within the input-output framework. Related to this, we call the agent of production and investment activity a "sector" or an "industry."

"static unit TFP" and "dynamic unit TFP." We formulate these two measures here using Leontief's static and dynamic input-output frameworks. While traditional TFP is defined in terms of the growth accounting of a specific sector, our proposed static unit TFP of a commodity evaluates productivity growth on an economy-wide basis, including the more efficient use of factor inputs in all linked industries. It can be interpreted as a specification of the true impacts of productivity change – the effective rate of TFP proposed by Hulten (1978). Effective TFP is also identical to the TFP of Peterson's "vertically integrated sector," where each assumptive sector produces one type of final output making use only of factor inputs. Peterson (1979) and Wolff (1985) have measured such TFP for the United Kingdom and the United States respectively, using Leontief's static input-output framework.

Dynamic unit TFP, as proposed here, can be evaluated through the total historical production of a specific commodity, where all the inputs are reduced only to dated labor inputs. Using Peterson's language, it implies the productivity index of a "dynamically vertical integrated sector," where each assumptive sector produces one type of final output making use only of dated labor inputs. Aulin-Ahmavaara (1999) has proposed a "fully effective" rate of TFP using the dynamic input-output framework to evaluate capital as a produced input. Her formulation is based on the balanced growth solution of the closed dynamic input-output model, where production technology is represented by two technology matrices – input coefficients and capital coefficients – as structural parameters. On the other hand, our dynamic unit TFP is backwardly evaluated and is based on the dynamic inverse model, in order to decompose economic growth using dynamic growth accounting. The two technology matrices are treated as historical structural parameters.

In input-output, an economy is depicted by static and dynamic interdependencies of commodity production. In particular, Ozaki's (1980) "unit structure" and Leontief's (1970) "dynamic inverse" are the bases of our accounting framework. In section 2 we introduce static and dynamic concepts of unit structure.

We formulate static unit TFP and dynamic unit TFP in section 3. The formulae are based upon the accounting balances of static and dynamic production linkages, as proposed in section 2. In the dynamic inverse, the capital coefficient matrix is usually assumed to be a constant matrix of structural parameters. Here, for each annual national input-output table for Japan from 1955 to 1992, we estimated a corresponding annual productive capital-stock matrix. During this period there were clear structural changes in Japan, which should be reflected in sectoral technological progress and not just by changes in industry mix.

In section 4 we briefly explain both our database on Japan's economy and our results for Japan's dynamic inverse. In section 5, using our proposed productivity formulae, we dynamically decompose Japan's productivity change from 1970 to 1990. Our results show that dynamic unit TFP's share of Japan's economic growth has risen gradually, and in the period 1985 to 1990 it contributed 16 percent of all TFP from the viewpoint of a traditional decomposition of economic growth, and a full 39 percent using a dynamic evaluation.

2.   Static and dynamic unit structure

2.1   Static structure

Let us begin with the definition of "unit structure." In the static input-output framework, the system of production at any time t can be described as follows in terms of the input coefficient matrix $\mathbf{A}_t$, column vectors of final demand $\mathbf{f}_t$ and output $\mathbf{x}_t$

$$\mathbf{A}_t \mathbf{x}_t + \mathbf{f}_t = \mathbf{x}_t$$

If $\mathbf{A}_t$ is non-singular, we obtain $\mathbf{x}_t = (\mathbf{I} - \mathbf{A}_t)^{-1}\mathbf{f}_t$ using identity matrix $\mathbf{I}$. Taking $\mathbf{f}_t^* = \mathbf{e}_{(i)}$, where $\mathbf{e}_{(i)}$ denotes the ith unit vector with a one in position i and all other entries equal to zero, the matrices of intermediate deliveries $\mathbf{X}_t^*$, labor $\mathbf{L}_t^*$ and capital $\mathbf{K}_t^*$ required for producing a single unit of final demand of commodity are then given by

$$\mathbf{U}_t \mid {}_{\mathbf{f}_t^*=\mathbf{e}_{(i)}} = \begin{bmatrix} \mathbf{X}_t^* \\ \mathbf{L}_t^* \\ \mathbf{K}_t^* \end{bmatrix} = \begin{bmatrix} \mathbf{A}_t \langle (\mathbf{I} - \mathbf{A}_t)^{-1}\mathbf{f}_t^* \rangle \\ \mathbf{B}_t^L \langle (\mathbf{I} - \mathbf{A}_t)^{-1}\mathbf{f}_t^* \rangle \\ \mathbf{B}_t^K \langle (\mathbf{I} - \mathbf{A}_t)^{-1}\mathbf{f}_t^* \rangle \end{bmatrix} \tag{1}$$

where $\langle \cdot \rangle$ is used to denote a diagonal matrix. $\mathbf{B}_t^L$ and $\mathbf{B}_t^K$ represent the labor coefficient matrix ($l \times n$) and capital coefficient matrix ($k \times n$) respectively. Equation (1) is termed the "static unit structure" or the "unit structure." The static unit structure is the basket of all the inputs required (directly and indirectly) to produce one unit of final demand of a commodity ($\mathbf{f}_t^* = \mathbf{e}_{(i)}$). It is the set of static linkages in the production of a commodity. The unit structure of any specific commodity is quite stable in a time series of input-output tables (see, e.g., Ozaki, 1980), although the input mix can change due to substitution motivated by changes in relative prices, scale economies, productivity change and so forth.

2.2   Dynamic inverse and dynamic structure

The above static unit structure concept corresponds to a measure of one module of a production system for a specific time period t. For commodity i in year t, the accumulation of capital needed for production is the result of past investments in *all* sectors. With this in mind, we define another concept – that of the "dynamic unit structure" – to evaluate the production linkages of commodity i in year t as a result of a dynamic process that includes capital accumulation. Leontief (1970) proposed the dynamic inverse to evaluate how technological change affects production. So, let us begin with an explanation of it, using our accounting framework.

Assume the following commodity balance equation

$$\mathbf{A}_t \mathbf{x}_t + \mathbf{I}_t^P \mathbf{i} + \mathbf{I}_t^G \Gamma \mathbf{i} + \mathbf{c}_t = \mathbf{x}_t \tag{2}$$

where $\mathbf{I}_t^P$ is the investment matrix of private and government enterprises, while $\mathbf{I}_t^G$ stands for the infrastructure investment matrix of dimension n (commodity) $\times$ m (infrastructure) and the bridge matrix $\Gamma (m \times n)$ is an array of 0s and 1s that allocates each type of infrastructure to the industries.[2] Further, assume that some industry-specific infrastructure is imputed only and that other more general infrastructure (e.g. parks, sewage facilities and so on) is ignored and treated as other final demand $\mathbf{c}_t$. Also, let $\mathbf{i}$ denote the summation vector consisting of 1s. We assume that $\mathbf{I}_t^P$ is defined using the perpetual inventory method with a column vector of constant replacement rates $\mathbf{\delta}^P$ and a capital stock matrix $\mathbf{S}_t^P$. That is,

$$\mathbf{I}_t^P = \mathbf{S}_{t+1}^P - (\mathbf{I} - \langle \mathbf{\delta}^P \rangle) \mathbf{S}_t^P = \mathbf{B}_{t+1}^P \langle \mathbf{x}_{t+1} \rangle - (\mathbf{I} - \langle \mathbf{\delta}^P \rangle) \mathbf{B}_t^P \langle \mathbf{x}_t \rangle \tag{3a}$$

Infrastructure investment is defined similarly

$$\mathbf{I}_t^G \Gamma = \mathbf{S}_{t+1}^G \Gamma - (\mathbf{I} - \langle \mathbf{\delta}^G \rangle) \mathbf{S}_t^G \Gamma = \mathbf{B}_{t+1}^G \langle \mathbf{x}_{t+1} \rangle - (\mathbf{I} - \langle \mathbf{\delta}^G \rangle) \mathbf{B}_t^G \langle \mathbf{x}_t \rangle \tag{3b}$$

Substituting (3a) and (3b) into (2), we obtain the following equation using the capital coefficients in $\mathbf{B}_t^P$ and $\mathbf{B}_t^G$

$$(\mathbf{I} - \mathbf{G}_t) \mathbf{x}_t - \mathbf{B}_{t+1}^K \mathbf{x}_{t+1} = \mathbf{c}_t \tag{4}$$

where $\mathbf{G}_t = \mathbf{A}_t - (\mathbf{I} - \langle \mathbf{\delta}^P \rangle) \mathbf{B}_t^P - (\mathbf{I} - \langle \mathbf{\delta}^G \rangle) \mathbf{B}_t^G$ with $\mathbf{B}_t^K = \mathbf{B}_t^P + \mathbf{B}_t^G$. The linear differences of these equations form the basis of Leontief's

---

[2] Generally, infrastructure for roads and highways is classified into Road transportation (sector 28), while that for marine and air transportation is classified into Water transportation (29) and Air transportation (30) respectively. Infrastructure for the conservation of land (forests, mountains, rivers, coasts and wetlands) is classified into Agriculture, forestry and fishing (1), while land improvement is classified into Real estate (38).

dynamic inverse approach. Note, in particular, that the stability of capital coefficients is not invoked here. They can change, as we will see in section 4. From the perspective of the base period t, the commodity balance equation for each past period can also be written as

$$x = (I - D)^{-1}c = Mc \tag{5}$$

where

$$D = \begin{pmatrix} G_{t-T} & B^K_{t-T+1} & & & \\ & \ddots & \ddots & & \\ & & G_{t-2} & B^K_{t-1} & \\ & & & G_{t-1} & B^K_t \\ & & & & G_t \end{pmatrix}$$

$$x = \begin{pmatrix} x_{t-T} \\ \vdots \\ x_{t-2} \\ x_{t-1} \\ x_t \end{pmatrix}$$

$$c = \begin{pmatrix} c_{t-T} \\ \vdots \\ c_{t-2} \\ c_{t-1} \\ c_t \end{pmatrix}$$

and $G_t = A_t$ in base period t. Assuming that the elements of final demand at t are exogenous, equation (5) yields the production series that must be satisfied, directly and indirectly in the static and dynamic process, by the given final demand levels. Equation (5) is consistent with the demand for direct and indirect transactions with static and dynamic linkages, where the accumulated capital must be produced prior to the previous year. Furthermore, we should mention that the system is satisfied by supply-side technological conditions identified by the capital coefficients.

The following equation represents the "dynamic unit system" of commodity i

$$DMc^* + c^* = Mc^* \tag{6}$$

where $\mathbf{c}^*$ denotes the final demand vector and $\mathbf{c}_t^* = \mathbf{e}_{(i)}$, and $\mathbf{c}_{t-\tau}^* = 0$ for $\tau = 1, \ldots, T$. In equation (6), the following matrix

$$
\mathbf{U}^D|_{\mathbf{c}^*} = \begin{bmatrix} \mathbf{X}^* \\ \mathbf{L}^* \\ \mathbf{K}^* \end{bmatrix} = \begin{bmatrix} \mathbf{D}\langle \mathbf{Mc}^* \rangle \\ \mathbf{B}^L \langle \mathbf{Mc}^* \rangle \\ \mathbf{B}^K \langle \mathbf{Mc}^* \rangle \end{bmatrix} \tag{7}
$$

is called the "dynamic unit structure". It is parallel in concept to the static unit structure formulated in the previous section.

3.   TFP and produced inputs

3.1   Static unit TFP

The rate of technological progress for a specific activity is defined as the difference between the growth rate of gross output and the weighted average growth rate of the various inputs of the activity. This traditional residual measure is called the growth rate of TFP. In order to construct a framework embracing both static unit TFP and dynamic unit TFP, we should review the concepts of the growth rate of sectoral TFP and the aggregate measure of sectoral TFP.

The rate of traditional TFP growth in an arbitrary sector j, assuming perfect competition and constant returns to scale, can be formulated as

$$
\left(\frac{\dot{T}_j}{T_j} \right)_t = \left(\frac{\dot{X}_j}{X_j} \right)_t - \sum_i \frac{p_{i,t} X_{ij,t}}{p_{j,t} X_{j,t}} \left(\frac{\dot{X}_{ij}}{X_{ij}} \right)_t - \sum_l \frac{p_{lj,t}^L L_{lj,t}}{p_{j,t} X_{j,t}} \left(\frac{\dot{L}_{lj}}{L_{lj}} \right)_t
$$
$$
- \sum_k \frac{p_{kj,t}^K K_{kj,t}}{p_{j,t} X_{j,t}} \left(\frac{\dot{K}_{kj}}{K_{kj}} \right)_t \tag{8a}
$$

where X_j denotes the real gross output of sector j. Likewise, X_{ij}, L_{lj} and K_{kj} denote for sector j, respectively, the intermediate input i, the input of labor of type l and input of capital of type k. The prices of gross output, labor and capital inputs are $p_{j,t}$, $p_{lj,t}^L$ and $p_{kj,t}^K$ respectively. In equation (8a) the weights of each input, which are defined by the nominal cost shares of the components in intermediate, labor and capital inputs, sum to unity under the accounting balance

$$
p_{j,t} X_{j,t} = \sum_i p_{i,t} X_{ij,t} + \sum_l p_{lj,t}^L L_{lj,t} + \sum_k p_{kj,t}^K K_{kj,t}
$$

Using a_{ij}, b_{lj}^L and b_{kj}^K as typical elements of the coefficient matrices $\mathbf{A}$, $\mathbf{B}^L$ and $\mathbf{B}^K$ respectively, we can also rewrite equation (8a) as

$$
\left(\frac{\dot{T}_j}{T_j}\right)_t = -\sum_i \frac{p_{i,t} X_{i,j,t}}{p_{j,t} X_{j,t}} \left(\frac{\dot{a}_{ij}}{a_{ij}}\right)_t - \sum_l \frac{p_{lj,t}^L L_{lj,t}}{p_{j,t} X_{j,t}} \left(\frac{\dot{b}_{lj}^L}{b_{lj}^L}\right)_t
$$

$$
- \sum_k \frac{p_{kj,t}^K K_{kj,t}}{p_{j,t} X_{j,t}} \left(\frac{\dot{b}_{kj}^K}{b_{kj}^K}\right)_t \tag{8b}
$$

This equation indicates that the growth rate of sectoral TFP is a continuous analogue of the Leontief (1953) structural change measure.[3] Next, based on the accounting identity for the national economy, we obtain the following equation for the growth rate of aggregate (overall) TFP

$$
\left(\frac{\dot{T}}{T}\right)_t = \sum_i \frac{p_{i,t} f_{i,t}}{\mathbf{p}_t' \mathbf{f}_t} \left(\frac{\dot{f}_i}{f_i}\right)_t - \sum_j \sum_l \frac{p_{lj,t}^L L_{lj,t}}{\mathbf{p}_t' \mathbf{f}_t} \left(\frac{\dot{L}_{lj}}{L_{lj}}\right)_t
$$

$$
- \sum_j \sum_k \frac{p_{kj,t}^K K_{kj,t}}{\mathbf{p}_t' \mathbf{f}_t} \left(\frac{\dot{K}_{kj}}{K_{kj}}\right)_t \tag{9a}
$$

and

$$
\left(\frac{\dot{T}}{T}\right)_t = \sum_j \frac{p_{j,t} X_{j,t}}{\mathbf{p}_t' \mathbf{f}_t} \left(\frac{\dot{T}_j}{T_j}\right)_t \tag{9b}
$$

where $\mathbf{p}_t' \mathbf{f}_t$ (which denotes aggregate nominal final demand $\Sigma_i p_{i,t} f_{i,t}$) is identical to aggregate nominal value added $\Sigma_j (\Sigma_l p_{lj,t}^L L_{lj,t} + \Sigma_k p_{kj,t}^K K_{kj,t})$. Equation (9a) shows that the growth rate of aggregate TFP is the difference between the growth rate of net outputs (aggregate final demand) and that of net inputs (aggregate factor inputs, decomposed here into labor and capital). The growth rate of aggregate final demand is defined by a Divisia aggregate index of the growth rate of final demand components, weighted by nominal shares of each component in nominal total final demand.

[3] If we define partial factor productivity of intermediate inputs $T_{ij}^A (=1/a_{ij})$, labor productivity $T_{lj}^L (=1/b_{lj}^L)$ and capital productivity $T_{kj}^K (=1/b_{kj}^K)$, it is easy to see that

$$
\left(\frac{\dot{T}_j}{T_j}\right)_t = \sum_i \frac{p_{i,t} X_{ij,t}}{p_{j,t} X_{j,t}} \left(\frac{\dot{T}_{ij}^A}{T_{ij}^A}\right)_t
$$

$$
+ \sum_l \frac{p_{lj,t}^L L_{lj,t}}{p_{j,t} X_{j,t}} \left(\frac{\dot{T}_{lj}^L}{T_{lj}^L}\right)_t + \sum_i \frac{p_{kj,t}^K K_{kj,t}}{p_{j,t} X_{j,t}} \left(\frac{\dot{T}_{kj}^K}{T_{kj}^K}\right)_t
$$

This implies that the growth rate of "total" factor productivity is identified by the weighted average of the growth rates of "partial" productivities of all the inputs.

Equation (9b) is also the formula of aggregate TFP growth as measured by the Domar-weighted average of the growth rates of sectoral TFP in (8a). The sum of sectoral weights is necessarily more than unity as a property of the Domar (1961) aggregation. Hulten (1978) also gives the detailed derivation of aggregate TFP in (9a) and (9b).

In (9a), labor and capital inputs can be interpreted as the direct and indirect requirements for the production of final demand $f_{i,t}$. Under the assumption of a homothetic production function in all sectors and exogenous factor prices, factor inputs required directly and indirectly for production are proportional to the scale of final demand. Because of this, aggregate TFP in equation (9a) can be interpreted as the aggregate TFP "function" for an arbitrary final demand $f_{i,t}$. Here the unit structure in a static input-output framework gives a specification. Applying the notion of the unit structure of commodity i in equation (1) to an aggregate measure of the production efficiency, we define the growth rate of "static unit TFP," or simply "unit TFP," as

$$\left(\frac{\dot{T_i}}{T_i}\right)_t^U = -\sum_j \sum_l \frac{p_{lj,t}^L L_{lj,t}^*}{p_{i,t}} \left(\frac{\dot{L_{lj}^*}}{L_{lj}^*}\right)_t - \sum_j \sum_k \frac{p_{kj,t}^K K_{kj,t}^*}{p_{i,t}} \left(\frac{\dot{K_{kj}^*}}{K_{kj}^*}\right)_t \quad (10)$$

where $\mathbf{L}_t^* = \mathbf{B}_t^L\langle(\mathbf{I} - \mathbf{A}_t)^{-1}\mathbf{e}_{(i)}\rangle$ and $\mathbf{K}_t^* = \mathbf{B}_t^K\langle(\mathbf{I} - \mathbf{A}_t)^{-1}\mathbf{e}_{(i)}\rangle$ at any moment of time. As expressed in the previous section, we denote with a superscript asterisk, *, all the variables related to Leontief's input-output framework. In case $\mathbf{f}_t^* = \mathbf{e}_{(i)}$, the nominal accounting balance for the economy yields $\mathbf{p}_t'\mathbf{e}_{(i)} = p_{i,t} = \Sigma_j(\Sigma_l p_{lj,t}^L L_{lj,t}^* + \Sigma_k p_{kj,t}^K K_{kj,t}^*)$. The growth rate of unit TFP is independent of the scale of final demand. The aggregate measure should be distinguished from the growth rate of aggregate TFP in equation (9b), although they may seem similar. The one in (10) corresponds to an aggregate measure of production efficiency in terms of the unit structure. This measure denotes the total production efficiency of a specific *commodity*, where the production efficiency is evaluated as a measure of TFP not of a specific activity but rather of a specific commodity's final demand. It is defined as an aggregate measure of the production efficiency in terms of all the activities (directly and indirectly induced) needed to deliver a specific commodity to final demand. The static unit TFP is identical to Peterson's (1979) TFP for a "vertically integrated sector," where each sector produces one final output and uses only primary inputs to do so.

Since $\mathbf{L}_t = \mathbf{L}_t^*\hat{\mathbf{f}}_t$ and $\mathbf{K}_t = \mathbf{K}_t^*\hat{\mathbf{f}}_t$,

$$\left(\frac{\dot{T}}{T}\right)_t = \sum_i \frac{p_{i,t} f_{i,t}}{\mathbf{p}_t'\mathbf{f}_t} \left(\frac{\dot{T_i}}{T_i}\right)_t^U \quad (11)$$

That is, the growth rate of aggregate TFP is the weighted average of the static unit TFP growth rates. The weights indicate the nominal final demand share and sum to unity. So, we can interpret the static unit TFP based on an input-output framework as an example of Hulten's (1978) effective rate of TFP. From equations (9b) and (11), the relationship between the traditional direct measure of TFP and static unit TFP is

$$\left(\frac{\dot{T_i}}{T_i}\right)^U_t = \sum_j \frac{p_{j,t}X^*_{j,t}}{p_{i,t}}\left(\frac{\dot{T_j}}{T_j}\right)_t = \sum_j \frac{p_{j,t}h_{ji,t}}{p_{i,t}}\left(\frac{\dot{T_j}}{T_j}\right)_t \tag{12}$$

Because $\mathbf{f}^*_t = \mathbf{e}_{(i)}$, $X^*_{j,t}$ equals element j of vector $(\mathbf{I} - \mathbf{A}_t)^{-1}\mathbf{e}_{(i)}$ – i.e. column i of the Leontief inverse. Using $\mathbf{H}_t = (\mathbf{I} - \mathbf{A}_t)^{-1}$ we have $X^*_{j,t} = h_{ji,t}$. The growth rate of unit TFP is defined by the weighted average of the growth rate of TFP for individual sectors. The weights are the Domar weights of a unit of final demand, concurring with Wolff (1985, p. 270) and Aulin-Ahmavaara (1999, p. 354).[4] When it is assumed that the direct activity for commodity i does not need intermediate inputs, then $h_{ji,t} = 0$ for $j \neq i$ and $h_{ii,t} = 1$, so that both TFP indices are identical. Assuming positive productivity progress, the growth of the unit TFP typically will be greater than that of the traditional TFP.

It is convenient to define the aggregate measure of unit TFP. Equation (10) can be extended for an arbitrary final demand $\mathbf{f}^*_t$

$$\left(\frac{\dot{T}}{T}\right)^{U(\mathbf{f}^*_t)}_t = \sum_i \frac{p_{i,t}f^*_{i,t}}{\mathbf{p}'_t\mathbf{f}^*_t}\left(\frac{\dot{f}^*_i}{f^*_i}\right)_t - \sum_j\sum_l \frac{p^L_{lj,t}L^*_{lj,t}}{\mathbf{p}'_t\mathbf{f}^*_t}\left(\frac{\dot{L}^*_{lj}}{L^*_{lj}}\right)_t$$
$$- \sum_j\sum_k \frac{p^K_{kj,t}K^*_{kj,t}}{\mathbf{p}'_t\mathbf{f}^*_t}\left(\frac{\dot{K}^*_{kj}}{K^*_{kj}}\right)_t \tag{13}$$

Let us refer to this aggregate TFP concept as "compound unit TFP." The first term of the right-hand side in (13) is zero when the final demand vector is constant ($\mathbf{f}^*_t = \mathbf{f}^*$). In the case of $\mathbf{f}^*_t = \mathbf{e}_{(i)}$, the measure in (13) is identical with unit TFP in (10), $(\dot{T}_i/T_i)^U_t = (\dot{T}/T)^{U(\mathbf{e}_{(i)})}_t$. In particular, if the actual final demand vector $\mathbf{f}_t$ is applied, the compound unit TFP returns to the growth rate of aggregate TFP in (9a): $(\dot{T}/T)_t = (\dot{T}/T)^{U(\mathbf{f}_t)}_t$. The compound unit TFP offers information on productivity change for any composite commodities, such as the commodity baskets of household consumption, exports and investment.

---

[4] When the growth rate of static unit TFP and traditional TFP are denoted by column vectors $d\mathbf{t}^U_t$ and $d\mathbf{t}_t$ respectively, we can rewrite the relationship in equation (12) as $(d\mathbf{t}^U_t)' = (d\mathbf{t}_t)'\hat{\mathbf{p}}_t(\mathbf{I} - \mathbf{A}_t)^{-1}\hat{\mathbf{p}}_t^{-1}$.

3.2   Dynamic unit TFP

The above concept of static unit TFP measures productivity change for a specific commodity at any time t. We should note that production is restricted by the technology embodied in accumulated capital. Through investment, accumulated productive capital is composed of the capital goods from prior periods. Moreover, capital goods are characterized by technological properties at the time of the investment, not at the time of their use. By focusing on the historical perspective of capital accumulation, we can develop a dynamic concept of the effective rate of productivity change. Here we formulate "dynamic unit TFP," based on the dynamic unit structure derived from Leontief's dynamic inverse in section 2.2

To link TFP growth and dynamic unit structure we first assume a proportional relationship between the quantity of capital service K_t and accumulated productive capital stock S_t. In particular, for simplicity in formulating dynamic unit TFP, assume K_t and S_t are proportional at the aggregate level. Then the Divisia aggregate inputs for capital are

$$\left(\frac{\dot{S}}{S}\right)_t = \left(\frac{\dot{K}}{K}\right)_t = \sum_j \sum_k \frac{p_{kj,t}^K K_{kj,t}}{\sum_j \sum_k p_{kj,t}^K K_{kj,t}} \left(\frac{\dot{K}_{kj}}{K_{kj}}\right)_t \qquad (14a)$$

and aggregate measures of labor and final demand can be defined

$$\left(\frac{\dot{L}}{L}\right)_t = \sum_j \sum_l \frac{p_{lj,t}^L L_{lj,t}}{\sum_j \sum_l p_{lj,t}^L L_{lj,t}} \left(\frac{\dot{L}_{lj}}{L_{lj}}\right)_t$$

$$\left(\frac{\dot{f}}{f}\right)_t = \sum_i \frac{p_{i,t} f_{i,t}}{\mathbf{p}_t' \mathbf{f}_t} \left(\frac{\dot{f}_i}{f_i}\right)_t \qquad (14b)$$

Second, assume a dynamic unit structure with discrete historical periods at any moment of continuous time. With this, we can formulate the relationship between productive capital stock and gross investment as

$$S_{t-\tau} = (1 - \delta) S_{t-\tau-1} + I_{t-\tau-1} \qquad (\tau = 0, 1, 2, \ldots)$$

where δ denotes the replacement rate for aggregate productive capital stock, which is constant over time for simplicity. Here $S_{t-\tau}$ indicates the stock at $t - \tau$, and is related to the stock and investment in the previous period $t - \tau - 1$ using a perpetual inventory formulation similar to that in equations (3a) and (3b). Differentiating with respect to time t, we obtain the following relationship

$$
\left(\frac{\dot{S}}{S}\right)_{t-\tau} = (1-\delta)\frac{S_{t-\tau-1}}{S_{t-\tau}}\left(\frac{\dot{S}}{S}\right)_{t-\tau-1}
$$

$$
+\frac{I_{t-\tau-1}}{S_{t-\tau}}\left(\frac{\dot{I}}{I}\right)_{t-\tau-1} \quad (\tau = 0, 1, 2, \ldots) \tag{15}
$$

Now we discuss the dynamic formulation in which one unit of a specific commodity is supplied at time t. Such a commodity not only has linkages to intermediate inputs and labor during that period, but also has dynamic linkages to them through the accumulation of capital. In order to clarify the relationship, let us briefly review the formula of compound unit TFP. Recall that the growth rate of compound unit TFP at $t - \tau$ is defined in equation (13). Thus, using (14a) and (14b),

$$
\left(\frac{\dot{T}}{T}\right)_{t-\tau}^{U(\mathbf{f}_{t-\tau}^*)} = \left(\frac{\dot{f}^*}{f^*}\right)_{t-\tau} - \sigma_{L,t-\tau}^*\left(\frac{\dot{L}^*}{L^*}\right)_{t-\tau} - \sigma_{K,t-\tau}^*\left(\frac{\dot{K}^*}{K^*}\right)_{t-\tau}
$$

$$
(\tau = 0, 1, 2, \ldots) \tag{16a}
$$

with $\quad \sigma_{L,t-\tau}^* = \Sigma_j\Sigma_l p_{lj,t-\tau}^L L_{lj,t-\tau}^*/\mathbf{p}_{t-\tau}'\mathbf{f}_{t-\tau}^* \quad$ and $\quad \sigma_{K,t-\tau}^* = \Sigma_j\Sigma_k p_{kj,t-\tau}^K K_{kj,t-\tau}^*/\mathbf{p}_{t-\tau}'\mathbf{f}_{t-\tau}^*$, and

$$
\left(\frac{\dot{T}}{T}\right)_{t-\tau}^{U(\mathbf{f}_{t-\tau}^*)} = \sum_j \frac{p_{j,t-\tau}X_{j,t-\tau}^*}{\mathbf{p}_{t-\tau}'\mathbf{f}_{t-\tau}^*}\left(\frac{\dot{T}_j}{T_j}\right)_{t-\tau} \quad (\tau = 0, 1, 2, \ldots)
$$

$$
\tag{16b}
$$

Note that (16a) is identical to (13) when $\tau = 0$. When we consider the dynamic process needed to satisfy the final demand for a single unit of a specific commodity at $t - \tau$, $\mathbf{f}_{t-\tau}^*$ – the real volume of final demand at $t - \tau$ in (16a) – must represent enough real gross investment to satisfy the capital service inputs required both at $t - \tau$ and the previous period, $t - \tau - 1$. Thus

$$
\left(\frac{\dot{I}^*}{I^*}\right)_{t-\tau} = \left(\frac{\dot{f}^*}{f^*}\right)_{t-\tau} \quad (\tau = 1, 2, \ldots) \tag{17}
$$

which implies that the period's aggregate growth rate of investment needed to satisfy the delivery of a single unit of a specific commodity at $t - \tau$ is identical to the Divisia aggregate growth rate of the capital goods that embody aggregate investment. Taking $\tau = 1$ and substituting equations (15) and (17) into (16a), we can rewrite the growth rate of aggregate capital service input at any time t – the third term of the right-hand side ($\tau = 0$) in (16a) – as

$$
\left(\frac{\dot{K}^*}{K^*}\right)_{t-\tau+1} = s^*_{t-\tau}\left\{\left(\frac{\dot{T}}{T}\right)^{U(f^*_{t-\tau})}_{t-\tau} + \sigma^*_{L,t-\tau}\left(\frac{\dot{L}^*}{L^*}\right)_{t-\tau}\right.
$$

$$
\left.+ \left(\frac{(1-\delta)S^*_{t-\tau}}{I^*_{t-\tau}} + \sigma^*_{K,t-\tau}\right)\left(\frac{\dot{S}^*}{S^*}\right)_{t-\tau}\right\}
$$

$$(\tau = 1) \qquad (18a)$$

where $s^*_{t-\tau} = I^*_{t-\tau}/S^*_{t-\tau+1}$.

This equality implies that the growth rate of the aggregate capital service input needed to deliver one unit of a specific commodity to final demand at any time t is decomposable according to the dynamic process that describes past capital accumulation. The right-hand side shows that the growth rate of capital service inputs at t decomposes into three parts. The first is the compound unit TFP growth in period $t - 1$, which is required to satisfy the investment demand of the previous period. The second shows labor's contribution in the production of the investment goods at $t - 1$. The third represents the contribution of capital services at $t - 1$ as well as the contributions of past capital accumulation. If we apply equations (15), (16a) and (17) to the previous period $\tau = 2$, we obtain the following as the third item in (18a)

$$
s^*_{t-\tau+1}\left(\frac{(1-\delta)S^*_{t-\tau+1}}{I^*_{t-\tau+1}} + \sigma^*_{K,t-\tau+1}\right)\left(\frac{\dot{S}^*}{S^*}\right)_{t-\tau+1}
$$

$$
= \Phi^*_{t-\tau}\left(\frac{\dot{T}}{T}\right)^{U(f^*_{t-\tau})}_{t-\tau} + \Phi^*_{t-\tau}\sigma^*_{L,t-\tau}\left(\frac{\dot{L}^*}{L^*}\right)_{t-\tau}
$$

$$
+ \Phi^*_{t-\tau}\left\{\frac{(1-\delta)S^*_{t-\tau}}{I^*_{t-\tau}} + \sigma^*_{K,t-\tau}\right\}\left(\frac{\dot{S}^*}{S^*}\right)_{t-\tau} \qquad (\tau = 2) \quad (18b)
$$

where

$$
\Phi^*_{t-\tau} = s^*_{t-\tau}s^*_{t-\tau+1}\left(\frac{(1-\delta)S^*_{t-\tau+1}}{I^*_{t-\tau+1}} + \sigma^*_{K,t-\tau+1}\right)
$$

We can decompose the contribution of the capital in (18b) at the period $t - 1$ into three components at $t - 2$ in a fashion similar to that shown in (18a).

Finally, repeating the same procedure, we can trace the dynamic production linkages that are required to satisfy the unit of final demand at any time t. Since we assume that the capital invested in the prior periods embodies properties of the technology in each successive period, we can define the dynamic impact of the growth of productivity by the following

$$\left(\frac{\dot{T}}{T}\right)_t^{D(f_t^*)} = \left(\frac{\dot{T}}{T}\right)_t^{U(f_t^*)} + \sigma_{K,t}^* \sum_{\tau=1}^{\infty} \Phi_{t-\tau}^* \left(\frac{\dot{T}}{T}\right)_{t-\tau}^{U(f_{t-\tau}^*)} \tag{19a}$$

and

$$\left(\frac{\dot{T}}{T}\right)_t^{D(f_t^*)} = \left(\frac{\dot{f}^*}{f^*}\right)_t - \sigma_{L,t}^* \left(\frac{\dot{L}^*}{L^*}\right)_t - \sigma_{K,t}^* \sum_{\tau=1}^{\infty} \Phi_{t-\tau}^* \sigma_{L,t-\tau}^* \left(\frac{\dot{L}^*}{L^*}\right)_{t-\tau} \tag{19b}$$

where

$$\Phi_{t-\tau}^* = \begin{cases} s_{t-\tau}^* & (\tau = 1) \\ s_{t-\tau}^* \Phi_{t-\tau+1}^* \left(\dfrac{(1-\delta) S_{t-\tau+1}^*}{I_{t-\tau+1}^*} + \sigma_{K,t-\tau+1}^* \right) & (\tau = 2, \dots, \infty) \end{cases}$$

We refer to $(\dot{T}/T)_t^{D(e_{(i)})}$ as the growth rate of dynamic unit TFP. We can interpret the measure in two ways. One is as the formulation in equation (19a), where it is defined as the weighted sum of static unit TFP at the period t and the compound unit TFP of the previous period $t - \tau$, where $\tau = 1, 2, \dots$ Here we should note that each compound unit TFP includes all of the sectoral TFP linkages made possible through the production of capital and intermediate goods as described in equation (16b). The other interpretation is that in (19b), where it is defined as the difference between the aggregate growth rate of final demand at t and the sum of all of the contributions attributable to dated labor. Through the formulation of the dynamic unit TFP we can now evaluate all the economic effects attributable to the technological properties involved in the production of a single unit of a specific commodity.

4.   Measurement

4.1   Data

The database upon which our framework is based consists of a time series of annual national input-output tables for Japan's economy from 1960 to 1992. These tables are consistent with the official quinquennial benchmark tables. Furthermore, we estimated the labor and capital inputs for each of the forty-three sectors (see table 15.1) of the input-output tables. Labor measures included in the series of tables are: number of workers (persons); hours worked; and wage per hour. Each of these is

Table 15.1 *Sector classification*

1. Agriculture, forestry and fishing	23. Motor vehicles
2. Coal mining	24. Other transportation equipment
3. Other mining	25. Precision instruments
4. Building and construction	26. Other manufacturing
5. Food manufacturing	27. Railway transportation
6. Textiles	28. Road transportation
7. Apparel	29. Water transportation
8. Wood and related products	30. Air transportation
9. Furniture and fixture	31. Storage facility services
10. Paper and pulp	32. Communication
11. Publishing and printing	33. Electricity
12. Chemical products	34. Gas supply
13. Petroleum refinery	35. Water supply
14. Coal products	36. Wholesale and retail trade
15. Rubber products	37. Finance and insurance
16. Leather products	38. Real estate
17. Stone and clay	39. Education
18. Iron and steel	40. Research
19. Non-ferrous metals	41. Medical care
20. Metal products	42. Other services
21. General machinery	43. Public services
22. Electric machinery	

cross-classified into 11,352 categories: by industry (forty-three categories), gender (two), age (eleven), employment status of workers (three) and education (four).[5]

The framework for the measurement of capital as a factor of production depends on the method proposed by Biørn (1989), Jorgenson (1989) and Hulten (1990). To better describe the properties of dynamic structural changes, we estimated a time series of productive capital-stock matrices for the 1955–1992 period. Capital flows and stocks are bifurcated into enterprises that are privately owned and those that are government owned. Social overhead capital is not allocated by industry. Both enterprise types are classified into the forty-three sectors of table 15.1. On the other hand, our capital flow and stock matrices are consolidated from the seventy-eight categories of capital goods in the official input-output accounts into forty-three categories of row-wise capital goods.[6]

[5] The number of workers includes proprietors, unpaid family workers and payroll employees. The totals are consistent with the numbers in the *Census of Manufactures*. Also, labor compensation in the input-output table is adjusted consistently with the definition of workers.

[6] Our measure of capital stock includes tangible assets, inventories and land. In constant prices, we account for any quality adjustments in capital goods. The series of productive

As a residual, TFP measurement depends entirely upon the growth rates of gross output and various inputs. Hence, measurement concepts are extremely important in interpreting the implications of TFP. We typically assume, for instance, that outputs and inputs are both measured as homogeneous in quality over time. In other words, if either output or inputs have quality differences over time, corrections for quality differences must be made in the output and input indices. This ensures that the effects of positive quality changes in "outputs" are embodied in TFP, while the impact of the positive quality changes in "inputs" are disembodied in TFP, as formulated by Jorgenson (1966) and Hulten (1992). In our estimates of the TFP growth rate, we make every attempt to evaluate quality changes in each input in as detailed a manner as possible. Our results for TFP growth should, nonetheless, be interpreted with care with regard to both quantity and quality.

4.2   Capital coefficients

Let us focus on trends of accumulated capital for the 1955–1992 period in Japan. Since 1960 the annual average growth rate of capital by sector has been significantly higher than that for labor. In particular, from 1960 to 1965, twenty-eight out of the forty-three sectors maintained capital growth of more than 10 percent annually. This trend continued through 1975. After the oil embargo almost all industries – except Electricity (sector 33), Gas supply (34), Medical care (41) and Other services (42) – experienced a dramatic slowdown in capital growth. From 1975 to 1980 capital growth dropped to less than half the rate experienced previously. One of the most intriguing characteristics of the economy after 1985 is that capital formation in specific industries – such as Electric machinery (sector 22), Precision instruments (25) and Communication (32) – increased rapidly.

Figure 15.1 shows the aggregate change in capital coefficients from 1960 to 1992. In the figure, the height of a bar represents the size of the corresponding capital coefficient. Each of the twelve segments on a bar

capital stock for tangible assets is estimated using the double-benchmark-years method. As benchmarks, we used the 1955 and 1970 National Wealth Surveys in Japan. Some age-efficiency profiles of each capital good were estimated from the observations from data on used cars, rental housing and so on. We assumed that the mortality distribution of each capital good was geometric. Also, we estimated the prices of capital service using imputations of capital assets and income by sector, taking account of Japan's detailed tax structure, including corporate tax, enterprise tax, property tax and acquisition tax with the institution of various types of allowances and reservations (see Nomura, 1998). See Kuroda et al. (1997) for more details about the input-output tables and related capital, labor, energy and materials (KLEM) information used in this paper.

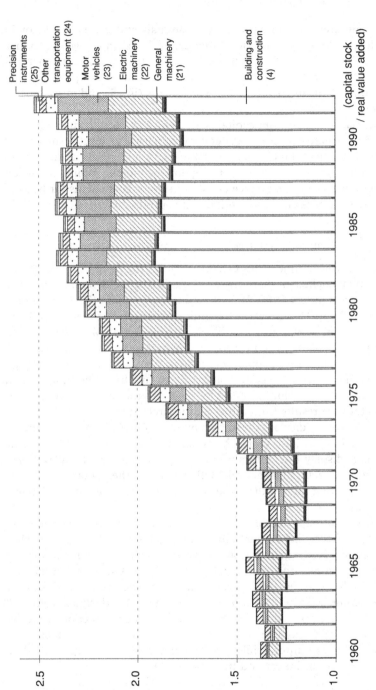

Figure 15.1 Trends of aggregated capital coefficients in Japan

represents the share of an asset type: animals and plants (in sector 1), building and construction (in 4), textile products (in 6), wood products (in 8), furniture (in 9), metal products (in 20), general machinery (in 21), electric machinery (in 22), motor vehicles (in 23), other transportation equipment (in 24), precision instruments (in 25) and miscellaneous products (in 26).

The nation's aggregate capital coefficient increased from 1.4 in 1960 to 2.5 in 1992. Moreover, general machinery and electric machinery gradually increased their shares among assets, apparently at the expense of building and construction. In Japan's economy, capital coefficient changes presumably influence changes in input coefficients for both intermediate inputs and labor and, thereby, productivity.

4.3   Dynamic unit structure

Equipped with a time series of estimated intermediate input coefficient and capital coefficient matrices, we can describe the dynamic unit structure in Japan for the 1960–1992 period using equation (7). For example, tables 15.2 and 15.3 show the dynamic unit structure for Motor vehicles (sector 23) in 1980 and 1992. The consumption of Motor vehicles for both years is assumed to be 100 million constant 1985 yen. Each table is composed of a set of subtables that describe the year-to-year linkages of dynamic spillover effects, working backward from the base year. In each subtable the column labeled "x" contains the vector of gross output by sector that results from direct and indirect spillovers, while the column labeled "c" displays the impact of 100 million yen of motor vehicles demanded in the base year. The columns labeled "I_p" and "I_g" in the subtables display the vectors of required investment in the private and government sectors respectively. Other parts of the subtables show the linkages among intermediate transactions in each stage of the dynamic spillover.

The top subtable in tables 15.2 and 15.3 corresponds to the static unit structure. According to our results, the production of Electric machinery (sector 22) – required as an intermediate input in terms of the unit structure – grows from 8 in 1980 to 18 in 1992. On the other hand, in terms of the static unit structure, Japan's intermediate demand for General machinery (sector 21) and of Iron and steel (18) declined from 1980 to 1992. This implies that efficiency changes in the production of Electric machinery gradually increased their influence upon the productivity of Motor vehicles output, while the influence of efficiency gains made in both General machinery and Iron and steel waned.

Table 15.2 Dynamic unit structure of sector 23 (Motor vehicles) (base year = 1980)

[1980]

[1980]	23	22	21	20	18	19	15	13	12	6	33	36	42	c	x
23.Vehicle	42.8													100	143
22.Elec.Mach.	4.9	0.7										0.2	0.1		8
21.Machinery	9.9	5.0										0.3	0.2		16
20.Metal Prod.	1.4	0.1	0.1		0.1							0.1	0.1		3
18.Iron&Steel	8.4	0.7	1.6	0.7	12.7							0.2			24
19.Non-ferrous	2.9	0.5	0.3	0.1	0.2	2.5									7
15.Rubber Prod.	6.7														7
13.Petroleum	0.7						0.1				1.5				6
12.Chemical	1.4	0.1			0.4	0.2	0.1	0.2	3.0	0.8					8
6.Textile	1.4								0.3						1
33.Electricity	1.4						0.1				0.1	0.2	0.3		5
44.Raw Oil											4.6				0
45.Natural Gas											0.3				0
28.Road Trans.	1.4														3
36.Trade	7.7	0.4	0.2	0.6	0.1	0.3	0.1	0.3	0.1			0.1	0.6		14
42.Other Serv.	6.4	0.8	0.9	1.0	0.1	0.5	0.5	0.7	0.3			0.9	1.4		16

Year blocks (columns: 4, 23, 22, 21, 20, 18, 19, lp, lg, x)

[1979]

[1979]	4	23	22	21	20	18	19	lp	lg	x
4.Build.&Const.								35.9	3.6	40.1
23.Vehicle	0.2							0.4		1.8
22.Elec.Mach.	0.6							5.1		10.0
21.Machinery	0.4							24.7		37.2
20.Metal Prod.	3.6									5.6
18.Iron&Steel	1.6	0.1								18.4
19.Non-ferrous	0.3									4.9
33.Electricity	0.3									3.3
36.Trade										
42.Other Serv.	2.9									3.7

[1978]

[1978]	4	23	22	21	20	18	19	lp	lg	x
4.Build.&Const.								20.9	6.8	28.0
23.Vehicle	0.3							1.8		3.5
22.Elec.Mach.	0.3							4.0		7.0
21.Machinery	0.3							9.9		15.8
20.Metal Prod.	2.3							0.3		10.4
18.Iron&Steel	1.0	0.2	0.9	0.2						
19.Non-ferrous	0.2									2.4
33.Electricity	0.2									2.3
36.Trade	0.2									5.8
42.Other Serv.	2.0									7.6

[1977]

[1977]	4	23	22	21	20	18	19	lp	lg	x
4.Build.&Const.								13.6	4.1	17.9
23.Vehicle	0.1	0.7						1.1		2.1
22.Elec.Mach.	0.2		1.0					2.4		4.2
21.Machinery	0.2	0.1		3.0				6.0		9.6
20.Metal Prod.	1.4				0.1			0.2		2.2
18.Iron&Steel	0.5	0.1	0.2	1.0	0.6	0.3		0.3		5.8
19.Non-ferrous	0.2				0.1	0.2	0.2			1.5
33.Electricity	0.1							0.1		1.4
36.Trade	0.3	0.1	0.2	0.5	0.1			0.2		3.6
42.Other Serv.	1.3			0.7	0.2					4.9

[1976]

[1976]	4	23	22	21	20	18	19	lp	lg	x
4.Build.&Const.								8.6	2.4	11.1
23.Vehicle	0.1	0.4						0.7		1.3
22.Elec.Mach.	0.6		0.7					1.5		2.6
21.Machinery	0.9			1.8				3.7		5.8
20.Metal Prod.	0.3			0.3	0.6	0.4	2.2	0.1		3.8
18.Iron&Steel	0.1		0.1	0.1	0.1	0.2				1.0
19.Non-ferrous							0.4			0.8
33.Electricity	0.9									2.2
36.Trade	0.8									2.9
42.Other Serv.										

[1975]

[1975]	4	23	22	21	20	18	19	lp	lg	x
4.Build.&Const.								4.9	1.6	6.6
23.Vehicle	0.3	0.3						0.5		0.9
22.Elec.Mach.	0.3		0.3		0.1			0.8		1.4
21.Machinery	0.3			1.0				2.3		3.6
20.Metal Prod.	0.5				0.4	0.2	1.3			0.8
18.Iron&Steel	0.2					0.1				0.5
19.Non-ferrous							0.2			0.5
33.Electricity	0.5									1.3
36.Trade	0.5									2.0
42.Other Serv.										

[1974]

[1974]	4	23	22	21	20	18	19	lp	lg	x
4.Build.&Const.								3.1	0.9	4.1
23.Vehicle	0.2	0.2						0.3		0.5
22.Elec.Mach.	0.2		0.3					0.6		1.1
21.Machinery	0.1			0.7				1.5		2.3
20.Metal Prod.	0.4				0.3	0.2	0.9			0.6
18.Iron&Steel	0.1					0.1				0.4
19.Non-ferrous							0.2			0.3
33.Electricity	0.3									0.9
36.Trade	0.4	0.1								1.4
42.Other Serv.										

[1973]

[1973]	4	23	22	21	20	18	19	lp	lg	x
4.Build.&Const.								1.9	0.6	2.6
23.Vehicle	0.1	0.2						0.3		0.3
22.Elec.Mach.			0.2					0.9		0.6
21.Machinery	0.3			0.4						1.4
20.Metal Prod.					0.2	0.1	0.6			0.4
18.Iron&Steel							0.1			1.1
19.Non-ferrous										0.3
33.Electricity	0.2									0.2
36.Trade	0.2									0.5
42.Other Serv.										

[1972]

[1972]	4	23	22	21	20	18	19	lp	lg	x
4.Build.&Const.								1.1	0.4	1.6
23.Vehicle	0.3							0.1		0.2
22.Elec.Mach.								0.2		0.3
21.Machinery								0.5		0.8
20.Metal Prod.				0.2			0.3			0.2
18.Iron&Steel	0.1									0.1
19.Non-ferrous										0.1
33.Electricity										0.3
36.Trade	0.1									0.5
42.Other Serv.										

[1971]

[1971]	4	23	22	21	20	18	19	lp	lg	x
4.Build.&Const.								0.6	0.2	0.9
23.Vehicle										0.1
22.Elec.Mach.				0.1						0.2
21.Machinery								0.3		0.5
20.Metal Prod.							0.2			0.1
18.Iron&Steel										0.3
19.Non-ferrous										
33.Electricity										0.2
36.Trade										0.3
42.Other Serv.										

unit: millions of constant 1985 yen

Table 15.3 Dynamic unit structure of sector 23 (Motor vehicles) (base year = 1992)

unit: millions of constant 1985 yen

[1992]	23	22	21	20	18	19	15	13	12	6	33	36	42	c	x
23 Vehicle	68.4													100	169
22.Elec.Mach.	11.7	5.8										0.1			18
21.Machinery	2.0	0.2	1.4	0.1									0.3		4
20.Metal Prod.	1.3	0.3	0.1	0.1									0.4		2
18.Iron&Steel	5.7	0.3	0.2	0.6	6.2										13
19.Non-ferrous	3.3	0.6	0.1	0.2	0.1	2.6									7
15.Rubber Prod.	4.5	0.1					0.2								5
13.Petroleum	0.5	0.1			0.1	0.1		0.1	0.5	0.1					3
12.Chemical	1.9	0.2			0.1		1.2		1.9	0.3					7
6.Textile	0.3						0.2			0.1					1
33.Electricity	2.0	0.2						2.2							5
45.Natural Gas															0
44.Raw Oil								0.3		0.4					0
28.Road Trans.	1.3	0.1			0.1	0.1	0.1			0.2					3
36.Trade	8.4	0.6	0.1	0.1	0.5	0.3			0.2	0.2	0.2	0.9			15
42.Other Serv.	7.5	0.8	0.1	0.1	0.4	0.3			0.4	1.0	1.0				15

[1991]	4	23	22	21	20	18	19	lp	lg	x
4.Build.&Const.	0.1							35.3	1.3	37.5
23.Vehicle	0.3	0.7						0.2		1.7
22.Elec.Mach.	0.7	0.1	5.1	2.6				6.6		15.7
21.Machinery	0.5			21.6				39.6		62.4
20.Metal Prod.	4.0		0.2	1.5	0.4			0.3		6.6
18.Iron&Steel	1.2		0.2	3.0	1.7	6.5				13.0
19.Non-ferrous	0.4		0.5	1.0	0.5	0.1	2.1			4.7
33.Electricity	0.3		0.5	0.2	0.5	0.2				3.1
36.Trade	2.8		0.5	1.9	0.4	0.5	0.2			3.4
42.Other Serv.	2.9		0.5	1.9	0.4	0.4	0.2			3.5

[1990]	4	23	22	21	20	18	19	lp	lg	x
4.Build.&Const.	0.1							20.5	6.1	27.2
23.Vehicle	0.2	0.4						2.0		4.2
22.Elec.Mach.	0.5	0.3	5.7	0.8				11.0		18.6
21.Machinery	0.4		0.2	7.0				13.1		21.0
20.Metal Prod.	2.8		0.3	0.5	0.3			0.3		4.5
18.Iron&Steel	0.9	0.1	0.3	1.2	1.2	4.0				7.9
19.Non-ferrous	0.3		0.4	0.4	0.3	0.1	1.4			3.1
33.Electricity	0.2		0.2	0.2	0.4	0.3				2.2
36.Trade	2.1		0.7	0.7	0.2	0.3	0.2			6.1
42.Other Serv.	1.9		1.1	0.6	0.2	0.2	0.1			7.3

[1989]	4	23	22	21	20	18	19	lp	lg	x
4.Build.&Const.	0.1							14.2	4.1	18.6
23.Vehicle	0.3	1.0						1.4		2.8
22.Elec.Mach.	0.3	0.2	3.4	0.5				6.2		10.9
21.Machinery	0.3		0.1	4.1				7.4		12.1
20.Metal Prod.	1.8		0.2	0.7	0.2			0.2		2.9
18.Iron&Steel	0.6	0.1	0.2	0.8	0.8	2.5				5.1
19.Non-ferrous	0.2		0.3	0.2	0.2		0.9			2.0
33.Electricity	0.1		0.1	0.1	0.2	0.2				1.4
36.Trade	1.2		0.2	0.4	0.1	0.2				3.5
42.Other Serv.	1.3		0.1	0.6	0.2	0.1				4.7

[1988]	4	23	22	21	20	18	19	lp	lg	x
4.Build.&Const.	0.2							8.9	3.3	12.4
23.Vehicle	0.2	0.7						0.9		1.8
22.Elec.Mach.	0.2	0.1	2.1	0.3				3.7		6.5
21.Machinery	1.2		0.1	2.6				4.6		7.5
20.Metal Prod.	0.5		0.4	0.4	0.5			0.1		1.9
18.Iron&Steel	0.1		0.2	0.1	0.1	1.7				3.4
19.Non-ferrous			0.2				0.6			1.3
33.Electricity	0.7		0.2	0.2	0.2	0.1	0.1			0.9
36.Trade	0.8		0.4	0.2	0.2		0.1			2.1
42.Other Serv.	0.3									2.9

[1987]	4	23	22	21	20	18	19	lp	lg	x
4.Build.&Const.								5.7	2.1	7.9
23.Vehicle	0.4									1.1
22.Elec.Mach.	0.1		1.2	0.2				0.5		4.8
21.Machinery				1.7				2.1		1.2
20.Metal Prod.	0.8		0.1	0.3	0.3			2.9		2.1
18.Iron&Steel	0.3		0.1	0.1	0.3	1.1				0.8
19.Non-ferrous										0.6
33.Electricity	0.5		0.1	0.2	0.1					1.3
36.Trade	0.5		0.2	0.1	0.1					1.9
42.Other Serv.										

[1986]	4	23	22	21	20	18	19	lp	lg	x
4.Build.&Const.								3.8	1.4	5.3
23.Vehicle	0.2							0.3		0.7
22.Elec.Mach.			0.7	0.1				1.3		2.3
21.Machinery				1.2				2.0		3.3
20.Metal Prod.	0.5			0.2	0.2	0.7				0.8
18.Iron&Steel	0.2		0.1				0.2			1.4
19.Non-ferrous										0.6
33.Electricity	0.3		0.1	0.1						0.4
36.Trade	0.3									0.9
42.Other Serv.	0.4		0.1	0.1						1.3

[1985]	4	23	22	21	20	18	19	lp	lg	x
4.Build.&Const.								2.6	0.8	3.5
23.Vehicle	0.2	0.2						0.2	0.2	0.4
22.Elec.Mach.		0.4		0.7				0.8	0.8	1.4
21.Machinery	1.2		0.1	0.4				1.3		2.1
20.Metal Prod.	0.3		0.1	0.4	0.5				1.0	0.5
18.Iron&Steel	0.1		0.2	0.1	0.1	0.5			0.3	1.0
19.Non-ferrous			0.1	0.1			0.1		0.3	0.3
33.Electricity	0.2		0.2	0.2	0.2	0.1			0.3	0.3
36.Trade	0.2		0.2	0.2	0.2		0.1		0.6	0.6
42.Other Serv.	0.3		0.4	0.1	0.1				0.9	0.9

[1984]	4	23	22	21	20	18	19	lp	lg	x
4.Build.&Const.								1.6	0.6	2.3
23.Vehicle	0.4	0.1						0.1		0.3
22.Elec.Mach.				0.2				0.1		0.8
21.Machinery			0.4	0.4				0.5		1.3
20.Metal Prod.	0.2				0.3			0.8		0.3
18.Iron&Steel				0.1	0.1	0.3				0.7
19.Non-ferrous										0.2
33.Electricity	0.1									0.2
36.Trade	0.1		0.1	0.1						0.4
42.Other Serv.	0.2		0.2	0.1						0.6

[1983]	4	23	22	21	20	18	19	lp	lg	x
4.Build.&Const.								1.0	0.4	1.5
23.Vehicle	0.2	1.0						0.1	0.2	0.4
22.Elec.Mach.		0.2	3.4	0.1				0.2	0.4	0.8
21.Machinery			0.1	4.1		0.3		0.5	0.8	0.2
20.Metal Prod.	0.5			0.2	0.7		0.2		0.2	0.4
18.Iron&Steel	0.2		0.1			0.1			0.1	0.2
19.Non-ferrous									0.1	0.1
33.Electricity	0.1		0.1	0.1					0.3	0.3
36.Trade	0.1			0.1					0.4	0.4
42.Other Serv.	0.1		0.1							

The story of dynamic linkages is slightly different. Investments required from both General machinery and Electric machinery increased from 1980 to 1992, as we can see in the series of subtables for past years in tables 15.2 and 15.3. These increasing shares imply that efficiency changes in General machinery and Electric machinery have increasingly spilled over into efficiency gains in the production of Motor vehicles via the latter sector's investment in capital goods. These spillover effects gradually diminished, becoming insignificant after ten years.

Figure 15.2 shows the extent of dynamic spillovers embodied in the past gross output of sectors strongly related to motor vehicle production. The impacts estimated are those backwardly derived from a 100 million (constant 1985) yen final demand for Motor vehicles (sector 23) in the base year. The spillovers last nearly ten years for each commodity. Backward dynamic linkages of the motor vehicle demand shock have gradually grown in magnitude and lengthened in temporal effect. It is also interesting that, for intermediate energy inputs such as Petroleum (13), the spillovers from added motor vehicle production began to diminish near the end of the study period. This means that increases in energy efficiency in motor vehicle production through such measures as energy conservation and substitution further contribute to productivity improvements in direct and indirect energy usage. Moreover, it should be noted that spillovers from Electric machinery (22) increased in terms of both intermediate transactions and required investment goods. As we mentioned above, the static spillovers of General machinery (21) were diminishing for intermediate transactions. Nonetheless, through its dynamic spillovers the sector increased its influence through required investment goods.

5.   Decomposition of Japan's economic growth

5.1   Static decomposition

We now decompose aggregate economic growth in Japan. Figure 15.3 shows the average annual growth rate of real GDP and the contributions of labor, capital and TFP as sources of the economic growth from 1960 to 1990. In figure 15.3 the bar for each five-year subperiod represents the subperiod's average annual real GDP growth rate. The segments of each bar show the average annual growth rate in each subperiod as decomposed into contributions of labor (shown as bricks in the figure), capital inputs (shaded with dots) and TFP (white) respectively.[7] Each

---

[7] Here labor and capital inputs are measured by Divisia aggregates. Note that, in this paper, we exclude inventories and land as capital inputs in each sector.

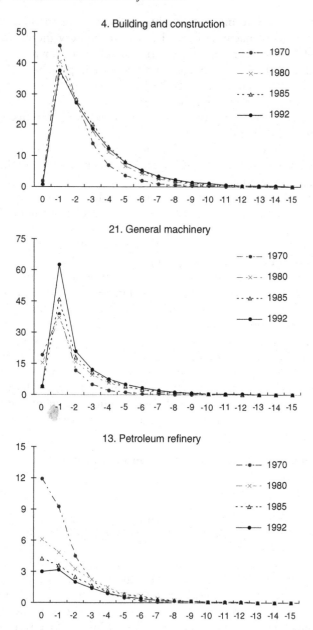

Figure 15.2   Output requirements for sector 23 (Motor vehicles)

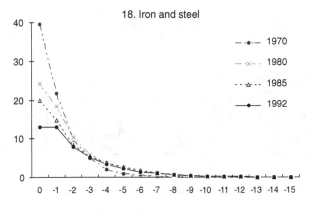

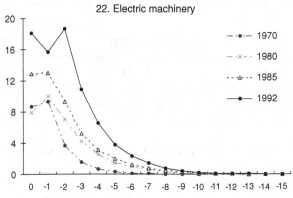

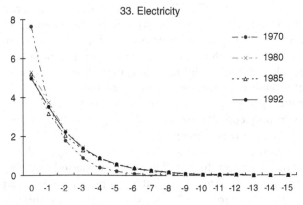

Figure 15.2   (*cont.*)

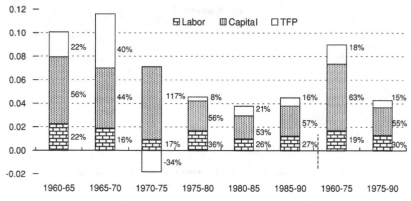

Figure 15.3   Decomposition of economic growth in Japan

decomposition share's bar segment is associated with its share percentage on the immediate right. During the rapid economic growth of the 1960s the average annual growth rate of real GDP exceeded 10 percent, while the annual TFP growth rates were 2.1 percent and 4.6 percent for the 1960–1965 and 1965–1970 periods respectively. During those periods the TFP's corresponding shares of the growth reached 22 percent and 40 percent.

The high growth rates of real GDP and TFP in the 1960s rapidly deteriorated in the first half of the 1970s. The average annual growth rate of TFP from 1970 to 1975 was −1.8 percent. The precipitous fall is largely attributable to a −6.0 percent annual growth rate of TFP during the first oil shock of 1973/1974. Nevertheless, a focus on the growth rate during the two-year period immediately before the oil shock reveals a clear slowdown in TFP growth never observed in the 1960s. Since the early 1970s the real growth rate of GDP has recovered slightly to 3 to 4 percent annually, although still lower than that of the 1960s. Moreover, annual TFP growth rates recovered slightly to 0.3, 0.8 and 0.7 percent respectively during the periods 1975 to 1980, 1980 to 1985 and 1985 to 1990, to which they contributed the following respective shares of real GDP growth: 8, 21 and 16 percent.

The results show that capital input's contribution to growth was stable at around 50 to 60 percent during all five-year subperiods except 1970 to 1975. The annual growth rate of capital input reached about 12 percent during the 1960s and early 1970s, but decreased to a stable 6 percent during the 1975–1990 period. Using the dynamic concept discussed earlier, we will decompose capital input's contribution for a specific period into portions attributable to dated labor and TFP growth. But, before we do, let us focus on sectoral growth rates of traditional TFP and static unit TFP.

Table 15.4 shows the average annual growth rate of traditional TFP by sector. Although the sectoral trends of TFP growth seem to be roughly the same as the aggregate trend, upon closer examination there are some distinguishable sectoral differences. In particular, there were some exceptional sectors. For example, during these periods, in Electric machinery (sector 22), Motor vehicles (23) and communication (32) TFP grew at high, stable rates, while for Agriculture, forestry and fishing (1), Coal products (14), Water supply (35) and Other services (42) it was generally negative. Here we will not analyze why TFP growth rates were high in some industries and low in others, especially since there were no large, multifarious differences in the patterns of the relative factor prices. In this paper we instead assume that sectoral TFP growth rates are exogenously given as a condition of technology. We focus on the spillover effect on TFP growth of the exogenously given technology through static and dynamic linkages among sectors.

In order to consider the interdependencies among sectors from the perspective of static intersectoral spillovers of TFP, we compare sectoral TFP with static unit TFP (see tables 15.4 and 15.5). Sectoral TFP by definition represents the efficiency of a specific sector's production. On the other hand, static unit TFP, which is based upon the unit structure, indicates the total efficiency of the linkages pertaining to a specific commodity's production. When we focus on the difference between static unit TFP and sectoral TFP, as shown in the columns marked "-TFP" of table 15.5, we see interesting characteristics of the spillovers through the commodity linkages in intermediate transactions. For example, the average annual growth rates of static unit TFP in Food manufacturing (sector 5) and Wood and related products (8) during the 1960–1975 period recorded large falls of 1.6 and 1.4 percent respectively, compared to the growth rates of each sector's traditional TFP during the same period. This is because the traditional TFP growth rate in Agriculture, forestry and fishing (1), which serves as an intermediate input to sectors 5 and 8, registered a 3.3 percent average annual fall during this period. One might naturally hypothesize that the deterioration of the efficiency in the Wood and related products sector (8) would have a deleterious impact on the efficiency of Furniture and fixture (9) through the transaction of its intermediate input. Contrarily, annual unit TFP growth in sector 9 during the same period was 1.0 percentage point higher than its TFP growth rate. This is because the production efficiency of its other main intermediate inputs, such as Metal products (20), increased by 2.5 percent as a measure of unit TFP, compensating for the deterioration of efficiency in

Table 15.4 Traditional TFP (average annual growth rate – percent)

	1960–65	1965–70	1970–75	1975–80	1980–85	1985–90	1960–75	1975–90
1. Agriculture	−1.646	−3.870	−4.288	−2.819	1.010	−0.416	−3.268	−0.742
2. Coal mining	7.286	5.443	−2.583	−4.187	0.118	−2.469	3.382	−2.179
3. Other mining	3.943	8.522	−3.776	5.012	−2.611	2.415	2.896	1.605
4. Build. & const.	−1.253	1.037	−0.602	−1.966	0.164	0.741	−0.273	−0.354
5. Food	−0.109	0.243	−0.593	0.818	−0.615	−1.316	−0.153	−0.371
6. Textile	0.829	1.308	0.677	1.405	0.873	1.415	0.938	1.231
7. Apparel	0.610	1.453	0.540	1.405	−0.234	−0.608	0.868	0.188
8. Wood	1.595	1.254	1.895	−3.308	4.354	−1.342	1.581	−0.099
9. Furniture	−0.872	1.177	0.164	1.052	0.920	0.181	0.156	0.718
10. Paper & pulp	2.142	2.459	−1.480	0.406	1.210	2.155	1.040	1.257
11. Publishing	−4.456	−3.594	−2.278	−0.242	0.087	0.637	−3.443	0.161
12. Chemical	2.685	4.710	−1.678	1.058	2.305	1.343	1.906	1.569
13. Petroleum	−0.816	−2.808	−4.384	−1.328	−0.274	5.901	−2.669	1.433
14. Coal prod.	−0.169	2.039	−5.034	−7.746	0.234	2.102	−1.055	−1.803
15. Rubber prod.	3.266	3.497	−3.578	−0.674	2.897	2.896	1.062	1.706
16. Leather prod.	3.133	−0.645	2.813	−2.197	1.523	−0.970	1.767	−0.548
17. Stone & clay	2.485	1.155	−2.192	0.599	0.954	0.924	0.482	0.826
18. Iron & steel	0.219	1.991	0.029	0.836	−0.441	0.126	0.746	0.174
19. Non-ferrous	−0.400	1.039	2.945	2.205	1.963	0.228	1.195	1.465
20. Metal prod.	2.140	3.607	−1.974	1.553	0.777	1.325	1.258	1.218
21. Machinery	−1.009	3.409	−1.709	3.094	1.366	0.337	0.230	1.599
22. Elec. mach.	2.852	6.140	1.228	5.374	1.752	3.068	3.407	3.398

23. Motor vehicles	1.131	4.487	1.999	3.184	0.254	0.817	2.539	1.418
24. Oth. trans. eq.	4.557	1.176	−5.048	0.594	1.377	1.932	0.228	1.301
25. Precision inst.	2.770	4.908	0.013	6.184	1.555	−0.320	2.564	2.473
26. Misc. mng. prod.	2.308	3.870	−2.388	1.431	0.663	0.773	1.263	0.956
27. Railway trans.	1.982	−2.491	5.667	−10.538	1.300	−1.748	1.719	−3.662
28. Road trans.	2.550	4.609	−5.813	2.302	−2.287	−0.246	0.449	−0.077
29. Water trans.	−0.598	7.449	2.025	−2.081	3.905	−3.820	2.958	−0.666
30. Air trans.	4.142	8.275	8.190	−0.617	2.035	−0.009	6.869	0.470
31. Storage	1.036	3.778	−6.321	8.487	0.866	−0.751	−0.502	2.867
32. Communication	1.815	2.102	0.427	2.342	5.714	2.173	1.448	3.410
33. Electricity	4.441	4.988	−3.409	−1.776	1.539	2.054	2.006	0.605
34. Gas	3.481	0.763	0.380	−0.319	1.314	2.950	1.541	1.315
35. Water	−2.742	−2.203	−2.351	−6.098	0.210	−1.129	−2.432	−2.339
36. Trade	5.505	5.452	−0.240	2.262	−0.448	3.196	3.572	1.670
37. Finance	5.479	1.466	−0.507	−0.410	3.361	1.024	2.146	1.325
38. Real estate	5.596	−0.204	−2.952	−0.402	0.658	−0.384	0.813	−0.042
39. Education	0.867	3.563	0.992	−5.010	−3.558	−1.481	1.808	−3.350
40. Research	5.950	2.653	−1.360	4.075	−1.863	0.013	2.415	0.742
41. Medical care	1.567	−0.511	5.186	−2.068	−1.134	−3.711	2.081	−2.304
42. Other serv.	−5.744	1.401	−3.932	0.092	−0.773	−2.601	−2.758	−1.094
43. Public serv.	4.089	2.467	6.905	−4.968	−0.844	0.450	4.487	−1.787

Table 15.5 Static unit TFP (average annual growth rate – percent)

	1960–65	1965–70	1970–75	1975–80	1980–85	1985–90	1960–75	-TFP	1975–90	-TFP
1. Agriculture	-1.535	-3.814	-6.018	-3.055	1.558	-0.145	-3.789	-0.52	-0.547	0.19
2. Coal mining	7.975	7.060	-4.138	-4.437	0.608	-2.187	3.632	0.25	-2.005	0.17
3. Other mining	4.720	9.763	-5.017	5.509	-2.142	3.458	3.155	0.26	2.275	0.67
4. Build. & const.	0.691	4.830	-2.509	-1.295	0.914	1.412	1.004	1.28	0.344	0.70
5. Food	-0.448	-0.563	-4.373	-0.167	0.150	-1.183	-1.794	-1.64	-0.400	-0.03
6. Textile	2.560	4.437	-1.177	2.408	2.539	3.060	1.940	1.00	2.669	1.44
7. Apparel	2.962	5.116	-0.790	2.683	0.943	1.016	2.429	1.56	1.547	1.36
8. Wood	1.579	0.318	-1.393	-4.996	5.964	-1.131	0.168	-1.41	-0.054	0.04
9. Furniture	0.983	4.028	-1.542	0.652	2.674	0.686	1.157	1.00	1.338	0.62
10. Paper & pulp	4.456	5.754	-4.541	0.156	3.041	3.895	1.890	0.85	2.364	1.11
11. Publishing	-3.217	-1.401	-4.506	-0.045	1.177	1.649	-3.042	0.40	0.927	0.77
12. Chemical	5.464	9.124	-4.667	1.765	4.080	2.623	3.307	1.40	2.823	1.25
13. Petroleum	-0.692	-2.462	-5.151	-1.324	-0.072	6.464	-2.768	-0.10	1.689	0.26
14. Coal prod.	3.930	7.089	-9.706	-11.388	0.669	1.558	0.438	1.49	-3.054	-1.25
15. Rubber prod.	5.429	7.321	-5.634	-0.033	4.403	4.121	2.372	1.31	2.831	1.12
16. Leather prod.	7.567	1.700	2.543	-2.655	2.826	-0.676	3.937	2.17	-0.169	0.38
17. Stone & clay	4.182	4.728	-4.582	1.539	1.236	1.920	1.442	0.96	1.565	0.74
18. Iron & steel	2.123	7.825	-2.109	0.292	-0.244	0.791	2.613	1.87	0.280	0.11
19. Non-ferrous	2.107	7.028	1.620	4.782	3.759	1.291	3.585	2.39	3.278	1.81
20. Metal prod.	3.480	7.390	-3.261	2.133	1.213	1.887	2.536	1.28	1.744	0.53
21. Machinery	0.086	8.260	-3.305	5.602	2.608	1.142	1.680	1.45	3.117	1.52
22. Elec. mach.	4.963	11.687	0.353	8.149	3.197	4.969	5.667	2.26	5.438	2.04

23. Motor vehicles	3.273	10.144	1.334	6.007	1.372	2.415	4.917	2.38	3.265	1.85
24. Oth. trans. eq.	6.639	5.705	−7.220	2.036	2.609	3.114	1.708	1.48	2.586	1.28
25. Precision inst.	4.503	9.043	−0.771	8.341	2.813	0.349	4.258	1.69	3.835	1.36
26. Misc. mng. prod.	4.645	7.932	−5.019	2.132	2.398	1.939	2.519	1.26	2.156	1.20
27. Railway trans.	3.569	−0.819	3.474	−9.996	1.818	−1.538	2.075	0.36	−3.239	0.42
28. Road trans.	3.092	5.963	−6.544	2.680	−2.047	0.182	0.837	0.39	0.272	0.35
29. Water trans.	−0.141	10.126	2.401	−2.944	6.065	−4.395	4.129	1.17	−0.425	0.24
30. Air trans.	5.486	10.379	6.936	−0.584	3.117	0.590	7.600	0.73	1.041	0.57
31. Storage	1.314	4.829	−8.252	8.415	1.326	−0.942	−0.703	−0.20	2.933	0.07
32. Communication	1.949	2.559	−0.257	2.552	5.701	2.128	1.417	−0.03	3.460	0.05
33. Electricity	5.153	5.641	−5.065	−2.280	1.671	2.309	1.910	−0.10	0.567	−0.04
34. Gas	4.335	1.869	−0.158	3.106	1.120	2.964	2.015	0.47	2.397	1.08
35. Water	−2.471	−1.267	−4.292	−6.679	0.957	−0.663	−2.677	−0.24	−2.129	0.21
36. Trade	6.344	6.780	−1.259	2.362	0.043	3.361	3.955	0.38	1.922	0.25
37. Finance	5.226	2.249	−1.598	−0.344	3.769	0.837	1.959	−0.19	1.421	0.10
38. Real estate	5.724	0.384	−3.306	−0.529	0.870	−0.346	0.934	0.12	−0.001	0.04
39. Education	0.497	4.429	0.517	−5.054	−3.430	−1.422	1.814	0.01	−3.302	0.05
40. Research	5.352	3.610	−2.590	4.080	−1.700	0.007	2.124	−0.29	0.796	0.05
41. Medical care	2.932	1.873	3.598	−1.669	−0.230	−2.977	2.801	0.72	−1.625	0.68
42. Other serv.	−4.936	3.361	−5.692	0.216	−0.183	−2.185	−2.422	0.34	−0.717	0.38
43. Public serv.	4.830	3.669	5.921	−4.905	−0.585	0.556	4.807	0.32	−1.645	0.14

sector 8. Reflecting the decline in the efficiency of wood products and the concomitant improvement in the efficiency of metal products, at least in terms of static unit TFP, we observe the trend that, in many sectors, wood products are substituted by metal products as intermediate inputs.

We also observe cases in which technological linkages had positive spillover effects on production efficiency. Let us focus on the linkage between Electric machinery (sector 22) and Motor vehicles (23). Differences in the growth rate between static unit TFP and traditional TFP in Motor vehicles reveal positive spillover effects: 2.4 percentage points in 1960 to 1975 and 1.9 percentage points in 1975 to 1990. We can identify the specific sectors from which the spillover effects mostly emanated by examining the relationship between traditional TFP and static unit TFP in equation (12). According to the results, during the 1960–1975 and 1975–1990 periods 13.7 and 18.7 percent respectively of all positive spillover effects in the Motor vehicles sector were due to efficiency improvements in Electric machinery. Growth rates of unit TFP in Electric machinery during the periods 1960 to 1975 and 1975 to 1990 exceeded 5 percent, and this was coupled with gradually increasing shares of direct and indirect requirements of intermediate goods from Electric machinery to Motor vehicles during these periods.

We can translate spillover effects in unit TFP into the framework of the commodity linkages in intermediate input transactions. End-use commodities might have larger impacts from spillover effects from other commodities because their production requires relatively many commodities as intermediate inputs. On the other hand, basic commodities have properties in which their efficiency change might have serious spillover effects on other commodities. A typical example of this is Communication (sector 32), which experienced small differences in the growth rates of unit and sectoral TFP. Nonetheless, its efficiency change had sizable impacts on the efficiency of various other sectors. This is because Communication is a sort of basic commodity.

5.2   *Dynamic decomposition*

Let us now evaluate our dynamic approach. In equation (19a) we defined dynamic unit TFP to evaluate, dynamically, the total efficiency of the production that is directly and indirectly required to deliver one unit of a specific commodity to final demand at any time. As we explained in section 2.2, the framework of the dynamic unit structure provides an accounting balance for measuring dynamic unit TFP. Since we have demonstrated that dynamic impacts of production linkages diminish within about a ten-year timeframe (see the case of Motor vehicles in figure 15.2 and tables 15.2 and 15.3), we evaluate our measures of dynamic unit TFP in the years following 1970 using the 1960–1990 period.

For a given sector and time period, table 15.6 presents the average annual growth rate of dynamic unit TFP and the differences between dynamic unit TFP and static unit TFP (the columns marked "-UTFP"). As shown in section 3.2, we try to evaluate the TFP growth embodied in the accumulated capital with the dynamic unit TFP measure. In its formula, once the contribution of capital in static unit TFP is decomposed into the contributions made by prior labor and TFP, the past TFP contribution is added to static unit TFP. Therefore, dynamic unit TFP should be greater than static unit TFP, assuming positive productivity progress, as shown by positive signs in the "-UTFP" columns in table 15.6.

In sectors in which capital accumulated smoothly and capital intensity was high, the growth rate of dynamic unit TFP was likely to be far larger than that for static unit TFP. This is even true for sectors in which the difference in the growth rates between static unit TFP and traditional TFP is relatively low, such as Communication (sector 32).

As discussed in section 4, the values of the capital coefficients of General machinery (sector 21) and Electric machinery (22) as capital goods increased rapidly during the study period. Growth rates of transitional TFP as well as static unit TFP in General machinery and Electric machinery were also fairly high during the entire 1960–1990 period. Due to the above two reasons, growth rates of dynamic unit TFP edged up in almost all sectors after 1975. For example, in the Motor vehicles sector (23) the differences in the growth rates of dynamic unit TFP and static unit TFP were 0.26, 0.61 and 0.86 percentage points for 1975 to 1980, 1980 to 1985 and 1985 to 1990 respectively, including the effects of accumulated capital enhanced dynamic unit TFP in almost all sectors.

We focus on several sectors in figure 15.4, in order to clarify the differences of the three productivity measures that we proposed in this paper. In figure 15.4 each index of the three TFP measures is assigned the value of 1 in 1970, the base year. Note that dynamic unit TFP can be measured only in the periods after 1970, due to the requisite ten-year lag in the effect of capital investment. For General machinery (sector 21), Electric machinery (22) and Motor vehicles (23) the index for dynamic unit TFP has the highest growth rate, while the index of sectoral TFP has the lowest. Among these sectors the growth rate for Electric machinery is the highest. In Agriculture, forestry and fishing (1), all three indices gradually declined through the second half of the 1970s and stabilized in the 1980s. Most interestingly, the index of dynamic unit TFP for this sector took an

Table 15.6 Dynamic unit TFP (average annual growth rate – percent)

	1970-75	-UTFP	1975-80	-UTFP	1980-85	-UTFP	1985-90	-UTFP	1975-90	-TFP	-UTFP
1. Agriculture	-4.522	1.50	-3.185	-0.13	1.994	0.44	0.865	1.01	-0.109	0.63	0.44
2. Coal mining	-2.883	1.26	-4.293	0.14	1.188	0.58	-1.383	0.80	-1.496	0.68	0.51
3. Other mining	-2.759	2.26	5.821	0.31	-1.325	0.82	4.500	1.04	2.998	1.39	0.72
4. Build. & const.	-0.865	1.64	-1.126	0.17	1.430	0.52	2.322	0.91	0.875	1.23	0.53
5. Food	-2.790	1.58	-0.189	-0.02	0.646	0.50	-0.235	0.95	0.074	0.45	0.47
6. Textile	0.169	1.35	2.535	0.13	2.925	0.39	3.641	0.58	3.033	1.80	0.36
7. Apparel	0.472	1.26	2.785	0.10	1.312	0.37	1.654	0.64	1.917	1.73	0.37
8. Wood	0.040	1.43	-5.025	-0.03	6.402	0.44	-0.302	0.83	0.358	0.46	0.41
9. Furniture	-0.078	1.46	0.711	0.06	3.108	0.43	1.571	0.89	1.797	1.08	0.46
10. Paper & pulp	-2.736	1.80	0.422	0.27	3.687	0.65	4.909	1.01	3.006	1.75	0.64
11. Publishing	-3.039	1.47	0.136	0.18	1.696	0.52	2.453	0.80	1.428	1.27	0.50
12. Chemical	-2.760	1.91	1.986	0.22	4.687	0.61	3.758	1.13	3.477	1.91	0.65
13. Petroleum	-3.618	1.53	-1.216	0.11	0.104	0.18	7.147	0.68	2.012	0.58	0.32
14. Coal prod.	-7.898	1.81	-11.276	0.11	1.418	0.75	2.640	1.08	-2.406	-0.60	0.65
15. Rubber prod.	-4.144	1.49	0.195	0.23	4.930	0.53	5.036	0.91	3.387	1.68	0.56
16. Leather prod.	3.934	1.39	-2.559	0.10	3.256	0.43	0.160	0.84	0.286	0.83	0.45
17. Stone & clay	-2.715	1.87	1.651	0.11	1.736	0.50	2.854	0.93	2.080	1.25	0.52
18. Iron & steel	-0.085	2.02	0.672	0.38	0.458	0.70	1.970	1.18	1.033	0.86	0.75
19. Non-ferrous	3.745	2.12	4.988	0.21	4.342	0.58	2.412	1.12	3.914	2.45	0.64
20. Metal prod.	-1.573	1.69	2.277	0.14	1.652	0.44	2.767	0.88	2.232	1.01	0.49
21. Machinery	-1.565	1.74	5.876	0.27	3.296	0.69	2.191	1.05	3.788	2.19	0.67
22. Elec. mach.	2.377	2.02	8.369	0.22	3.778	0.58	6.053	1.08	6.067	2.67	0.63

23. Motor vehicles	3.054	1.72	6.264	0.26	1.984	0.61	3.275	0.86	3.841	2.42	0.58
24. Oth. trans. eq.	-5.462	1.76	2.200	0.16	3.117	0.51	3.932	0.82	3.083	1.78	0.50
25. Precision inst.	0.833	1.60	8.626	0.28	3.398	0.58	1.233	0.88	4.419	1.95	0.58
26. Misc. mng. prod.	-3.332	1.69	2.287	0.16	2.953	0.56	2.943	1.00	2.728	1.77	0.57
27. Railway trans.	4.539	1.07	-10.043	-0.05	2.102	0.28	-0.726	0.81	-2.889	0.77	0.35
28. Road trans.	-5.779	0.76	2.677	0.00	-1.850	0.20	0.792	0.61	0.540	0.62	0.27
29. Water trans.	4.360	1.96	-3.207	-0.26	6.492	0.43	-3.444	0.95	-0.053	0.61	0.37
30. Air trans.	9.238	2.30	-0.796	-0.21	3.616	0.50	1.569	0.98	1.463	0.99	0.42
31. Storage	-7.074	1.18	8.623	0.21	1.919	0.59	0.056	1.00	3.533	0.67	0.60
32. Communication	1.401	1.66	2.768	0.22	6.267	0.57	3.371	1.24	4.135	0.73	0.67
33. Electricity	-2.567	2.50	-2.070	0.21	2.329	0.66	3.898	1.59	1.386	0.78	0.82
34. Gas	1.641	1.80	3.391	0.29	1.529	0.41	3.922	0.96	2.947	1.63	0.55
35. Water	-2.738	1.55	-6.614	0.07	1.403	0.45	0.461	1.12	-1.583	0.76	0.55
36. Trade	0.438	1.70	2.479	0.12	0.520	0.48	4.211	0.85	2.403	0.73	0.48
37. Finance	0.269	1.87	-0.180	0.16	4.335	0.57	1.883	1.05	2.013	0.69	0.59
38. Real estate	-0.762	2.54	-0.644	-0.11	1.704	0.83	1.628	1.97	0.896	0.94	0.90
39. Education	1.088	0.57	-5.039	0.01	-3.260	0.17	-1.073	0.35	-3.124	0.23	0.18
40. Research	-1.913	0.68	4.174	0.09	-1.421	0.28	0.559	0.55	1.104	0.36	0.31
41. Medical care	5.320	1.72	-1.484	0.19	0.294	0.52	-2.058	0.92	-1.083	1.22	0.54
42. Other serv.	-3.845	1.85	0.465	0.25	0.429	0.61	-1.196	0.99	-0.101	0.99	0.62
43. Public serv.	6.667	0.75	-4.826	0.08	-0.353	0.23	0.930	0.37	-1.416	0.37	0.23

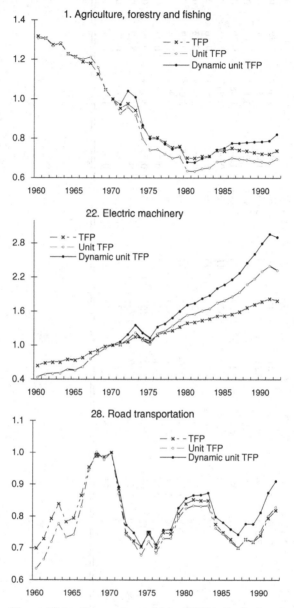

Figure 15.4   Comparison of three TFP indexes, in selected sectors

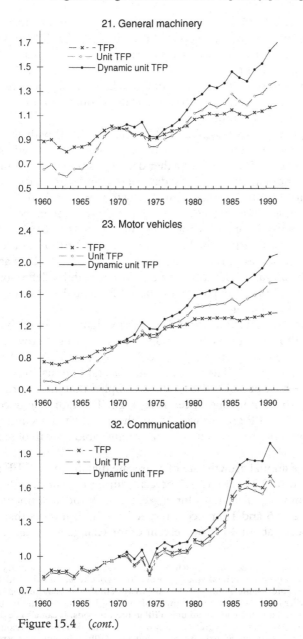

Figure 15.4   (*cont.*)

upward turn after 1985.[8] In Road transportation (28) and Communication (32), the indexes of static unit TFP and traditional TFP followed the pattern of their main commodity linkage (i.e. services), while the index of dynamic unit TFP in these sectors rapidly rose after 1985. This is because the capital coefficients of motor vehicles as an asset in Road transportation (28) and those of communication equipment in Communication (32) increased strongly.

We attempt to evaluate aggregate dynamic unit TFP with the hope of decomposing the sources of economic growth, as pointed out in figure 15.3. Figure 15.5 shows a further decomposition of the contribution of capital input into two sources: dated labor, and dated TFP growth. Thus, in figure 15.5 the average annual growth rate of real GDP during the five-year subperiods is decomposed into *four* component sources of growth: the contributions of labor at the base year ($t = 0$); past labor ($t = -1, \ldots, -\infty$); TFP at the base year; and past TFP. In figure 15.5 the contributive shares of each source are shown along the bars as percentages of the annual GDP growth in each subperiod. By definition, the sum of the contributions of past labor and TFP is equal to the contribution of capital input in figure 15.3.[9]

The dynamic unit TFP contribution is the weighted sum of the contribution of TFP in the base period and of all past TFP growth. The average annual growth rate of aggregate dynamic unit TFP for 1970 to 1975 was −0.16 percent. The rather negative average annual growth rate of TFP for the base period (−1.81 percent) implies that the contribution of past TFP growth must have been fairly high. The rather large contribution from past TFP growth was due to the accelerated accumulation of capital from 1960 to 1975 and a concomitant rapid growth of sectoral TFP.

The average annual growth rate of aggregate dynamic unit TFP gradually increased to 0.5, 1.3 and 1.7 percent during the subperiods since 1975. The annual growth rates for aggregate TFP for the same subperiods were 0.2, 0.5 and 1.0 percent respectively. This implies that prior TFP contributed about 40 to 60 percent of the change in dynamic TFP

---

[8] We include social overhead capital such as agricultural land reform, forestry roads and fishing harbors in the capital stock measure for Agriculture, forestry and fishing (sector 1). Thus, the decline in the capital productivity of this sector may be exaggerated.

[9] As defined earlier in equation (19a), dynamic unit TFP is the weighted sum of the unit TFP at the period t and the compound unit TFP in prior periods. It can also be defined as the difference between the aggregate growth rate of final demand in period t and all past contributions of the growth of labor – equation (19b). Here we first estimated the contribution of past TFP growth and defined the past contribution of labor as the difference between the contribution of capital input and the contribution of past TFP growth.

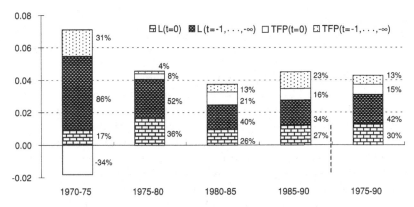

Figure 15.5   Dynamic decomposition of economic growth in Japan

growth. Figure 15.5 also shows that the contributive shares of past TFP to dynamic TFP growth rose gradually from 4 to 13 percent and further to 23 percent for the three subperiods after 1975. On the other hand, the contributive share of past labor declined, from 52, to 40 and to 34 percent.

After the first oil shock capital input in Japan accumulated steadily at a rate of 5 to 6 percent annually. This means that capital accumulation did not contribute as much then to increases in dynamic unit TFP as it had during the 1960s. An interesting characteristic of recent Japanese capital accumulation, however, is that the shares of General machinery (sector 21) and Electric machinery (22) in capital goods have increased rapidly. Hence, high growth rates of traditional TFP in both sectors have enhanced dynamic unit TFP growth rates in almost all sectors. In other words, we could say that recent technological progress in the General and electric machinery sectors has improved the production efficiency of almost all sectors through capital accumulation. We might further conclude that new technology developed in commodities such as semiconductors and computers has become embodied in capital goods, and will likely spill over in a big way to all sectors through the dynamic accumulation process of investment.

Figure 15.3 reveals that, from a static perspective, capital, labor and TFP stimulated, respectively, 55, 30 and 15 percent of Japan's economic growth from 1975 to 1990. From a dynamic perspective (figure 15.5) TFP's share was 28 percent for the entire 1975–1990 period and 39 percent during the last five years of that period (1985 to 1990). This means that Japanese policy-makers should encourage technological progress in the name of dynamic economic growth.

6.   Conclusion

How can we *observe* and *translate* the dynamic TFP contribution through accumulated capital? In this paper we have proposed two productivity formulae based on Leontief's input-output framework – static unit TFP and dynamic unit TFP – and evaluated the historical spillovers of productivity change as the dynamic decomposition of Japan's growth from 1960 to 1990. Our results show that the contributive shares of dynamic unit TFP in Japan's economic growth rose gradually. In the period 1985 to 1990 the 16 percent TFP contribution to economic growth in a traditional decomposition expands to 39 percent with a dynamic evaluation.

In economic development the current technological state is constrained by past technological progress, which, in its turn, constrains future economic growth. Technological progress in an activity or commodity has a role in an economic system that is different from that of intermediate or consumption goods. This is because the accumulating capital that defines technological progress promotes production efficiency not only now but also many years into the future.

This effect of accumulated capital on production efficiency is also transmitted through international trade. The international shipment of capital goods represents the transfer not only of current technology but also of future production efficiency. The technological progress embodied in traded capital goods can raise economic growth in the importing country through the substitution of goods it subsequently induces in the future.

ACKNOWLEDGEMENTS

We are indebted to the two editors, Erik Dietzenbacher and Michael Lahr, for their many helpful comments and suggestions.

REFERENCES

Aulin-Ahmavaara, P. (1999) Effective rates of sectoral productivity change, *Economic Systems Research*, 11, 349–363.
Biørn, E. (1989) *Taxation, Technology and the User Cost of Capital* (Amsterdam, Elsevier Science).
Domar, E. D. (1961) On the measurement of technological change, *Economic Journal*, 71, 709–729.
Hulten, C. R. (1978) Growth accounting with intermediate inputs, *Review of Economic Studies*, 45, 511–518.
    (1990) The measurement of capital, in E. R. Berndt and J. E. Triplett (eds.) *Fifty Years of Economic Measurement: The Jubilee of the Conference on Research in Income and Wealth* (Chicago, University of Chicago Press), 119–158.

(1992) Growth accounting when technical change is embodied in capital, *American Economic Review*, 82, 964–980.

Jorgenson, D. W. (1966) The embodiment hypothesis, *Journal of Political Economy*, 74, 1–17.

(1989) Capital as a factor of production, in D. W. Jorgenson and R. Landau (eds.) *Technology and Capital Formation* (Cambridge, MA, MIT Press), 1–35.

Kuroda, M., K. Shimpo, K. Nomura and N. Kobayashi (1997) *Keio Economic Observatory Database – Measurement of Output, Labor and Capital Inputs* (Tokyo, Keio University Press) [in Japanese].

Leontief, W. W. (1970) The dynamic inverse, in A. P. Carter and A. Brody (eds.) *Contributions to Input-Output Analysis* (Amsterdam, North-Holland), 17–46.

Leontief, W. W., et al. (1953) *Studies in the Structure of the American Economy* (New York, Oxford University Press).

Nomura, K. (1998) The measurement of capital service price, *Keio Economic Observatory Discussion Paper 53* [in Japanese].

Ozaki, I. (1980) The structure of economic development (III) – a determination of economic fundamental structure, *Mita Journal of Economics*, 73, 66–94 [in Japanese].

Peterson, W. (1979) Total factor productivity in the UK: a disaggregated analysis, in K. D. Patterson and K. Schott (eds.) *The Measurement of Capital: Theory and Practice* (London, Macmillan), 212–225.

Wolff, E. N. (1985) Industrial composition, interindustry effects and the U.S. productivity slowdown, *Review of Economics and Statistics*, 67, 268–277.

16 Japan's economic growth and policy-making in the context of input-output models

Shuntaro Shishido

1. Introduction

The contributions of Leontief's input-output analysis to economic theory are discussed by many others in this volume. So, I focus, instead, upon applied aspects and the policy implications of his theory. In particular, I emphasize the role and impacts of his model in Japanese national economic policy and development planning in terms of macroeconomic and industry structural changes since the mid-1950s. While regional input-output models also have been widely used for regional development issues by Japan's local governments and related institutions, I shall touch on them only in the context of national development policy. Although national input-output models have been extensively used by Japan's government agencies, especially the Economic Planning Agency (EPA) and the former Ministry of International Trade and Industry (MITI, now METI), the enthusiasm for using the model that existed between the 1950s and 1970s seems to have gradually cooled down, except for the case of environmental policy. The dramatic turning point occurred in the early 1980s, when the cabinet of the then Prime Minister, Yasuhiro Nakasone, instituted a neo-liberal economic policy. This policy declared an over-abundance of quantitative guidelines and opted to maintain only a little of what had been the core of the government's economic planning. Even though important improvements by the government continued to accumulate in the form of input-output table compilation and related modeling techniques, the downgrading of the status of quantitative macroeconomic and sectoral targets generally has been observed.

In the second half of this chapter the long-term consequences of the neglect of (even the development of) quantitative guidelines by Japan's government since the early 1980s are discussed. This discussion focuses upon such measures as output capacity, production, employment, the rate of capacity utilization and productivity, on both a sectoral and macroeconomic basis. Although the analysis needs further extension, our tentative findings suggest that there are huge imbalances between supply capacity and demand in every sector of the Japanese economy. Thus, it is clear that there is a huge role that the government can play in narrowing economic gaps.

2. Japan's medium-term planning and Leontief models

It was not until 1965 that the Japanese government officially adopted Leontief's model in the framework of comprehensive planning for the period between 1964 and 1968. At that time its system of planning models had three components: (1) a macroeconometric model with forty-three equations; (2) an input-output model with sixty output and trade sectors and twenty-five subsectors for value added, employment, investment and capital stock; and (3) an integrated economic model composed of the two models above.

The idea was that the first model (i.e. a macro-model built on Keynesian ideals) needed to be constrained a bit by supply-side relationships: output, imports, employment, capacity constraints, etc. The input-output model tested for potential bottlenecks. The third model integrated the macro- and input-output systems for the target year, assuming full capacity utilization and full employment. This model was mostly used to estimate desirable policy values for target years, four years ahead, without consideration of economic cyclicity during the intermediate period.

Since the first two models were combined almost strictly via a one-way linkage, i.e. "macro-model to input-output model," violations of the economy's constraints were possible, e.g. labor shortages, accelerated inflation, balance of payments difficulties or bottlenecks in the availability of specific resources. The existence of these problems was tested and handled by appropriate policy measures through the application of the third model, which enabled a two-way feedback between the macro-model and the input-output system.

The Japanese economy was enjoying fairly rapid economic growth when this model was first used. Nonetheless, the dangers of trade imbalance and bottlenecks in specific sectors – including social overhead – always existed, requiring a deliberate macroeconomic policy and structural adjustment formulated within an input-output framework. The relationship between the three models is shown in figure 16.1.

Forecasts from this fully integrated model as produced by the Econometric Committee of the EPA were well received by the business world, and the stock market soared. Its popularity was at least partly due to the enhanced sectoral detail contained in the alternative forecasts. The response of the stock market and the economy to announcements from the new model was much stronger than expected. While the National

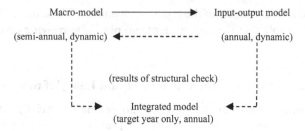

Figure 16.1   The relationships between the three models

Income Doubling Plan prepared by the cabinet of the then Prime Minister, Hayato Ikeda, had included forecasts for sectoral output, it had no
means to reconcile its GDP growth forecast – which was based almost
exclusively on business opinion – with the various sectoral output forecasts. The models upon which the Econometric Committee's report were
based, on the other hand, were well documented and theoretically sound.
Thus they promoted policy modeling, especially input-output modeling,
for government agencies and businesses (EPA, 1965, and 1979; Tatemoto
et al., 1967; Watanabe and Shishido, 1970).

Although the government's official plan concentrated upon a four-year
period (examined through several scenarios), a longer-term analysis of the
Japanese economy was also conducted. The data used for this model ran
from 1906 to 1960. The analysis relied heavily on production functions
with technological progress for agriculture and non-agriculture sectors.
This supply-side growth model assumed that savings were fully absorbed
in fixed investment and that a trade surplus would persist. Its ten-year
projections provided useful information on exogenous variables, such as
the demand for social overhead capital and private housing stock, used
within the aforementioned medium-term macroeconomic model.

In summary, the Econometric Committee, represented by leading
scholars and analysts in those days, contributed to the progress of a
sound and balanced development of policy modeling for both (a) short-
or medium-term macroeconomic demand management on the one hand
and (b) sectoral supply and capacity building with structural changes
on the other. Particularly important, as discussed later, is the integrated study and policy analysis of the Keynesian type from the demand side and the structural analysis of the Leontief type from the
supply side, including capacity utilization. Issues regarding such matters as technological and environmental progress, as well as international
competitiveness, were successfully dealt with through the latter type of
analysis.

3.   Later developments of policy guidelines

The combined use of Leontief and Keynesian models by the EPA was further improved in 1977. The official medium-term macro-model was transformed into a ten-sector econometric model. This semi-annual model can be regarded as a kind of macro-model including a general-equilibrium-type elaboration with respect to the interdependence between sectoral quantities and prices. Sectoral capacity variables were also added to the main body of the model, although they were never officially published. The input-output model, which had been extensively used as a guideline by businesses, virtually disappeared from official targets. Nonetheless, it appeared again as a long-term optimum growth model with turnpike properties. Although the model was reduced from sixty to twenty-seven sectors, it was characterized as a model for the optimal allocation of welfare and environmental resources. Pollution abatement was critical, so three types of pollutants (SOx, BOx and BOD, i.e. biological oxygen demand) were explicitly included in the model. The model was used between 1975 and 1990 for alternative policy packages (for technical discussions, see EPA, 1979).

Despite important contributions by the Econometric Committee of the EPA during the 1970s, public expectations for a reasonable GDP growth rate waned gradually from about 8 to 10 percent in the 1960s to around 5 percent. This remarkable degradation was fueled by mounting anti-growth sentiments. This in turn was induced by the oil price shock of 1973/1974 and an increasing environmental awareness. Academic monetarists gradually became more skeptical about the effectiveness of conventional macroeconomic policy. When some major economists in developed countries joined this campaign, the influence of mainstream macroeconomic policy began to weaken.

With these ideological shifts as the background, the Nakasone cabinet decided to cut back drastically on the number of target figures. It also substantially weakened the role of the EPA as an analytical core within the government. Although the activity of the Econometric Committee continued, their analyses with policy implications have rarely been published in recent years. As a consequence of all this, interest among Japanese policy-makers and media with regard to economic forecasts and the models that produce them also began to fade.

Within Japan's government agencies, besides the EPA, however, intellectual development of Leontief-type models was *never* discontinued. The developments can be grouped into three categories. First, the compilation of an international input-output table by MITI and the Institute of Developing Economies greatly contributed to the strengthening of the intellectual infrastructure within East Asian countries in the context of the Japanese and the US economies. The MITI project was later extended with linkages to European input-output tables. It also stimulated academics to collaborate internationally on multi-country, multisectoral econometric models. Second, the Environment Agency undertook a vigorous research program that included such notable studies as those on global environment modeling with a 60-sector Leontief matrix (Shishido, 1998) and technological aspects of environmental and recycling activities (Hayami et al., 1993). Third, interest in regional input-output models, the first of which was produced by the Kansai district and MITI in the early 1960s, spread gradually. By the end of the 1990s all prefectures had their own tables for 1990. At the time of writing this paper regional tables for 1995 are due to be released for most prefectures; policy implications derived from them will surely enhance the quality of Japan's regional development. The continued application of the Leontief model as discussed in the three points above suggests that it may be more flexible for multi-purpose policy analyses than conventional aggregate models.

4.   Capacity output at macro- and sectoral levels

4.1   *Purpose of the study and database*

A consensus prevails today that the slowdown in growth rates during the 1990s was mostly due to structural factors, such as Japan's aging demographic composition, consumer concerns about likely future rises in taxes, and capital outflows due to the decline in the relative value of the yen. Pundits argue that the potential GDP or aggregate capacity of Japan's economy has also been stagnant and that the gap between GDP capacity and actual GDP is negligible – say around 5 percent. This implies that accelerated growth will result only in chronic inflation. As pointed out by Niwa (2000) and Sato (2001a), this low ceiling hypothesis is founded upon fragile empirics that rely on limited samples for estimating production functions and unrealistic procedures for normalizing capacity output. As observed by the Econometric Committee, realistic estimates are more likely to be obtained if samples spanning a much longer period are obtained or if a better-specified production function is employed.

In the present paper, the production functions for the 1955–1998 period are mostly derived from updated EPA data on value added and gross capital stock (in 1990 prices), employment and working hours for the following eight sectors: (1) Agriculture; (2) Mining; (3) Manufacturing;

(4) Construction; (5) Electricity and gas; (6) Wholesale and retail trade; (7) Transport and communication; and (8) Finance and services.[1]

For continuity's sake, the time series for capital stock was adjusted so that the capital stock owned before 1990 by the national railway and the public corporation for telephone service and communication were integrated into the private capital stock series of Transport and communication.

Working hours data were gathered by the Ministry of Labor for establishments employing thirty or more employees. The period for the present analysis covers the historical development of nearly half a century and, therefore, includes nine business cycles, as compared with the three – or so – business cycles used by recent quarterly studies on capacity estimation. With regard to the industries covered, the present study is still tentative in the sense that the Agriculture, forestry and fishing sector is excluded because of the time needed to adjust such data. Manufacturing is only a single sector in the present paper.

4.2   The model

Ideally, in estimating production functions the concept of production should be gross rather than net output or value added (see, for instance, Klein and Kumasaka, 1995). For convention and for comparability, however, we have tentatively adopted a sectoral production function approach on a value-added basis, disregarding the contributions of intermediate inputs. Although we are fully aware of the bias caused by this approach, we are obliged to be satisfied at this stage, because our present purpose is to measure the output capacity rather than to elaborate the estimation of sectoral production functions.

The following four logarithmic specifications were tested for each sector

$$\ln V = a_0 + a_1 \ln K + a_2 \ln(LH) + a_3 \ln u + a_4 t \tag{1}$$

$$\ln(V/LH) - \sigma \ln(K/LH) = b_0 + b_1 \ln u + b_2 \ln V_{-i} + b_3 t \tag{2}$$

$$\ln(V/LH) - \overline{\sigma} \ln(K/LH) = c_0 + c_1 \ln u + c_2 \ln V_{-i} + c_3 t \tag{3}$$

$$\ln(V/LH) = d_0 + d_1 \ln(\sigma K/LH) + d_2 \ln u + d_3 \ln V_{-i} + d_4 t \tag{4}$$

where V = real value added (GDP), K = gross capital stock, L = number of employment, H = hours worked, u = the rate of unemployment, t = time trend, V_{-i} = scale factor (i.e. lagged GDP), σ = current share of capital and $\overline{\sigma}$ = fixed share of capital, i.e. the average of the σ's.

---

[1] Government services and non-profit organization services are excluded from the sector Finance and services.

Specification (1) is an unconstrained function in the sense that $a_1 \neq \bar{\sigma}$ and $a_1 + a_2 \neq 1$. The unemployment rate u represents a short-run reaction, i.e. a short-run shift of the aggregate demand curve. This variable is important, reflecting a cyclical economic change (e.g. an output rise in construction and trade sectors in a boom year accompanied by lower unemployment – as observed later).

Specification (2) is a TFP function in logarithms, where TFP is defined in terms of growth accounting as

$$TFP = \frac{V}{K^{\sigma}(LH)^{1-\sigma}} = \frac{V/LH}{(K/LH)^{\sigma}} \tag{5}$$

This equation implies that the production function is constrained with the current share of capital σ.

Specification (3) indicates a similar constrained function with a fixed share of capital $\bar{\sigma}$. Both specifications (2) and (3) have the same explanatory variables (u, V_{-i} and t), where V_{-i} is a shift parameter for a scale effect with a certain time lag, representing a shift of the long-run supply curve, and t is a parameter representing Hicks-neutral technical change, which is usually positive. A negative t is observed for some sectors, as noted later.

Specification (4) is a hybrid of type (1) and type (2). The dependent explanatory variable is not TFP but labor productivity, which is a function of the current share of the capital-labor input ratio $\sigma K/LH$, and the variables u, t and V_{-i}. This type can also be regarded as a variant of specification (2), since it expects an adjusted value of σ with the help of regression. A possibility of a more flexible time lag searching for K, L and V_{-i} is regarded as the advantage of this approach.

4.3   The results

Before estimating the sectoral functions, we first estimated each of the four types for the aggregate economy for illustrative purposes. The best estimate for non-agricultural private GDP for 1957 to 1998 turned out to be specification (4), as shown below.

$$\ln(V/LH) = \underset{(4.161)}{-4.143} + \underset{(7.372)}{0.626 \ln(\sigma K_{-2}/LH)} - \underset{(3.791)}{0.181 \ln u}$$
$$+ \underset{(6.361)}{0.020\, t} + \underset{(4.537)}{2.189\, IPR} + \underset{(2.276)}{0.200 \ln V_{-7}} \tag{6}$$

$$\bar{R}^2 = 0.997, \text{S.E.} = 0.027, \text{D-W} = 1.16$$

where $IPR = \ln(K/V)$ indicates the net fixed investment ratio, subscripts denote time lags, and numbers in parentheses give t-statistics. This result

Table 16.1 *Relative contributions of various factors (percent)*

	Growth rate of V	Factor input	TFP	Technological progress	Residual
	A	B	$C(=A-B)$	D	$E(=C-D)$
1955–1973	9.4	4.3	5.1	2.0	3.1
1973–1998	3.2	1.8	1.4	2.0	−0.6

was selected after discovering the lag structure and considering the appropriateness and balances between parameter estimates.

Regarding the contributions of capital and labor, the long-run elasticities are about 0.7 for capital and 0.3 for labor, while the elasticity for economies of scale is 0.2. This value is relatively low and reveals a long delay compared with the results from the alternative specifications. Strikingly, the value on technological progress remains as high as 2 percent over the past forty years with a significant t-statistic. This is particularly remarkable when we consider the fact that the growth rate of real GDP fell sharply after 1974 due to the oil price shock, and that it declined further during the 1990s.

The relative contributions of all the factors in our production function are summarized in table 16.1. The last column (E) is interesting, since in the latter period the demand effects of u and *IPR* weakened substantially, resulting in a negative value of −0.6 percent, in sharp contrast with the positive 3.1 percent during the previous period.

Now let us turn to the sectoral breakdown of these macroeconomic changes using sector-to-sector differences in production functions and capacity building. After testing the four alternative functions, we decided to use specification (3), the version with fixed factor shares. An exception was made for Manufacturing, for which specification (2), a flexible share version, was used. The rationale for this is founded mostly upon the continuity of the factor share data from SNA statistics for all sectors but Manufacturing. Another reason is that the long-run shift from capital to labor in terms of factor share is quite important in Manufacturing compared with other sectors.

The results of our regression analyses are summarized in table 16.2. Factor shares $\bar{\sigma}$ represent the relative contribution of capital compared to labor input $(1 - \bar{\sigma})$ and with values that are generally in accordance with the conventional findings of economists, especially in input-output analysis. As noted before, the short-term aggregate demand effect (i.e. the unemployment rate u) is significant, and especially so for Construction,

Wholesale and retail trade, and Transport and communication. The scale effect V_{-i} is important in Mining, Electricity and gas, and Wholesale and retail trade, while Construction is least responsive. For other sectors the scale effect is also significant, with coefficient values between 0.1 and 0.2. Values for technological progress (i.e. the time parameter t) are relatively high for Mining, Manufacturing, Wholesale and retail trade, and Transport and communication. The high values of t in Mining and Manufacturing roughly parallel the aggregate production function mentioned earlier. A striking observation is the negative trend values for Electricity and gas and for Finance and services. In view of increasing environmental costs, the negative value in Electric power and gas industries seems to be understandable. For Finance and services, heavy protection by the Japanese government for the banking and insurance sectors, which continued until the early 1990s, might be the culprit, but a more detailed examination is required to confirm this suspicion.

Finally, the Durbin-Watson statistics in table 16.2 are generally low, indicating the possibility of a finer model specification. By enhancing the quality of the basic data, particularly on current sectoral shares of capital and by outlying irregular samples, there is room for improvement. Regarding the $\overline{R}^2$ statistics, Construction and Electricity and gas both show low values, reflecting high volatility in the business cycle and weather conditions respectively.

4.4   Capacity output and the rate of operation

Having discussed macroeconomic and sectoral production functions, we can now estimate sectoral capacity output and the rate of operation by sector, and also aggregate GDP capacity by summing the sectoral estimates. In estimating the capacity, we opted for the approach of measuring maximum output levels by normalizing the unemployment rate and hours worked and by accounting for scale effects.

For simplicity we selected 1973 as the base year with the maximum rate of utilization for all sectors in terms of working hours and the unemployment rate. For two sectors (i.e. Transport and communication and Finance and services), however, the year 1970 was used as the maximum. The lowest rate of unemployment of 1.1 percent was observed in 1964. It was omitted, however, due to the inflationary tendency of the period. In 1973 the unemployment rate was 1.3 percent.[2] The normalized figures

---

[2] The Japanese concept of the unemployment rate is similar to that in other industrial countries, but underemployment in Agriculture, trade and services is traditionally excluded from open unemployment, making Japan's rate lower than others. Even in recession, Japan's unemployment rate tends to rise fairly slowly because of this accounting anomaly.

Table 16.2 *Summary of regression analyses of sectoral production functions*

	Mining	Manufacturing[a]	Construction	Electricity and gas	Wholesale and retail trade	Transport and communication	Finance and services
Unemployment	-0.137	-0.190	-0.330	-0.233	-0.318	-0.295	-0.031
	(1.550)	(5.112)	(6.128)	(3.658)	(11.665)	(7.390)	(1.513)
Scale	0.750	0.122	0.059	0.432	0.515	0.124	0.238
	(9.342)	(3.865)	(1.289)	(7.226)	(25.383)	(2.941)	(5.132)
Time (t)	0.020	0.021	0.006	-0.011	0.013	0.013	-0.024
	(5.654)	(7.521)	(1.670)	(2.268)	(6.012)	(4.192)	(8.340)
Time lag for scale	3	4	4	4	2	1	1
Factor share ($\bar{\sigma}$)	0.379	0.149 to 0.515	0.325	0.519	0.240	0.510	0.451
$\bar{R}^2$	0.938	0.979	0.524	0.841	0.997	0.958	0.962
Durbin-Watson	0.974	1.229	0.708	0.551	1.164	0.766	1.064
Observation period	1958–98	1959–98	1959–98	1959–98	1957–98	1956–98	1956–98

[a] Current share σ for the observation period (instead of $\bar{\sigma}$).

for the monthly working hours per sector in 1973 are as follows: 192 for Mining; 182 for Manufacturing; 197 for Construction; 176 for Electricity and gas; 183 for Wholesale and retail trade; 192 for Transport and communication (in 1970); and 180 for Finance and services (in 1970). The average amount of working hours per month was 183.

Regarding the scale effect, we normalized the output by assuming a long-run stationary value when $V = V_{-i}$ (with i the time lag). Mining and Wholesale and retail trade tend to have higher values of capacity because of their larger values for V_{-i}.

Sectoral capacities were estimated by solving the equations underlying table 16.2 by substituting the above normalized values and scaling. The results for these sectoral capacity outputs (or values added) and the rates of operation are indicated in figures 16.2 and 16.3.

First we take an aggregate figure that is not taken from the aggregate production function of equation (6), discussed earlier, but from the summations of the above sectoral output and capacity estimates. Figure 16.2 (panel A) clearly indicates a faster growth of GDP capacity or GDP potential with a widening gap between actual GDP and its potential. Figure 16.2 (panel B) shows a falling trend for the rate of operation (V/V_c), where V_c represents GDP capacity. It is rather surprising that, even during the "bubble" period (1988–1991), the operation rate grew rather modestly. Interestingly, this result is broadly embraced by Niwa's (2000) estimate of the aggregate capacity and the operation rate, although his GDP covers all sectors, including Agriculture and Government. An alternative estimate of GDP potential on an aggregate basis was conducted recently by Sato (2001b) using a reduced form of CES-type production function. His result lies between ours and conventional low estimates. The difference is mostly attributable to the assumptions for the normalization of unemployment and hours worked and the use of net capital stock instead of gross, which he originally estimated.

Sectoral cycles and trends are shown in figure 16.3. Manufacturing in figure 16.3 (panel A) also indicates a growing gap, but its performance is slightly better than the average operation rate. A more detailed study on subsectors of Manufacturing can easily be conducted using MITI data from monthly reports on the capacities and their rates of operation. Generally, our estimate for the Manufacturing sector as a whole agrees with MITI's official figures since 1973 (see Yoshioka et al., 1994, for details).

Figure 16.3 (panel B) indicates a widely fluctuating pattern for Construction. But its downward trend is faster than the average. The industries in Electricity and gas seem to suffer from low rates of operation

A: Growth of actual GDP and GDP capacity in billions of 1990 yen

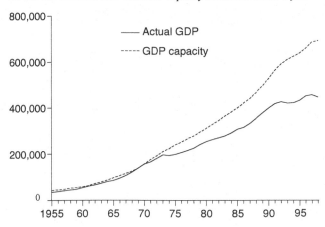

B: Average GDP utilization rate

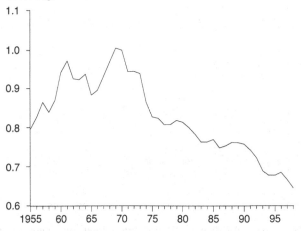

Figure 16.2   Japan's private non-agricultural sectors, 1955–1998

during the entire study period, except for a boom between 1967 and 1973. This is mostly attributable to relatively high seasonal variations in temperature, especially radical in Japan, that tend to force heavy capital spending by the Electric power industry.

A similar tendency can be observed in figure 16.3 (panel C) for Whole-sale and retail trade, which operates under the worst conditions. In the 1990s its deterioration seems to be accelerating, reflecting the recent

A. Manufacturing v. industry average

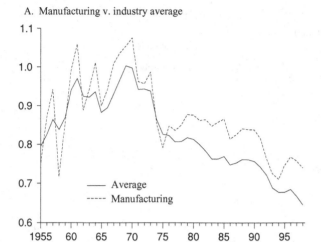

B. Construction and Electricity and gas v. industry average

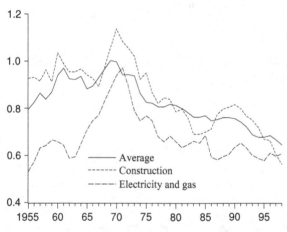

Figure 16.3   Average GDP utilization rates by major industries in Japan, 1955–1998

conservative behavior of consumers. Transport and communication also shows low operation, but in the 1990s it remains at a slightly higher level than the average. A downward trend, however, has continued in recent years.

The Finance and services sector in figure 16.3 (panel D) seems to record the least deterioration. Although the rate has fallen substantially since 1985, it appears to have hit the bottom at a higher level than the economy average. Also the Mining sector – for which no figure is

C. Wholesale and retail trade and Transport and communication v. industry average

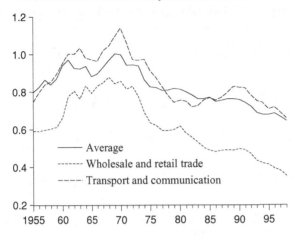

D. Finance and services v. industry average

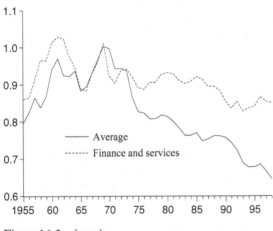

Figure 16.3   (*cont.*)

presented here, because of its small share in GDP – exhibits an inactive rate of operation that is significantly lower than the average, especially after the early 1980s.

Finally, we need to discuss the rate of capacity growth as compared with the actual rate of growth of GDP at the aggregate level, integrating all sectors except Agriculture. As shown in table 16.3, Japan's capacity tended to grow as rapidly as official GDP until 1973. At that point the growth significantly decelerated in the late 1970s. The average capacity growth rate in the 1980s was around 5.4 percent, while the pace decelerated further in the 1990s to around 3.3 percent. However, as shown in

Table 16.3 *Non-agricultural private GDP: rate of change in GDP capacity, actual GDP and utilization rate (percent)*

	Capacity (V_c)	Actual GDP (V)	Utilization rate (V/V_c)
1955	n.a.	n.a.	79.6
1960	6.7	10.4	94.0
1965	11.1	9.7	88.2
1970	10.2	13.0	99.7
1975	9.0	4.9	82.6
1980	5.3	5.0	81.3
1985	5.2	4.0	76.9
1990	5.7	5.3	75.7
1995	3.9	1.6	67.7
1998	2.7	1.1	64.5

Note: The rate of change is the annual average over the preceding five years, while the rate of capacity utilization is for the current year. Data were unavailable prior to 1955.

the right-hand column, the gap between the potential and actual GDP continued to widen.

5.   Concluding remarks

As discussed in the earlier sections, the Japanese government's medium-term plan and its growth target, though supported by its econometric model, have gradually diverged from their optimum track of securing full capacity and full employment growth. This tendency accelerated after the two oil price shocks in the 1970s and the political climate of neo-liberalism in the early 1980s. An explicit link between macroeconometric and input-output models, formerly the theoretical core for formulating medium- and long-term policy programs, has substantially weakened so that the idea of macro- and sectoral capacity utilization has gradually been disregarded. Behind this historical backdrop it should, especially, be noted that there was a relative change in the power balance within the government toward a stronger influence by the fiscal monetary authorities, which tend to be conservative compared to other government agencies, such as EPA, METI or those concerned with construction and transportation activities. Interestingly, these agencies remain active users of input-output models and are by nature growth minded. Also, in business and trade organizations the deflationary gap, though increasingly widening, has tended to be regarded less seriously. Political parties, especially the Liberal Democratic Party, which used to be a leading party in terms of pursuing economic growth, also seem to have lost the desire for returning to the vigorous growth of the 1980s.

The growing imbalance discussed above, however, has been causing various adverse impacts. Included among them are: a huge trade surplus with resultant upward pressure on the yen; stagnant imports, discouraging growth in neighboring countries and the world market; steadily accumulating fiscal debt; and excessive unemployment, breeding serious social unrest. In order to rejuvenate the Japanese economy so as to narrow the present gap, we need a vigorous policy package from the demand side and concrete targets at macro- and sectoral levels. Although our current study continues to examine broader categories of the economy, the findings obtained so far suggest a great deal of promise if we concentrate upon several strategic sectors in Manufacturing and expand our coverage to Agriculture and Government services, especially infrastructure. Under the present huge deflationary gap, a "big push" on both private consumption and fixed investment seems to be essential. This will require an elaborate Leontief-Keynesian mapping of the Japanese economy, because the market mechanism, or "invisible hand," seems unable to readily solve the current situation. As strongly experienced during the 1960s and early 1970s, a consistent policy package of growth targets at both macro- and sectoral levels, with an explicit outlook on capacity utilization, is very likely to reduce the investment risk premium, stimulating business investment as well as the stock market and foreign investors.

ACKNOWLEDGEMENTS

The author is indebted to Kazutaka Takechi for research assistance.

REFERENCES

Economic Planning Agency (1965) *Econometric Models for Medium-term Economic Planning 1964–1968*, report by the Committee on Econometric Methods, Tokyo.

(1979) *Econometric Model for the New Economic and Social Seven-year Plan: A Preliminary*, paper attached to the Official Report by the Committee for Econometric Model Analysis, Tokyo.

Hayami, H., A. Ikeda, M. Suga and K. Yoshioka (1993) Estimation of air pollutions and evaluating CO_2 emissions from production activities: using Japan's 1985 input-output tables, *Journal of Applied Input-Output Analysis*, 1, 29–45.

Klein, L. R., and Y. Kumasaka (1995) The reopening of the US productivity-led growth era, *NLI Research*, 76, 3–19.

Niwa, H. (2000) The recent deflationary gap in Japan: a quantitative measurement, *Journal of Asian Economics*, 11, 245–258.

Sato, K. (2001a) Japan's GDP estimates: a critical review, *Journal of Asian Economics*, 12, 21–36.

(2001b) Japan's potential output and the GDP gap: a new estimate, *Journal of Asian Economics*, 12, 183–196.

Shishido, S. (1998) Long-term impacts of carbon taxes on global environment and growth, in B. G. Hickman and L. Klein (eds.) *LINK Proceedings 1991, 1992: Selected Papers from Meetings in Moscow, 1991, and Ankara, 1992* (Singapore, World Scientific Press), 153–171.

Tatemoto, M., T. Uchida and T. Watanabe (1967) A stabilization model for the post-war Japanese economy: 1954–1962, *International Economic Review*, 8, 13–44.

Yoshioka, K., T. Nakajima and M. Nakamura (1994) *Sources of Total Factor Productivity for Japanese Manufacturing Industry, 1964–1988: Issues in Scale Economies, Technical Progress, Industrial Policies and Measurement Methodologies*, Keio Economic Observatory Monograph, Series No. 5 (Tokyo, Keio University Press).

Watanabe, T., and S. Shishido (1970) Planning applications of the Leontief model in Japan, in A. P. Carter and A. Brody (eds.) *Applications of Input-Output Analysis* (Amsterdam, North-Holland), 9–23.

17 Contributions of input-output analysis to the understanding of technological change: the information sector in the United States

Lawrence R. Klein, Vijaya G. Duggal and Cynthia Saltzman

> By means of reckoning appropriate to such interdependence [as that of input-output analysis], the quantification can do much to clarify otherwise elusive structural relations. These relations, moreover, may be consequential for one or another practical purpose.
>
> (Bergson, 2000)

1. Methodological issues

The outcome of years of technical change *within* the economy of the United States is impressive, and of great importance in interpreting the economic performance of the 1990s (and before) and the early twenty-first century. Macrodynamic statistics are both indicative and provocative, but they do not tell the story of what has been going on *within* the economy. The purpose of the present paper is to investigate some of the internal workings of information technology (IT) through the eyes of the input-output accounts for 1972 to 1996.

Semi-annually, the Bureau of Labor Statistics publishes *International Comparisons of Manufacturing Productivity and Unit Labor Cost Trends*. In its release of October 17, 2000, it reports the percentage change in manufacturing output per hour during 1999. The bar for the United States in figure 17.1, covering comparable data for ten major industrial countries, shows a towering figure of 6.2% growth for 1999, far above the other bars.

It has not always been so, but in many respects the performance of the US economy in the 1990s has been excellent in producing record non-inflationary output expansion, and much of this success rests upon the productivity performance of the economy. This is in sharp contrast to the dismal figures for the 1970s and the stumbling results in the 1980s. The time-series aggregates suggest that some firms' developments have occurred since the energy shocks of the 1970s, and a number of ideas are worth pursuing for the analysis of what has happened over three decades; but time-series aggregates can take us only so far in explanation. As we

(Percent)

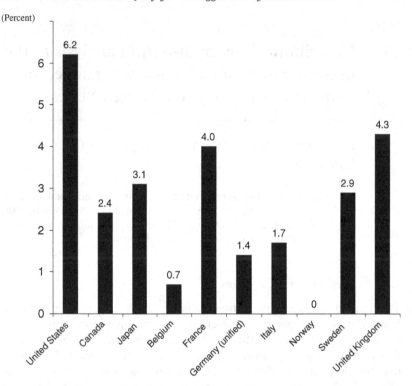

Figure 17.1   Percentage change in manufacturing output per hour, 1999

often heard from the lips of Wassily Leontief, we have to look *inside* the economic mechanism to get a fuller understanding of what went wrong, on some occasions, and what went right on others.

Input-output analysis is a natural tool, but surely not the only tool, for looking at the workings of the economy from the inside. At the very beginning of the first energy shock, at the time of the oil embargo of autumn 1973, input-output analysis was instrumental in assessing the magnitude of the shock and its lasting consequences. Less than a month after the shock, in October 1973, it was possible to predict a recession in the United States and, indeed, in the whole world economy (Klein, 1974).

To interpret the expansion of the US economy in the 1990s it is fruitful again to consult the input-output accounts. Suggestions along this line of thought have come from the research arm of Goldman, Sachs & Co. and from the US Bureau of Economic Analysis (BEA), the home of input-output accounts for the economy of the United States.[1] It was seen, from the input-output tables for 1996, 1992 and 1987, that one of the fastest-growing sectors was that for Computer and data processing services, especially in connection with deliveries from this "software" sector to other business users (hence the use of the term "B2B" to describe this kind of activity within the intermediate sectors of the US input-output table).

Macrodynamic analysis is mainly concerned with final, as distinct from *intermediate*, transactions. Therefore this important aspect of IT activity could easily be overlooked in trying to interpret the contributions of the information sector to the advancement of technology, increasing productivity, and the role of technological change in achieving the long-term expansion of the US economy, at a relatively high rate, with little inflation – certainly without accelerating inflation, as in the elusive quest for such a concept as NAIRU (non-accelerating inflation rate of unemployment), the very existence of which as a useful macroeconomic concept is in doubt.

The attention to B2B activity was sometimes set aside, on the grounds that it was too small to be of much importance. This is reminiscent of the comments in 1973/1974 that energy prices could not have a significant effect on the US economy because the sector's output was only a small fraction of total GDP. This turn of analysis prompted use of the input-output accounts in 1973, where all the intermediate flows of energy could be seen to have importance for input-output accounting, even though they may be washed out for final demand analysis at the macrolevel.

Of course, the full effect of IT must involve both intermediate flows (B2B) and final flows (deliveries for export, fixed capital formation, consumption and public sector use), and, indeed, we shall work up to this point in the present paper. When the BEA decided to treat own-account software activity as capital expenditure for building up human capital this changed the situation somewhat, because a significant part of software expenditures was transferred to capital outlays and showed up more in GDP (both level and growth). In our attempt to establish a longer time linkage among US input-output accounts, we shall have to treat own-account software as an intermediate expense in order to preserve time consistency among six input-output tables going back to 1972.

---

[1] See Brookes and Wakhay (2000) and Okubo et al. (2000). It should be pointed out that the 1996 input-output table was prepared by the BEA but is not a benchmark table.

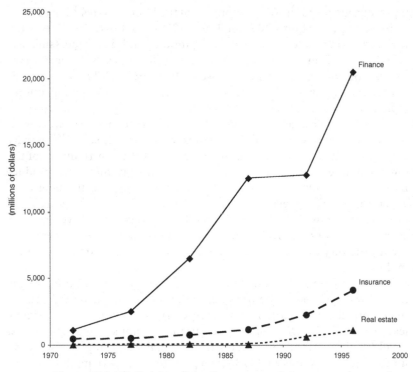

Figure 17.2   Deliveries of the Computer and data processing services sector to Finance, Insurance and Real estate

2.   Some properties of the US input-output accounts for 1972 to 1996

The BEA has supplied us with six tables, two per decade (1970s, 1980s and 1990s), with identical classification of ninety sectors.[2] These tables do not treat own-account software as expenditures for enhancement of human capital, and that means that deliveries to final investment demand are lower, for that reason, but such outlays are consistently treated in all six tables.

A sector of special interest to us is the one covering Computer and data processing services, i.e. sector 73A in the current input-output table. In figure 17.2 we plot the dollar values, at six time points, for deliveries to Finance, Insurance and Real estate. It is evident that Finance is an outstanding sector; it was one of the first to use software services on a large

[2] We are indebted to Mark Planting of the BEA for the preparation of the tables on a consistent classification basis.

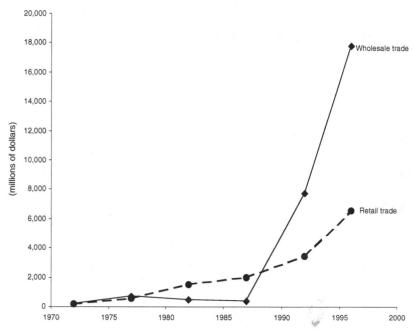

Figure 17.3   Deliveries of the Computer and data processing services
sector to Wholesale trade and Retail trade

scale, taking off by about 1980 in using electronic transfer, automated
teller machines, automatic accounting systems and other automated
"back office" services to keep abreast of global markets and provide almost instantaneous services to customers. There is a tendency for Insurance to begin its increasing use of software on a large scale by introducing
new processes in office and any other financial work. For those who think
that IT technology is something that began only in the second half of the
1990s, we recommend that they look at the impressive ascent of the curve
for Finance, starting in the early 1980s.

    In figure 17.3 it is evident that Wholesale trade and Retail trade started
to use software on a larger scale in the late 1980s, but the shift was made
sooner and at a higher rate of expansion in Wholesale trade. This is a point
in the supply chain where more sophisticated ordering and inventory
control can be important.

    Since we do not have the finest degree of classification that careful
input-output analysis deserves, we have some fairly large entries along
the diagonal of the intermediate square matrix showing the inter-business
deliveries. In a sense, this plotting in figure 17.4 of sector 73A's deliveries

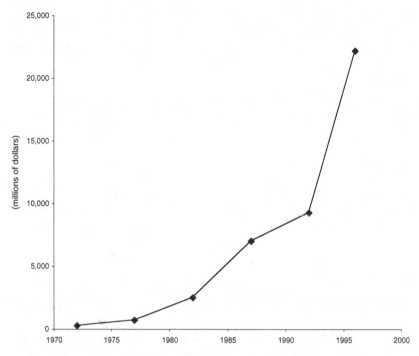

Figure 17.4   Deliveries of the Computer and data processing services sector to itself

to itself shows how work on own-account software has grown: very rapidly since the early 1980s.

The final demand deliveries in figures 17.5 and 17.6 show a large upturn after the middle of the 1980s for delivery to consumers (households), business investment (in the physical sense) and exports. All levels of government are significant users of software services, and this began in the early 1980s. Both defense and non-defense agencies or departments are big users.

This is an unusual set of tabulations, enabling us to trace intermediate deliveries amounting to scores of billions of dollars from the early beginnings of computer information activity to the present. It is not something new – i.e. in some sectors it is less than a decade old – but it has considerably more room to grow. All the figures presented here are drawn up in current prices; so there is an inflation factor. We have not attempted to present the tables, or their entries, in constant prices on a broad scale, but in the next section, on production function analysis, we have used deflated entries in order to make some judgments about constant dollar production functions.

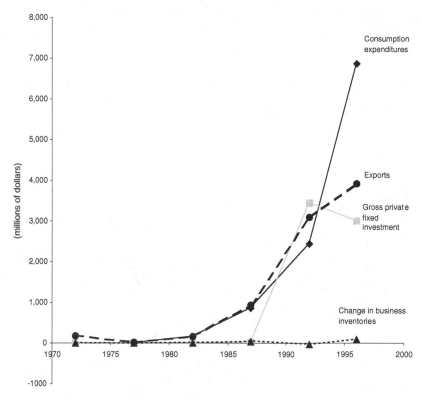

Figure 17.5   Final demand expenditures on the Computer and data processing services sector: consumption, investment and exports

3.   KLEMI

One of the truly interesting econometric developments of the era of energy problems was the introduction of the concept of the KLEM (capital, labor, energy, and materials) production function.[3] In the usual specification and estimation of the aggregate production function, following the work of Paul Douglas (1948), output is defined as (real) value added. The inputs are capital and labor, which are rewarded with profits, interest and rent for the return to capital, and wages for the return to labor. If intermediate inputs are added, as in the case of energy and materials, then output must be "grossed up" by adding the real cost of the intermediate inputs to (real) value added – to obtain an appropriate gross measure of output.

---

[3] For a discussion of KLEM production functions see Jorgenson (2000). During the oil crisis of the early 1970s it became important to explicitly introduce energy and other intermediate products into the study of productivity (see Klein, 1974).

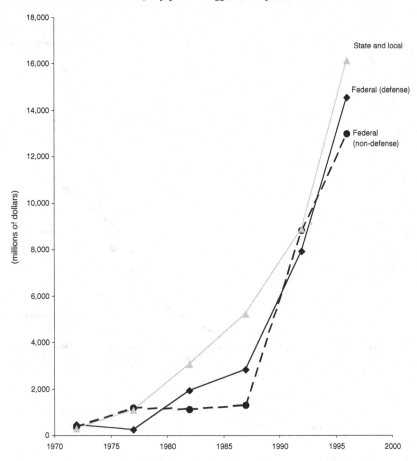

Figure 17.6   Final demand expenditures on the Computer and data processing services sector: government

If we want to study the productive power, at the margin, for information, treated as an intermediate input, we must split the *M*-factor input into non-information materials and services, and information services – the "I" of KLEMI. The hardware contributions to output should properly be studied by having two types of *K* and two types of *L*: information and non-information capital and labor. Lacking that split at the detailed industry level we might use total *K* and total *L* for an industry sector and *E*, *M* and *I* pertaining to the same sector. In some sectors, however, it has been possible to find data on information capital.

In an input-output table there should be a square matrix array for flows of intermediate goods and services. That is what we find in our sequence of six tables from 1972 to 1996, treating own-account software as an intermediate item and not a capital item. We take this from the deliveries of row 73A (Computer and data processing services) in the US table to a using industry that has been selected for a special study of technological change. Energy deliveries to the sector being studied and other intermediate deliveries (besides energy and software) constitute the input values of the M-factor. We then proceed to study the relationship between gross output X_i and K_i, L_i, E_i, M_i and I_i in the i-th sector.

It is unfortunate that the United States does not produce annual input-output tables, at least of moderate size, yet we are extremely appreciative of having approximately quinquennial tables. We could not, however, make meaningful samples for the estimation of KLEMI production functions from just six tables; so we improvised. We interpolated linearly between successive tables to construct "pseudo-samples" of annual data. We might have gone a step further and tried to re-balance tables by RAS-type procedures for annual periods between actual table dates, but we simply stayed with linearly interpolated table values, and estimated production functions from twenty-five pseudo- plus actual observations.

Our first choice of an industry for which to estimate a KLEMI production function was Automobiles and parts, since this sector was one of the first to modernize by drawing heavily on robotic technology in the late 1970s and early 1980s. The sector also followed the Japanese innovation of just-in-time (JIT) inventory practices. These two characteristics of the use of information technology in the Automobiles and parts sector need to be accommodated in the structural specification of the estimated production function. For example, robotic technology would be associated with an increase in the information technology capital stock (*ITS*). In many ways, this robotic technology capital stock mimics the labor input. On the other hand, JIT inventory practices would tend to correlate with the information technology service input (*I*), and one might expect that JIT inventory practices, and information technology services in general, would increase the marginal product of labor relative to the marginal product of capital.

One might also expect that the information technology capital stock, particularly the robotic technology, would require a large share of any information technology service input, with a mutually enhancing interaction. There are also the issues of potential increasing returns to scale and increases in the marginal product of information technology, in its roles both as a component of the capital stock (hardware) and as a service input (software). This is really the crux of the debate concerning the longevity of the productivity impact of information technology, and, hence, any structural specification would have to allow for increasing returns. For comparison purposes we will also estimate a production function for the Transportation equipment sector, since the Automobiles and parts sector is a component of this larger industry classification.

An important advantage found in the empirical determination of production functions, especially of the KLEMI type, is that we have a quantitative tool for formulating and estimating the degree of returns to scale. In general, we have found the tendencies toward mergers and acquisitions to be highly suggestive of increasing returns to scale, for that is a reason frequently given for merging already large corporations – i.e. to realize the perceived economies of scale. We shall examine the statistics for the degree of returns to scale from our estimated production function, and we are led in this direction by some insightful analyses of the automobile industry in the context of trade agreements between the United States and Canada, and also the more recent North American Free Trade Agreement institution, which brings Mexican production into consideration. Daly (1998) finds "lower average (and marginal) costs per unit with greater output." He finds in Canada "the increased use of computer-assisted design, computer assisted manufacturing (CAD-CAM) and more flexible production systems . . . A further development is the increased outsourcing of components by large plants and firms to smaller plants. Improved communication by fax and e-mail and more flexible transportation by trucks . . ." These cost-effective techniques, he finds, have been prominent in the large multinational automobile companies involved in US-Canadian trade agreements.

In order to incorporate all of the characteristics discussed above, the following production function specification is hypothesized

$$X = K^{c_1} L^{c_2} M^{c_3} e^{[c_4(ITS)I - \frac{c_5}{I k_I}]} e^{[\frac{c_6 K}{(ITS)L}]} e^{t^{c_7}} e^{c_8} \tag{1}$$

where X represents real output; K is the total real stock of capital ($KO + ITS$), with ITS the information technology capital stock and KO all other capital; L is labor hours; I is the information technology service input; M is all other intermediate inputs, including energy; k_I is the ratio of the stock of information technology capital to labor; and t is the time trend to proxy disembodied technological change.[4] To show some of the properties of this function we first focus on the term containing the IT activity, using the expanded term ITS/L for k_I

$$e^{[c_4(ITS)I - \frac{c_4 L}{(ITS)I}]} \tag{2}$$

---

[4] The functional form $e^{t^{c_7}}$ for the time trend is used instead of the more common $e^{c_7 t}$ because it allows for a non-constant growth rate over time and is more likely to yield a trend stationary dependent variable (see Duggal et al., 1999).

The derivatives of the marginal products of this function, with respect to both I and ITS, can be expressed as a fourth-order polynomial of their inverses. This means, depending on the values of c_4 and c_5, that the rate of change of the marginal products can be positive or negative, and switch from positive to negative or vice versa, over a large range of I and ITS values. Additionally, the labor value in the numerator of the negative term means that changes in either I or ITS will increase the total marginal product of labor relative to the marginal product of KO.

The production function specified in equation (1) can also be written in the following form

$$X = K^{c_1} L^{c_2} M^{c_3} e^{[c_4(ITS)I - \frac{c_5 L}{(ITS)I} + \frac{c_6 K}{(ITS)L} + t^{c_7} + c_8]} \tag{3}$$

In this form one might consider technological change as having both dis-embodied and embodied elements, where disembodied change is prox-ied by the time trend and embodied change is inherent in an increasing capital/labor ratio, with labor weighted by the information technology capital stock. Note that, as specified, disembodied technological change would be characterized as Hicks-neutral in that it does not impact the ra-tio of the marginal products of capital and labor. Embodied technological change will be neutral only when KO, and its percentage change, is equal to ITS and its percentage change respectively. Barring this exception, embodied technological change would increase or decrease the marginal product of labor relative to the marginal product of capital depending on the interaction of the values of c_4, c_5, KO, ITS, I and L. The functional form for the information technology service input, depending on the co-efficient value c_4, specifically allows for an increasing marginal product of I over some initial range of I values. As part of the larger exponen-tial form, the role of information technology in enhancing technological change, both embodied and disembodied, is highlighted.

By forming the natural logarithm of equation (3) we have the structural equation to be estimated

$$\ln X = c_1 \ln K + c_2 \ln L + c_3 \ln M + c_4 (ITS)I$$
$$- \frac{c_5 L}{(ITS)I} + \frac{c_6 K}{(ITS)L} + t^{c_7} + c_8 \tag{4}$$

This appears, admittedly, to be a very stylized specification. However, it is important to emphasize that the functional form was developed to incorporate the particular assumptions made regarding the Automobiles and parts sector. In doing so we used a variant of the transcendental production function classification, which is one – of several – functional forms used to generalize a Cobb-Douglas production function (see, e.g., Intriligator et al., 1996).

The implication of this generalization is to allow for the possibility of a variable returns to scale coefficient, as well as a variable elasticity of substitution. Previously we have used a transcendental production function specification in our examination of the macro-impacts of public infrastructure, with very good results (Duggal et al., 1999). Given that information technology is very much associated with an information and communications infrastructure, one would anticipate a similar need for generalizing the standard Cobb-Douglas production function. As shown by the estimation results following the data section, the specification of equation (4), with minor refinements, produces remarkable results in estimating output and productivity changes in the Automobiles and parts sector over the sample period.

4.   Data

4.1   *Gross output*

The value added data for each of the two sectors (Automobiles and parts, and the Transportation equipment sector as a whole) has been grossed up to incorporate all intermediate inputs using the nominal dollar values from the six input-output tables described above. The six gross values thus calculated for each sector are linearly interpolated to construct nominal pseudo-series for gross output (X) on an annual basis. The data are then deflated by the US Bureau of Labor Statistics (BLS) producer price index for each sector to convert it to 1996 prices.

4.2   *Labor*

Labor (L) is expressed in billions of man-hours on an annual basis. It is the product of the BLS data on employment for the two sectors and the average weekly hours of production and non-supervisory workers in the transportation equipment sector as a whole.

4.3   *Stock of capital*

The BEA provides current dollar data on the stock of capital (K) by sector. It also provides the corresponding quantity indexes in chained 1996 dollars. Real stock was calculated by multiplying the quantity index for each year by the nominal dollar value of the 1996 stock. The chained 1996 stock value was then adjusted by the annual sectoral Federal Reserve capacity utilization index. The real stock of capital is expressed in billions of chained 1996 dollars.

4.4   Stock of information technology capital

The CD-ROM from the BEA gives detailed fixed tangible wealth data by sector.[5] It is expressed in billions of chained 1992 dollars. The stock of information technology capital (ITS) for each sector consists of the following asset classes: mainframe computers; personal computers; direct access storage devices; computer printers; computer terminals; computer tape drives; computer storage devices; other office equipment; communication equipment; instruments; photocopy and related equipment; and telecommunications.

4.5   Information technology service B2B input

The information technology service B2B inputs (I) from the following sectors into the two industries under investigation were aggregated in nominal terms from the six input-output tables: Computer and office equipment; Audio, video and communication equipment; Communications, except radio and TV; and Computer and data processing services. The aggregate input was linearly interpolated and the annual series was deflated by the price index for custom software and, alternatively, by the price index for own-account software.[6]

4.6   All intermediate B2B inputs, other than information technology service input

The B2B energy input was aggregated using Coal mining, Crude petroleum and natural gas, and Petroleum refining and related products from the six input-output tables. The annual series were then developed by linear interpolation. The aggregate energy input was converted to 1996 prices using the BLS producer price index for intermediate energy inputs. All intermediate B2B inputs, other than those of information technology and of energy, were aggregated, interpolated and adjusted by the BLS producer price index for intermediate inputs other than energy. The 1996 dollar value for energy and other intermediate inputs were added to obtain M measured in billions of 1996 dollars.

[5] Courtesy of the NLI Research Institute.
[6] Mark Planting at the BEA provided the price indexes.

5.   Estimation results

5.1   Automobiles and parts

Estimating equation (4), as specified initially, we obtained somewhat lack-luster results; the estimated coefficient values attached to the capital stock variables and the time trend were negative and, in some cases, statistically significant, with a very low Durbin-Watson statistic. For comparison purposes a standard KLEMI log-linear Cobb-Douglas production function was estimated, but the capital and time trend estimated coefficients were negative, with an equally low Durbin-Watson statistic. It was then that recent discussions concerning an observed lag effect in the productivity of capital in the automobile industry were brought to mind. Additionally, the possibility of interaction between embodied and disembodied technological change was considered. Taking these ideas into account we obtained the following estimation results (with t-statistics in parentheses) when using the price index for own-account software to deflate the information technology service input

$$\ln X = \underset{(6.2)}{0.16} \ln K_{-2} + \underset{(4.6)}{0.27} \ln L + \underset{(12.4)}{0.61} \ln M + \left(\frac{t}{(ITS)KO}\right)^{0.15}_{(4.3)}$$

$$+ \underset{(3.4)}{0.0027}\left(\frac{K}{(ITS)L}\right) + \underset{(2.2)}{0.017}(ITS_{-1})I$$

$$- \underset{(3.2)}{0.057}\left(\frac{L}{(ITS)(I + L_{-1})}\right) + \underset{(1.9)}{0.41} \tag{5}$$

$$\overline{R}^2 = 0.995, \text{ D.W.} = 2.2$$

Besides the presence of lags[7] for the capital stock variables, the only noteworthy change from the specification of equation (4) is the interaction effect between technology and the capital stock variables. This interactive impact is such that increases in the capital stock variables decrease the marginal impact of disembodied technological change as compared to equation (4). Likewise, disembodied technological change will not be Hicks-neutral in that it would now increase the marginal product of labor relative to the marginal product of capital.

---

[7] These lags, and other data limitations, truncate the sample period to twenty-two data points.

The results are very similar when using a different data set, namely the price index for custom software, to deflate the I values

$$\ln X = \underset{(5.9)}{0.15} \ln K_{-2} + \underset{(4.5)}{0.31} \ln L + \underset{(10.7)}{0.60} \ln M + \left(\frac{t}{(ITS)KO}\right)^{0.17}_{(4.0)}$$

$$+ \underset{(3.4)}{0.0020} \left(\frac{K}{(ITS)L}\right) + \underset{(1.8)}{0.016(ITS_{-1})I}$$

$$- \underset{(3.1)}{0.097} \left(\frac{L}{(ITS)(I + L_{-1})}\right) + \underset{(1.9)}{0.51} \tag{6}$$

$$\overline{R}^2 = 0.995, \text{D.W.} = 1.9$$

These estimation results shed interesting light on the historical trends in the Automobiles and parts industry and the impact of information technology. All subsequent calculations are based on the estimated coefficient values in equation (5).

Given our interest in B2B activity, we begin by examining the role of the information technology services input. Calculating the marginal product of this input, holding all other variables at their 1996 values, we found that – on average – over 90 percent of the total change occurred through the change in the current period value. Hence, given this, along with the fact that I_t and I_{t-1} are modeled in the equation as a summation (for simplicity), only the current period marginal productivity was analyzed. This was done by calculating the change in output over an array of potential I_t values ranging from \$0.5 to \$8.5 billion at 1996 prices and increasing by \$0.1 billion increments; I_{t-1} was held constant at its 1995 value. Figure 17.7 illustrates this marginal product relationship in 1996. As can be seen, over an initial range of I values the marginal product decreases. However, at an I value of \$1.57 billion at 1996 prices the marginal product begins to increase. In 1996 expenditures on information technology services equal \$2.05 billion. Hence, the Automobiles and parts sector is operating with increasing marginal productivity for I services.

Figure 17.8 makes it very clear that there is still a very large range of I values associated with increasing marginal productivity for the information technology service input. This is in sharp contrast to the marginal product of information technology services that existed in 1985. Figure 17.9 shows a downward-sloping marginal product curve over a fairly large range of I values.

More importantly, the output elasticity of I services has increased from 0.045 in 1985 to 0.087 at 1996 values, and continues to increase with

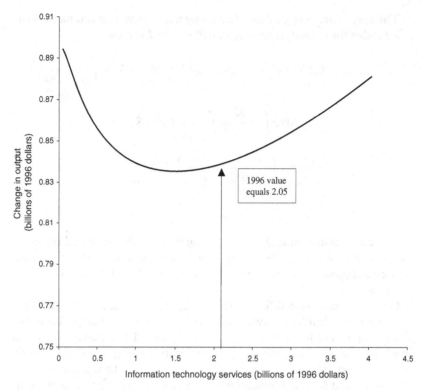

Figure 17.7   Current period change in output given a $0.1 billion increment in information technology services inputs; all other variables held at their 1996 values

rising values of *I*. Output elasticities are presented in table 17.1 for a range of *I* values, holding all other variables at their 1985 and 1996 values respectively.

The story is equally compelling with respect to the information technology capital stock. Figure 17.10 presents the two-period marginal product relationship, with all other variables at their 1996 values. Low values of information technology capital stock have a negative marginal product; there is a threshold amount required to reap the productivity benefits. However, once that threshold is reached, further increases in *ITS* generate increasing returns. At current values, the percentage increase in the marginal product is roughly equal to the percentage increase in the information technology stock. Hence, at present, we are not near a point of diminishing marginal productivity.

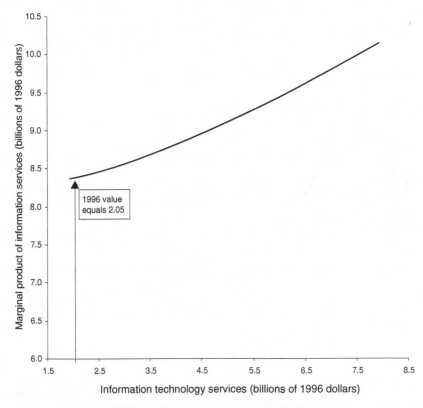

Figure 17.8   Marginal product of information technology services at higher potential values; all other variables held at their 1996 values

As with *I* services, the output elasticity of *ITS* also increases with increasing values for *ITS*, equaling approximately 0.10 at the 1996 value of *ITS*. Table 17.2 presents the output elasticity over a range of *ITS* values. In the case of *ITS*, doubling its value more than doubles the output elasticity.

Turning our attention to the labor input, we find in figure 17.11 a changing marginal product of labor over the period 1985 to 1996. For a given range of labor values, table 17.3 shows an increasing output elasticity over the same time period. The first point to note is that, for a given year, even with the relative complexity of the estimated production function, the estimated output elasticity of labor is fairly constant over the reported range of labor values. The second – and more important – point is the increase in the output elasticity over time. Converting equation (5)

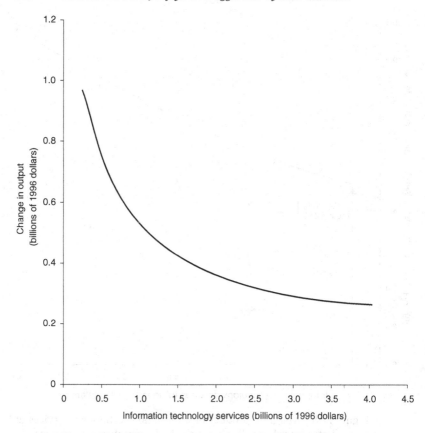

Figure 17.9   Change in output given a $0.1 billion increment in information technology services; all other variables held at their 1985 values

back to the functional specification of the production function, and deriving the output elasticity of labor, one sees that this output elasticity is determined by the KO/L, K/L and $t/(ITS)KO$ ratios, as well as the exponent

$$e^{[c_4(ITS_{-1})I - \frac{c_5 L}{(ITS)(I + I_{-1})} + \frac{c_6 K}{(ITS)L} + (\frac{t}{(ITS)KO})^{c_7} + c_8]}$$

The major part of the increase in the labor output elasticity, particularly between 1985 and 1990, is attributable to information technology, in its roles both as a service input and part of the capital stock. This is true because the KO/L, K/L and $t/(ITS)KO$ ratios are all virtually unchanged between 1985 and 1990, with only modest changes between 1985 and 1996.

Table 17.1 *Output elasticity of* I *in the Automobiles and parts sector; all other variables held at their actual values in 1985 and 1996*

I	1985	1996
1.95	0.051	0.083
2.95	0.060	0.123
3.45	0.066	0.143
4.35	0.076	0.179
5.35	0.087	0.218
6.25	0.099	0.254
7.25	0.111	0.294

Note: Actual values of *I* in 1985 and 1996 were 1.20 and 2.05 respectively, and these correspond to elasticities of 0.045 in 1985 and 0.087 in 1996.

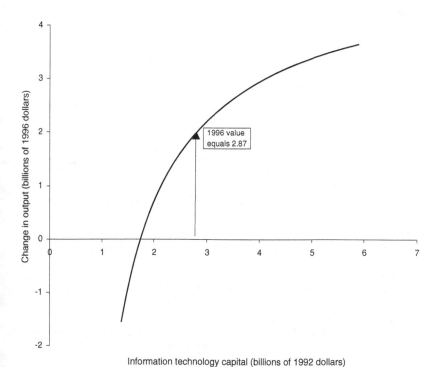

Figure 17.10 Two-period change in output given a $0.3 billion increment in information technology capital; all other variables held at their 1996 values

Table 17.2 *Output elasticity of* ITS *in the Automobiles and parts sector; all other variables held at their 1996 values*

ITS	ε_{ITS}
2.0	0.022
2.6	0.076
3.2	0.128
3.8	0.176
4.4	0.229
5.0	0.278
5.6	0.327
5.9	0.351

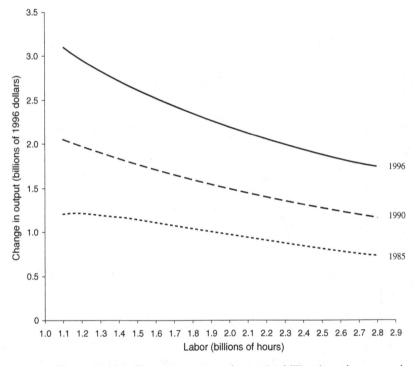

Figure 17.11　Change in output given a 0.1 billion hour increment in the labor input; all other variables held constant at a given year

Table 17.3 *Output elasticity of labor in the Automobiles and parts sector; all other variables held at their actual values in 1985, 1990 and 1996*

L	1996	1990	1985
1.5	0.215	0.174	0.130
1.7	0.220	0.181	0.136
1.9	0.224	0.186	0.139
2.1	0.227	0.189	0.141
2.3	0.229	0.191	0.143
2.5	0.231	0.192	0.143
2.7	0.233	0.193	0.142
2.9	0.234	0.193	0.142

Table 17.4 *Average annual growth rates of factor inputs in the Automobiles and parts sector for the 1991–1996 period*

Input	L	KO	ITS	I	M
Percentage change	5.0	8.65	15.0	7.0	6.0

Perhaps, however, the most important information derived from the estimation results is the calculated returns to scale coefficient using the estimated coefficient values. Because of the presence of lagged variables, the returns to scale coefficient is calculated over two periods. Starting with the actual values existing in 1996 and increasing all inputs by 10 percent results in a 13.5 percent two-period increase in output. This corresponds to a returns to scale coefficient of 1.35, representing sizable increasing returns to scale in the Automobiles and parts sector; no wonder there have been significant mergers in the auto industry over the last five years. The two-period percentage increase is broken down approximately as a 7 percent increase in the current year, a 5 percent increase the following year, and a 1 percent increase in the second period.

It is also possible to use the estimated results to project potential growth in the sector in the near term. Using the average annual growth rates of the factor inputs over the period 1991 to 1996, we calculated projected growth rates in output five periods forward. Starting with 1996 actual values, the resulting projected annual growth for the next five periods would be 6.2, 6.7, 7.3, 8.1 and 9.0 percent respectively. It is noteworthy that, in each year, less than 0.50 percentage points of the projected growth is due to the increasing value of the time trend. Table 17.4 presents the average annual growth rate for each of the factor inputs over the 1991–1996 period.

5.2   Transportation equipment

Estimating equation (4) using the price index for own-account software to deflate I provides the following results

$$\ln X = \underset{(3.4)}{0.13 \ln K_{-2}} + \underset{(6.9)}{0.42 \ln L} + \underset{(5.9)}{0.40 \ln M}$$

$$+ \underset{(1.8)}{t^{0.04}} + \underset{(4.4)}{0.013} \left(\frac{K}{(ITS)L} \right)$$

$$+ \underset{(2.0)}{0.0025(ITS_{-1})I_{-1}} \mid \underset{(4.1)}{1.31} \tag{7}$$

$$\overline{R}^2 = 0.989, \text{D.W.} = 2.5$$

Using the price index for custom software to deflate I causes very little variation in the results

$$\ln X = \underset{(2.4)}{0.10 \ln K_{-2}} + \underset{(7.6)}{0.40 \ln L} + \underset{(4.6)}{0.36 \ln M}$$

$$+ \underset{(2.2)}{t^{0.05}} + \underset{(4.7)}{0.015} \left(\frac{K}{(ITS)L} \right)$$

$$+ \underset{(2.3)}{0.0037(ITS_{-1})I_{-1}} + \underset{(4.0)}{1.61} \tag{8}$$

$$\overline{R}^2 = 0.989, \text{D.W.} = 2.5$$

All subsequent calculations are made using the estimated results of equation (7). The estimated coefficient value for c_5 was positive, but statistically insignificant. This is the major distinguishing feature when compared to the estimation results for the Automobiles and parts sector. A second distinguishing feature is that disembodied technological change is Hicks-neutral for the Transportation equipment sector.

In comparing the marginal product with respect to I for the two sectors, we find that, for a given range of I values (between \$2.5 and \$9.5 billion at 1996 prices), the calculated marginal products are very close. It is interesting to note, however, that the marginal product with respect to I in the Transportation equipment sector starts out about 5 percent higher than that for the Automobiles and parts sector at the lower initial values for I. This differential is gradually eliminated and then reversed at

Table 17.5 *Output elasticity of I in the Transportation equipment sector; all other variables held at their 1996 values*

I	ε_I
2.5	0.051
3.5	0.072
4.5	0.093
6.5	0.136
7.5	0.157
8.5	0.178
9.5	0.199

an *I* value of approximately $7.25 billion at 1996 prices. At the upper end of *I* values the marginal product in the Automobiles and parts sector is approximately 5 percent higher than that in the Transportation equipment sector.

When looking at the output elasticity of the information technology service input, we see that it equals approximately 0.11 at the 1996 *I* value in the Transportation equipment sector. This is a little higher than the 1996 value for the Automobiles and parts sector. However, as shown by table 17.5, over a similar range of *I* values the output elasticity of *I* in the Transportation equipment sector is consistently about half the output elasticity in the Automobiles and parts sector.

Figure 17.12 illustrates the marginal product with respect to the information technology capital stock. As with Automobiles and parts, a threshold level must be reached, albeit at a higher *ITS* value for the Transportation equipment sector. Output elasticities for a range of *ITS* values are reported in table 17.6. The output elasticity is approximately 0.09 at the 1996 *ITS* value. The two-period returns to scale coefficient for Transportation equipment is somewhat larger than for Automobiles and parts. This is of interest since the Transportation equipment sector encompasses the Automobiles and parts sector, implying that the non-auto transportation equipment sectors experienced even higher returns to scale. Starting with the 1996 values for all inputs and increasing them by 10 percent results in a 14.8 percent increase in output over two periods. This corresponds to a returns to scale coefficient of 1.48.

The average annual growth rate was calculated for each input over the period 1991 to 1996. These figures are presented in table 17.7. Projecting these input factor growth rates forward for five periods would result in output growth rates of 3.8, 4.2, 4.6, 5.1 and 5.7 percent respectively. Of

Table 17.6 *Output elasticity of* ITS *in the
Transportation equipment sector; all other
variables held at their 1996 values*

ITS	ε_{ITS}
7.0	0.038
7.5	0.048
8.0	0.057
8.5	0.065
9.0	0.074
9.5	0.082
10.0	0.089
10.5	0.098
11.0	0.105
11.5	0.113
12.0	0.120

Table 17.7 *Average annual growth rates of factor inputs in the
Transportation equipment sector for the 1991–1996 period*

Input	L	KO	ITS	I	M
Percentage change	−0.2	2.5	10.5	6.8	4.7

these projected annual percentage changes, fewer than 0.20 percentage
points each year are attributable to the advancing time trend.

6.   Summary remarks

In this paper we have tried to bring the analysis and discussion of the
influences of IT on productivity change in the US economy to a finer
level of observation and measurement. We focused on the industry level,
rather than the macro-level, in order to observe where and how unusual
technical progress occurred. A natural tool in this search for the explanation of the observed technical progress has been input-output analysis.
It has not been totally neglected in the present debates about the identification of technical change, its sustainability and its magnitude, but this
tool has been inadequately used.

Through the help of the BEA we have obtained a remarkable data
source in the form of six input-output tables, sequenced from 1972 to
1996, with uniform industry classification. These tables show strikingly

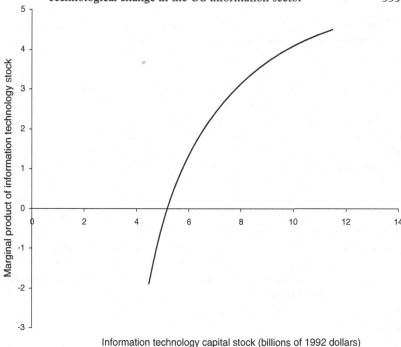

Figure 17.12   Two-period marginal product of information technology
capital stock; all other variables held at their 1996 values

how intermediate and final deliveries of computing and software services
to various sectors of the economy have grown, over three decades. In the
BEA's macroeconomic time series of NIPA tables, these trends would
not have been visible.

In a second use of these input-output tables we have applied econometric methods of production function estimation to estimate how original
factor inputs (capital and labor) interact with intermediate flows in extensions of KLEM production functions to KLEMI functions. This is a
time-series analysis for given industries. We selected, as an example, the
Automobiles and parts sector, and also the larger industry that encompasses it, namely Transportation equipment. The larger industry includes
aircraft and other moving vehicles.

A principal finding of our study is that this industry is significantly affected by IT (stocks and flows, final and intermediate) and that it appears
to be operating under conditions of increasing returns to scale. It is our
view that these findings help to explain how IT developments are showing
up in American industry.

These are not small matters. Our estimated production functions, from the supply side of the economy alone, indicate that a sustained industry output stream growing at 6 to 8 percent yearly could be produced by the Automobiles and parts sector, by itself, if adequate demand were present. For the larger sector, Transportation equipment, sustained growth of 4 to 6 percent could be supplied if demand were present.

Although we are highly appreciative of the provision of this remarkable database contained in six successive input-output tables, we realize its shortcomings for the issues that we are investigating. When estimating the KLEMI production functions we made calculations as though we had samples of annual data for the period 1974 to 1996. While this is the case for the macroeconomic magnitudes such as capital and labor inputs, it is not the case for gross output and intermediate input flows. These are clearly pseudo-samples, with interpolated values between the reference periods of the six input-output tables. In spite of this deficiency, we feel that underlying production trends are discernible. Our findings are sufficiently encouraging to lead us to make KLEMI estimates for other industrial sectors.

REFERENCES

Bergson, A. (2000) Biographical memoir of Wassily Leontief, *Proceedings of the American Philosophical Society*, 144, 465–468.

Brookes, M., and Z. Wakhay (2000) The shocking effect of B2B, *Global Economics Paper*, No. 37, Goldman Sachs.

Daly, D. J. (1998) Canadian research on the production effects of free trade: a summary and implications for Mexico, *North American Journal of Economics and Finance*, 9, 147–167.

Douglas, P. H. (1948) Are there laws of production?, *American Economic Review*, 38, 1–41.

Duggal, V. G., C. Saltzman and L. R. Klein (1999) Infrastructure and productivity: a nonlinear approach, *Journal of Econometrics*, 92, 47–74.

Intriligator, M. D., R. G. Bodkin and C. Hsiao (1996) *Econometric Models, Techniques, and Applications* (Englewood Cliffs, NJ, Prentice Hall).

Jorgenson, D. W. (2000) *Econometrics: Econometric Modeling of Producer Behavior* (Cambridge, MA, MIT Press).

Klein, L. R. (1974) Supply constraints in demand-oriented systems: an interpretation of the oil crisis, *Zeitschrift für Nationalökonomie*, 34, 45–56.

Okubo, S. O., A. M. Lawson and M. A. Planting (2000) Annual input-output accounts of the US economy, 1996, *Survey of Current Business*, 7 (1), 37–46.

18   How much can investment change trade patterns? An application of dynamic input-output models linked by international trade to an Italian policy question

Clopper Almon and Maurizio Grassini

1.   The problem and our approach to it

In an earlier paper (Almon and Grassini, 1999) we compared the shifts in the industrial structure of employment in seven countries – Italy, France, Spain, Germany, the United States, Japan and China – over the years 1980 to 1995. Among these countries, Italy was outstanding for its slow rate of decline in the share of non-agricultural employment in Textiles and clothing, in Leather and footwear, in Agricultural and industrial machinery, and in Non-metallic mineral products (stone, clay and glass products). By contrast, in comparison to the other countries, the share of non-agricultural employment declined particularly rapidly – one of the two fastest or a close third – in Chemical products, Metal products, Electrical goods, Office and computing machinery, Motor vehicles, Food and tobacco, Wood and furniture, Paper and printing products, Plastic products and rubber, and Recovery and repair services. The list of sectors

Prefatory note: This paper is not about Wassily Leontief or about my working relationship with him. That relationship during my seven years (1959 to 1966) at his research project at Harvard was always warm but strictly professional. I think I was in his home once and he never in mine, though our houses were but a few minutes' walk apart. On the other hand, this paper has grown from those years together, from his stimulation to find out about the economy from all possible sources, from his interest in international trade, and from his concern about investment in the dynamic process of economic growth. Leontief was not a champion of regression-based econometrics. This paper – and all my modeling work, then as now – is full of it. He never once in my presence belittled it or criticized my use of it in general, though he might express doubt about a particular equation. His concern was not to eliminate a particular way of investigating the economy but to insist that there are many sources of information. He loved the idea of using engineering sources of information, but he never thought they would be the key to the consumption behavior of households. He was quite prepared to admit that investment behavior was more complicated than just maintaining a constant capital-output ratio. Thus, although this paper goes beyond Leontief's own empirical and modeling work, I am confident that it is squarely in his tradition. It is that tradition of concern for real world relevance that I would like to celebrate in this collection of papers. (Clopper Almon)

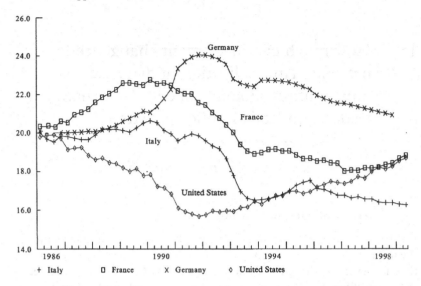

Figure 18.1   Percentage share of gross investment in GDP

where Italy is distinguished by hanging on to employment share are those generally connected with low wages, while those where Italy is leading the decline include most of the high-wage, high-tech sectors. This pattern may be called "low-tech drift."

The standard forecasts for Italy made with INTIMO – the *Int*erindustry *It*alian *Mo*del, a multisectoral macroeconomic (MM) model – show accelerating rates of decline in Electricity, Non-metallic mineral products, Chemicals, Metal products, Office and computing machinery, Electrical goods, Motor vehicles, Other transportation equipment, Textiles, Leather, Paper, and Plastic products. Accelerated positive growth in employment share appears in Petroleum refining, Hotels and restaurants, and Private health services. In other words, a continuation of low-tech drift.

Over this same period fixed investment in Italy fell from over 24 percent of GDP in 1980 to under 17 percent in 1997. Figure 18.1 shows this ratio for Italy in comparison with France, Germany and the United States for the years 1986 to 1998. In 1986 there was surprising similarity among the countries in this ratio: all four had investment at, essentially, 20 percent of GDP. Since then Italy has fallen below its two close European neighbors in every year. Each of them has had a period of expansion of the investment share followed more recently by declining ratios, which, however, remain well above the Italian ratio. The American ratio has been growing since a low in 1990 and now surpasses the Italian ratio.

The coincidence of the low-tech shift with the fall in the investment/ GDP ratio suggests – though it certainly does not prove – a connection between the two. We were therefore led to ask: to what extent can Italy influence its industrial structure by increasing investment? We do not pretend to offer a complete answer; we just take a look at the changes that would come about through a connection between Italian exports and investment in Italy. In doing so we use the Inforum international system of MM models, and particularly the bilateral trade model that links them.

The mechanism we use to generate this effect is somewhat unconventional, not because we wish to innovate but because we are not able to resolve statistically what form of the conventional mechanism should be used. Conventional microeconomic theory suggests that increasing investment increases the capital/output ratio and therefore should reduce the labor/output ratio. The reduced labor/output ratio would lead to lower unit costs of production, which would lead to lower prices, which would lead to increased exports, which would stimulate domestic production. That process should be simple to model. But it is not.

The problem is that industry capital stocks – at least, as measured by the Istituto Nazionale di Statistica (ISTAT) – have maintained an almost constant ratio to output over the last two decades while output per employee has increased *steadily*. Clearly, this development is not the work of a static production function. Some sort of technological change has to be introduced. There is no shortage of possible ways to do so. The problem is that there are very slim statistical grounds for preferring one form of technological change to another, but the different forms may have very different implications for the effects of a policy of stimulating investment. At one extreme, capital per unit of output may be fixed and all technical progress affects employment only. In this case, extra investment is simply wasted. At the other extreme, all technical progress may be embodied in new capital and all progress is due ultimately to investment, but investment has been smooth enough that the progress looks steady. In this case, increasing investment would be very important. We are not trying to say that the determination of the correct explanation is either unimportant or ultimately impossible. We say only that it is not simple, and that we, therefore, have taken a different, less conventional approach to the question at the cost of accepting that our answers may be very partial.

The heart of our approach lies in the bilateral trade model that links the multisectoral macroeconomic models of fourteen countries and two broad regions. In the linking model, the share of Italy in the imports of – say – Agricultural machinery in – say – Germany depends, in part, on the growth of the capital stock of the Agricultural machinery industry in Italy relative to the growth of the capital stock in this industry in all countries in the system from which Germany imports Agricultural machines. Prices also enter into the determination of import shares, but in many cases they prove incapable of explaining the changes in these shares. Why? Probably because there have been changes in the quality of products from different countries that are not reflected in the reported prices. This quality effect may be the result of investment in the exporting industry. The classic example is the automobile industry in Japan, which "bought" a sizable share of the world market by investing in the machinery necessary to make high-quality cars at affordable prices. Car buyers realized that they could get "a lot of car for the money" with the Japanese brands, though the price statistics showed no big drop. The purpose of the relative capital stock variable is to pick up such quality effects.

The bilateral trade model works at the level of 120 products and shows the flows of these products between each pair of countries or regions in the system. This system includes Canada, the United States, Mexico, Austria, Belgium, France, Germany, Italy, Spain, the United Kingdom, Japan, China, Korea, Taiwan, other OECD, and the rest of the world. The models of the various countries are "macro" in the sense that they generate the main variables of concern in macroeconomics: GDP, employment, unemployment, inflation, interest rates, government deficits or surpluses, the balance of payments, and so on. But they are also multisectoral; and, in so far as possible, they build up aggregates from industry-level data, which is the real center of interest in them. Thus, employment is the sum of employment in all industries, investment is the sum of investment in all industries, the total compensation of employees is the sum of the compensation of employees in all industries, imports are the sum of imports by products, and so on. Of course, some variables, such as the interest rate, have no industry dimension.

This study begins from a base run of the entire system. All the country models and the bilateral trade model are run iteratively until mutually consistent solutions are found. Then we run an Italian scenario with a stimulus to investment and rerun the models for France, Germany, Spain, the United States, Japan and China to get a new solution consistent with the Italian high-investment scenario. We then look at the changes in the outputs of the Italian industries between the base and the high-investment scenario.

Conceptually, therefore, the experiment is quite simple. There is, however, a considerable amount of machinery brought to bear on the question. We must try to explain the essence of that machinery without burdening the reader with an indigestible mass of information. In section 2 the Italian model is described. It is a fairly representative model of the system; some are more developed, some less. Most are, like the Italian one, built by a partner in the country and adapted to the statistics and the economy of the country. Section 3 gives a brief description of the bilateral trade model. Section 4 lays out the scenarios; section 5 examines the effects of the investment stimulus; and section 6 summarizes the paper and its results.

2.   The Italian model

2.1   The accounting structure and data

A structural model of an economy begins with an accounting system. In fact, an accounting system is already a model, since each balance in the accounts is an equation. Their number is also the number of the endogenous variables, which are necessarily accompanied by a large number of exogenous variables. Adding econometrically estimated equations among variables in the accounting system reduces the number of exogenous variables but at the same time introduces the thinking of the model builder. We shall, therefore, begin with a description of the accounting framework and then move to the econometric equations.

INTIMO begins with the Italian input-output table (Tavola dell'Economia Italiana) and the institutional accounts. The input-output table used in the model has forty-four sectors. Forty sectors represent the private component of the economy; four sectors represent non-market sectors: three for government and one for non-profits. The table distinguishes between domestic and foreign production in each cell, and the model preserves this distinction.

The table used in the model has had non-deductible value added tax (VAT) removed from intermediate and final demand flows. A fundamental assumption of input-output is that a lira's worth of a particular product requires the same inputs no matter where across the product's row that lira of sales appears. This assumption is flagrantly violated in the tables published with flows including non-deductible VAT. For example, in such a table, paper sold to firms appears without VAT while the same paper sold to households appears with VAT. The removal of the non-deductible VAT, therefore, makes the input-output calculations more valid and moves the table much closer to a factor-cost rather than a market-price basis. Besides the VAT matrix, the bundle of excise and other *ad valorem* taxes has been represented in a matrix specifically built for the model, where about thirty different indirect taxes are listed.

The institutional accounts have been aggregated into three sectors: enterprises, households and government. In the European System of Accounts (ESA) there are seven institutional accounts: 1) production; 2) generation of income; 3) distribution of income; 4) use of income; 5) capital; 6) financial; and 7) current transactions (with the rest of the world). The input-output table and the institutional accounts are closely linked. Aggregates from the intermediate consumption and value added matrices in the input-output table go into the first two accounts, production and generation. INTIMO then models the third and seventh accounts, the distribution of income and current transactions accounts, to calculate disposable income. The use of income and capital accounts allow computation of macroeconomic variables such as saving, investment, consumption, and inventory changes in nominal terms. Needless to say, the household disposable income, which results from the computation in the institutional accounts, is not necessarily the one that was assumed in the computation of households in the input-output accounts. The model must be solved iteratively to insure that the two are equal.

2.2   Equations from input-output identities

In an input-output table there are two sets of accounting identities

$$\mathbf{Aq} + \mathbf{f} = \mathbf{q} \quad \text{and} \quad \mathbf{p}'\mathbf{A} + \mathbf{v}' = \mathbf{p}' \tag{1}$$

where $\mathbf{q}$ is the vector of sectoral outputs, $\mathbf{f}$ is the vector of final demand (the sum of consumption, investment, inventory changes and net exports) $\mathbf{v}$ is the value added vector per unit of output, $\mathbf{p}$ is the vector of sectoral prices, vectors are columns, and a prime is used to indicate transposition. $\mathbf{A} = [a_{ij}]$ is the matrix of coefficients so that $a_{ij}q_j = q_{ij}$, where q_{ij} is the flow from sector i to sector j in the input-output table; matrix $\mathbf{A}$ is also known as the "input-output technical coefficient matrix." In our case, the matrix $\mathbf{A}$ includes imported intermediate deliveries. The set of equations on the left side are known as the "fundamental equation in the input-output analysis," or "the Leontief equation"; the set of equations on the right side may be named as the "Leontief price equation."

In INTIMO, all these variables should also have a subscript t to emphasize that they vary over time, so the equation for the determination of output is

$$\mathbf{q}_t = \mathbf{A}_t \mathbf{q}_t + \mathbf{f}_t \tag{2a}$$

The vectors $\mathbf{q}_t$ and $\mathbf{f}_t$ are to be thought of as real outputs and final demands, measured in constant prices. For the determination of prices the distinction between foreign and domestic products is important. For the price equations we need to separate the $\mathbf{A}_t$ into a matrix of domestic inputs $\mathbf{H}_t$ and imported inputs $\mathbf{T}_t$, such that $\mathbf{A}_t = \mathbf{H}_t + \mathbf{T}_t$. Then the equation for determining domestic prices is

$$\mathbf{p}_t' = \mathbf{p}_t'\mathbf{H}_t + (\mathbf{p}_t^m)'\mathbf{T}_t + \mathbf{v}_t' \qquad (2b)$$

where $\mathbf{p}_t^m$ is the vector of import prices. While the elements of matrix $\mathbf{A}$ may be interpreted as "technical" coefficients, matrices $\mathbf{H}$ and $\mathbf{T}$ simply distinguish the origin of inputs – a distinction that is useful for analyzing the impact of foreign prices on domestic prices but independent of any technological consideration. We do not have annual input-output tables in Italy, but we have historical series on outputs, final demands, imports, domestic prices and foreign prices. From these series and the 1988 input-output table we have made a series of $\mathbf{A}$, $\mathbf{H}$ and $\mathbf{T}$ matrices, from which we project future matrices.

2.3   Behavioral equations

In very general terms, the real and price sides of INTIMO (or any MM model) can be presented in the following form

$$\mathbf{q} = \mathbf{A}\mathbf{q} + f(\mathbf{q}, \mathbf{p}, \mathbf{z}_R) \quad \text{and} \quad \mathbf{p}' = \mathbf{p}'\mathbf{H} + (\mathbf{p}^m)'\mathbf{T} + v(\mathbf{p}, \mathbf{q}, \mathbf{z}_N)$$
$$(3)$$

where f and v are functions that generate the vectors $\mathbf{f}$ and $\mathbf{v}'$ respectively, and where $\mathbf{z}_R$ and $\mathbf{z}_N$ are vectors of variables not appearing in the input-output table, such as interest rates, money supply or population. Note the "crossovers"; prices appear in the final demands and physical outputs appear in the price equations. We omit the t subscripts, which should be understood on each matrix or vector. We have not included a dependence of the matrices on prices because that dependence has not been built into the present version of INTIMO. There is no problem in principle or theory in doing so, but there are very substantial empirical problems. Besides these equations, there are equations that do not have a sectoral dimension, such as the equations for collecting personal taxes or making up the government accounts. We now turn to the forms and content of the various behavioral equations that make up the f and v functions in these equations.

Let us begin with the description of a demand system used to model personal consumption expenditure. It is hard to judge the usefulness of a demand system without any reference to the use to be made of it. Thus, an MM model is a good testing ground for a demand system because it is fairly clear what it has to do. It will be used for fairly long-term growth studies so it must have an analytical form able to deal with significant growth in real income, with demographic and other trends, and with changes in relative prices. It must allow both complementarity and substitution among the different goods. Prices should affect the marginal propensity to consume with respect to income and the extent of that influence should be an empirical question and not decided by the form of the function. Following the same reasoning, income will surely make the demand for any good vary according to its specific propensity to consume, but increasing income should surely not make any demand go negative.

INTIMO now uses the Perhaps Adequate Demand System (PADS – see Almon, 1997; and Bardazzi and Barnabani, 2001). PADS demand equations have a form with a multiplicative relation between the income term and the price term. The income term has a linear form with a constant, real income per capita, its first difference and a time trend. By the use of adult equivalency weights, the effect of the age structure of the population on consumption is reflected in the forecasts. This age structure, in turn, is derived from a demographic submodel in INTIMO that computes population year by year in a hundred one-year cohorts on the basis of fertility by age, net immigration by age, and survival rates from one age to the next.

The price term in PADS is non-linear and designed to allow every product to have its own own-price elasticity and to exploit the idea of groups and sub-groups of closely related commodities where intra-group complementarity or substitutability may be important. Not all commodities need be forced into a group; some of them, given the detail of the available statistics, do not fit into any group. Other commodities or services such as Medical service and Education are recorded as household consumption expenditure, but they are mainly government expenditure so they do not fall under the consumer's budget constraint. They can be given special treatment.

The PADS system in INTIMO models forty categories of personal consumption expenditure found in the national accounts. The vector of a consumption in these categories is then multiplied by a "bridge matrix" to convert them into the forty-four sectors of the input-output table. Though the numbers of sectors in the two classifications are nearly equal, the classifications are actually quite different.

Investment equations are based on capital stock gross investment data available for twenty-one sectors, which are easily related to the forty-four sectors of the input-output table. Gross investment is assumed to be composed of two parts: expansion investments, and replacement investments. The latter are considered equal to the amount of investments required to maintain the level of capital stock constant; these investments are related to past investment and capital stock by means of a replacement rate implied by investments and ISTAT capital stock data. The capital stocks are, in fact, computed according to the perpetual inventory principle, so that, given the investments and the stocks, the "average" replacement rate can be calculated. The expansion investments are dependent on changes in output with lags of up to three or four years. The model is thus dynamic and must be solved year by year. No other explanatory variables are used. We are, of course, aware that investment functions should consider the cost of capital, but we do not have such information at the sectoral level and the use of aggregate measures has not been particularly successful.

These equations explain investment demanded by purchasing industry. As in the case of personal consumption expenditure, a bridge matrix is needed to convert investment by purchaser into investment by type of product purchased.

Imports are modeled by import share equations. The share is the ratio of sectoral imports to sectoral output. These shares are not constant over time; they are modeled by a price term and a sort of time trend. The price term for each sector is a moving average of the ratio of import price to domestic price for that sector; the moving average covers the current year and the two previous years. The domestic price is computed inside the model while the import price is supplied by the "bilateral trade model." The "sort of time trend," known as a Nyhus's trend, is obtained by cumulating over time the variable $1-s$, where s is the import share. If the import share is close to 0, this variable grows by nearly 1 each year and is thus nearly a time trend. If, however, the import share rises, this "time" slows down. If the share reaches 1, this "time trend" stops growing altogether. Exports are supplied by the bilateral trade model.

Government expenditure, which is here represented in terms of purchases for sectors, is treated as an exogenous variable; it belongs to the scenario variables and allows us to investigate the impact on the economy when the level or the structure of the expenditure is changed. For example, it can be used to study the industrial effects of a shift of government expenses between defense and education.

In the model simulations reported in this paper, labor productivity for each sector is modeled with the rate of output growth of the sector and either the level of output or a time trend. This device is not our favorite theory. We outlined in the introduction the problems in connecting labor productivity with investment. In the case of the United States we are trying to estimate the connection between investment and productivity using cross-sections across firms within an industry. At one time INTIMO used an equation based on "Verdoorn's law" (Verdoorn, 1949), which states that empirical evidence supports "a fairly constant relation over a long period between the growth of labor productivity and the [cumulated] volume of industrial production." That idea was abandoned in this study when it became clear that the equations were such that increasing outputs reduced employment in many industries.

We have investigated a number of other analytical forms for modeling labor productivity. We tried labor-capital ratios; that is to say, a step toward the total factor productivity definition. In many cases the estimation of the labor productivity equations seemed successful and gratifying. Unfortunately, good fitting and excellent statistical testing do not prevent the equation from giving highly anomalous results in alternative scenarios. We consider the modeling of labor productivity as one of the most challenging topics in building an MM model.

Wages are modeled at sectoral level and at aggregated level. There are forty-two sectoral equations and one "macro" equation. The macro-equation is an indicator for wages in industry – the energy, manufacturing and construction sectors. It explains the index of nominal wage as a function of the personal consumption deflator, and labor productivity is defined as the ratio of total output over employment. Both variables enter the equation with the current and one lagged value. The macro-equation has been designed for long-term forecasting. The personal consumption deflator represents wage indexation, whether as a legal *scala mobile* or as just the working of labor markets. Labor productivity appears in the equation because productivity increases are often used as an argument for wage increases in labor negotiations. The "macro" equation is viewed as a sort of "helper" indicator to incorporate influences on the overall wage level, which, were they put into the sectoral equations, could also influence relative wages – which they should not. On the other hand, this helper indicator is not used as a control total on the sectoral equations.

Besides the "macro" equation there are sectoral equations for each industry, except that the government sectors are aggregated into a single sector. The dependent variable of these equations is the ratio of the sectoral wage index over the aggregate wage index. There are two types of sectoral equations. One uses the rates of growth of employment and output plus a trend. The other uses the ratios between sectoral employment and sectoral output to industry employment and industry output respectively, with industry as defined above. It is these sectoral wage indexes that ultimately determine aggregate wages.

Contributions for social security are computed at the sectoral level. From the time series of (sectoral) wage and social security contributions, a time series of social securities rates is computed. These rates are exogenous variables that vary over time to reflect policy actions. Contributions for social security are derived by applying such rates to sectoral wages.

Gross operating surplus (profits, for short) are explained at the sectoral level – the same forty-two sectors for which wages were computed. The profit equations work in terms of profits per unit of output and list among the explanatory variables sectoral price, change in sectoral output, sectoral foreign price for non-sheltered sectors, and a time trend.

Besides the many equations that explain a single cell in the input-output accounting scheme, INTIMO has a growing number of equations dealing with variables from the institutional accounts. (Their number is growing because these accounts have only fairly recently been incorporated into INTIMO.) The institutional accounts properly belonging to the model are the distribution of income and current transactions accounts. In them, the institutions have been aggregated into three: enterprises, government and households. The households account has received special attention in order to model household disposable income (the balance line), which enters the personal consumption expenditure demand system. Some items (which are macroeconomic variables) of this account are obtained by aggregation of sectoral flows; for example, gross operating surplus, compensation of employees and actual social contribution. Other items need to be modeled. In some cases, a simple relationship among macroeconomic variables suffices. For example, profits distributed to employees can be taken as a proportion of the gross operating surplus of the private sector. In other cases, modeling the item may be more complex. For example, social benefits and current taxes on income and wealth both deserve special attention.

3. The bilateral trade model

The models of the Inforum international system (see Nyhus, 1991), such as the INTIMO model, are linked together with a model of bilateral trade flow in merchandise at the level of 120 products (see, e.g., Grassini, 1998). This bilateral trade model was created and originally estimated by Ma (1996). His work added countries, including China, and the influence of capital to that of Nyhus (1991). It has subsequently been revised and updated with more recent data. The following explanation of the model is taken directly, with only minor modification, from Ma's work. This model takes imports (from all sources) by product, prices by product, and capital investment by industry from the national models. From these data it distributes the imports of each country among supplying countries. The crucial work of the model is, therefore, to calculate the movement in 120 import-share matrices. In any one of these matrices, which we denote by **S** (for share), the element s_{ijt} is the share of country i in the imports of country j of the product in question in year t. (This t is 0 in 1990.) The equation for this typical element is

$$s_{ijt} = \beta_{ij0} \left(\frac{p_{eit}}{p_{wjt}} \right)^{\beta_{ij1}} \left(\frac{k_{eit}}{k_{wjt}} \right)^{\beta_{ij2}} e^{\beta_{ij3}\tau_t} \tag{4}$$

where p_{eit} is the effective price of the good in question in country i (exporter) in year t, defined as a moving average of domestic market prices for the last three years; p_{wjt} is the world price of the good in question as seen from country j (importer) in year t (see fuller description below); k_{eit} is an index of effective capital stock in the industry in question in country i in year t, defined as a moving average of the capital stock indexes for the last three years; k_{wjt} is an index of world average capital stock in the industry in question as seen from country j in year t (see fuller description below); τ_t is the Nyhus trend variable, set to 0 in the base year, 1990; and β_{ij0}, β_{ij1}, β_{ij2} and β_{ij3} are estimated parameters.

The world price p_{wjt} is defined as a fixed-weighted average of effective prices in all exporting countries of the good in question in year t

$$p_{wjt} = \sum_i s_{ij0} p_{eit},$$

$$\text{with } \sum_i s_{ij0} = 1 \tag{5}$$

and the world average capital stock k_{wjt} is defined as a fixed-weighted average of capital stocks in all exporting countries of the sector in question in year t

$$k_{wjt} = \sum_i s_{ij0} k_{eit} \tag{6}$$

The fixed weights s_{ij0} in equations (5) and (6) are the trade shares for the base year 1990. The use of the fixed weights ensures that the share equation satisfies the "homogeneity" condition as suggested by demand theory. For example, if all effective domestic prices p_{eit} are doubled, then a doubling of the world prices as seen by each importing country (or its import prices) leaves the price ratio unchanged.

The parameters were estimated using ordinary least squares in the following specification

$$\log s_{ijt} = \log\beta_{ij0} + \beta_{ij1} \log(p_{eit}/p_{wjt}) + \beta_{ij2} \log(k_{eit}/k_{wjt}) + \beta_{ij3}\tau_t \tag{7}$$

Ma (1996) searched the parameter space for estimates of β_{ij0}, β_{ij1}, β_{ij2} and β_{ij3}, and included only estimates with correct signs – namely $\beta_{ij1} < 0$ and $\beta_{ij2} > 0$. The search procedure explored seven alternative functional forms as follows, beginning with the form in equation (4). If the estimated price parameter or capital parameter was of the wrong sign, various combinations of a subset of the three explanatory variables were then used in the regression. If either price parameter or capital parameter still had a wrong sign, then the share equation was regressed on the Nyhus trend variable alone, because there was no sign restriction on the Nyhus trend variable.

It should also be noted that in any forecast period each trade share must be non-negative, and that the sum of the shares from all sources in a given market must add up to 1 (i.e. $\Sigma_i s_{ijt} = 1$ for all j and t). The non-negativity condition is automatically satisfied through the use of the logarithmic functional form, but the adding-up condition is not. Methods must, therefore, be found for modifying the forecast trade shares so that the adding-up condition is met. Estimates of all of the n shares are made separately and then adjusted to meet the adding-up condition. In this way the forecast shares in each market will satisfy both the adding-up condition and the non-negativity condition. In scaling the forecast shares to meet the adding-up condition in each import market, those with the best fits should be adjusted proportionally less than those with poor fits. There is a set of good weights at hand: the standard errors of the estimated equations. Thus, the adding-up condition in each import market is imposed by distributing the residual in proportion to the standard error of each estimated share equation.

Ma (1996) estimated equations for over nineteen thousand trade flows. The capital term entered equations accounting for some 60 percent of total trade flow. It should be emphasized that the estimation used time-series, not cross-section, data. Thus, the coefficients showing the effect of investment in Italy on Italian shares in the imports of other countries reflected only Italian experience. They were in no way based on, say, the effects of Japanese investment on Japanese exports.

Ma (1996) reports a variety of tests and experiments with the system. The best summary for Italy, however, is the experiment reported below.

4.   The base and alternative scenarios

The baseline scenario is given by the models as they stand in the Inforum international system. It represents a sort of business-as-usual, middle-of-the-road projection for the period 1999 to 2010. The alternative stimulated investment in Italy so that it reached levels ever higher relative to the

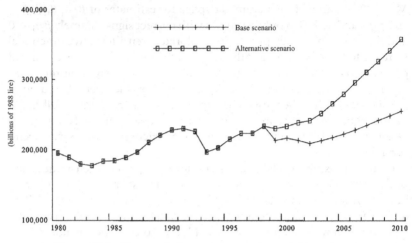

Figure 18.2   Base and alternative scenarios: total investment

base. The ratio of total investment in the alternative to total investment in the base increased roughly 4.25 percent every year. Figure 18.2 compares the base and the alternative in total investment. In the alternative, the investment in the individual industries was scaled so that the total reached the levels shown in this graph. Obviously, the alternative shows the results of a highly successful program of investment stimulation.

It is not our purpose here to make proposals about how this level of investment could be reached, but only to look at its effects coming about through increases in the Italian share of other countries' imports. It should also be emphasized that it takes a number of years of increased investment to change the capital stock significantly, and that the capital stock works with a lag of up to three years on import shares.

5.   The effects of investment stimulus

To quickly summarize the working of the model, increased investment increases capital stocks so that Italy's share in the imports of other countries is increased, thus implying that Italy's exports increase. Table 18.1 shows the percentages by which Italian manufacturing exports are increased in the high investment scenario. The largest effects are in Plastic and rubber products – up 20.9 percent in 2010 – followed by Non-metallic mineral products at 13.2 percent. Nine of the twenty mining and manufacturing industries have export increases of over 5 percent. In all but two of the industries the effect is positive. The negative effects in Textiles and clothing

Table 18.1 *Percentage increases in exports from investment program*

Sector	2005	2010
7 Ores	4.3	9.8
8 Non-metallic mineral products	7.0	13.2
9 Chemical products	2.2	3.8
10 Metal products	3.7	8.5
11 Agricultural and industrial machinery	2.5	5.0
12 Office, precision and optical machinery	2.8	5.2
13 Electrical goods	2.8	5.5
14 Motor vehicles	2.5	4.9
15 Other transport equipment	1.9	2.2
16 Meat and preserved meat	0.9	1.8
17 Dairy products	1.5	−1.8
18 Other foods	1.7	3.2
19 Beverages	1.4	2.6
20 Tobacco	0.3	0.7
21 Textiles and clothing	−1.5	−1.8
22 Leather and footwear	2.1	4.5
23 Wood, wooden products and furniture	2.2	3.4
24 Paper and printing products	2.4	8.4
25 Plastic and rubber products	10.5	20.9
26 Other manufacturing industries	3.3	5.4

come about because Italy's capital investment has little or no effect on its shares in other countries' imports in these products, but the increase in domestic demand for these particular products, due to the economic stimulus, does not increase labor productivity (as it does in some industries) and has thus led to an increase in their prices, and this increase reduced the share of Italian exports in the imports of other countries. By contrast, in the other industries (with the exception of Dairy products), the growing demand did lead to productivity increases and thus to reduced prices, which worked in the same direction as the capital effect in the equations of the trade model.

Given that the increase in investment reaches 40 percent only in the last year, 2010, these increases in exports seem satisfying and certainly plausible. The projected changes of investment and capital stocks are shown graphically in figure 18.4 at the end of this section.

Of more immediate interest are the following graphs, collectively referred to as figure 18.3, which show the export projections for France, Germany and the United States, and for Italy both with and without the investment stimulus. All lines are indexes with 1997 equal to 100. In general, US exports continue to grow more rapidly than those of the

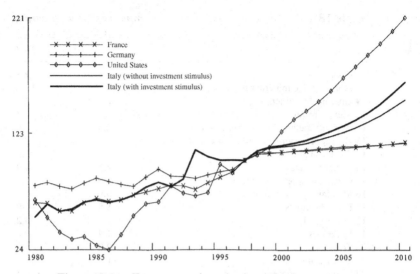

Figure 18.3a   Export growth projections: Ores

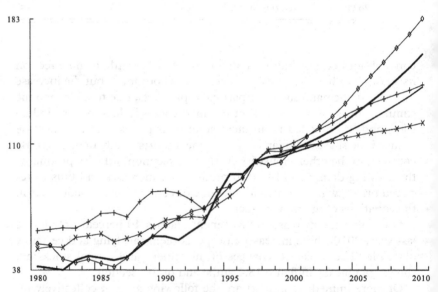

Figure 18.3b   Export growth projections: Non-metallic minerals and products

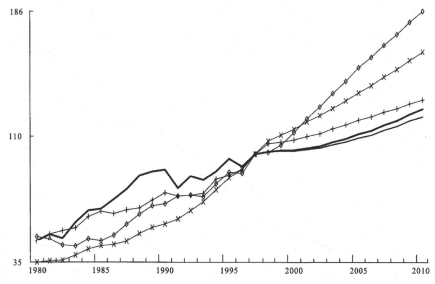

Figure 18.3c   Export growth projections: Chemical products

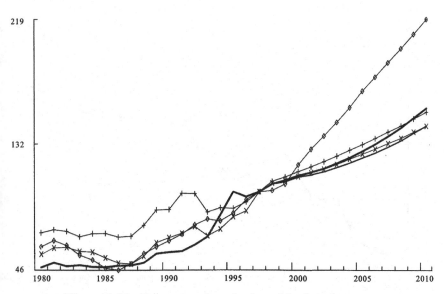

Figure 18.3d   Export growth projections: Metal products

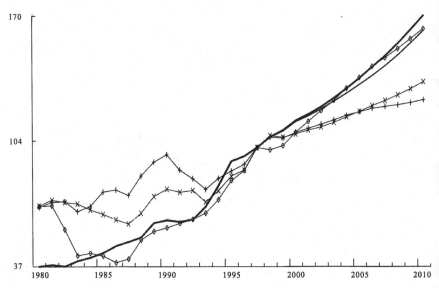

Figure 18.3e   Export growth projections: Agricultural and industrial machinery

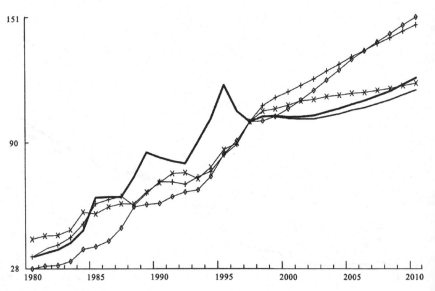

Figure 18.3f   Export growth projections: Office, precision and optical machinery

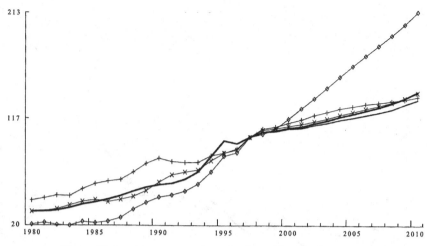

Figure 18.3g   Export growth projections: Electrical goods

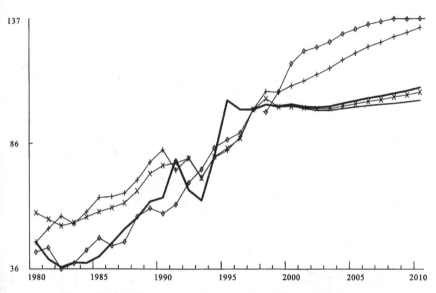

Figure 18.3h   Export growth projections: Motor vehicles

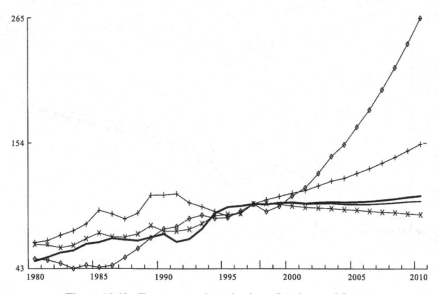

Figure 18.3i   Export growth projections: Leather and footwear

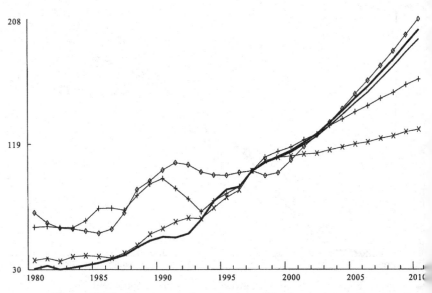

Figure 18.3j   Export growth projections: Wood, wooden products and furniture

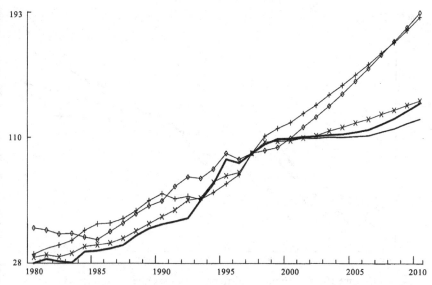

Figure 18.3k   Export growth projections: Paper and printing products

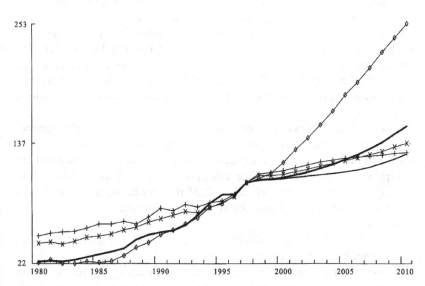

Figure 18.3l   Export growth projections: Plastic and rubber products

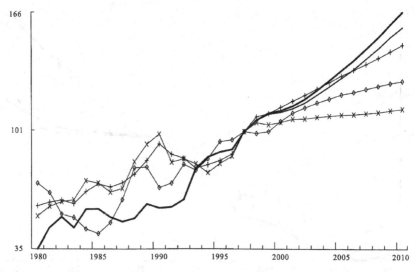

Figure 18.3m   Export growth projections: Other manufacturing industries

European countries. Relative to France and Germany, Italy has good prospects in: Metals; Agricultural and industrial machinery; Wood, wooden products and furniture; and Other manufacturing. It is weak in the Chemicals, Motor vehicles, Paper, and Food industries. The investment program makes a noticeable difference in the comparisons with the European neighbors. The most striking case is Plastics and rubber, where it moves Italy from being the slowest grower to the fastest among the Europeans.

The positive effects of the investment program show up in the changes in the annual rates of change of the shares of non-agricultural employment shown in table 18.2. For example, the annual rate of change of the share of Ores in non-agricultural employment between 1995 and 2010 is −3.49 percent in the base run. It rises to −2.95 percent in the high investment alternative. The table shows the second figure minus the first, or 0.54 percentage points.

These beneficiaries are, with perhaps the exception of the last, the ones to be expected. On the one hand, they include the direct beneficiaries of the stimulus: the capital-supplying industries, such as Agricultural and industrial machinery and Building. On the other, they include those such as Plastic and rubber products that benefited most from an increase in exports. Since the total shares in non-agricultural employment must add to 100, increases in these shares must necessarily reduce other shares.

Table 18.2 *Sectors with increased rate of change of employment share, 1995–2010*

Sector	Difference in rate of change of share in non-agricultural employment 1995–2010
Ores	0.54
Non-metallic mineral products	1.11
Metal products	0.37
Agricultural and industrial machinery	0.37
Wood, wooden products and furniture	0.26
Paper and printing products	0.08
Plastic and rubber products	0.35
Other manufacturing	0.28
Building	1.78
Trade	0.06
Inland transport	0.02
Private education	0.68

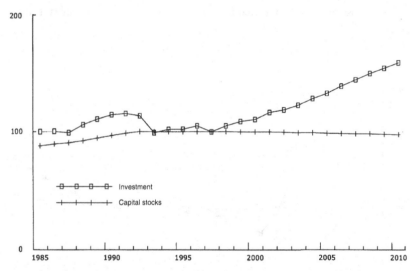

Figure 18.4a Projected investment and capital stock changes: Agriculture

That does not mean that the industries losing share would consider them-selves hurt by the increase in investment.

It may be felt that the effect on exports was fairly small given the size of the increase in investment, but it should be pointed out that the increased investment lifts Italian capital stocks only slightly. The following graphs, collectively referred to as figure 18.4, show Italian investment and capital

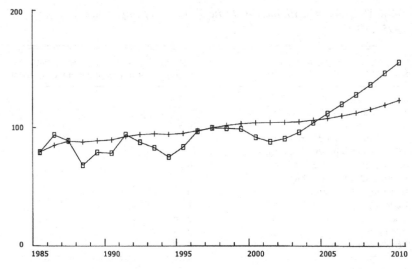

Figure 18.4b   Projected investment and capital stock changes: Energy sectors

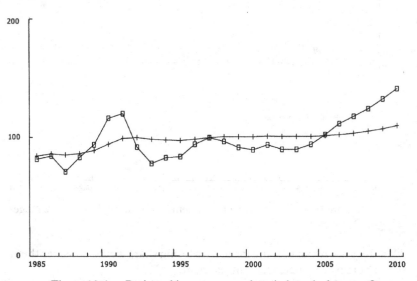

Figure 18.4c   Projected investment and capital stock changes: Ores

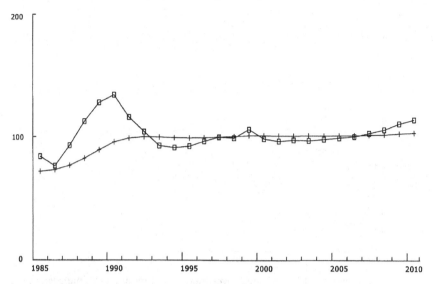

Figure 18.4d   Projected investment and capital stock changes: Chemical products

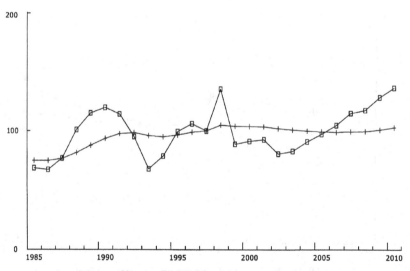

Figure 18.4e   Projected investment and capital stock changes: Electrical goods

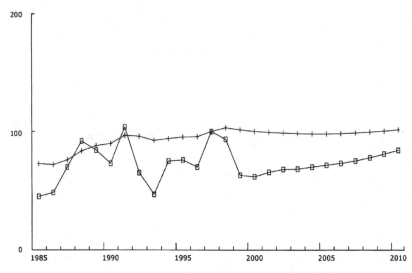

Figure 18.4f   Projected investment and capital stock changes: Motor vehicles

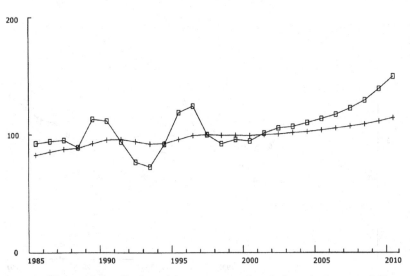

Figure 18.4g   Projected investment and capital stock changes: Office, precision and optical machinery

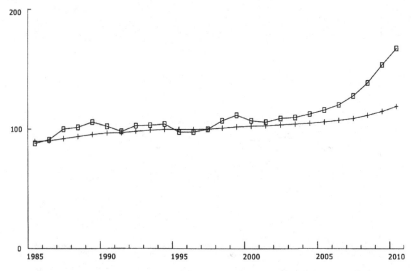

Figure 18.4h   Projected investment and capital stock changes: Food and tobacco

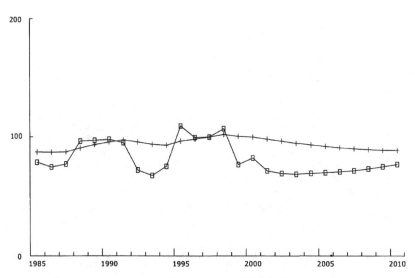

Figure 18.4i   Projected investment and capital stock changes: Textiles, clothing and footwear

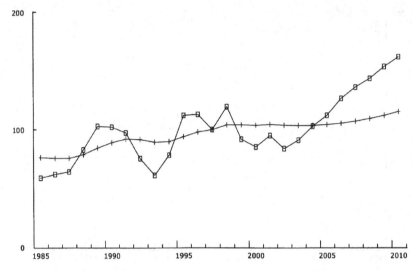

Figure 18.4j   Projected investment and capital stock changes: Metals and metal products

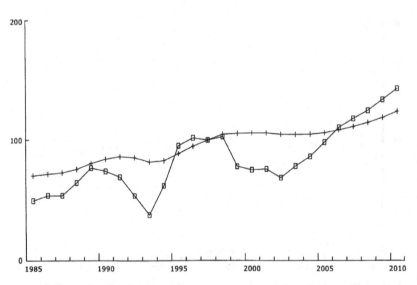

Figure 18.4k   Projected investment and capital stock changes: Agricultural and industrial machinery

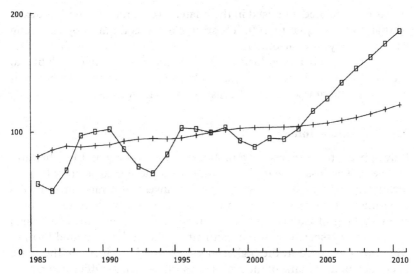

Figure 18.4l Projected investment and capital stock changes: Non-metallic mineral products

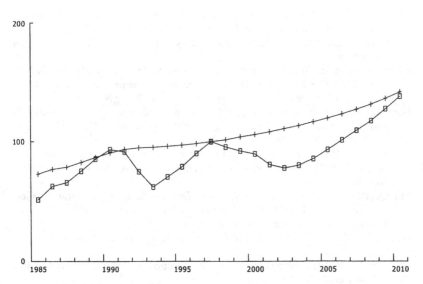

Figure 18.4m Projected investment and capital stock changes: Other manufacturing industries

stocks as calculated and used in the bilateral trade model – both indexed so that 1997 is equal to 100. These stocks are computed by assuming 8 percent per year wear-out. They show remarkably little growth. In other words, in a number of industries the increase in investment, relative to the base forecast, is necessary just to keep capital constant. In others it produces a slight rise only in the last years of the forecast.

6.   Conclusion

Italy appears to be specializing in Textiles and clothing and Leather and footwear. The loss of share in the industries more associated with high technology may be a consequence of low investment rates in Italy. An experiment in increasing investment spending uniformly leads to some strengthening of exports and some increase in the employment shares of industries associated with investment. In the undifferentiated form in which we have used it, the higher investment did not increase the share of employment in some of the high-tech sectors such as Office machinery and Chemicals.

REFERENCES

Almon, C. (1997) A perhaps adequate demand system, in *The Inforum Approach to Household Consumption: a Collection of Papers*, Inforum Working Paper 97–001 (College Park, MD, Interindustry Forecasting at the University of Maryland).

Almon, C., and M. Grassini (1999) *The Changing Structure of Employment in Italy 1980–2010: Can Investment Affect the Outcome?*, paper presented to the Banca d'Italia conference on macroeconomic studies in Perugia, Italy.

Bardazzi, R., and M. Barnabani (2001) A long-run disaggregated cross-section and time-series demand system: an application to Italy, *Economic Systems Research*, 13, 365–389.

Grassini, M. (1998) *The Core of the Multisectoral Inforum Model*, paper presented at the Twelfth International Conference on Input-Output Techniques, New York.

Ma, Q. (1996) *A Multisectoral Bilateral World Trade Model*, Ph.D. dissertation (College Park, MD, University of Maryland). [Available in portable document format from www.inforum.umd.edu.]

Nyhus, D. (1991) The Inforum international system, *Economic Systems Research*, 3, 55–64.

Verdoorn, P. (1949) Fattori che regolano lo sviluppo della produttivita del lavoro, *L'Industria*, 1, 3–10.

19   Social cost in the Leontief environmental model: rules and limits to policy

Albert E. Steenge

1.   Introduction

Leontief was one of the first to address issues of social cost in an input-output context, proposing a particular model to deal with it (Leontief, 1970; Leontief and Ford, 1972).[1] The basis of Leontief's environmental model (LEM for short) is a traditional open input-output model. His extension meant the introduction of coefficients representing the outputs of noxious substances and the introduction of specific anti-pollution processes or activities. Leontief formulated environmental policy in terms of a program aimed at reducing emissions into the environment. Abatement involved the operation of anti-pollution activities. Inputs to these new activities consisted of traditional goods (such as machinery, electronics or labor) and the – jointly produced and "free" – toxic substances. Outputs consisted of the elimination of the toxic substances. Thus, in Leontief's view, the "physical costs" of environmental policy were expressed as additional need for the traditional goods and labor, the model's primary factor.

How to address issues of social cost is an old problem. Many proposed solutions are based on a complex system of taxes and subsidies throughout the economy (e.g. Baumol and Oates, 1975). As such, they depend on detailed knowledge of the origin and type of pollution. Input-output analysis, with its focus on technology, therefore, is a good candidate for policy analysis in such cases. The development of the LEM, and subsequent work on it, illustrates this. However, many aspects, both of a theoretical and a practical nature, still need further investigation. For example, the theory of allocation and distribution of social cost is not well developed in the currently available models. In fact, at present a well-established theory of supporting prices is still not available (Steenge, 1999). Leontief's

---

[1] I follow the standard definition. Social costs are the costs incurred by society as a whole as a result of the production of a set of commodities. They are equal to the sum of private and external costs. In this contribution they depend on the level of tolerated environmental emissions.

seminal contribution has been to introduce the basic concepts. He left it up to others to interpret and extend the foundation he provided.

In my view, a number of fundamental problems with regard to social cost in an input-output setting are particularly pressing. First of all, there are several model specifications in existence, the relative merits of which remain unclear. In itself it would be a major task to systematize the present categories of models and sub-models. We are also faced with persistent issues regarding the economy's environmental objective. Is it primarily about the minimization of the output of noxious chemicals and substances, or is it rather about the maximization of the production of an elusive commodity such as "clean air"? Related to this are many open questions about fundamental aspects of the model(s). Can we be sure, for example, that core values are positive, or non-negative, when prescribed by economic logic? What is the precise role of technology? And how much of the product "pollution abatement" can be produced anyway?

In this contribution I shall propose a methodology to deal with these issues. In my view, we should return first to the old open input-output model. Its task always was very clear. It should enable us to calculate the cost of final consumption demand in physical terms, including labor, and the accompanying prices. To this end it distinguishes between purpose (satisfaction of final demand) and the technologies in the industries. Circularity next does the job; in exchange for their consumption package, households sell their labor to the industries. There is only one limiting factor: homogeneous labor. If there is not enough labor to satisfy demand, preferences should be adjusted.

The situation changes suddenly, however, when it is realized that production produces public "bads." New rules are added to the game: the aim of production for final demand is maintained, but in addition we have to satisfy certain environmental constraints that were not included previously. In particular, two types of rules emerge. One type deals with the physical limits to be set to pollution. A second type gives rules for the allocation of costs. The well-known "polluter pays" principle is one such rule, but others are known from practice or the literature. Next to thinking about the form of the new rules, we have to think about their nature. What precisely do they accomplish? Clearly, they aim at reducing pollution, but can the economy comply? And what is the nature of the constraints on emissions? Do they perhaps generate *new limiting factors*, or not?

A problem is that the LEM allows two different views of abatement costs. On the one hand, it tells us that environmental policy boils down to additional goods and services being asked for in exchange for a particular service (i.e. the elimination of noxious substances). This is analogous to households asking for consumer goods in exchange for a particular service, i.e. labor. This suggests viewing abatement services as a new type of primary factor, which implies that limits to the scale and scope of environmental policy should be found here. But then, where precisely should the limiting factor be found? If environmental policy is about the production of extra goods and services, shouldn't that mean that labor alone is the ultimate primary factor (just as in the model without pollution)? And doesn't that suggest that the LEM is telling us that, provided there is a sufficient amount of labor around, there is *no* technological barrier to a program of zero pollution? (Which again raises the question of what precisely the rules bring about.) On the other hand, in terms of the LEM, we may just as well argue the other way around. If environmental activities become a part of normal duty, they also become part of normal technology, and rather should be considered as belonging to the intermediate inputs. That would mean that the "limits to policy" should lie there.

So, apparently, there is a certain ambiguity in the model. Below I shall try to clarify the origin and nature of this. I shall illustrate my approach with a number of numerical examples based on earlier work by Leontief.

2.   The Leontief environmental model

2.1   *Methodology*

The LEM's task is to calculate the real and price effects of environmental policy. It differs from the traditional open input-output model in that it describes the emissions of noxious substances – the so-called pollutants – in terms of quantities per unit of good produced. That is, emissions are described in terms of a new type of output coefficient. Environmental policy is introduced in the form of curbs on the quantities of emissions that may be released into the environment, and in a cost allocation scheme being imposed.[2]

The model is a typical "construct" in the sense that it requires several sets of coefficients that must be configured in a specific way. First of all, there are the traditional input coefficients, representing inputs in the production of conventional goods, such as wheat and steel. Second, we need information on pollution, i.e. coefficients registering the outputs of noxious substances (such as the chemicals that cause the greenhouse effect or depletion of the ozone layer) per unit of wheat or steel produced. Third, we need information on the technology of abatement processes in the

---

[2] More or less simultaneously several authors have proposed models sharing a number of traits with the Leontief approach; see, e.g., Isard (1972) or Victor (1972). I shall abstract from these efforts because the proposed model structure in these cases is not along established input-output lines.

form of inputs of traditional goods. Fourth, we need labor input coefficients for both the traditional goods and the abatement activities. Finally, we need a description of policy: how much should be abated and which party should pay for it? It is the task of the economic modeler to put these building blocks together in a way suitable for the problem at hand.

The building blocks are as follows. A_{11} is the traditional input coefficients matrix, A_{21} the matrix of emission coefficients, A_{12} the matrix of input coefficients of the abatement industries, A_{22} the matrix of output of pollutants per unit of eliminated pollutant,[3] v_1' the vector of direct labor input coefficients, and v_2' the vector of direct labor input coefficients for the abatement activities. Vectors are columns by definition and a prime is used to indicate transposition. Furthermore, we have c_1 for the vector of final consumption of the traditional goods, c_2 for the vector of tolerated levels of pollutants, x_1 for the vector of total outputs of traditional goods, and x_2 for the vector of the total of pollutants being abated.

Next the building blocks are put together. Following Leontief (1970) we have for the real side

$$
\begin{bmatrix}
I - A_{11} & -A_{12} \\
\hline
A_{21} & -I + A_{22}
\end{bmatrix}
\begin{bmatrix}
x_1 \\
\hline
x_2
\end{bmatrix}
=
\begin{bmatrix}
c_1 \\
\hline
c_2
\end{bmatrix}
\tag{1}
$$

We also may encounter an alternative form

$$
\begin{bmatrix}
I - A_{11} & -A_{12} \\
\hline
-A_{21} & I - A_{22}
\end{bmatrix}
\begin{bmatrix}
x_1 \\
\hline
x_2
\end{bmatrix}
=
\begin{bmatrix}
c_1 \\
\hline
-c_2
\end{bmatrix}
\tag{2}
$$

Leontief's price equation is

$$
\begin{bmatrix}
p_1' & p_2'
\end{bmatrix}
\begin{bmatrix}
I - A_{11} & -A_{12} \\
\hline
-Q_{21} & I - Q_{22}
\end{bmatrix}
=
\begin{bmatrix}
v_1' & v_2'
\end{bmatrix}
\tag{3}
$$

[3] Also, the production of abatement facilities may generate pollution.

where Q_{21} and Q_{22} are expressions for the proportions of each pollutant "eliminated at the expense of the originating industry" (Leontief, 1970, p. 271). In his numerical examples Leontief discusses the case of equal sectoral proportions (I come back to this extensively below). We also encounter quite different price equations, such as[4]

$$
\begin{bmatrix} \mathbf{p}'_1 & \mathbf{p}'_2 \end{bmatrix}
\begin{bmatrix} \mathbf{I} - \mathbf{A}_{11} & -\mathbf{A}_{12} \\ -\mathbf{A}_{21} & \mathbf{I} - \mathbf{A}_{22} \end{bmatrix}
= \begin{bmatrix} \mathbf{v}'_1 & \mathbf{v}'_2 \end{bmatrix}
\tag{4}
$$

In equations (3) and (4) $\mathbf{p}_1$ and $\mathbf{p}_2$ denote, respectively, the prices of the conventional goods and the prices of the pollutants being eliminated. In fact, the literature has produced quite a few specifications both for the real and the price side. This can be seen as illustrative of the long quest for a definite form of the basic model. We observe that equations (3) and (4) are not precise mathematical duals of (1) or (2) respectively. In fact, (1) and (2) are, rather, input-output accounting identities, while (3) and (4) reflect policy characteristics.

The real model looks deceptively simple. Writing out both "rows" of (1) or (2) separately we have

$$
\left.\begin{array}{l} \mathbf{x}_1 = \mathbf{A}_{11}\mathbf{x}_1 + \mathbf{A}_{12}\mathbf{x}_2 + \mathbf{c}_1 \\ \mathbf{x}_2 = \mathbf{A}_{21}\mathbf{x}_1 + \mathbf{A}_{22}\mathbf{x}_2 - \mathbf{c}_2 \end{array}\right\}
\tag{5}
$$

Equations (5) tell us that total production of conventional goods should cover requirements for the production of these conventional goods, inputs for abatement processes and final demand for conventional goods.[5] The second equation says that the total of abated and tolerated pollution equals total generated pollution. Despite its simple appearance, a substantial literature has been devoted to finding conditions that guarantee the economic interpretability of solutions, particularly regarding the non-negativity of $\mathbf{x}_1$ and $\mathbf{x}_2$, given $\mathbf{c}_1$ and $\mathbf{c}_2$.[6] To see that non-negativity is not "automatically" guaranteed, consider (5) again; $\mathbf{x}_2$ can be written as

$$
\mathbf{x}_2 = (\mathbf{I} - \mathbf{A}_{22})^{-1}(\mathbf{A}_{21}\mathbf{x}_1 - \mathbf{c}_2)
\tag{6}
$$

---

[4] See, e.g., Luptacik and Böhm (1994, and 1999) for a discussion of equations (2) and (4).
[5] I follow tradition in supposing that matrix $\mathbf{A}_{11}$ is indecomposable with a Perron-Frobenius eigenvalue less than unity.
[6] See, e.g., Stone (1972), Flick (1974), Steenge (1978), Lowe (1979), Moore (1981), Lee (1982), Rhee and Miranowski (1984), Dufournaud et al. (1988), Qayum (1991), Arrous (1994) or Lager (1998).

where we assume that the Perron-Frobenius eigenvalue of A_{22} is less than unity. We see that, in any case, we have to address the possibility of the second term on the right-hand side of (6) becoming negative. Subsequent substitution in (1) and rearrangement gives $(I - A_{11})x_1 - A_{12}(I - A_{22})^{-1} (A_{21}x_1 - c_2) = c_1$, or

$$x_1 = [A_{11} + A_{12}(I - A_{22})^{-1}A_{21}]x_1 + [c_1 - A_{12}(I - A_{22})^{-1}c_2]$$
(7)

From x_1 we now straightforwardly may obtain x_2. At first glance, (7) looks like a normal input-output model, where, for the moment, we may think of matrix $A_{11} + A_{12}(I - A_{22})^{-1}A_{21}$ as an "enlarged" input coefficients matrix. We also encounter the term $c_1 - A_{12}(I - A_{22})^{-1}c_2$. The "final demand term" thus consists of (functions of) the two variables c_1 and c_2. In (7) the sign that the elements of $c_1 - A_{12}(I - A_{22})^{-1}c_2$ will have is not immediately clear. Situations characterized by relatively small c_1 and relatively large c_2 may occur. In such a case, even if matrix $A_{11} + A_{12}(I - A_{22})^{-1}A_{21}$ has a Perron-Frobenius eigenvalue less than one, the model will tell us that one or more elements of x_1 may become negative (because of the negativity of one or more elements of the final demand term). Remarks of a similar nature can be made regarding L, the required amount of labor, and regarding implied prices (e.g. by taking a closer look at equation (4) above). Another point concerns matrix $A_{11} + A_{12}(I - A_{22})^{-1}A_{21}$ itself. Should we interpret this matrix as a "normal" coefficients matrix and apply standard input-output theory?[7] If so, this would mean that *adding* terms such as (sub)matrix $A_{12}(I - A_{22})^{-1}A_{21}$ may invoke a situation where the model loses its economic interpretability because the Perron-Frobenius eigenvalue of the enlarged matrix exceeds unity.[8]

A major source of confusion is that the connection between the real and the price side is not particularly transparent in the LEM. The LEM simultaneously provides information on the technical side (the quantity of polluting substances produced, and the abatement technologies that are available), and on the cost allocation mechanism. We should realize that the model thus tries to combine two tasks which, really, are quite different. As a consequence, we may end up with specifications of the real and price sides that reflect different ideas. Recall, of course, that in the original models without pollution this was never a problem because the price

---

[7] The habit of working with increased coefficients is itself well established in certain fields. We may think here of methods that are based on adding competitive imports to the production structure to obtain more realistic technical coefficients.

[8] For further discussion, particularly regarding the positioning of the model amongst alternatives, see Duchin and Steenge (1999).

equation followed the description of technology. In the LEM, as proposed by Leontief, this cannot be maintained because behavioral and policy aspects have entered. Consequently, the relation between the physical and the price side has become less transparent. Below, to obtain a better insight into the structural relations, I shall adopt a specification of the environmental rules that restores transparency. In doing so I shall follow Leontief's price equation (3) and assume identical sectoral abatement rates. In addition, I shall assume that the polluting industries pay for the costs of abatement. This can be accomplished by focusing primarily on the quantities to be abated (i.e. x_2) rather than on the tolerated emissions, c_2.[9] So, x_2 in equation (5) will now be specified as

$$x_2 = \alpha(A_{21}x_1 + A_{22}x_2) \tag{8}$$

where α is the uniform abatement rate. Imposing identical sectoral abatement rates in combination with the "polluter pays" principle results in a system matrix, as given by (9). The advantage is that we can now employ the same matrix of input coefficients for the real part and for price analysis. Model (1) becomes

$$
\begin{bmatrix}
I - A_{11} & -A_{12} \\
-\alpha A_{21} & I - \alpha A_{22}
\end{bmatrix}
\begin{bmatrix}
x_1 \\
x_2
\end{bmatrix}
=
\begin{bmatrix}
c_1 \\
0
\end{bmatrix}
\tag{9}
$$

However, it is not difficult to show that we still need additional structural analysis. For example, here also overall non-negativity is not guaranteed. To see this, we calculate the corresponding value of x_1. We obtain

$$x_1 = A_{11}x_1 + \alpha[A_{12}(I - \alpha A_{22})^{-1}A_{21}]x_1 + c_1$$
$$= [A_{11} + \alpha A_{12}(I - \alpha A_{22})^{-1}A_{21}]x_1 + c_1$$

Whether or not x_1 is an economically interpretable value now depends on the Perron-Frobenius eigenvalue of matrix $A^* \equiv A_{11} + \alpha A_{12}(I - \alpha A_{22})^{-1}A_{21}$. This eigenvalue, however, depends on α, the adopted sectoral abatement rate. So, because of the "sudden" appearance of α at a strategic place in the model (apparently), we have to investigate the relation between $\lambda(A^*)$ and α.[10] Most importantly of course, is the question

---

[9] That is, I leave these to be calculated at a later stage.
[10] I shall use the symbol $\lambda(.)$ to denote the Perron-Frobenius or dominant eigenvalue of the corresponding matrix.

Table 19.1 *Leontief tableau with pollution*

	Agriculture	Manufacturing	Households	Total output
Agriculture	25	20	55	100
Manufacturing	14	6	30	50
Labor	80	180	0	260
Pollution	50	10	0	60

as to whether there is a particular value of α – say α^{max} – for which $\lambda(\mathbf{A}^*)$ becomes unity, since in that case the above open model would lose its economic meaning.[11] This suggests that "simply" imposing values for α in the range $0 \leq \alpha \leq 1$ may be hazardous. We may "guess right" (say, based on actual pre-policy observations), but we have no guarantee that $\lambda(\mathbf{A}^*)$ will be less than unity. In section 4 I shall come back to this. First, however, I shall discuss in section 3 the question of whether imposing the new environmental rules introduces additional primary factors into the model. If so, that would have direct implications for our price theory.

2.2   A numerical example

Below I shall refer to a numerical example first put forward by Leontief (1970) – a physical input-output tableau that includes produced emissions. Assuming, with Leontief, that households do not produce any pollution, we start from table 19.1 (units are, say, in appropriate quantities of grain, steel, man-years and emitted substances). This yields the input coefficients matrix $\mathbf{A}_{11}$

$$\mathbf{A}_{11} = \begin{bmatrix} 0.25 & 0.40 \\ 0.14 & 0.12 \end{bmatrix}$$

and the following vector of pollution (output) coefficients: $\mathbf{A}_{21} = [0.50 \; 0.20]$. The vector of labor input coefficients is $\mathbf{v}'_1 = [0.80 \; 3.60]$.

The next step is to introduce anti-pollution or abatement technologies. Following Leontief, we identify a single abatement activity that eliminates the pollution as follows

$$\mathbf{A}_{12} = \begin{bmatrix} 0 \\ 0.20 \end{bmatrix}$$

---

[11] This is based on the fact that the Perron-Frobenius eigenvalue of $\mathbf{A}^*$ increases when α increases. A limit on this eigenvalue thus also implies a limit on α.

The abatement activity also uses labor inputs, so $v'_2 = 2.00$. We assume that it does not produce any emissions: $A_{22} = 0$. Finally,

$$c_1 = \begin{bmatrix} 55 \\ 30 \end{bmatrix}$$

Leontief (1970) provides a number of examples. We may calculate the prices of grain and steel, say, using a standard input-output model. Given these prices, the price of eliminating one unit of pollutant in the anti-pollution industry may be calculated. The resulting prices, in arbitrary monetary units, are $p_1 = 2.00$, $p_2 = 5.00$ and $p_3 = 3.00$, where p_1 and p_2 stand for the prices of agricultural and manufactured goods respectively, and p_3 for the costs of eliminating one unit of the pollutant. The problem rapidly gets more complex if we adopt a more integrated framework. As an illustration, if society set the abatement level at 50 percent, and if we allocated on the basis of "the polluter pays," prices become, respectively, 3.234, 5.923 and 3.185. Below I shall further explore this example, using Leontief's numerical values. Although several cost allocation schemes are possible, I shall follow Leontief and pay particular attention to the "polluter pays" principle as a device for allocating the cost of abatement to the polluting sectors.

3. Intermediate or primary inputs?

In the introduction I mentioned that it is not immediately clear how to interpret the anti-pollution activities in terms of the model. Abatement expenses are analogous to final demand in that the LEM views them as net output in exchange for a particular service called abatement activity. On the other hand, if taking care of environmental quality becomes part of normal production, the corresponding outlays will obtain the character of necessary intermediate inputs into production. So we have a certain ambiguity here that makes the message of the model unclear. Let us see now if these ideas can be made more concrete, and if the different views really make a difference.

I propose to explore the model's properties in terms of an augmented system matrix.[12] As we shall see below, this allows us to employ a single equation formulation that contains the basic information we need. This also means that we shall work with a model that, in certain respects, resembles the *closed* Leontief model. A major advantage of this is that the

---

[12] See, for example, Seton (1977) for an exposition.

structure of the model (including the choices involved) becomes more transparent.

We start from a situation where there is no environmental policy at all. In that case, the economy is described as

$$\left. \begin{array}{l} \mathbf{x}_1 = \mathbf{A}_{11}\mathbf{x}_1 + \mathbf{c}_1 \\ L = \mathbf{v}_1'\mathbf{x}_1 \end{array} \right\} \tag{10}$$

which is just the standard form of the traditional *open* model. Substitution of the labor equation gives $\mathbf{x}_1 = \mathbf{A}_{11}\mathbf{x}_1 + (1/L)\mathbf{c}_1\mathbf{v}_1'\mathbf{x}_1$, or $\mathbf{x}_1 = [\mathbf{A}_{11} + (1/L)\mathbf{c}_1\mathbf{v}_1']\mathbf{x}_1$. So our basic model becomes

$$\mathbf{x}_1 = \mathbf{A}^1\mathbf{x}_1 \tag{11}$$

with augmented system matrix

$$\mathbf{A}^1 \equiv \mathbf{A}_{11} + (1/L)\mathbf{c}_1\mathbf{v}_1' \tag{12}$$

Equation (11) tells us that we have rewritten the open model (10) in the standard form of the closed Leontief model. The model, evidently, differs from a typical closed model because $\mathbf{c}_1$ is of a different nature from the fixed coefficient production functions in $\mathbf{A}$. Thus, the interpretation of $\mathbf{A}^1$ should be as follows: once we know $\mathbf{x}_1$ and L in (10), we know that they must satisfy equation (11) as well. From (11) we also have $\lambda(\mathbf{A}^1) = 1$.[13] Equilibrium prices $\mathbf{p}_1'$ satisfy

$$\mathbf{p}_1' = \mathbf{p}_1'[\mathbf{A}_{11} + (1/L)\mathbf{c}_1\mathbf{v}_1'] \tag{13}$$

Because (13) only determines prices up to scalar multiplication, we need a standardization for $\mathbf{p}_1$. A standard approach would be to impose $(1/L)\mathbf{p}_1'\mathbf{c}_1 = w$, where w is the wage rate.

Let us return to (8), and assume that the value of the abatement parameter α has been set exogenously. If the abatement expenses are viewed as additions to final demand, the system, including labor, would become[14]

$$\left. \begin{array}{l} \mathbf{x}_1 = \mathbf{A}_{11}\mathbf{x}_1 + \mathbf{A}_{12}\mathbf{x}_2 + \mathbf{c}_1 \\ \mathbf{x}_2 = \alpha\mathbf{A}_{21}\mathbf{x}_1 \\ L = \mathbf{v}_1'\mathbf{x}_1 \end{array} \right\} \tag{14}$$

Eliminating $\mathbf{x}_2$ gives

$$\mathbf{x}_1 = \mathbf{A}_{11}\mathbf{x}_1 + \alpha\mathbf{A}_{12}\mathbf{A}_{21}\mathbf{x}_1 + \mathbf{c}_1 \tag{15}$$

---

[13] When consumption $\mathbf{c}_1$ changes, required labor L changes correspondingly. We then obtain a new augmented matrix, again with dominant eigenvalue equal to unity.
[14] In order not to complicate the formulas too much, I shall henceforth assume $\mathbf{A}_{22} = 0$.

Including the labor equation gives $x_1 = [A_{11} + \alpha A_{12}A_{21} + (1/L)c_1 v'_1]x_1$; that is

$$x_1 = A^2 x_1 \qquad (16)$$

with

$$A^2 \equiv A_{11} + \alpha A_{12}A_{21} + (1/L)c_1 v'_1 \qquad (17)$$

Equation (16) is quite an interesting equation. It looks like a straightforward extension of (11). However, can we, given our a priori choice of α, be so sure of its economic interpretation? For example, can we be sure – also in the light of the discussion in the previous section – of the signs of the core variables? A moment's reflection will show that we should take a close look at (15). We have started from an exogenously given value of α. This value reflects a certain level of aspiration from the side of the environmental policy-makers. However, we have not yet considered the issue of possible limits set by technology. These limits are not difficult to find, though. Equation (15) straightforwardly tells us that economic interpretability of the model requires that α must be such that the Perron-Frobenius eigenvalue of matrix $A_{11} + \alpha A_{12}A_{21}$ is smaller than unity. If that is the case, x_1, x_2 and L will all be positive. If not, the model ceases to reflect an economic problem. I shall return to this point in section 4.

Let us now address the question of whether the abatement activities should be considered as a new type of primary inputs, or rather as intermediate inputs. As a first step, let us explore the notion that abatement expenses just amount to extra production of conventional goods, comparable to the production for final consumption demand. That is, we assume that some institution buys those goods and gives "abatement services" in return. In this sense, abatement then resembles households' consumption in the open model.[15] In the case where $\alpha = 0.5$, we now have straightforwardly in our 2×2 economy

$$x_1 = \begin{bmatrix} 104.218 \\ 57.909 \end{bmatrix}$$

This gives $L = 291.845$ and $x_2 = 31.845$. We thus find

$$A^2 = \begin{bmatrix} 0.25 & 0.40 \\ 0.14 & 0.12 \end{bmatrix} + \begin{bmatrix} 0 & 0 \\ 0.050 & 0.020 \end{bmatrix} + \begin{bmatrix} 0.151 & 0.678 \\ 0.082 & 0.370 \end{bmatrix}$$

Prices p'_1 (standardized such that the price of wheat is unity) are found to be $[1.000 \quad 2.201]$.

---

[15] Also note that, for the moment, I assume that the abatement process does not need any labor; i.e. $v'_2 = 0$.

Looking at $\mathbf{A}^2$, we see that the issue of the nature of the abatement expenses now can be solved neatly. In fact, it appears that we have a *choice* whether to classify them as intermediate or primary inputs. First, we can look at the coefficients matrix in a traditional way and adopt labor as the single primary factor. This implies that the intermediate coefficients matrix becomes

$$\overline{\mathbf{A}}^2 = \begin{bmatrix} 0.25 & 0.40 \\ 0.14 & 0.12 \end{bmatrix} + \begin{bmatrix} 0 & 0 \\ 0.050 & 0.020 \end{bmatrix}$$

In this case, we find for corresponding prices $\overline{\mathbf{p}}'_1$ that $\overline{\mathbf{p}}'_1 \propto \mathbf{v}'_1 (\mathbf{I} - \overline{\mathbf{A}}^2)^{-1}$.

Alternatively, we may see the abatement sectors as providing the primary inputs (thereby relegating labor to the intermediates). This leads to another intermediate coefficients matrix

$$\widetilde{\mathbf{A}}^2 = \begin{bmatrix} 0.25 & 0.40 \\ 0.14 & 0.12 \end{bmatrix} + \begin{bmatrix} 0.151 & 0.678 \\ 0.082 & 0.370 \end{bmatrix}$$

The environmental services now being considered as primary factor, we obtain $\widetilde{\mathbf{p}}'_1 \propto \mathbf{A}_{21} (\mathbf{I} - \widetilde{\mathbf{A}}^2)^{-1}$.

Because there is only one set of equilibrium prices, we must have, after proper standardization, $\overline{\mathbf{p}}'_1 = \widetilde{\mathbf{p}}'_1$. It thus turns out that our choice (primary or intermediate input) is not relevant as far as prices are concerned.

The above, however, does not yet capture the full flavor of the LEM. We have (deliberately) neglected the fact that Leontief's anti-pollution activities also require labor input. To see what this implies, consider the following equation, which is just a rewritten form of equation (14) with the labor inputs for the abatement activities added

$$\left. \begin{array}{l} \mathbf{x}_1 = \mathbf{A}_{11}\mathbf{x}_1 + \mathbf{A}_{12}(\alpha \mathbf{A}_{21}\mathbf{x}_1) + \mathbf{c}_1 \\ L = \mathbf{v}'_1 \mathbf{x}_1 + \mathbf{v}'_2 (\alpha \mathbf{A}_{21}\mathbf{x}_1) \end{array} \right\} \tag{18}$$

Assuming that exogenous α is in the correct range, we can calculate $\mathbf{x}_1$ from the first equation of (18). Next we find L from the second. We observe directly that we find the same vector $\mathbf{x}_1$ as before. Only the quantity of required labor will be much larger. After rearranging we have

$$\mathbf{x}_1 = \mathbf{A}^3 \mathbf{x}_1 \tag{19}$$

with

$$\mathbf{A}^3 \equiv \mathbf{A}_{11} + \alpha \mathbf{A}_{12} \mathbf{A}_{21} + (\mathbf{c}_1/L)(\mathbf{v}'_1 + \alpha \mathbf{v}'_2 \mathbf{A}_{21}) \tag{20}$$

as the new system matrix. In terms of our example, we have

$$\mathbf{A}^3 = \begin{bmatrix} 0.25 & 0.40 \\ 0.14 & 0.12 \end{bmatrix} + \alpha \begin{bmatrix} 0 & 0 \\ 0.100 & 0.040 \end{bmatrix} + \frac{1}{L} \begin{bmatrix} 44 & 198 \\ 24 & 108 \end{bmatrix}$$
$$+ \frac{\alpha}{L} \begin{bmatrix} 55 & 22 \\ 30 & 12 \end{bmatrix} \tag{21}$$

In the case $\alpha = 0.5$ we have straightforwardly, as mentioned, the same total output vector. For required labor we find that $L = 355.538$. Substitution gives

$$\mathbf{A}^3 = \begin{bmatrix} 0.25 & 0.40 \\ 0.14 & 0.12 \end{bmatrix} + \begin{bmatrix} 0 & 0 \\ 0.050 & 0.020 \end{bmatrix} + \begin{bmatrix} 0.124 & 0.557 \\ 0.068 & 0.304 \end{bmatrix}$$
$$+ \begin{bmatrix} 0.077 & 0.031 \\ 0.042 & 0.017 \end{bmatrix}$$
$$= \begin{bmatrix} 0.451 & 0.988 \\ 0.300 & 0.461 \end{bmatrix}$$

Standardized prices are $\mathbf{p}'_1 = [1.000 \quad 1.832]$.

From (20) and (21), we see very clearly that we may "pick" the system matrix that best fits our ideas about the role of abatement activities. If we view these, given prevailing legislation, as part of the technology, we may "compose" our intermediate input coefficients matrix by selecting the first, second and fourth constituent matrix of $\mathbf{A}^3$ to obtain

$$\overline{\mathbf{A}}^3 = \begin{bmatrix} 0.327 & 0.431 \\ 0.232 & 0.157 \end{bmatrix}$$

Labor now is the single primary factor. (If we do so, the corresponding vector of primary (labor) inputs again is $\mathbf{v}'_1$.) However, we may also wish to express a somewhat different philosophy. That is, we may wish to bring together the first and second terms in (20) to form the intermediate part and the last two for the primary input part. We then have

$$\mathbf{A}^3 = \begin{bmatrix} 0.250 & 0.400 \\ 0.190 & 0.140 \end{bmatrix} + \begin{bmatrix} 0.201 & 0.588 \\ 0.110 & 0.321 \end{bmatrix}$$

where the first matrix on the right-hand side represents the redefined intermediate input coefficients and the second the coefficients for the combined primary inputs. Prices, after standardization, would be the same, naturally. There is no compelling reason not to explore a further possibility. We just note that we may even wish to view the first three terms of (20) as the intermediate part and the last matrix as the primary input part. Finally, we should observe that the value of α that satisfies

$\lambda(\mathbf{A}_{11} + \alpha\mathbf{A}_{12}\mathbf{A}_{21}) = 1$ also satisfies $\lambda[\mathbf{A}_{11} + \alpha\mathbf{A}_{12}\mathbf{A}_{21} + (\mathbf{c}_1/L)(\mathbf{v}'_1 + \alpha\mathbf{v}'_2\mathbf{A}_{21})] = 1$.

4.   The role of α

Below I shall explore the model further, thereby concentrating on the behaviour of α as a limiting factor. I shall again use Leontief's data of section 2.2. Let us adopt the notation $\mathbf{A}^* \equiv \mathbf{A}_{11} + \alpha\mathbf{A}_{12}\mathbf{A}_{21}$.[16] To determine $\alpha^{\max}$, the critical value of α that makes $\lambda(\mathbf{A}^*)$ equal to unity, we should realize that this is also the value that assures that the determinant of matrix $(\mathbf{I} - \mathbf{A}^*)$ vanishes. So, to find $\alpha^{\max}$, we need only look for the value of α for which

$$\det(\mathbf{I} - \mathbf{A}^*) = 0 \qquad (22)$$

Below I shall, for reasons of space, not present a fully developed exposition of the available possibilities. To give an example of the type of relation we may expect I shall discuss a number of cases and leave further work for a later occasion. First, let us take a brief look into the relation between $\alpha^{\max}$ and the elements of the available abatement technology. So, let us see what happens if the first element of $\mathbf{A}_{12}$ (0 in the Leontief example) is increased. Such an action can be interpreted, naturally, as raising the cost of abatement technology. Thus, for the economy as a whole we have the same set of coefficients as used by Leontief, the single exception being the first coefficient in matrix $\mathbf{A}_{12}$, which now is written as

$$\mathbf{A}_{12} = \begin{bmatrix} k \\ 0.20 \end{bmatrix}$$

From equation (22) we obtain straightforwardly $0.604 - 0.070\alpha - 0.468k\alpha = 0$. This gives $\alpha = -0.604/(-0.070 - 0.468k)$, which is graphed in figure 19.1.

As we may see, the value of α for which (22) is satisfied (i.e. $\alpha^{\max}$) depends significantly on k. The abatement rates that can be reached sharply decrease with increasing k. From the above, we also may conclude that the "limits to environmental policy" (as expressed by the value of $\alpha^{\max}$) will not be reached under a policy for an economy characterized by the Leontief set of technological coefficients (where $k = 0$). That is, emissions can be completely curbed. However, we may encounter quite different situations. Suppose the economy's data had been

$$\mathbf{A}_{12} = \begin{bmatrix} 0.60 \\ 0.50 \end{bmatrix}$$

[16] Recall that I imposed $\mathbf{A}_{22} = 0$.

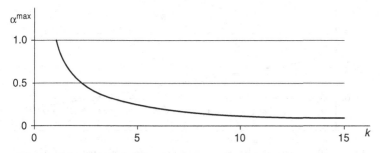

Figure 19.1   Relation between α^{max} and k

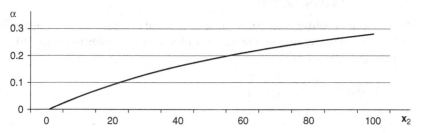

Figure 19.2   Relation between α and x_2 for selected values of A_{12} and A_{21}

and $A_{21} = [1.00 \quad 1.20]$. This would give $\alpha = x_2/(160 + 2.117x_2)$, which is depicted in figure 19.2.

Thus, we can only eliminate a relatively small part of total pollution. This leads us to consider the case where policy-makers have agreed on a value for the tolerated level of emissions. Suppose we impose $c_2 = 65$. Using equations (5) we then obtain

$$\mathbf{x}_1 = \begin{bmatrix} 99.3 \\ 48.6 \end{bmatrix}$$

From $x_2 + c_2 = A_{21}x_1$ we have $x_2 = -5.655$. That is, we encounter an example where certain core values are negative. We may translate this result in a common value for α that will also turn out to be negative. We conclude (also) that the tolerated level of emissions has to be chosen within boundaries determined by the available technologies. Via direct substitution we can find the relation between α and c_2.

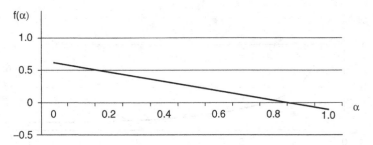

Figure 19.3   Relation between $f(\alpha)$ and α for selected values of A_{12} and A_{21}, $m = 2$

5.   The scope for policy

Next, let us consider briefly the consequences of increasing the scope for policy, i.e. of increasing m, the number of toxic substances to be abated. Let us first consider the following values

$$A_{12} = \begin{bmatrix} 0.17 & 0.25 \\ 0.20 & 0.15 \end{bmatrix}$$

and

$$A_{21} = \begin{bmatrix} 1.50 & 1.80 \\ 0.30 & 0.25 \end{bmatrix}$$

With $f(\alpha) = \det(I\text{-}A^*)$, to find α^{max} we put $f(\alpha) = 0$. This gives $0.604 - 0.778\alpha + 0.004\alpha^2 = 0$ (see figure 19.3). Thus $\alpha^{max} = 0.779$.

Let us now jump to the case where $m = 4$. Suppose we have

$$A_{12} = \begin{bmatrix} 0.17 & 0.25 & 0.12 & 0.10 \\ 0.20 & 0.15 & 0.18 & 0.18 \end{bmatrix}$$

and

$$A_{21} = \begin{bmatrix} 1.50 & 1.80 \\ 0.30 & 0.25 \\ 0.85 & 1.25 \\ 1.00 & 0.60 \end{bmatrix}$$

Again, with $f(\alpha) = \det(I\text{-}A^*)$, equation (22) now gives $f(\alpha) = 0.604 - 1.368\alpha - 0.004\alpha^2 = 0$, and $\alpha^{max} = 0.441$ (see figure 19.4).

Comparing figures 19.3 and 19.4 we observe that the drop in α^{max} can be quite dramatic with increasing m. This may be an important observation for current empirical research in anti-emission policies. To give an example, in the Dutch National Accounts system environmental data are compiled in a set of so-called satellite accounts. Together these form the

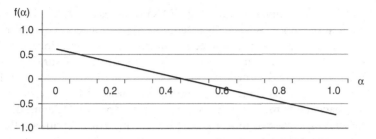

Figure 19.4   Relation between $f(\alpha)$ and α for selected values of $\mathbf{A}_{12}$ and $\mathbf{A}_{21}$, $m = 4$

NAMEA system[17] – see de Haan and Keuning (1996) or Keuning et al. (1999). In the system five "environmental themes" are distinguished as a consequence of the emission of chemical substances. These themes are, respectively, the greenhouse effect, ozone layer depletion, acidification, eutrophication and waste. It will be interesting to see if the variety of reductions talked about in today's political arena can also be obtained as economically realistic values using models of the type we have been discussing. If indeed the critical value of α drops sharply with an increasing number of noxious substances, this may reflect a reduction in the options for cleaning up in practice. Therefore, our enlarged model may give us a method to calculate rates of economically and technologically realistic emission clean-ups when policy-makers are confronted with a multitude of choices.[18]

Finally, let us return for a moment to equation (7). We encountered the term $\mathbf{c}_1 - \mathbf{A}_{12}(\mathbf{I} - \mathbf{A}_{22})^{-1}\mathbf{c}_2$, and asked if this term could become negative. By now it will be clear that we will not have a problem if α in $\mathbf{x}_2 = \alpha(\mathbf{A}_{21}\mathbf{x}_1 + \mathbf{A}_{22}\mathbf{x}_2)$ is in the accepted range. Substitution then will tell us that (7) can readily be interpreted along the lines presented above.

6.   Final remarks and conclusion

I hope I have shown that the Leontief environmental model is quite surprising, turning out to be an input-output model of hybrid character. We have seen that the abatement sectors have properties that remind us of both the intermediate input structure and the final demand or primary input structure.

---

[17] The acronym stands for "National Accounting Matrix including Environmental Accounts."
[18] See Steenge and Voogt (1995) for a discussion of options in an optimization model for "green national income" research.

I pointed out that many of the LEM's problems can be attributed to the fact that the model is basically a "composite," a collection of sub-models, whether already existing or specially devised for the occasion. This led to a number of "consistency issues" – the consequence of our desire to put these various models or sub-models under one conceptual umbrella. In view of this, to tackle the problems I have proposed a strategy that first goes back to the much less ambitious original open Leontief model. Then the LEM was viewed in terms of this basic model, but with a difference: two new rules have been imposed. These rules make the economy operate under a set of new constraints regarding the output of its pollutants and the way costs should be allocated. The question to be addressed now becomes one of the integration of the new rules.

I have pointed out that today's literature on the LEM is well aware of these two rules, but basically it works with only one rule, which has to combine the two tasks of describing the physical and the price structure. This imposed double task is, in my view, a major source of misunderstanding. To remove it, I have proposed to decide first which part of the industrial emissions should be eliminated. Hereafter, this decision should be coupled to a scheme in which the sources pay for this part. The problem then disappears, and we can work with only one specification.

As we have seen, the character of the abatement expenses gives the LEM a built-in ambiguity. To address this problem an approach in terms of augmented system matrices was proposed. This led, via a number of substitutions, to a model that shares a number of properties with the closed Leontief model. It was shown (end of section 3) that, on this basis, we can construct a system matrix that is the sum of four submatrices. The LEM's ambiguity can now be handled by making new coefficients matrices via combinations of the submatrices. The conclusion is that the abatement activities can be classified twofold: belonging either to final demand or to intermediate production, in both instances in various combinations with the other activities. In this sense the LEM really is a most interesting hybrid.

The proposed approach afforded me a systematic view of prices and price formation. I did so under the "polluter pays" principle, i.e. the polluter ends up paying the social cost. However, we should realize that this is not the end of the story. There are other interesting possibilities. So, let me end on a speculative note. The results of this contribution remind me of Coase's theorem (Coase, 1960, and 1988), which deals with the efficiency of social cost allocation mechanisms. It establishes the efficiency of a system of tradable property rights vis-à-vis other systems, such as "polluter pays" systems. Primarily by trading their "pollution rights," parties may be expected to reach a social optimum. This optimum is normally preferable to the outcomes of a discretionary public policy. Particularly in the presence of alternatives (such as cleaner but more expensive production technologies), trading off can become efficient. This will also provide a fresh look at the non-substitution theorem. It will be interesting to see if a link can be established between standard Leontief accounting and Coasean optimization procedures. If so, it will provide further proof of the versatility of the input-output framework.

REFERENCES

Arrous, J. (1994) The Leontief pollution model: a systematic formulation, *Economic Systems Research*, 6, 105–107.
Baumol, W. J., and W. E. Oates (1975) *The Theory of Environmental Policy* (Englewood Cliffs, NJ, Prentice-Hall).
Coase, R. H. (1960) The problem of social cost, *Journal of Law and Economics*, 3, 1–44.
———— (1988) *The Firm, the Market and the Law* (Chicago, University of Chicago Press).
Duchin, F., and A. E. Steenge (1999) Input-output analysis, technology and the environment, in J. C. J. M. van den Bergh (ed.) *Handbook of Environmental and Resource Economics* (Cheltenham, Edward Elgar Publishing), 1,037–1,059.
Dufournaud, C. M., J. J. Harrington and P. P. Rogers (1988) Leontief's "Environmental repercussions and the economic structure . . ." revisited: a general equilibrium formulation, *Geographical Analysis*, 20, 318–327.
Flick, W. A. (1974) "Environmental repercussions and the economic structure: an input-output approach": a comment, *Review of Economics and Statistics*, 56, 107–109.
de Haan, M., and S. J. Keuning (1996) Taking the environment into account: the NAMEA approach, *Review of Income and Wealth*, 42, 131–148.
Isard, W. (1972) *Ecologic-Economic Analysis for Regional Development* (New York, Free Press).
Keuning, S. J., J. van Dalen and M. de Haan (1999) The Netherlands' NAMEA; presentation, usage and future extensions, *Structural Change and Economic Dynamics*, 10, 15–37.
Lager, C. (1998) Prices of 'goods' and 'bads': an application of the Ricardian theory of differential rent, *Economic Systems Research*, 10, 203–222.
Lee, K.-S. (1982) A generalized input-output model of an economy with environmental protection, *Review of Economics and Statistics*, 64, 466–473.
Leontief, W. W. (1970) Environmental repercussions and the economic structure: an input-output approach, *Review of Economics and Statistics*, 52, 262–271.
Leontief, W. W., and D. Ford (1972) Air pollution and the economic structure: empirical results of input-output computations, in A. Brody and A. P. Carter (eds.) *Input-Output Techniques* (Amsterdam, North-Holland), 9–30.
Lowe, P. D. (1979) Pricing problems in an input-output approach to environmental protection, *Review of Economics and Statistics*, 61, 110–117.

Luptacik, M., and B. Böhm (1994) Reconsideration of non-negative solutions for the augmented Leontief model, *Economic Systems Research*, 6, 167–170.

—— (1999) A consistent formulation of the Leontief pollution model, *Economic Systems Research*, 11, 263–275.

Moore, S. A. (1981) "Environmental repercussions and the economic structure": some further comments, *Review of Economics and Statistics*, 63, 139–142.

Qayum, A. (1991) A reformulation of the Leontief pollution model, *Economic Systems Research*, 3, 428–430.

Rhee, J. J., and J. A. Miranowski (1984) Determination of income, production, and employment under pollution control: an input-output approach, *Review of Economics and Statistics*, 66, 146–150.

Seton, F. (1977) The question of ideological obstacles to rational price setting in communist countries, in A. Abouchar (ed.) *The Socialist Price Mechanism* (Durham, NC, Duke University Press), 10–39.

Steenge, A. E. (1978) "Environmental repercussions and the economic structure": further comments, *Review of Economics and Statistics*, 60, 482–486.

—— (1999) Input-output theory and institutional aspects of environmental policy, *Structural Change and Economic Dynamics*, 10, 161–176.

Steenge, A. E., and M. H. Voogt (1995) A linear programming model for calculating green national incomes, in U. Derigs, A. Bachem and A. Drexl (eds.) *Operations Research Proceedings 1994: Selected Papers of the International Conference on Operations Research, TU Berlin, August 30–September 2, 1994* (Berlin, Springer-Verlag), 376–381.

Stone, R. (1972) The evaluation of pollution: balancing gains and losses, *Minerva*, 10, 412–425.

Victor, P. A. (1972) *Economics of Pollution* (London, Macmillan).

Subject index

abatement (see pollution, abatement)
accounts (see system, national accounts, of)
allotopy 108, 118
American Academy of Arts and Sciences 16
American Economic Association (AEA) 3, 10, 90
armament 14, 166
Asia 40
automation 9, 13
automobile (see motor vehicle)

balance of payments 39, 40, 41, 44, 295, 340
Baumol's disease 190–191
BEA (see Bureau of Economic Analysis)
Berlin 7, 137, 143
"best practice" approach (see input-output, "best practice")
bilateral
    flows 37, 56, 57
    trade (see trade, bilateral)
BLS (see Bureau of Labor Statistics)
"Blue Book" 13
Brandeis University 24
Bretton Woods 42
Bureau of Economic Analysis (BEA) 183, 188, 191, 199–202, 312–313, 323, 334
Bureau of Labor Statistics (BLS) 12, 14, 92, 183, 188, 199–202, 311

Canada 320
capacity 294
    plant 232–254
    utilization 294, 308, 323
capital 18, 91, 167, 169, 172, 173, 256, 275, 298, 305
    accumulation 234, 256–292
    coefficients 91, 92, 95, 169, 176, 232–255, 259–290

expansion coefficient(s) 95
flow 269
formation 30, 35, 37, 313
-intensive 18, 54, 55, 131, 166–168, 172–174, 176–177, 181, 189, 233, 250–255
-labor ratio 168, 174–176, 247, 255
-output ratio 339
productivity (see productivity, capital)
replacement coefficients 95
rich 51, 52
-saving 239–244
service 266
social overhead 269
stock 35, 40, 95, 183, 184, 186, 232–247, 265, 269, 290, 304, 319, 324, 328, 339–340, 344–345, 348, 350, 351, 359–365
-stock matrix 257
-using 239–247
Center for Economic Data Development and Research 234
CGE (see computable general equilibrium)
China 11, 135, 139, 337, 347
closed model 90, 375
club 105
Club of Rome 30
collusion 220, 221, 226, 227, 231, 233
commodity
    content 18, 19, 21
Communist(s) 65, 68, 137, 144
    Party 66, 70
comparative advantage 19, 20, 47, 55, 56, 58, 62, 172, 174, 182
compensation (see labor, compensation)
competition, perfect 153, 154, 156, 160, 164, 214, 261
computable general equilibrium (CGE) xx, 59, 60
Conference on Human Environment 31

Author index